Mastering CyberSecurity Defense

A comprehensive guide to command CyberSecurity, threat intelligence, and compliance strategies

Santosh Kumar Tripathi

bpb

www.bpbonline.com

First Edition 2025

Copyright © BPB Publications, India

ISBN: 978-93-65897-869

LIMITS OF LIABILITY AND DISCLAIMER OF WARRANTY

To View Complete
BPB Publications Catalogue
Scan the QR Code:

www.bpbonline.com

Dedicated to

To my beloved mother, **Late Madhuri Tripathi**, *whose wisdom and unwavering support continue to guide me even beyond this world.*

To my father, **Uday Bhan Tripathi**, *whose values, strength, and encouragement have shaped my journey in life and profession.*

To my wife, **Dr. Aparna Tripathi**, *whose patience, encouragement, and belief in me have been my pillars of strength throughout this journey.*

To my daughter, **Ayantika Tripathi**, *and my son,* **Abhyuday Tripathi**, *whose curiosity and bright minds inspire me to make the digital world safer for the next generation.*

This book is a tribute to your love, sacrifices, and the endless motivation you have given me.

About the Author

Santosh Kumar Tripathi is a **renowned CyberSecurity leader, educator, and strategist** with over **17 years of experience** in CyberSecurity and Compliance. His journey in CyberSecurity began with the **Indian Navy**, where he served in the **Information Warfare Cell**, playing a crucial role in **hardening security infrastructure** and **defending critical systems against Cyber threats**. This experience laid the foundation for his deep expertise in **Cyber defense, risk management, and security operations**.

Currently, he is the **Director of Information Security and Compliance** at a leading security product company *"Virsec"*, where he leads **enterprise security initiatives, risk mitigation strategies, and regulatory compliance efforts** aligned with frameworks like **NIST, FISMA, ISO 27001, and SOC 2**.

He holds a **Master's in Information Security and Cyber Forensics** from the **University of Madras, Chennai**, and an **MBA from GITAM University, Visakhapatnam**. He is **pursuing a Ph.D. in CyberSecurity** from **Suresh Gyan Vihar University, Jaipur**. He also holds **globally recognized security certifications**, including **Certified Information Systems Auditor (CISA), Certified Data Privacy Solutions Engineer (CDPSE), Computer Hacking Forensic Investigator (CHFI), Certified Ethical Hacker (CEH), ISO 27001 Lead Auditor, ISO 31000 Lead Risk Manager, and Certified in Cloud Security Knowledge (CCSK)**, among others.

A **passionate CyberSecurity advocate**, he has conducted **CyberSecurity awareness sessions in 12+ universities** and delivered insights at **50+ security events at** national and international levels, educating professionals and students on emerging **Cyber threats, mitigation strategies, and best security practices**. His thought leadership extends to **LinkedIn**, where he actively engages with the CyberSecurity community, mentors aspiring professionals, and shares industry insights.

His contributions to the field have earned him **multiple prestigious national and international awards**, recognizing his excellence in **CyberSecurity, compliance, innovation, leadership, and security strategy**. Titles such as **Cyber Chanakya, CyberSecurity Influencer, Innovation Leader, Compliance Champion, and Aspiring CXO** reflect his impact on the industry.

With *Mastering CyberSecurity Defense*, he aims to provide a **comprehensive, practical, and insightful guide** to modern CyberSecurity challenges. This will make it an invaluable resource for **individuals, security professionals, students, and organizations** striving to strengthen their security posture in today's digital age.

About the Reviewers

❖ **Parth Shah, CISSP**, is a Senior Security Research PM at Microsoft with over 15 years of experience in cybersecurity, specializing in application security, cloud security, AI security, and incident response. He holds a Master's in Cybersecurity and Leadership from the University of Washington. Parth serves as President of the ISSA Rainier Chapter, where he drives cybersecurity education and professional development. He is also an AI Frontier Network (AIFN) Ambassador, contributing to global AI security initiatives, and an honorary member of the Center for Cyber Security Studies and Research (CFCS2R).

Parth is a Hall of Fame inductee for international bug bounty programs and published articles in IEEE conferences and AI journals.

❖ **Sanyam Jain** is a distinguished Cloud Security Engineer with extensive expertise in cybersecurity. Known for his dedication to securing digital environments, Sanyam's achievements reflect his deep commitment to protecting critical infrastructure and contributing to the broader security community. He has excelled across Cloud Security, Security Operations, Application Security, Compliance, and Security Automation, consistently developing strategies that help organizations exceed their security objectives.

His technical proficiency spans network security, threat detection, data encryption, and access control, with expertise across AWS, Azure, and Google Cloud. Sanyam's discovery of security vulnerabilities has earned recognition in leading publications like Forbes, TechCrunch, ZDNet, and Bleeping Computer, underscoring his thought leadership in the field.

In addition to his corporate work, Sanyam collaborates with NGOs such as GDI Foundation and CSIRT.Global, supporting the protection of critical internet infrastructures. He also serves as a judge for Bintelligence and has evaluated projects in India's largest hackathon. Academically, he holds a Master's degree in Technology from BITS Pilani, graduating with distinction, and is CKA certified in Kubernetes. His contributions extend to book reviews on cybersecurity and cloud computing, reflecting his commitment to advancing knowledge and best practices in the industry.

Acknowledgement

Writing *Mastering CyberSecurity Defense* has been an incredible journey, one that would not have been possible without the support, encouragement, and inspiration of many individuals.

First and foremost, I express my deepest gratitude to my parents, *Late Madhuri Tripathi* and *Uday Bhan Tripathi*, whose values, wisdom, and unwavering support have shaped me. To my wife, *Dr. Aparna Tripathi*, for her constant encouragement, patience, and belief in my aspirations, even during the countless hours I spent writing this book. To my wonderful children, *Ayantika Tripathi* and *Abhyuday Tripathi*, for being my source of inspiration and reminding me why CyberSecurity is crucial for the next generation.

I extend my sincere appreciation to my mentors, *Dr. Ram Kumar G* and *Dr. Swati Mishra*. Your guidance, thought-provoking discussions, and shared experiences have greatly enriched my knowledge and perspectives. A special thanks also to my professional network, including security leaders, researchers, and practitioners, whose insights and collaboration have been instrumental in shaping the ideas presented in this book.

To my friends and well-wishers, thank you for your unwavering support and encouragement. Your belief in my vision motivated me to push forward, even in challenging times.

A heartfelt thank you to *BPB Publications* for trusting my ability and providing this incredible platform to publish my book. Their support and guidance were invaluable in navigating the complexities of the publishing process. I would also like to acknowledge the reviewers, technical experts, and editors who offered valuable feedback and played a crucial role in refining this manuscript. Their insights and suggestions have significantly enhanced the quality of this book.

Finally, I extend my gratitude to my readers. Whether you are a CyberSecurity leader, professional, student, enthusiast, or individual, I hope this book serves as a valuable resource in your journey to mastering CyberSecurity. Your pursuit of knowledge and passion for securing the digital world inspire me to continue sharing and contributing to this ever-evolving field.

This book is the culmination of the collective efforts and encouragement of many, and I am deeply grateful for each contribution.

Preface

In an era where digital threats are growing at an unprecedented rate, CyberSecurity is no longer just an IT concern, it is a business imperative, a regulatory requirement, and a fundamental aspect of modern life. Organizations and individuals must adopt proactive security strategies to protect sensitive data, maintain business continuity, and mitigate Cyber risks. However, understanding CyberSecurity requires more than technical expertise; it demands a comprehensive approach integrating governance, risk management, and emerging technologies.

Mastering CyberSecurity Defense is my attempt to bridge the gap between theory and practical implementation, offering a structured approach to understanding, managing, and mitigating Cyber risks. This book is not just for security professionals but for anyone looking to develop a strong foundational and advanced understanding of CyberSecurity concepts. Whether you are an intern, student, professional, business leader, or someone simply concerned about digital security, this book provides a well-rounded perspective on CyberSecurity challenges and best practices.

One key motivation for writing this book was to make CyberSecurity knowledge more accessible and actionable. I have included real-world examples, industry best practices, and insights professionals can apply daily. Additionally, emerging technologies such as Artificial Intelligence, Blockchain, and Quantum Computing are explored to give readers a glimpse into the future of CyberSecurity.

I hope this book serves as a valuable guide in your CyberSecurity journey. Whether you are taking your first steps into this field or looking to deepen your expertise, *Mastering CyberSecurity Defense* will equip you with the knowledge and strategies to navigate the ever-evolving digital threat landscape.

Chapter 1: Introduction to CyberSecurity - CyberSecurity is the practice of protecting systems, networks, and data from Cyber threats. This chapter provides a foundational understanding of CyberSecurity concepts, their importance in today's world, and the various domains it encompasses. It traces the evolution of CyberSecurity, highlighting how digital transformation has led to increased attack surfaces. The chapter introduces key terminologies such as threat actors, vulnerabilities, exploits, and attack vectors.

It also covers different branches of CyberSecurity, including network security, cloud security, endpoint protection, and application security. Readers will gain insights into the impact of Cyberattacks on businesses, governments, and individuals, emphasizing the need for a proactive security mindset. By the end of this chapter, readers will have a clear understanding of why CyberSecurity is critical and how it plays a crucial role in protecting digital assets in an increasingly interconnected world.

Chapter 2: Understanding Cyber Threat Landscape - The Cyber threat landscape is constantly evolving, with attackers using sophisticated techniques to exploit vulnerabilities. This chapter delves into different types of Cyber threats, including malware, phishing, ransomware, **denial-of-service (DoS)** attacks, insider threats, and **advanced persistent threats (APTs)**. Readers will understand the motivations behind Cyberattacks, such as financial gain, state-sponsored espionage, and hacktivism.

The chapter also explores the **tactics, techniques, and procedures (TTPs)** used by Cybercriminals and how organizations can proactively monitor and mitigate these threats. Real-world case studies are presented to illustrate the consequences of Cyberattacks on businesses and governments. By understanding the attack lifecycle and emerging threat vectors, readers will be better equipped to anticipate and defend against Cyber risks. The importance of continuous threat intelligence and risk assessment is also emphasized, preparing readers for the complexities of modern CyberSecurity challenges.

Chapter 3: Building a Secure Infrastructure - A strong security posture begins with a well-protected IT infrastructure. This chapter focuses on designing and implementing security architectures that safeguard networks, endpoints, cloud environments, and applications. Readers will explore core security principles such as defense in depth, least privilege access, and zero trust security.

It covers various security controls, including firewalls, **intrusion detection and prevention systems (IDPS)**, **endpoint detection and response (EDR)**, and encryption techniques. Cloud security strategies, including securing workloads in AWS, Azure, and Google Cloud, are also discussed. Additionally, network segmentation, micro-segmentation, and secure coding practices are explained to minimize vulnerabilities.

By the end of this chapter, readers will understand how to implement a multi-layered defense strategy to reduce attack surfaces and enhance infrastructure security. The chapter also introduces security frameworks such as NIST, ISO 27001, and CIS controls to guide best practices in building a resilient security infrastructure.

Chapter 4: Defending Data Strategies - Data is one of the most valuable digital assets, making it a prime target for Cybercriminals. This chapter explores various strategies for securing data at rest, in transit, and in use. It introduces encryption techniques, data masking, and tokenization as essential methods for protecting sensitive information.

The importance of access controls, database security, and **data loss prevention (DLP)** mechanisms is also discussed. Additionally, compliance requirements such as GDPR, HIPAA, and PCI DSS are explained to help organizations align with regulatory standards. Readers will learn how to classify and secure different types of data based on sensitivity levels.

The chapter emphasizes the significance of secure data storage, backup strategies, and disaster recovery planning. Real-world scenarios highlight how poor data protection can lead to financial losses and reputational damage. By implementing robust data security measures, organizations can ensure confidentiality, integrity, and availability of their critical assets.

Chapter 5: Identity and Access Management - IAM is a crucial component of CyberSecurity that ensures only authorized individuals have access to critical systems and data. This chapter introduces IAM concepts, including **authentication, authorization**, and **accounting (AAA)** principles.

It explores different authentication methods such as **single sign-on (SSO), multi-factor authentication (MFA)**, and biometric security. The chapter also explains **Role-Based Access Control (RBAC)**, **Attribute-Based Access Control (ABAC)**, and **Privileged Access Management (PAM)**. Readers will understand the risks associated with weak credentials and how to implement secure identity policies.

The chapter further discusses **Identity-as-a-Service (IDaaS)** and modern trends in identity security, including password-less authentication and zero-trust identity models. Real-world use cases highlight the consequences of poor access management and how organizations can mitigate identity-based threats. By the end of this chapter, readers will be well-equipped to establish strong IAM policies and enhance organizational security.

Chapter 6: Security Policies and Procedures - A well-defined security policy framework is essential for maintaining a strong CyberSecurity posture. This chapter explains how organizations can develop, implement, and enforce security policies tailored to their business needs. It covers key security frameworks such as NIST, ISO 27001, and CIS controls, providing a structured approach to risk management.

Topics include third-party security management, vendor risk assessments, and security awareness training. The chapter emphasizes the importance of establishing clear security guidelines for employees, vendors, and stakeholders. Additionally, incident handling procedures, security audits, and compliance management are discussed.

By implementing effective security policies and procedures, organizations can create a security-conscious culture that minimizes human error and enhances regulatory compliance. Case studies demonstrate how well-defined policies have prevented major security breaches, reinforcing the need for structured security governance.

Chapter 7: Incident Response - Despite strong security measures, Cyber incidents are inevitable. This chapter focuses on incident response planning, detection, mitigation, and recovery strategies. Readers will learn about the incident response lifecycle, including preparation, identification, containment, eradication, recovery, and lessons learned.

Key incident response tools such as SIEM (Security Information and Event Management), forensic investigation techniques, and automated threat detection solutions are explored. The chapter also explains how organizations can develop an effective Cyber Incident Response Plan (CIRP) to minimize downtime and financial losses during a security breach.

Real-world case studies illustrate how organizations have successfully responded to major Cyberattacks. The chapter highlights the importance of tabletop exercises and simulations to prepare for CyberSecurity incidents proactively. By the end, readers will understand how to build a resilient incident response strategy to mitigate risks effectively.

Chapter 8: Legal and Ethical Considerations - CyberSecurity is not just a technical challenge, it also involves legal and ethical responsibilities. This chapter discusses global CyberSecurity laws, data privacy regulations, and compliance requirements. It explains GDPR, CCPA, HIPAA, and industry-specific legal frameworks that govern CyberSecurity practices.

The chapter also explores ethical hacking, responsible disclosure policies, and digital forensics. Readers will gain insights into the legal consequences of Cybercrime, including penalties for data breaches and intellectual property theft. Additionally, the role of ethics in CyberSecurity decision-making is highlighted.

CyberSecurity professionals can ensure compliance while maintaining high ethical standards by understanding legal and ethical considerations. Real-world legal cases and regulatory violations are lessons for organizations to strengthen their security and legal posture.

Chapter 9: Emerging Trends in CyberSecurity - As technology advances, so do Cyber threats. This chapter explores future CyberSecurity trends, including AI-driven security, blockchain for security applications, IoT security challenges, quantum computing threats, and Cyber resilience strategies.

Readers will learn how organizations leverage machine learning for threat detection and how blockchain enhances data integrity. They will also cover the impact of Zero-Trust Architecture and automation in CyberSecurity operations.

This chapter provides a forward-looking perspective, helping readers stay ahead in the rapidly evolving CyberSecurity landscape. Organizations that embrace these emerging technologies will be better prepared to tackle future threats effectively.

Coloured Images

Please follow the link to download the
Coloured Images of the book:

https://rebrand.ly/ndv6gee

We have code bundles from our rich catalogue of books and videos available at **https://github.com/bpbpublications**. Check them out!

Errata

We take immense pride in our work at BPB Publications and follow best practices to ensure the accuracy of our content to provide with an indulging reading experience to our subscribers. Our readers are our mirrors, and we use their inputs to reflect and improve upon human errors, if any, that may have occurred during the publishing processes involved. To let us maintain the quality and help us reach out to any readers who might be having difficulties due to any unforeseen errors, please write to us at :

errata@bpbonline.com

Your support, suggestions and feedbacks are highly appreciated by the BPB Publications' Family.

Did you know that BPB offers eBook versions of every book published, with PDF and ePub files available? You can upgrade to the eBook version at www.bpbonline. com and as a print book customer, you are entitled to a discount on the eBook copy. Get in touch with us at :

business@bpbonline.com for more details.

At **www.bpbonline.com**, you can also read a collection of free technical articles, sign up for a range of free newsletters, and receive exclusive discounts and offers on BPB books and eBooks.

Piracy

If you come across any illegal copies of our works in any form on the internet, we would be grateful if you would provide us with the location address or website name. Please contact us at **business@bpbonline.com** with a link to the material.

If you are interested in becoming an author

If there is a topic that you have expertise in, and you are interested in either writing or contributing to a book, please visit **www.bpbonline.com**. We have worked with thousands of developers and tech professionals, just like you, to help them share their insights with the global tech community. You can make a general application, apply for a specific hot topic that we are recruiting an author for, or submit your own idea.

Reviews

Please leave a review. Once you have read and used this book, why not leave a review on the site that you purchased it from? Potential readers can then see and use your unbiased opinion to make purchase decisions. We at BPB can understand what you think about our products, and our authors can see your feedback on their book. Thank you!

For more information about BPB, please visit **www.bpbonline.com**.

Join our book's Discord space

Join the book's Discord Workspace for Latest updates, Offers, Tech happenings around the world, New Release and Sessions with the Authors:

https://discord.bpbonline.com

Table of Contents

CHAPTER 1

Introduction to CyberSecurity

Introduction

Welcome to the invisible battleground of cyberspace, where digital threats lurk in the shadows, waiting to strike. Let us unveil the indispensable role of CyberSecurity in safeguarding our digital world!

Technology has become an integral part of our daily lives in the ever-changing digital world. From waking up to the sound of our digital alarms to the instant chats or messages we send on our smartphones, brewing a cup of coffee with a programmable machine, using GPS to navigate to work, the online **Teams** or **Zoom** meetings we attend, and the digital content we consume every day, technology is omnipresent. It has made our lives more convenient and transformed how we work, learn, communicate, and entertain ourselves. However, with the prevalent use of technology comes a significant concern, **CyberSecurity**.

CyberSecurity is no longer a back-office IT function or a concern limited to tech giants and governments; today, it is the **bedrock of trust** in our digitally interconnected world. There is quite literally no sphere of life untouched by CyberSecurity. Whether a financial transaction in a bustling metro city or a remote healthcare consultation in a village, it plays a vital, though often invisible, role in protecting data, identities, and critical infrastructure.

In this digital era, CyberSecurity is not just relevant, **it is essential**. A depiction of CyberSpace is shown in *Figure 1.1*:

Figure 1.1: *Cyberspace*

Structure

The following sections will be covered:

- Transformation of CyberSecurity into a necessity
- Importance of CyberSecurity
- Historical overview
- Current landscape
- Emerging cyber threats
- Regulatory framework

Objectives

In this chapter, we will learn why CyberSecurity is crucial in today's digital age, protecting personal, organizational, and national data from cyber threats. We will also gain insights into the evolution of CyberSecurity, understanding how past events and technological advancements have shaped the current landscape. Identify and comprehend the major cyber threats facing us today, such as ransomware and phishing, as well as future risks posed by AI and quantum computing will also be covered. Under **Regulatory Frameworks**, we will explore the key data protection laws and regulations, such as GDPR, HIPAA, and CCPA, that govern CyberSecurity practices and ensure compliance. By the end of this chapter, you will build a solid foundation of CyberSecurity concepts and principles, preparing you for deeper discussions on specific strategies, tools, and best practices in subsequent chapters.

Transformation of CyberSecurity into a necessity

During the computing phases, CyberSecurity was often seen as a topic in science fiction or only relevant to a selected group of researchers. Computers were machines kept in controlled environments away from the daily lives of most individuals. Security risks were minimal. The notion of a cyberattack appeared like something from a movie rather than a real worry.

Yet, with progress and increased computer accessibility, things began to shift. The rise of the Internet marked a new era of connectivity that altered how we **communicate, work, and engage** with our environment. This enhanced connectivity also introduced vulnerabilities as hackers and cybercriminals discovered ways to exploit network and system weaknesses.

The 21st century witnessed an influx of cyberattacks that rocked our society's core. From data breaches to ransomware assaults, the threat landscape evolved continuously, posing fresh obstacles for individuals, businesses, and governments alike.

As our reliance on digital platforms for personal and professional activities grows, the security of our data and digital identities becomes a pressing concern. Cyber threats like **hacking, phishing,** and **ransomware** are not just abstract concepts but real dangers that can jeopardize our privacy and financial stability. In this digital age, neglecting robust CyberSecurity measures is like leaving our homes unlocked in a bustling city. The consequences can be severe, ranging from data breaches and financial loss to widespread disruptions. Therefore, CyberSecurity is not a luxury but a **necessity** in our technology-driven lives, protecting us as we navigate the digital landscape. This realization sets the stage for our exploration of CyberSecurity in this book.

Let us look at the origins of CyberSecurity, following its path from the days of computing to the interconnected world we live in today. Explore the events, progress, and shifts in thinking that have influenced the current state of CyberSecurity. From the groundbreaking work of CyberSecurity pioneers to today's fight against cyber threats, this journey is captivating and essential. **Come along** as we journey through CyberSecurity's past, present, and future, discovering why this field holds greater significance now than before. By the end of this chapter, you will have a solid understanding of why CyberSecurity is crucial in our digital age.

Importance of CyberSecurity

*In today's digital age, where a single click can unlock a world of convenience—or unleash a torrent of chaos—understanding CyberSecurity is no longer optional; it is **essential**. Dive into why protecting your digital life should matter to you now more than ever.*

CyberSecurity is not just about stopping hackers; it is a comprehensive system that safeguards sensitive data, defends against malicious threats, and preserves trust in digital interactions. It is a shield that protects individuals, businesses, and nations from unprecedented risks of data breaches, financial loss, and even systemic disruptions. Understanding its importance is **the first step** towards ensuring digital safety and security.

When the internet was starting out, CyberSecurity was mainly used by researchers and academics. Nowadays, it is an aspect of our daily routines. We do our banking, shopping, work tasks, and socializing online. However, some risks come with this convenience. If we do not properly safeguard our information, financial details, and identities, they could be vulnerable to theft.

CyberSecurity is the **cornerstone** of our digital resilience, ensuring information confidentiality, **integrity**, and **availability (CIA)** in an increasingly complex and interconnected landscape.

CyberSecurity safeguards our defenses, ensuring the security, privacy, and accessibility of information in an ever-evolving and interconnected online environment. Recognizing the significance of CyberSecurity is crucial, as a single breach can lead to losses in millions or even billions of dollars. Such breaches can tarnish a company's image and customer confidence and may result in legal consequences. At times, the repercussions of a cyberattack can extend beyond entities to impact nations by disrupting economies and affecting people's lives.

However, CyberSecurity is not solely the concern of corporations and governments as it affects everyone. Whenever we engage online, we enter the realm of cyberspace, where risks exist akin to those in the world. Cybercriminals operate like real-world thieves, constantly seeking chances to exploit vulnerabilities. Employing tactics, they infiltrate systems, pilfer data, and disrupt our routines.

The reason why CyberSecurity is crucial for everyone, not just for tech gurus, is as follows:

- **Protecting personal information**: Picture someone intruding into your home and walking away with your possessions. Cybercriminals target assets like the data stored on your computer, phone, or digital devices. They might snatch your passwords, financial details, or cherished photos. CyberSecurity plays a role in thwarting these individuals from accessing your information and ensuring it remains secure.

- **Safeguarding your devices**: Our laptops, smartphones, smartwatches, and tablets store a wealth of work-related data. CyberSecurity protects against malware, software that could compromise data integrity, tamper with files, or disrupt device functionality.

- **Securing your online identity**: Social media accounts and online profiles are integral to our digital footprint. Strong CyberSecurity practices prevent unauthorized access to these accounts, protecting us from reputational damage and social engineering scams.

- **Ensuring business continuity**: Businesses rely heavily on digital infrastructure for operations, communication, and data storage. Big companies have important data like secrets about their products, information about their customers, and future plans. CyberSecurity is like a big lock on all this valuable information, ensuring that only the right people can access it. Companies could lose their secrets, customers' trust, and business without CyberSecurity.

- **Making sure everything keeps running**: Do you face interruptions in Internet connectivity? It is frustrating, right? Cyber-attacks can cause interruptions to the Internet connectivity in companies. With good CyberSecurity in place, companies can keep their websites, apps, and other services running smoothly, even if someone tries to mess with them.

- **Saving money**: When cybercriminals attack, fixing the damage can cost a lot of money. Think about it like **repairing a house after a storm**. CyberSecurity helps prevent the attacks from happening in the first place, saving companies money in repair costs and lost business.

- **Protecting our country**: Just like how soldiers defend our country from enemies, CyberSecurity protects our country from cyber-attacks. These attacks can target important things like government websites, power plants, and hospitals. Nations invest in CyberSecurity to defend against cyber threats, deter adversaries, and ensure the security and sovereignty of their territories. We can keep our country safe from digital threats by having strong CyberSecurity defenses.

- **Building trust and confidence**: Trust is essential for conducting transactions, sharing information, and collaborating online. When we shop online, we trust websites with our credit card information and social media platforms with our personal photos and messages. CyberSecurity helps keep these platforms safe and trustworthy so we can feel confident using them.

- **Encouraging new ideas**: Without CyberSecurity, businesses might be too scared to try new things like developing cool apps or using new technology. But with good CyberSecurity in place, they can explore new ideas and innovate without worrying about cyber threats holding them back.

- **Navigating legal waters**: The maze of CyberSecurity is not just about technology; it is also about compliance with laws and regulations. From the DPDPA in India to the GDPR in Europe to the CCPA in California, these frameworks are designed to ensure the responsible handling of our digital footprints.

- **Fostering digital innovation:** Despite the threats, CyberSecurity is not just a defensive strategy; it is an enabler of digital progress. Knowing our digital playgrounds are secure allows us to confidently embrace cloud computing, IoT devices, and AI innovations.

CyberSecurity is a collective responsibility that extends to every individual, organization, and community. By promoting CyberSecurity awareness and education, we can empower users to recognize and mitigate cyber threats, fostering a culture of cyber hygiene and resilience. We can equip individuals with the knowledge, skills, and tools needed to navigate cyberspace safely and securely through training programs, awareness campaigns, and collaboration initiatives.

Historical overview

Step back in time with us to the early days of computers and the birth of cyber threats. Let us unravel the history of CyberSecurity and how it shaped the world we live in today!

Imagine a time when computers were room-sized behemoths, their capabilities limited to basic calculations. Back then, the idea of cyber threats seemed like a distant fantasy, but the dawn of the digital age changed everything.

Figure 1.2: The Manchester Baby, the first computer to store programs digitally [1]

The 1970s: ARPANET and the Creeper

The journey of CyberSecurity began in the **1970s** with the creation of **ARPANET**, a precursor to the modern internet. ARPANET was a project funded by the U.S. Department of Defense. It was the **first network** to implement the protocol suite TCP/IP, which became the technical foundation of the modern Internet.

During this time, researcher *Bob Thomas* created a computer program called **Creeper** that could move across ARPANET's network. Creeper was not malicious, it displayed a message saying, *I'm the creeper; catch me if you can!*. This was followed by the development of **Reaper**, a program written by *Ray Tomlinson*, the inventor of email. Reaper was designed to chase and delete Creeper, marking the birth of the first antivirus software and the first self-replicating program.

---

1. **https://www.bricsys.com/en-eu/blog/who-invented-computers**

The 1980s: Birth of commercial antivirus

The 1980s marked the birth of commercial antivirus software. As personal computers became more common, so did computer viruses. In 1987, **Andreas Lüning** and **Kai Figge** released their first antivirus product for the **Atari ST**. This software was one of the first to use heuristics to detect viruses.

In the same year, three Czechoslovakians created the first version of the **NOD antivirus**. Meanwhile, in the US, *John McAfee (Figure 1.3)* founded **McAfee** and released **VirusScan**, one of the first antivirus programs available to home users.

Figure 1.3: John David McAfee, Developer of first commercial AntiVirus program [2]

The 1990s: The world goes online

With the advent of the internet, more people began putting their personal information online. This led to an increase in identity theft and other forms of cybercrime. Organized crime entities saw this as a potential source of revenue and started to steal data from people and governments via the web.

By the mid-1990s, network security threats had increased exponentially, massively producing firewalls and antivirus programs to protect the public. These tools were designed to detect and block malicious activity on the internet.

The 2000s: Threats diversify and multiply

The 2000s marked a significant shift in the landscape of CyberSecurity. The diversification and multiplication of cyber threats characterized this era.

Emergence of professional cyberattacks

In the early 2000s, cyberattacks started to become more professional and consistent. Crime organizations began to heavily fund these attacks, recognizing the potential for significant financial gain. These professional cyberattacks were serious and damaging compared to the relatively amateur hacking attempts of the past.

---

2. https://en.wikipedia.org/wiki/John_McAfee

Government response

In response to the increasing threat, governments worldwide began to clamp down on the criminality of hacking. Laws that imposed much more serious sentences for those guilty of cybercrimes were enacted. This represented a significant shift in the perception of cybercrime from a relatively minor nuisance to a major criminal activity.

Advancement of information security

Despite the growing threat, the field of information security continued to advance. As the internet grew, so did the complexity and sophistication of security measures. New defense mechanisms were developed, including intrusion prevention systems and secure coding practices.

Growth of viruses

Unfortunately, the growth of the internet also led to an increase in the number and variety of computer viruses. These viruses became sophisticated and harder to detect, posing a challenge to information security professionals.

The 2000s was a pivotal decade in the history of CyberSecurity. The professionalization of cyberattacks, a strong government response, advances in information security, and the growth of computer viruses marked it.

Present-day

The field of CyberSecurity is experiencing tremendous growth every day. The global CyberSecurity market is projected to reach **$345.4 billion by 2026**. Ransomware, a threat to organizations' data security, is expected to continue its trend in the coming years.

CyberSecurity has become a priority for governments, businesses, and individuals worldwide as our reliance on digital technology increases. Its significance will only increase in the future.

The realm of cybercrime has seen a rise, with escalated losses each year due to such activities. In 2023, the average cost of cybercrime amounted to **$1.54 million**, double the figure from 2022, at **$812,3804**. The United States faced high-profile cyberattacks, with 156 incidents recorded between May 2006 and June 2020. In India, which boasts the world's largest internet user base, cybercrimes have kept pace with technological advancements.

Ransomware remains a cyber threat. In 2021, ransomware inflicted losses of **$20 billion** worldwide, projected to soar to **$265 billion** by 2031. The first half of 2022 witnessed around **236.1 million** ransomware attacks globally.

In 2023, the average ransom was **$1.54 million**, twice that of 2022 at **$812,380**.

Penalties for cyber offenses

Numerous countries have established penalties for cyber offenses. For example, India's *Information Technology Act* of *2000* outlines cyber offenses and their corresponding penalties, such as altering computer source documents, computer hacking, and sharing images without consent. Globally, fines, penalties, and settlements for breaching data privacy have soared into millions of dollars. Notably, GDPR violations have led to fines totaling billions of euros.

Government regulations

Governments worldwide have enforced regulations to combat cyber offenses. The primary law that addresses cybercrime in India is the Information Technology Act of 2000. Other significant regulations include the **Personal Data Protection Bill of 2019** and the National **CyberSecurity Policy 2013**. In the US, key CyberSecurity regulations include **Health Insurance Portability and Accountability Act (HIPAA)**, the **Gramm Leach Bliley Act**, and the **Homeland Security Act** encompassing **Federal Information Security Management Act (FISMA)**.

Technological innovations in cyber fraud detection

Technological advancements have played a crucial role in detecting cyber fraud. Advanced algorithms, AI systems, and machine learning capabilities are being leveraged to analyze vast amounts of data, identify patterns or anomalies, and proactively detect unusual activities.

Law enforcement efforts against cyber crimes

Police agencies worldwide are intensifying their actions to combat cybercrimes. The Indian government has launched a National Cyber Crime Reporting Portal in India to enable victims/complainants to lodge complaints about cybercrimes online. Law enforcement departments in the United States and other nations are embracing technologies to analyze data and identify, prevent, and capture cybercriminals.

Significance of CyberSecurity awareness

CyberSecurity awareness is crucial in our increasingly digital world. It is about understanding the various threats that lurk online, like phishing scams, malware, and data breaches, and knowing how to protect ourselves from them. This awareness is not just for tech experts, it is for everyone who uses the internet, from checking emails to online shopping. Knowing these cyber risks, we can better protect our personal information and secure our digital lives. It is essential to keep intruders out.

By staying informed about CyberSecurity, we can **avoid** potential disasters that could cost us money, damage our reputation, or disrupt our daily lives. Plus, when everyone tries to be cyber aware, it creates a **safer online environment** for all of us. It is about being proactive, learning continuously, and staying one step ahead of cyber threats. This shared responsibility helps ensure that our digital world remains safe to work, play, and connect.

The evolution of CyberSecurity is a narrative marked by innovation, adjustment, and the ongoing battle with cyber criminals. One fact remains evident from the stages of computing to today's intricate landscape, CyberSecurity is not merely an academic subject, it is a fundamental pillar of our contemporary society.

Current landscape

Buckle up for a journey through the digital landscape of CyberSecurity today. From ransomware nightmares to phishing schemes, let us navigate the challenges of the digital Wild West!

The only certainty is uncertainty. This phrase is particularly true in the field of CyberSecurity. The CyberSecurity environment constantly evolves, shaped by ongoing technological progress, and increased cyber threats.

In today's world, we are more interconnected than ever. The rise of the **Internet of Things (IoT)**, **cloud computing**, **artificial intelligence**, and **machine learning** has revolutionized our lifestyles and work habits. However, these advancements have also broadened the attack surface for cybercriminals, making CyberSecurity more intricate than ever.

Cyber threats

A diverse array of cyber threats marks the present CyberSecurity environment. These threats can be broadly divided into two categories: threats to data **confidentiality, integrity, availability (CIA)** and privacy threats.

- **Threats to Confidentiality:** Confidentiality threats in the CyberSecurity landscape focus on unauthorized access to sensitive data, aiming to compromise the privacy and security of information. Malicious actors often use **phishing**, **malware**, and **ransomware** to steal or expose personal, financial, or corporate data. Phishing attacks trick individuals into revealing confidential information by masquerading as trusted entities. **Malware** and **ransomware** can infiltrate systems to steal sensitive data or lock users out, demanding payment for its release. These threats jeopardize the confidentiality of data, leading to financial loss, reputational damage, or breach of trust. Protecting sensitive information from unauthorized access remains one of the core goals of CyberSecurity, ensuring that only authorized individuals or systems can view or alter critical data. This is particularly important for organizations handling **personally identifiable information (PII)** or intellectual property, where a breach of confidentiality could have severe consequences.

- **Threats to Identity**: Identity-based cyber threats pose significant risks to individuals and organizations by compromising personal and organizational identities. **Phishing** is one of the most common methods that attackers use to steal login credentials or personal information. By disguising themselves as legitimate entities, attackers deceive users into revealing sensitive data like passwords or social security numbers. Another rising threat involves **identity theft**, where cybercriminals use stolen information to impersonate others for financial gain or malicious activities. In such cases, attackers can open fraudulent accounts, make unauthorized transactions, or carry out other harmful actions under a stolen identity. As more personal and professional activities move online, protecting one's digital identity becomes critical. These identity-related threats lead to financial loss, tarnish reputations, and erode trust between users and systems, making robust identity verification systems and user awareness essential in the fight against such attacks.

- **Threats to Availability**: Availability threats primarily target the accessibility and functionality of data and systems, aiming to disrupt or completely halt their operations. A typical example is the **Denial of Service (DoS)** attack, where an overwhelming amount of traffic floods a system, causing it to slow down or become utterly unavailable to users. **Distributed Denial of Service (DDoS)** attacks, which involve multiple sources bombarding a server with requests, are even more difficult to defend against. Another threat comes from **ransomware**, which locks users out of their systems or data unless a ransom is paid, effectively blocking access to critical resources. Ensuring availability is vital for businesses that rely on real-time data, such as financial institutions or healthcare providers, where downtime can result in significant operational and economic losses. These attacks disrupt business continuity, hamper productivity, and create financial strain, highlighting the need for robust system monitoring and timely threat detection to maintain the availability of critical infrastructure.

- **Threats to Privacy**: Privacy threats target individuals' or organizations' personal and sensitive information, aiming to exploit it for malicious purposes. **Data breaches** are a common type of privacy threat where unauthorized parties gain access to confidential data, often resulting in the exposure of sensitive information such as financial records, healthcare details, or personal identification numbers. **Identity theft** is another severe privacy threat where cybercriminals steal personal information, such as names, addresses, or social security numbers, to commit fraud or other illegal activities. This can lead to financial loss, damage to reputation, and long-term legal issues for the victims. **Tracking** is a more subtle privacy threat that involves collecting personal data without the individual's knowledge or consent, often through cookies or other digital tracking tools. This information is then used for targeted advertising, surveillance, or identity profiling. Such privacy threats can erode trust and undermine individuals' control over their data, making it critical for organizations to implement stringent privacy safeguards and transparency measures to protect against these growing risks.

CyberSecurity measures

Various CyberSecurity measures have been developed to combat these threats. These measures can be broadly categorized into three types, as follows:

- **Preventive measures**: These measures aim to prevent cyber threats from occurring. They include firewalls, antivirus software, and encryption. Firewalls control network traffic, blocking unauthorized access while permitting authorized communications. Antivirus software detects and removes malware. Encryption converts data into code to prevent unauthorized access.

- **Detective measures**: These measures aim to detect cyber threats. They include **intrusion detection systems (IDS)**, **security information and event management (SIEM)** systems, Network monitoring systems, and **artificial intelligence (AI)**. IDS monitors networks for malicious activity. SIEM systems collect and analyze security data. AI uses machine learning algorithms to detect patterns and anomalies that indicate cyber threats.

- **Corrective measures**: These measures aim to correct the damage caused by cyber threats. They include disaster recovery plans, incident response plans, and backups. Disaster recovery plans outline how to restore normal operations after a cyberattack. Incident response plans outline how to respond to a security breach. Backups are copies of data that can be used to restore data.

CyberSecurity challenges

Despite these measures, the current CyberSecurity landscape is fraught with challenges. These challenges can be broadly categorized into technical, human, legal, and ethical. The explanations for each are as follows:

- **Technical challenges**: Technical challenges in CyberSecurity are the specific difficulties we face when protecting our digital world from online threats. These issues arise because of the complexity and constantly changing nature of technology and the tactics used by cybercriminals. Some of the technical challenges are listed as follows:

  - **Complex systems**: Our digital lives are supported by many interconnected devices and networks. The more complex these systems are, the harder it is to keep everything secure.

  - **Advanced attacks**: Cybercriminals are always devising new, more sophisticated ways to break into systems. They use clever techniques that can sometimes slip past even the best security defenses.

  - **Unknown vulnerabilities (zero-day)**: Sometimes, software has security flaws that no one knows about until attackers exploit them. These are called zero-day vulnerabilities and are tough to defend against because they are discovered only after being used in an attack. It is like fixing a hole in your roof only after it starts raining inside.

- **Outdated software**: Many systems do not get updated regularly, which leaves them open to attacks that could have been prevented with the latest security patches.

- **Data overload**: So much data is created daily that tracking it all is hard. This makes it difficult to spot suspicious activities or breaches quickly.

- **Lack of CyberSecurity experts**: There are not enough trained CyberSecurity professionals to meet the demand. This shortage makes it harder for organizations to protect themselves effectively, like a city needing more police officers to maintain safety.

- **New technologies**: Emerging technologies like the IoT, AI, and cloud computing bring new security challenges. Each new technology adds another layer of complexity that needs securing.

In simple terms, the technical challenges of CyberSecurity involve dealing with the complicated and ever-changing nature of technology and cyber threats, human mistakes, and the lack of enough skilled professionals to handle these issues effectively.

- **Human challenges**: Human challenges in CyberSecurity are the obstacles that come from how people interact with technology and each other. These challenges are just as important as technical issues and often involve human error, lack of knowledge, and workplace culture.

  - **Human error**: CyberSecurity issues can include using easy-to-guess passwords, falling for phishing emails, or accidentally clicking on dangerous links. These simple errors can let hackers in, even if all other defenses are strong.

  - **Lack of awareness**: Many people are not fully aware of the dangers online. They might not recognize a phishing scam or know why updating the software is essential. Without this awareness, people might engage in risky behaviors that compromise security.

  - **Insufficient training**: Without proper training, employees might not know how to handle sensitive information or react to potential security threats. Good training programs are essential to teach staff the best practices and how to stay alert to cyber threats.

  - **Neglecting security protocols**: Sometimes, people ignore security rules because they find them inconvenient or do not understand their importance. This can include sharing passwords or leaving devices unattended, making it easier for cybercriminals to gain access.

o **Resistance to change**: New security measures often require changing routines or learning new tools. Some people resist these changes because they prefer sticking to what they know, even if it is less secure. This resistance can slow down the implementation of better security practices.

o **Threats**: Not all threats come from outside. Sometimes, employees with bad intentions or who are careless can cause significant security breaches. These insider threats are often the hardest to detect and prevent.

o **Overconfidence**: Some people think they are not likely to be targeted by cyber-attacks, so they do not take the necessary precautions. This overconfidence can lead to poor security habits and increased vulnerability.

o **Communication barriers**: Effective CyberSecurity needs good communication between IT and the rest of the organization. Miscommunication or lack of communication can lead to security gaps and confusion about who is responsible for what.

Human challenges in CyberSecurity involve dealing with people's mistakes, behaviors, and attitudes. Tackling these challenges requires continuous education, clear communication, and a culture emphasizing security. We can better protect our digital lives and workspaces by addressing these human factors.

- **Legal and ethical challenges**: Navigating CyberSecurity's legal and ethical landscape is crucial in today's digital world. Organizations must balance privacy and security, comply with data protection laws, ensure consent and transparency, and uphold responsibility and accountability. These challenges relate to the legal and ethical aspects of CyberSecurity. They primarily include the following:

o **Privacy versus security**: We all want to feel safe but also value our personal space. Balancing privacy and security is a major challenge in CyberSecurity. While security measures are essential to protect data and systems, they can sometimes infringe on individual privacy. Extensive surveillance can help prevent cyber-attacks but may also lead to concerns about personal privacy violations. Organizations must find a middle ground where security measures do not excessively intrude on personal privacy, maintaining trust and compliance with privacy laws.

o **Data protection laws**: Companies must juggle regulations from all over the world just to keep our info safe. Data protection laws like the GDPR, HIPAA, and CCPA set standards for how organizations handle personal data. These laws require businesses to implement robust security measures to protect data from breaches and unauthorized access. Compliance with these regulations is mandatory, and non-compliance can result in severe penalties. Adhering to these laws helps protect individual privacy and builds customer trust by ensuring their data is handled responsibly.

o **Consent and transparency**: We should know exactly what is happening with our data and have a say in it. Obtaining informed consent and maintaining transparency in data practices are ethical imperatives in CyberSecurity. Users must fully know how their data is collected, used, and shared. Transparent practices include clear privacy policies and regular updates about data breaches or changes in data handling procedures. Ensuring that users give informed consent builds trust and aligns with legal requirements, fostering a more ethical approach to data management.

o **Responsibility and accountability**: When there is a security breach, someone must own up to it, but it is not always clear whose mistake it was. Organizations must take responsibility and be accountable for their CyberSecurity practices. This involves implementing strong security measures, regularly auditing systems, and responding promptly to breaches. Accountability means organizations must own up to their mistakes and take corrective actions to prevent future incidents. This ethical approach protects data and builds a culture of trust and integrity within the organization and with its customers.

o **Ethical hacking**: It is like trying to outsmart the bad guys before they cause any harm. But sometimes, the line between hero and villain gets a bit blurry. Ethical hacking involves using hacking skills for defensive purposes, identifying and fixing vulnerabilities before malicious hackers can exploit them. White hat hackers play a crucial role in strengthening CyberSecurity by conducting penetration tests and security audits. While their activities might seem invasive, they are performed with permission and aim to improve security. Ethical hacking helps organizations avoid cyber threats and reinforces a proactive security posture.

o **Cyberwarfare and espionage**: The governments are playing a high-stakes game with our security, and it is hard to tell who is on our side. Cyberwarfare and espionage present significant legal and ethical challenges. Nation-states engage in cyber operations to disrupt other countries' infrastructure or steal sensitive information. These actions can lead to substantial geopolitical tensions and moral dilemmas. The covert nature of cyber espionage makes it hard to detect and attribute, complicating international relations and raising questions about the ethics of state-sponsored cyber activities.

o **Access to information**: It is like having a treasure trove of secrets that everyone wants a piece of. Who gets to hold the key, and how do we ensure they are not peeking where they should not? Another ethical challenge is balancing security and the public's right to access information. While sensitive data must be protected, overly restrictive access controls can impede transparency and freedom of information. Striking the right balance is essential to ensure that necessary information is available to the public without compromising security. This balance fosters an informed society while protecting critical data from cyber threats.

o **Employee surveillance**: We all want to feel trusted at work, but sometimes security measures can feel a bit too much like "**big brother**". Employee surveillance for security purposes raises ethical privacy concerns. While monitoring can help prevent insider threats and ensure compliance with security policies, it can also be perceived as intrusive. Organizations must implement surveillance measures judiciously, ensuring they are proportionate and transparent. Clear policies on what is monitored and why, as well as employee consent, help maintain trust and respect privacy rights.

o **Misinformation and deepfakes**: It is difficult to tell what is real and what is fake in a world where everything looks legitimate. We must be extra careful about what we believe and share online, but spotting the phonies is not always easy. The rise of misinformation and deepfakes presents new ethical challenges in CyberSecurity. These tools can spread false information, manipulate public opinion, and damage reputations. Combating misinformation requires robust verification processes and public awareness campaigns. Deepfakes, which use AI to create convincing but false videos, pose significant threats to truth and trust. Addressing these challenges involves developing technologies to detect deepfakes and educating the public about the dangers of misinformation.

CyberSecurity is not just about stopping the bad guys; it is also about navigating through a maze of legal and ethical challenges where the rules are not always clear, and the stakes are high.

In the next section, we will explore strategies for building a secure infrastructure, emerging trends in CyberSecurity, and legal and ethical considerations in this field.

Emerging cyber threats

Fasten your seatbelts as we dive into the future of cyber threats. From AI-driven dangers to Zero-day attacks, the horizon is filled with unseen challenges!

Technology is like a coin with two sides; it makes life easier and gives troublemakers new ways to cause chaos. Cyber threats refer to actions that target computer systems, networks, and data with the intent of causing disruption, harm, or unauthorized entry. These dangers manifest in multiple ways, including posing risks to individuals, businesses, and governmental entities. Let us understand the seven types of troubles or **cyber threats** that have come up. They are as follows:

Emerging Cyber Attacks

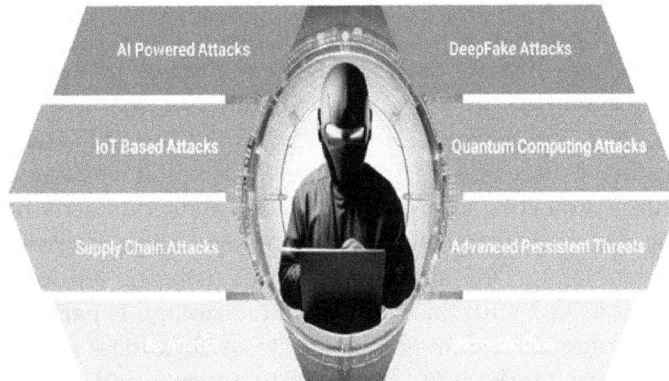

AI Powered Attacks   DeepFake Attacks

IoT Based Attacks   Quantum Computing Attacks

Supply Chain Attacks   Advanced Persistent Threats

Figure 1.4: Emerging cyber attacks

- **Artificial Intelligence-powered attacks**: AI-powered attacks leverage AI and machine learning techniques to carry out sophisticated cyberattacks. These attacks utilize AI algorithms to automate and optimize various stages of the attack lifecycle, making them faster, targeted, and harder to detect. AI can analyze vast amounts of data to identify vulnerabilities, craft convincing phishing emails, generate realistic deepfake content for social engineering, or even develop malware that can adapt and evolve to evade detection by traditional security measures. As AI technology advances, so will the capabilities of AI-powered attacks, posing significant challenges for CyberSecurity professionals in defending against these increasingly sophisticated threats.

- **IoT-based attacks**: IoT attacks target weaknesses in IoT gadgets to breach networks and access sensitive information. With the rise of devices ranging from household gadgets to industrial sensors, cybercriminals now have more targets. These attacks focus on protected devices by exploiting default passwords, unpatched vulnerabilities, or insecure network setups to gain unauthorized entry. Once compromised, these devices can be utilized for launching DoS attacks, data theft, or as gateways for network breaches. As IoT technology becomes more integrated into life and critical systems, tackling the security issues linked to devices is crucial in reducing the risks of IoT-related attacks and defending against potential cyber threats.

- **Supply chain attacks**: Supply chain attacks involve cyberattacks that exploit weaknesses in the network of suppliers and vendors supporting an organization's operations. These attacks target vulnerabilities within the supply chain to breach trusted systems and networks, aiming to compromise data or disrupt services. Attackers might infiltrate a supplier's systems to access the target organization's network or tamper with supply chain components to introduce code or backdoors. The impact of attacks extends beyond the targeted organization, affecting customers, partners, and stakeholders. With supply chains growing more intricate and interconnected, addressing security risks in these relationships is crucial for preventing supply chain attacks and safeguarding against CyberSecurity breaches.

- **5G attacks**: Attacks on 5G networks take advantage of vulnerabilities in fifth-generation technology to carry out cyberattacks that can compromise data security, privacy, and network availability. As the use of 5G technology becomes more widespread, attackers are finding ways to exploit weaknesses in the network infrastructure, protocols, and devices. These malicious activities could involve intercepting and modifying communications, exploiting network slicing for access to data, or launching DoS attacks to disrupt network services. Addressing the security issues linked with this innovative technology is paramount to safeguard against cyber threats and maintain the trustworthiness and dependability of communication networks as 5G continues to advance and grow.

- **Deepfakes**: Deepfakes use AI to create videos and audio clips that look and sound real but are totally made up. These manipulated media can deceive people by showing information or events. Deepfake technology can potentially damage trust in the media, public figures, and organizations, leading to turmoil, spreading information, and harming reputations. Moreover, deepfake attacks present CyberSecurity threats as they can facilitate impersonation, fraud, and manipulation for purposes. Combating the dangers posed by deepfake attacks necessitates a blend of solutions, such as detection algorithms and authentication methods, along with raising awareness and educating individuals on how to identify and minimize the impact of manipulated media.

- **Quantum computing**: It is like the next level of computing, super powerful and super-fast. However, it got CyberSecurity folks sweating bullets because it could break our current encryption methods. Quantum computing threats exploit the computing abilities of quantum computers to bypass encryption methods and compromise confidential information. The emergence of quantum computing threats could potentially make current encryption techniques outdated, leaving data vulnerable to access and manipulation. Mitigating the impact of quantum computing threats involves creating encryption algorithms for quantum attacks and enforcing quantum cryptographic standards for safeguarding digital communications and data amidst the era of quantum computing.

- **Advanced Persistent Threats**: Sophisticated cyberattacks known as **Advanced Persistent Threats (APTs)** are orchestrated by threat actors with goals. Unlike other cyberattacks, APTs are characterized by their term and persistent nature. These attacks involve stages like reconnaissance, infiltration, and data exfiltration. They are meticulously planned to go undetected for extended periods. APT attackers possess the resources and expertise to bypass security measures and avoid detection by security systems. They risk organizations by causing data breaches, stealing property, financial losses, and reputational damage. Combating

APT threats requires combining measures such as network segmentation, user training, threat intelligence utilization, and constant monitoring to promptly identify and mitigate APT activities.

- **Biometric data**: Cyberattacks that target biometric data exploit vulnerabilities in systems that rely on characteristics like fingerprints, facial features, or iris patterns for authentication or identification purposes. Biometric information, once compromised, cannot be altered like passwords, making it highly valuable to cybercriminals. These attacks may involve stealing data from compromised databases using altered biometric samples to trick authentication systems or exploiting flaws in biometric recognition algorithms to circumvent security measures. The theft or alteration of data poses privacy and security risks by potentially leading to identity theft, unauthorized access to sensitive information, and misuse of biometric credentials. Safeguarding data from attacks necessitates implementing strong security measures such as encryption, multi-factor authentication, and ongoing monitoring to uphold the confidentiality and integrity of this information.

- **Cyber-physical attacks**: Cyber-physical attacks focus on disrupting the connection between physical systems, posing threats to essential infrastructure, industrial controls, and everyday gadgets. These attacks exploit weaknesses in interconnected networks to interfere with operations like power distribution, transport systems, or manufacturing plants. By compromising elements, attackers can take control of physical systems, leading to operational disruptions, safety risks, or financial harm. Cyber-physical attacks may involve software targeting controls, ransomware impacting critical infrastructure, or exploiting IoT devices remotely. The consequences of attacks can be severe and vary from service interruptions and equipment damage to public safety concerns and environmental crises. Safeguarding against cyber-attacks requires a CyberSecurity approach that combines physical security measures with strong network defenses and proactive threat intelligence to manage the risks posed by these sophisticated and ever-evolving threats.

- **Zero-day exploit**: Zero-day exploits are essentially security weaknesses in software or hardware that the vendor is unaware of and has not provided a patch or solution for. Hackers can use these vulnerabilities to access systems that run code without permission or steal data. The danger with zero-day exploits lies in attackers finding and exploiting them before developers can fix them, making systems susceptible to attacks. Cybercriminals and government-backed groups often target these exploits to attack assets. To minimize the risk of zero-day exploits, organizations should take security steps like managing vulnerabilities using threat intelligence and employing intrusion detection methods to identify and counter attacks promptly. It is also crucial for organizations to prioritize installing software updates and patches to narrow the window of opportunity for attackers looking to exploit zero-day vulnerabilities.

The world of CyberSecurity is like a never-ending adventure, with new challenges always cropping up. We must stay sharp, keep learning, and be ready to tackle whatever comes our way. Because in this digital journey, the only way to stay ahead is to evolve right alongside it.

Regulatory framework

Embark on a journey through the maze of CyberSecurity regulations, where laws shape the landscape of our digital rights. From GDPR to HIPAA, let us unravel the rules that govern our data.

The CyberSecurity regulatory framework is a set of rules and guidelines designed to protect digital lives in an increasingly connected world. As we rely more on technology for everything from banking to healthcare, safeguarding sensitive information and critical systems has become paramount. Different countries have developed their own regulations, reflecting their unique legal, cultural, and technological landscapes. However, common principles like data protection, incident reporting, and cybercrime prevention form the backbone of these frameworks. By adhering to these standards, organizations can enhance their security measures, foster trust with users, and navigate the complex web of global cyber threats. There are some common themes and principles we see in many of these regulatory frameworks, which are as follows:

- **Data protection and privacy**: Ensuring the security and confidentiality of users' data is crucial to prevent access and misuse of it. It is comparable to securing a diary with a lock to ensure that only the owner can access its contents. Various security regulations and laws worldwide are designed to safeguard users' data. For instance, Europe's **General Data Protection Regulation (GDPR)** establishes strict rules for handling personal information. The **California Consumer Privacy Act (CCPA)** grants residents more control over their data in the United States. China's **Personal Information Protection Law (PIPL)** also prioritizes protecting personal data. Moreover, India's **Digital Personal Data Protection Act (DPDP)** outlines regulations for handling data and empowers individuals with control over their information. These frameworks promote a secure digital landscape by upholding strong data protection measures.

- **Incident reporting and response**: Incident reporting and response are critical parts of a security framework, ensuring that any breaches or attacks are quickly addressed to minimize damage. Organizations must report it promptly to authorities and affected parties when a cyber incident occurs, like a data breach or malware attack. This quick action helps contain the threat and prevent it from spreading further. Having a solid incident response plan also means that organizations are prepared to investigate the incident, fix vulnerabilities, and restore normal operations swiftly. By fostering transparency and readiness, incident reporting and response contribute significantly to overall CyberSecurity, making digital environments safer for everyone.

- **Cybercrime and law enforcement**: Cybercrime encompasses actions carried out using computers or the internet, like hacking, fraudulent activities, and stealing identities. Law enforcement agencies have a crucial role in fighting against these offenses by looking into incidents, collecting evidence, and bringing offenders to justice. They operate on a global scale to locate cybercriminals, often working in conjunction with agencies and groups. Effective law enforcement efforts serve to discourage cybercrime by holding wrongdoers accountable and improving security. This collaborative approach ensures that the Internet remains an environment for both individuals and businesses.

  The following are a few key law enforcement agencies around the world that are involved in combating cybercrime:

    o **Federal Bureau of Investigation (FBI)**, United States

    ·o Europol - European Union

    o **National Crime** Agency (**NCA**), United Kingdom

    o **Australian CyberSecurity Centre (ACSC)**, Australia

    o **Cyber Crime Investigation Cell (CCIC)**, India

    o **INTERPOL**, International

    o **Canadian Centre for CyberSecurity (CCCS)**, Canada

    o China's **Ministry of Public Security (MPS)**, China

    o Japan's **National Police Agency (NPA)**, Japan

    o **National CyberSecurity Agency (ANSSI)**, France

  These agencies work to investigate and combat cybercrimes, often collaborating with each other to tackle cross-border cyber threats.

- **Critical infrastructure protection**: Safeguarding critical infrastructure is essential to protecting systems and assets that contribute to national security, public health, and safety. This includes sectors such as energy, water, transportation, and telecommunications. Defending these infrastructures from cyber threats is vital, as any disruption can severely affect society.

  Security and regulatory frameworks such as the NIST CyberSecurity Framework, ISO/IEC 27001, **European Programme for Critical Infrastructure Protection (EPCIP)**, and **critical infrastructure protection (CIP)** Standards play a vigorous role in safeguarding infrastructure by offering guidelines and best practices for securing these systems.

- **Key global CyberSecurity regulations**: Numerous important CyberSecurity regulatory frameworks have been established to safeguard data and ensure CyberSecurity practices across various regions and industries. These frameworks establish standards and recommendations that organizations must adhere to in order to protect information and uphold the integrity of their operations. Some of those are as follows:

- o **General Data Protection Regulation**: The GDPR is a set of data protection rules enforced within the European Union dictating procedures for gathering, handling, and storing personal information. Its primary goal is to empower individuals with authority over their data by promoting organizational transparency and accountability. Companies must adhere to security protocols to safeguard data and promptly inform authorities and affected individuals in case of a data breach. Failure to comply can lead to penalties, underscoring the significance of data privacy. Moreover, GDPR affords individuals rights, like accessing their information, requesting corrections, and seeking deletion, fostering a culture that values data integrity.

- o **Sarbanes Oxley Act (SOX):** The SOX is a US law designed to safeguard investors from fraudulent financial reporting by companies. While it mainly focuses on ensuring transparency and responsibility, SOX also emphasizes CyberSecurity. Businesses are mandated to set up controls to protect the accuracy and security of their data. These controls involve tactics to prevent data breaches and unauthorized access to information. Regular audits and reports must be conducted to show adherence to penalties for any violations. SOX encourages a culture of honesty and precision in governance, establishing itself as an aspect of financial and CyberSecurity protocols in the U.S.

- o **NIST CyberSecurity Framework:** The NIST CyberSecurity Framework, created by the National Institute of Standards and Technology in the United States, offers a risk-focused approach to enhance CyberSecurity. It has five core functions: **Identification**, **Protection**, **Detection**, **Response**, and **Recovery**. These functions assist companies in recognizing their CyberSecurity vulnerabilities, safeguarding assets, identifying cyber incidents, effectively responding to crises, and restoring operations after disruptions. Due to its adaptability and thoroughness, this framework has been widely embraced across sectors. It aids organizations of all sizes to bolster their CyberSecurity defenses and resilience against threats.

- o **Payment Card Industry Data Security Standard**: The **Payment Card Industry Data Security Standard (PCI DSS)** serves as a framework of security measures to ensure that all businesses handling credit card details uphold a secure and monitored environment. Established by the Payment Card Industry Security Standards Council, the PCI DSS sets out guidelines for safeguarding cardholder information through practices like encryption, access control, and routine security assessments. Every entity involved in processing, storing, or transmitting credit card data must adhere to PCI DSS to safeguard against data breaches and fraudulent activities. Compliance plays a major role in safeguarding consumer information and fostering trust in payment systems, highlighting its significance in upholding the reliability and safety of financial transactions.

o   **Health Insurance Portability and Accountability Act**: HIPAA is a US law that focuses on safeguarding individuals' medical information. HIPAA was established in 1996. The Privacy Rule establishes guidelines for protecting **protected health information** (**PHI**) and gives patients control over their records. The Security Rule mandates physical and technical safeguards to secure PHI (ePHI), including access controls and encryption. In case of a breach of PHI, the Breach Notification Rule requires entities to inform affected individuals and authorities. The Enforcement Rule sets out procedures for investigations and penalties for noncompliance overseen by the HHS **Office for Civil Rights** (**OCR**). HIPAA plays a vital role in maintaining the confidentiality and security of health data, fostering trust between patients and healthcare providers.

o   **Digital Personal Data Protection Act**: The DPDPA is India's first data protection law, enacted to safeguard digital personal data. The DPDPA outlines the responsibilities of organizations in processing personal data and grants individuals' rights over their information. It emphasizes the lawful basis for data processing, requiring explicit consent or legitimate use. The act includes provisions for data localization, mandatory data processing agreements with third parties, and significant penalties for non-compliance. By establishing a legal framework for data protection, the DPDPA aims to enhance privacy, encourage responsible data handling, and protect individuals' personal information in the digital age.

o   **Personal Information Protection Law**: China's PIPL sets stringent requirements for processing personal data within its borders. Effective in 2021, PIPL mandates that organizations obtain user consent before collecting data and adhere to legality, fairness, and necessity principles. It also requires data localization, meaning personal information must be stored within China, and it restricts cross-border data transfers unless stringent conditions are met. PIPL grants individuals rights like those under the GDPR, such as accessing, correcting, and deleting their data. The law protects individuals' privacy and ensures that personal information is processed securely and responsibly. The major CyberSecurity regulations are as follows:

Major Global CyberSecurity Regulations

Cybersecurity regulations refer to laws, policies, and standards that protect digital information, systems, and infrastructure from cyber threats.

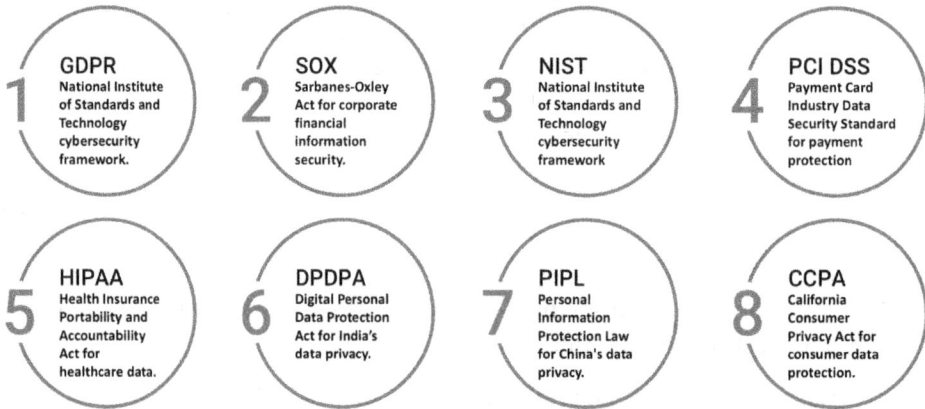

1 **GDPR** National Institute of Standards and Technology cybersecurity framework.

2 **SOX** Sarbanes-Oxley Act for corporate financial information security.

3 **NIST** National Institute of Standards and Technology cybersecurity framework

4 **PCI DSS** Payment Card Industry Data Security Standard for payment protection

5 **HIPAA** Health Insurance Portability and Accountability Act for healthcare data.

6 **DPDPA** Digital Personal Data Protection Act for India's data privacy.

7 **PIPL** Personal Information Protection Law for China's data privacy.

8 **CCPA** California Consumer Privacy Act for consumer data protection.

Figure 1.5: Major CyberSecurity regulations

o **California Consumer Privacy Act**: The CCPA gives people in California control over their information and privacy. It was implemented in 2018, allowing individuals to find out what data is being collected about them and who it is shared with and to opt out of selling their information. Additionally, it grants the right to ask for the removal of data stored by companies. The legislation applies to businesses that meet requirements, like having revenue or dealing with large amounts of personal data. CCPA aims to enhance transparency and responsibility, ensuring that companies uphold consumer privacy and manage data ethically.

o **Navigating the Complexities of Global Compliance**: Navigating the complexities of global compliance is challenging but essential for organizations operating in multiple jurisdictions. Each country has its own set of CyberSecurity laws and regulations, reflecting unique legal, cultural, and technological contexts. This creates a patchwork of requirements that businesses must adhere to, making compliance a formidable endeavor. To manage these challenges, organizations must conduct thorough compliance assessments to understand the specific laws and standards applicable to their operations. Developing a robust compliance program that includes regular audits, employee awareness training, and prompt monitoring of CyberSecurity measures is crucial.

Cross-functional collaboration between legal, Infosec, IT, HR, Product, and business teams can ensure a holistic approach to compliance. Leveraging technology and automation can also streamline compliance processes, reducing administrative burdens. Staying informed about emerging threats and regulatory changes helps organizations adapt and maintain compliance, ultimately building customer trust and safeguarding their digital assets.

Conclusion

This chapter laid the groundwork for understanding the critical role of CyberSecurity in today's digital world. The chapter illustrated the significant impact of security breaches on trust and operations through the lens of a real-world cyber-attack on a financial firm. It traced the evolution of CyberSecurity from early computing to the current landscape, highlighting major threats like ransomware and phishing. Emerging risks tied to AI and quantum computing were also discussed, emphasizing the need for proactive defense strategies. Additionally, the chapter reviewed important regulatory frameworks such as GDPR and HIPAA, underscoring the necessity for compliance to protect data and maintain trust. Overall, this chapter provided a comprehensive introduction to the multifaceted nature of CyberSecurity, preparing us for a deeper exploration of strategies and best practices in subsequent chapters.

Points to remember

- CyberSecurity is crucial for protecting digital assets and maintaining trust.
- Cyber-attacks can cause major disruptions and damage reputations.
- CyberSecurity has evolved from basic protections to addressing complex threats.
- Ransomware, phishing, and supply chain vulnerabilities are significant current threats.
- Emerging technologies like AI, 5G, and quantum computing present new security challenges.
- Adhering to regulations like GDPR and HIPAA is essential for protecting data and maintaining trust.

Join our book's Discord space

Join the book's Discord Workspace for Latest updates, Offers, Tech happenings around the world, New Release and Sessions with the Authors:

https://discord.bpbonline.com

CHAPTER 2
Understanding Cyber Threats Landscape

Introduction

In today's interconnected world, understanding the cyber threats landscape is akin to deciphering a complex puzzle with high stakes. From stealthy malware to nation-state espionage, this chapter illuminates the multifaceted dangers lurking in the digital realm and equips readers with the knowledge to navigate them safely!

In the dynamic arena of CyberSecurity, understanding the threats we face is paramount to devising effective defenses. Cyber threats have evolved dramatically over the years, transforming from simple hacks into sophisticated, multifaceted attacks that can cripple entire organizations. This chapter looks at the intricate landscape of cyber threats, providing a comprehensive overview that will equip readers with the knowledge to anticipate, recognize, and mitigate these ever-present dangers. By examining the evolution of cyber threats, the types of attacks, and the vectors and methods used by adversaries, we aim to foster a deeper understanding of the challenges in securing our digital world. A pictorial description of a cyberthreat landscape is as follows:

Figure 2.1: *Cyberthreat landscape across the globe*

Structure

The following sections will be covered:

- Evolution of cyber threats
- Types of cyber attacks
- Attack vector and methods

Objectives

By the end of this chapter, readers should be able to understand the historical progression of cyber threats from early viruses to sophisticated malware. The reader will be able to recognize various types of cyber-attacks, including APTs and targeted attacks. They will gain insight into attack vectors and methods such as phishing, social engineering, and DoS/DDoS attacks. By assessing the impact of cyber threats on organizations and individuals, the reader will be able to formulate defensive strategies against different types of cyber threats. All in all, the reader will enhance overall **CyberSecurity** awareness and proactive vigilance.

Evolution of cyber threats

From the playful pranks of early hackers to the calculated moves of modern cybercriminals, the evolution of cyber threats tells a tale of increasing complexity and peril.

The evolution of cyber threats is a journey through the history of digital innovation and exploitation. This subchapter explores the significant milestones in developing cyber threats, from the first computer viruses to today's **advanced persistent threats** (**APTs**). It highlights how technological advancements and increased connectivity have expanded the attack surface, making organizations more vulnerable to various threats.

Early computer viruses and worms

The nascent days of computing were marked by curiosity and experimentation, which inadvertently gave rise to the first computer viruses and worms. These early threats were not always malicious in intent but demonstrated the potential for significant disruption. This section looks at the origins of these pioneering cyber threats, examining the infamous Creeper and Morris Worm and their impact on early computing environments. In the early 1970s, the concept of self-replicating programs was introduced through the development of Creeper, often recognized as the first computer virus. The 1980s saw the creation of the Morris Worm, authored by *Robert Tappan Morris* in 1988. Unlike Creeper, the Morris Worm was a self-replicating program that caused significant disruption.

Impact on early computing environments

While often born from intellectual curiosity rather than malicious intent, the early viruses and worms profoundly impacted computing environments. Creeper demonstrated that programs could move autonomously across networks, raising awareness about the need for security in networked systems. The Morris Worm highlighted the real-world implications of such vulnerabilities, as it rendered many systems inoperable and caused widespread panic.

The aftermath of the Morris Worm underscored the importance of robust security measures and incident response protocols. It prompted significant changes in how software vulnerabilities were perceived and managed, leading to the establishment of CERT and the subsequent development of more sophisticated security practices. These early incidents laid the groundwork for the evolution of CyberSecurity as a critical discipline.

Rise of malware and automated attacks

As personal computing became more widespread in the 1990s, the landscape of cyber threats evolved to include more insidious forms of malware. This era saw the emergence of Trojan horses, spyware, and ransomware, alongside the development of automated attack tools that increased the scale and frequency of cyber incidents. This section explores the development and impact of these threats.

Development of trojan horses, spyware, and ransomware

Trojan horses, named after the deceptive wooden horse from Greek mythology, emerged as a prevalent threat in the 1990s. These malicious programs disguised themselves as legitimate software, tricking users into installing them. Once inside, Trojans could perform various malicious activities, such as stealing data, installing other malware, or creating backdoors for remote access. A notable example is the **Back Orifice** Trojan, released in 1998, allowing attackers to control Windows-based systems remotely.

Spyware, designed to monitor and collect user information secretly, became widespread with the rise of the internet. Programs like **Gator** and **CoolWebSearch** infiltrated systems to track user behavior, often for advertising purposes but also for more nefarious uses like identity theft.

Ransomware, which encrypts a user's data and demands payment for its release, first gained notoriety with the **AIDS Trojan** in 1989. However, it was in the mid-2000s that ransomware attacks became more frequent and financially motivated. Notable incidents include the **CryptoLocker** outbreak in 2013, which used strong encryption to lock victims' files and demanded Bitcoin payments for decryption keys.

Automation and the proliferation of attack tools

The automation of cyber-attacks significantly increased their scale and impact. Script kiddies, or inexperienced hackers, could leverage automated tools to launch attacks without deep technical knowledge. Tools like **Sub7** and **Metasploit** democratized hacking, enabling widespread exploitation of vulnerabilities.

Automation also facilitated the development of botnets, compromised computer networks controlled remotely by attackers. Botnets like **Storm** and **Zeus** were used for a variety of malicious purposes, including sending spam, launching **Distributed Denial of Service** (**DDoS**) attacks, and stealing sensitive information.

The proliferation of these tools led to an explosion in the number and severity of cyber-attacks, affecting individuals, businesses, and governments alike. The rise of malware and automated attacks marked a significant shift in the cyber threat landscape, necessitating more advanced security measures and a greater emphasis on CyberSecurity awareness and education.

Sophistication and coordination

The advent of the 21st century brought a new level of sophistication in cyber threats, characterized by APTs and coordinated attacks by nation-state actors. These threats posed significant challenges to CyberSecurity professionals, involving highly skilled adversaries employing advanced techniques for prolonged and targeted campaigns. This section explores the nature of APTs and the involvement of nation-states in cyber espionage.

Advanced persistent threats

APTs are a class of threats distinguished by their sophistication, persistence, and specific targeting. Unlike traditional cyber-attacks that aim for quick gains, APTs involve long-term, stealthy infiltration of networks, often targeting critical infrastructure, intellectual property, or sensitive governmental data. APTs typically employ a multi-phase approach: initial access, foothold establishment, privilege escalation, internal reconnaissance, data exfiltration, and maintaining persistence.

One of the most notable examples of an APT is the Stuxnet worm, discovered in 2010. Stuxnet targeted Iran's nuclear facilities and was designed to sabotage centrifuges used in uranium enrichment. The worm's complexity and specificity were unprecedented, demonstrating the potential for cyber weapons to cause physical damage.

Nation-state actors and cyber espionage

Nation-state actors have become significant players in cyber threats, conducting espionage, sabotage, and influence operations. These actors leverage their substantial resources and expertise to conduct sophisticated cyber campaigns that serve their strategic interests.

Cyber espionage has become a prevalent activity among nation-states. Operations such as **Operation Aurora**, attributed to Chinese state-sponsored actors, targeted major U.S. companies, including *Google*, to steal intellectual property and gather intelligence. Similarly, the *APT28* group, linked to Russian intelligence, has been involved in numerous espionage campaigns targeting governments, military organizations, and media entities.

These state-sponsored activities are often highly coordinated, involving multiple tactics such as spear-phishing, zero-day exploits, and custom malware. The involvement of nation-states in cyber operations has led to significant geopolitical tensions and has underscored the need for robust cyber defense capabilities at the national level.

Targeted attacks and cybercrime syndicates

The evolution of cyber threats has also seen the rise of organized cybercrime syndicates, targeted attacks aimed at financial gain, and data breaches. These well-organized groups operate with a level of sophistication that rivals nation-state actors, driven by substantial financial incentives. This section examines the emergence of cybercrime syndicates and their impact on the global CyberSecurity landscape.

Emergence of organized cybercrime groups

Organized cybercrime groups have become increasingly prominent in the digital age. These groups operate much like traditional criminal enterprises but in the virtual realm. They are often highly structured, with distinct roles ranging from developers who create malware to operators who deploy it and money mules who launder the proceeds.

One of the most notorious examples is the **Russian Business Network (RBN)**, which emerged in the mid-2000s. RBN provided a range of illegal services, including hosting for phishing sites, distribution of malware, and facilitation of child pornography. Their operations highlighted the sophisticated and business-like nature of modern cybercrime syndicates.

Financially motivated attacks and data breaches

Financially motivated attacks have become a major focus for cybercriminals, with tactics evolving to maximize profit. Ransomware attacks, like the **WannaCry** outbreak in 2017, have targeted organizations worldwide, demanding payments in cryptocurrency to unlock encrypted data. Similarly, the rise of *banking Trojans* such as **Zeus** and **Dridex** has allowed criminals to steal vast amounts of money directly from online banking accounts.

Data breaches have also become lucrative targets, with cybercriminals stealing personal information to sell on the dark web or use in identity theft schemes. High-profile breaches, such as the **Equifax breach** in 2017, exposed the sensitive data of millions of individuals, causing widespread financial and reputational damage.

The sophistication of these attacks often involves advanced techniques like social engineering, phishing, and exploitation of zero-day vulnerabilities. Organized cybercrime syndicates operate efficiently and effectively, posing significant challenges for CyberSecurity professionals and necessitating advanced detection and response strategies.

Current trends and future outlook

As the cyber threat landscape continues to evolve, new trends and technologies are emerging that will shape the future of CyberSecurity. This section explores current trends, such as using **artificial intelligence** (**AI**) and machine learning in cyber-attacks. It anticipates future threats and the role of emerging technologies in combating them.

AI and machine learning in cyber attacks

Integrating AI and machine learning into cyber attacks has significantly increased their sophistication and effectiveness. AI-powered attacks can adapt to defenses in real-time, making them harder to detect and mitigate. For instance, AI algorithms can analyze vast amounts of data to identify vulnerabilities, automate phishing campaigns, or develop polymorphic malware that changes its code to evade detection.

Machine learning techniques have also created more effective social engineering attacks. By analyzing social media and publicly available information, AI can craft highly personalized and convincing phishing emails, increasing the likelihood of success.

Future threats and the role of emerging technologies

Emerging technologies and the ever-increasing sophistication of cyber threats will continue to shape the CyberSecurity landscape. Quantum computing, for example, poses both opportunities and challenges. While it has the potential to revolutionize encryption methods, it also threatens to break current cryptographic algorithms, necessitating the development of quantum-resistant cryptography.

The **Internet of Things** (**IoT**) will also present new challenges as the proliferation of connected devices expands the attack surface. Ensuring the security of these devices, which often have limited computational resources and security features, will be critical in preventing large-scale attacks.

Blockchain technology holds promise for enhancing security through its decentralized and immutable nature, yet it is not without vulnerabilities. As blockchain applications grow, so will the attacks targeting these systems.

In conclusion, staying ahead of the cyber threat landscape requires continuous innovation and adaptation. By leveraging advanced technologies and fostering a proactive CyberSecurity culture, we can anticipate and mitigate future threats, ensuring the resilience and security of our digital world.

Types of cyber attacks

Cyber-attacks come in many forms, each with its unique method of infliction, from the silent theft of data to the loud disruption of services!

Cyber-attacks are diverse and continually evolving. This subchapter categorizes the various types of cyber-attacks, detailing their mechanisms and the potential damage they can cause. Understanding these attack types is essential for developing targeted defensive strategies and mitigating the impact of breaches.

Malware definition, types, and its operational mechanisms

Malware, short for malicious software, encompasses a variety of harmful programs designed to disrupt, damage, or gain unauthorized access to computer systems. Understanding the different types of malware and their operational mechanisms is crucial for developing effective CyberSecurity strategies. This section delves into the definitions and functions of viruses, worms, Trojans, and ransomware, providing insight into how they operate and the threats they pose. The types of malware are as shown in the following figure:

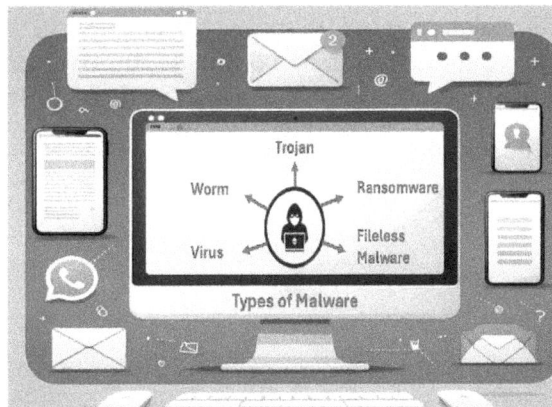

Figure 2.2: Types of malware

Definition and types of malware

The types of malware and their definitions are as follows:

- **Viruses:** Viruses are one of the earliest forms of malware. They attach themselves to legitimate files or programs and spread when the infected file or program is executed. Viruses can corrupt or delete data, disrupt system operations, and render systems inoperable. The **ILOVEYOU** virus, which spread via email in 2000, is a notorious example that caused extensive damage worldwide.

- **Worms:** Unlike viruses, worms are standalone programs that can replicate themselves without any human action, spreading across networks by exploiting vulnerabilities. Worms can cause significant network congestion and system disruptions. The **Blaster Worm** of 2003 is a well-known example, which exploited a vulnerability in Microsoft Windows to spread rapidly and cause widespread system failures.

- **Trojans:** Trojans, named after the deceptive wooden horse from Greek mythology, disguise themselves as legitimate software to trick users into installing them. Once installed, they can create backdoors, steal information, or download additional malware. A famous example is the **Zeus Trojan**, which steals banking information by logging keystrokes and capturing screenshots.

- **Ransomware:** Ransomware encrypts a victim's files, rendering them inaccessible until a ransom is paid. This type of malware has become increasingly prevalent and profitable for cybercriminals. **CryptoLocker**, which emerged in 2013, is a prime example of ransomware that caused extensive financial damage by encrypting files and demanding payment for release.

- **Fileless malware:** Fileless malware represents a significant shift in cyberattacks, operating without relying on traditional executable files. Instead, it leverages legitimate system tools and processes, such as PowerShell or WMI, to execute malicious code directly in a computer's memory. This approach makes it exceptionally difficult to detect with conventional antivirus software that primarily scans files. By leaving minimal traces on the hard drive, fileless malware evades detection and persists stealthily, posing a serious threat to systems and data.

Table 2.1 tabulates the comparison of different malware types:

Malware type	How it spreads	Primary target	Damage caused	Detection and prevention
Viruses	Attaches to legitimate files and requires user execution	Personal computers, corporate networks	Data corruption, file destruction	Antivirus software, regular updates
Worms	Self-replicates and spreads without user interaction	Networks, servers	Network congestion, slowing down systems	Firewalls, intrusion detection systems
Trojans	Disguised as legitimate software, executed by users	Individuals, enterprises	Data theft, remote access, unauthorized control	Endpoint protection, software whitelisting
Ransomware	Encrypts files and demands ransom for decryption	Businesses, hospitals, financial institutions	Data loss, financial extortion	Regular backups, email security training
Fileless malware	Resides in memory and exploits legitimate system processes	Government agencies, corporations	Hard to detect, executes stealth attacks	Behavioral analytics, advanced endpoint protection

Table 2.1: Comparison of malware types

Operational mechanisms

The operational mechanisms are as follows:

- **Propagation and infection:** Malware propagates through various vectors, including email attachments, malicious websites, and infected software downloads. Social engineering techniques, such as phishing, are often used to trick users into executing malware. Once executed, the malware replicates or installs itself, establishing a foothold in the system.

- **Execution and payload delivery:** After infection, the malware executes its payload, ranging from data corruption and theft to system disruption and espionage. Viruses and worms typically spread further, while Trojans and ransomware focus on stealing information or extorting money.

- **Persistence and evasion:** Advanced malware employs techniques to maintain persistence and evade detection. These include hiding in legitimate processes, using rootkits to mask their presence, and encrypting their communications. Malware may also disable security software to prevent its removal.

- **Impact and consequences:** Malware can have devastating impacts, from financial losses and operational disruptions to data breaches and reputational damage.

Organizations must implement robust security measures, including antivirus software, firewalls, and employee training, to mitigate the risk of malware infections.

Social engineering

Social engineering is a psychological manipulation technique used by cybercriminals to deceive individuals into revealing confidential information, granting unauthorized access, or performing actions that compromise security. Unlike traditional hacking, which exploits technical vulnerabilities, social engineering targets human behavior, relying on trust, curiosity, urgency, or fear to trick victims.

Attackers use tactics such as impersonation, phishing, or pretexting to access sensitive data like passwords, financial details, or company secrets. Social engineering remains one of the most effective cyber-attack methods because humans, despite security measures, can be the weakest link in **CyberSecurity**.

Types of social engineering

Cybercriminals employ various social engineering techniques, each designed to manipulate victims differently. The following are some of the most common methods:

- **Phishing**: A fraudulent attempt to obtain sensitive data by masquerading as a trustworthy entity via email, messages, or websites. Attackers create urgency or fear to manipulate victims into clicking malicious links or providing credentials.

    Example: A fake email from a bank warns of unauthorized access and urges the recipient to reset their password through a malicious link. This is depicted in *Figure 2.3*:

Figure 2.3: An illustration of a Phishing attack

Phishing is considered an **insider attack** because it manipulates authorized users within an organization to compromise security. Unlike external attacks, which directly exploit system vulnerabilities, phishing tricks employees or users into **unknowingly aiding attackers** by disclosing credentials, clicking malicious links, or downloading infected files.

- o Reasons phishing resembles an insider threat:

    - **Access via trusted users:** Since phishing exploits employees or users with legitimate access, it mimics an insider threat by using their credentials.

    - **Bypassing security measures:** Firewalls and intrusion detection systems often fail against phishing because it exploits human behavior rather than software vulnerabilities.

    - **Internal spread:** Once attackers gain access via phishing, they can escalate privileges, spread malware, or steal sensitive company data like an insider.

    - **Business Email Compromise (BEC):** Attackers use phishing to compromise corporate email accounts, then send fraudulent messages internally, making them appear as legitimate communications from trusted colleagues.

- o **Phishing types**: Various types of phishing attacks are described as follows:

    - **Email phishing:** Email phishing is the most common form of phishing, where attackers send emails that appear to be from legitimate sources, such as banks or popular websites. These emails often contain urgent messages designed to prompt recipients to click on malicious links or download attachments, leading to the theft of personal information.

    - **Spear phishing:** Spear phishing targets specific individuals or organizations, often using information gathered from social media or previous breaches to craft personalized and convincing messages. This tailored approach increases the likelihood of the victim falling for the scam. For example, attackers might impersonate a CEO and request the finance department to transfer funds.

    - **Clone phishing:** In clone phishing, attackers create a replica of a legitimate email previously sent by a trusted source. They modify the content slightly, often replacing legitimate links with malicious ones, and resend it to the victim. The familiarity of the email increases the chances of the recipient clicking on the compromised links.

    - **Whaling:** Whaling targets high-profile individuals, such as executives and politicians, with meticulously crafted and highly personalized phishing emails. These attacks steal sensitive information or trick victims into authorizing high-value transactions.

- **Pretexting**: Pretexting involves an attacker creating a fabricated scenario (pretext) to obtain information from the target. For example, an attacker might pose as a tech support representative and convince the victim to provide their login credentials to resolve a technical issue.

- **Baiting**: Baiting uses the promise of something desirable to lure victims into a trap. For example, infected USB drives could be left in public places with enticing labels, hoping someone will pick them up and connect them to their computer, thereby installing malware.

- **Quid pro quo**: Quid pro quo attacks involve exchanging services or favors to obtain information. For example, an attacker might call random numbers within an organization, offering free IT assistance in exchange for login credentials. This method exploits the victim's willingness to receive help in return for providing information.

- **Tailgating:** Tailgating, or *piggybacking*, involves an attacker gaining physical access to a secure area by following an authorized individual. This technique relies on the attacker's ability to blend in and exploit the victim's trust or courtesy.

- **Impersonation**: Impersonation is a social engineering tactic where attackers pose as trusted individuals, such as company employees, IT staff, or law enforcement, to manipulate victims into providing sensitive data or access. This technique is often used in phishing emails, phone calls, or face-to-face interactions. By gaining the victim's trust, attackers can extract passwords, financial details, or confidential business information, ultimately leading to data breaches, identity theft, or unauthorized access to secure systems.

- **Reverse social engineering**: Reverse social engineering is an advanced technique where attackers create a problem for the victim and then position themselves as the solution. Instead of directly requesting information, they trick victims into approaching them for help. For example, an attacker might disable an employee's computer remotely, then impersonate IT support and request login credentials to "fix" the issue. This method exploits trust and urgency, making victims more likely to comply without questioning.

- **Dumpster diving**: Dumpster diving involves searching through discarded materials, such as physical documents, hard drives, or old devices, to retrieve confidential information. Many organizations dispose of valuable data without proper shredding or erasure, making it an easy target for cybercriminals. Attackers can recover sensitive files, passwords, customer records, or financial details from trash bins, recycling centers, or e-waste disposals. This low-tech yet effective technique highlights the importance of secure disposal methods to prevent data leaks.

Impact and mitigation

The impact and mitigation are as follows:

- **Impact:** Phishing and social engineering attacks can lead to significant financial losses, data breaches, and reputational damage. Successful attacks often compromise sensitive information, which can be used for identity theft, fraud, or further attacks.

- **Mitigation:** Mitigating phishing and social engineering attacks requires a multi-faceted approach. Organizations should implement email filtering and anti-phishing technologies, conduct regular security awareness training, and establish clear protocols for verifying the authenticity of requests for sensitive information. Encouraging a culture of skepticism and caution can significantly reduce the effectiveness of these attacks.

Denial of Service and Distributed Denial of Service attacks

Denial of Service (DoS) and DDoS attacks aim to render systems and networks unavailable by overwhelming them with excessive traffic or requests, as shown in *Figure 2.4*. These attacks can cause significant disruption to online services, leading to financial losses and reputational damage. This section explains how DoS and DDoS attacks work, as well as their impact and mitigation strategies.

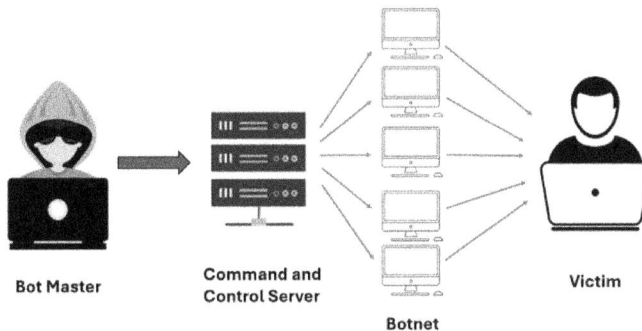

Bot Master   **Command and Control Server**   **Botnet**   **Victim**

Figure 2.4: Distributed Denial of Service

Working of DoS and DDoS attacks

The working of these attacks is as follows:

- **DoS attacks:** A DoS attack involves a single source generating a large volume of traffic or requests to overwhelm a target system or network. The goal is to exhaust the target's resources, such as bandwidth, processing power, or memory, causing it to slow down or become completely unresponsive.

- **DDoS attacks:** DDoS attacks are a more powerful variant of DoS attacks. They involve multiple compromised systems (often part of a botnet) simultaneously directing traffic towards the target. The distributed nature of DDoS attacks makes them more challenging to mitigate, as the traffic originates from numerous sources, making it difficult to distinguish between legitimate and malicious traffic.

Types of DoS and DDoS attacks

The types of attacks are as follows:

- **Volumetric attacks:** Volumetric attacks aim to consume the target's bandwidth by flooding it with a high traffic volume. Examples include UDP floods and ICMP floods, where large packets are sent to the target to saturate its internet connection.

- **Protocol attacks:** Protocol attacks exploit weaknesses in network protocols to deplete resources. SYN floods, for instance, exploit the TCP handshake process by sending many SYN requests to a server without completing the handshake, causing the server to consume resources waiting for responses that never arrive.

- **Application layer attacks:** Application layer attacks target specific applications or services, generating requests that appear legitimate but overwhelm the application's ability to respond. HTTP floods, where attackers send numerous HTTP requests to a web server, are a common example of application-layer attacks.

Impact of DoS and DDoS attacks

DoS and DDoS attacks can have severe consequences for organizations, including the following:

- **Service disruption:** The primary impact is the disruption of services, making websites, applications, or networks unavailable to legitimate users. This can result in lost revenue, especially for e-commerce and online service providers.

- **Reputational damage:** Prolonged downtime can harm an organization's reputation, leading to a loss of customer trust and potential long-term damage to the brand.

- **Financial losses:** In addition to lost revenue, organizations may incur significant costs in responding to and mitigating attacks, including investing in additional infrastructure and security measures.

Mitigation strategies

The mitigation strategies are as follows:

- **Rate limiting:** Rate limiting controls the number of requests a server will accept from a single IP address within a given timeframe, helping to mitigate the impact of DoS attacks.

- **Traffic analysis and filtering:** Advanced AI traffic analysis tools can help distinguish between legitimate and malicious traffic. Implementing filters to block suspicious traffic can reduce the effectiveness of DDoS attacks.

- **DDoS protection services:** Many organizations use DDoS protection services, such as those offered by **content delivery networks (CDNs)** or specialized security firms. These firms have the infrastructure and expertise to absorb and mitigate large-scale attacks.

- **Redundancy and load balancing:** Building redundancy into network infrastructure and using load balancers to distribute traffic across multiple servers can help ensure that services remain available even during an attack.

In conclusion, understanding the mechanisms and impact of DoS and DDoS attacks is crucial for developing effective defense strategies. By implementing robust mitigation measures and staying vigilant, organizations can protect their online services from these disruptive threats.

Man-in-the-Middle attacks

Man-in-the-Middle (MitM) attacks involve an attacker intercepting and potentially altering the communication between two parties without their knowledge. These attacks can compromise the confidentiality and integrity of sensitive information, leading to data breaches and financial loss. This section explores the methods and impact of MitM attacks (*Figure 2.5*) and how to defend against them.

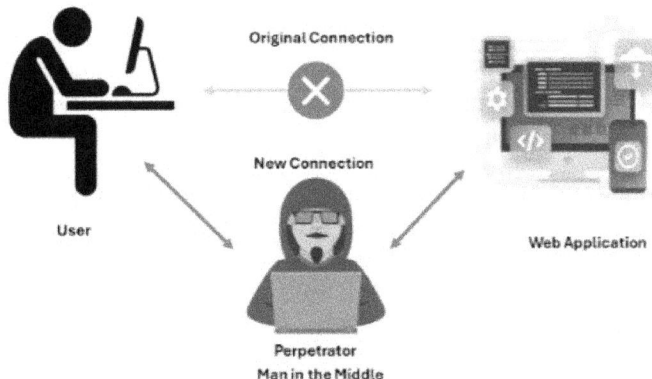

Figure 2.5: Man in the Middle Attack

Methods of MitM attacks

The methods used during MitM attacks are as follows:

- **Eavesdropping:** In eavesdropping attacks, the attacker intercepts communications between two parties to steal information such as login credentials, financial data, or personal information. This can be done through packet sniffing, where network traffic is captured and analyzed.

- **Session hijacking:** Session hijacking involves an attacker taking over an active session between a user and a service. By stealing session cookies or tokens, the attacker can impersonate the user and gain unauthorized access to sensitive information or perform actions on behalf of the user.

- **SSL stripping:** SSL stripping downgrades the security of an HTTPS connection to an unencrypted HTTP connection. The attacker intercepts the initial connection request and redirects it to an HTTP version of the website, making the communication vulnerable to interception and manipulation. Public Wi-Fi networks are prime targets due to their lack of security and shared nature.

- **DNS spoofing:** DNS spoofing, or DNS cache poisoning, involves an attacker altering DNS records to redirect traffic from a legitimate website to a malicious one. This can be used to steal credentials, install malware, or conduct phishing attacks.

Impact of MitM attacks

MitM attacks can have severe consequences for both individuals and organizations, including the following:

- **Data theft:** Sensitive information such as login credentials, financial data, and personal details can be stolen, leading to identity theft, financial loss, and unauthorized access to accounts.

- **Financial losses:** MitM attacks can result in significant financial losses, especially if attackers gain access to online banking or payment systems. Unauthorized transactions and fraudulent activities can cause substantial damage.

- **Reputational damage:** If customer data is compromised, organizations targeted by MitM attacks may suffer reputational damage. Loss of trust can lead to a decline in customer loyalty and long-term business impact.

Defense against MitM attacks

The defenses against MitM attacks are as follows:

- **Encryption:** Using strong encryption protocols such as HTTPS and **Virtual Private Networks** (**VPNs**) ensures that communications are encrypted, making it difficult for attackers to intercept and read data.

- **Two-Factor Authentication:** Implementing **Two-Factor Authentication** (**2FA**) adds an extra layer of security by requiring a second form of verification, reducing the risk of unauthorized access even if credentials are stolen.

- **Public Key Infrastructure: Public Key Infrastructure (PKI)** uses digital certificates and public-private key pairs to establish secure communications. Certificates authenticate the identity of communicating parties, ensuring that data is exchanged between trusted entities.

- **DNS Security Extensions**: **DNS Security Extensions (DNSSEC)** add cryptographic signatures to DNS records, ensuring the authenticity and integrity of DNS responses and protecting against DNS spoofing attacks.

- **Security awareness training:** Educating users about the risks of MitM attacks and safe online practices can help prevent these attacks. Users should be cautious about connecting to unsecured Wi-Fi networks and be aware of phishing attempts.

In summary, MitM attacks pose a significant threat to the confidentiality and integrity of communications. By understanding the methods used by attackers and implementing robust security measures, individuals and organizations can protect themselves from these insidious attacks.

SQL injection and other web-based attacks

Web-based attacks exploit vulnerabilities in web applications to gain unauthorized access, manipulate data, or disrupt services. SQL injection (*Figure 2.6*), one of the most common and dangerous web-based attacks, targets an application's database layer. This section examines SQL injection and other web-based attacks, as well as their methods, impact, and mitigation strategies.

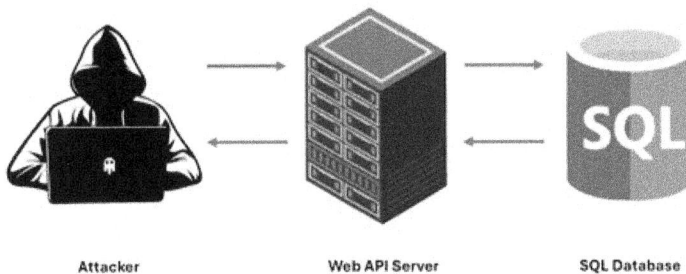

Attacker   Web API Server   SQL Database

Figure 2.6: *SQL injection*

SQL injection

SQL injection involves inserting malicious SQL code into a query through input fields such as forms or URL parameters. If the application does not properly sanitize inputs, the database executes the injected code, allowing the attacker to manipulate the database.

Examples: A typical example of SQL injection is using a ' **OR '1'='1'** string in a login form to bypass authentication. The attacker can gain unauthorized access to the application by altering the query logic.

Impact: SQL injection can lead to unauthorized data access, modification, and even complete database compromise. Sensitive information such as user credentials, financial records, and personal data can be stolen or altered.

Other web-based attacks

Other web-based attacks are as follows:

- **Cross-Site Scripting**: **Cross-Site Scripting (XSS)** attacks inject malicious scripts into web pages viewed by other users. These scripts can steal session cookies, deface websites, or redirect users to malicious sites. XSS attacks exploit vulnerabilities in web applications that fail to validate and encode user inputs properly.

- **Cross-Site Request Forgery**: **Cross-Site Request Forgery (CSRF)** attacks trick authenticated users into performing unintended actions on a web application. By exploiting the user's active session, attackers can perform actions such as changing account settings or making unauthorized transactions.

- **File inclusion attacks:** File inclusion attacks involve tricking a web application into including and executing unauthorized files. **Local File Inclusion (LFI)** targets files on the server, while **Remote File Inclusion (RFI)** involves including files from external sources. These attacks can lead to code execution and data leakage.

- **Directory traversal:** Directory traversal attacks manipulate input paths to access files and directories outside the intended scope. This can expose sensitive files such as configuration files, passwords, and database backups.

Mitigation strategies

The mitigation strategies are as follows:

- **Input validation and sanitization:** Implementing strict input validation and sanitization prevents the application from processing malicious inputs. Using parameterized queries or prepared statements ensures that user inputs are treated as data, not executable code.

- **Encoding outputs:** Properly encoding outputs ensures that any injected scripts are rendered harmless. For example, HTML encoding can prevent XSS attacks by converting special characters into their respective HTML entities.

- **CSRF tokens:** Including unique tokens in forms and validating them on the server side can prevent CSRF attacks. These tokens ensure that requests are legitimate and originate from the authenticated user.

- **Access controls:** Implementing strict access controls and permissions ensures that users and processes only have access to the necessary resources. This minimizes the impact of successful attacks by limiting access to sensitive data and functionality.

- **Regular security testing:** Regular security testing, including vulnerability assessments and penetration testing, helps identify and remediate vulnerabilities before attackers can exploit them. Automated tools and manual testing can uncover many web application flaws.

In conclusion, SQL injection and other web-based attacks pose significant risks to web applications and their users. By understanding these threats and implementing robust security measures, developers and organizations can protect their applications and data from unauthorized access and manipulation.

Insider threats

Insider threats originate from within an organization and can be perpetrated by employees, contractors, or other trusted individuals. These threats can be malicious, involving deliberate actions to harm the organization, or negligent, resulting from careless behavior. This section explores the nature of insider threats, their impact, and strategies for mitigation.

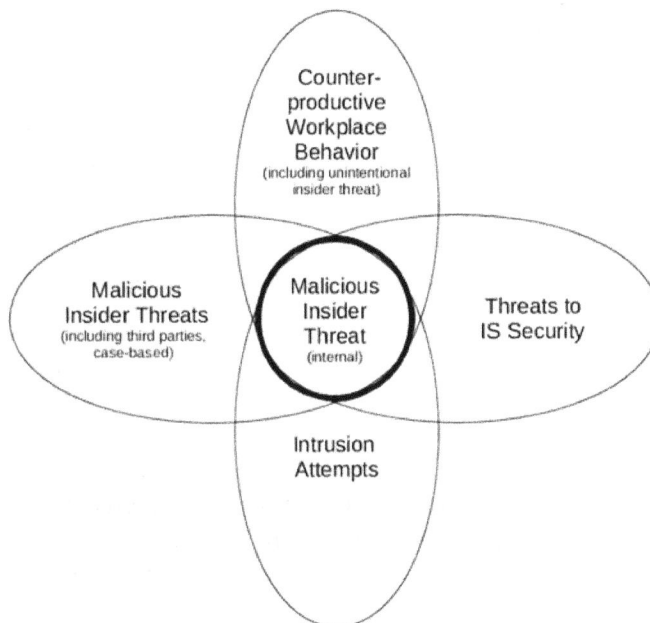

Figure 2.7: Insider threat

Types of insider threats

The types of insider threats are as follows:

- **Malicious insiders:** Malicious insiders intentionally seek to cause harm to the organization. This can include stealing sensitive information, sabotaging systems, or leaking confidential data. Motivations for malicious actions can vary, including financial gain, revenge, or ideological reasons.

- **Negligent insiders:** Negligent insiders pose a threat through carelessness or ignorance. This can involve failing to follow security protocols, mishandling sensitive data, or inadvertently introducing malware. Negligence can result from a lack of awareness or training.

- **Compromised insiders:** Compromised insiders are those whose accounts or credentials have been taken over by external attackers. This can occur through phishing, social engineering, or other means. The attacker then uses the insider's access to infiltrate the organization.

Impact of insider threats

The impacts of insider threats are as follows:

- **Data breaches:** Insider threats can lead to significant data breaches, exposing sensitive information such as customer data, intellectual property, and financial records. This can result in financial losses, legal repercussions, and reputational damage.

- **Operational disruption:** Malicious actions by insiders can disrupt operations, causing downtime, loss of productivity, and damage to critical systems. This can have a cascading effect on business continuity and service delivery.

- **Financial losses:** The financial impact of insider threats can be substantial, including direct losses from theft or fraud, costs associated with incident response and remediation, and potential regulatory fines.

Mitigation strategies

The mitigation strategies are as follows:

- **Access controls:** Implementing strict access controls ensures that employees and contractors only have access to the information and systems necessary for their roles. Regularly reviewing and adjusting access permissions can minimize the risk of unauthorized access.

- **Monitoring and logging:** Continuous monitoring and logging of user activity can help detect suspicious behavior early. Anomalies such as unusual login times, access patterns, or data transfers can indicate potential insider threats.

- **Security awareness training:** Regular security awareness training for employees can reduce the risk of negligence and increase vigilance against potential threats. Training should cover best practices for data handling, recognizing phishing attempts, and adhering to security policies.

- **Data Loss Prevention (DLP):** DLP solutions can monitor and control the movement of sensitive data within and outside the organization. Implementing DLP policies helps prevent unauthorized data transfers and alerts security teams to potential breaches.

- **Behavioral analytics:** Behavioral analytics tools use machine learning to establish baseline behavior patterns for users. Deviations from these patterns can trigger alerts, helping to identify potential insider threats before they cause significant damage.

- **Incident response plans:** Developing and regularly updating incident response plans ensures that the organization is prepared to respond swiftly and effectively to insider threats. This includes clear procedures for identifying, containing, and mitigating threats and communication strategies for stakeholders.

In summary, insider threats represent a significant risk to organizations due to the inherent trust placed in insiders. By implementing robust access controls, continuous monitoring, and comprehensive security training, organizations can mitigate the risks posed by malicious and negligent insiders, protecting their assets and maintaining operational integrity.

The battle against cyber threats requires unwavering vigilance, continuous education, and adaptive defense strategies in the ever-evolving digital landscape. Understanding the diverse nature of these threats is the cornerstone of building a resilient CyberSecurity framework. As we fortify our defenses against malware, phishing, DoS attacks, MitM intrusions, web-based exploits, and insider threats, we pave the way for a safer and more secure digital future. By staying informed and proactive, we protect our valuable data and systems and uphold the trust and integrity that are the bedrock of our interconnected world.

Attack vectors and methods

The pathways cyber attackers use to breach defenses are as varied as the attacks themselves, exploiting any vulnerability to gain entry and wreak havoc!

Attack vectors are the routes or methods that attackers use to infiltrate systems. This subchapter delves into common attack vectors and their methods to exploit them. Understanding these vectors is vital for fortifying defenses and reducing the likelihood of successful attacks.

Network-based attacks

Network-based attacks exploit network infrastructure and protocol vulnerabilities to gain unauthorized access, disrupt services, or steal sensitive information. These attacks can target many network components, including routers, switches, firewalls, and protocols like TCP/IP. Understanding these attacks is essential for securing network environments.

Types of network-based attacks

The types of network-based attacks are as follows:

- **MitM attacks:** MitM attacks involve intercepting and potentially altering the communication between two parties without their knowledge. Attackers position themselves between the communicating parties and can eavesdrop or inject malicious content into the communication stream. Techniques such as ARP spoofing and DNS poisoning are commonly used to facilitate MitM attacks.

- **DDoS attacks:** DDoS attacks overwhelm network resources by flooding them with excessive traffic from multiple sources, often using a botnet. These attacks can cause significant service disruptions, making websites or services unavailable to legitimate users. DDoS attacks can target various network stack layers, from network bandwidth to application-specific endpoints.

- **Packet sniffing:** Packet sniffing involves capturing and analyzing network traffic to intercept sensitive information such as passwords, session tokens, and personal data. Attackers use tools like **Wireshark** or **tcpdump** to perform packet sniffing. Encrypted communication protocols (for example, HTTPS, VPN) can mitigate the risk of packet sniffing by making intercepted data unreadable.

- **IP spoofing:** IP spoofing involves sending packets with a forged source IP address, making it appear as though the packets are coming from a trusted source. This technique is often used in DDoS attacks and to bypass IP-based authentication mechanisms. Network-level security measures such as ingress and egress filtering can help prevent IP spoofing.

Mitigation strategies

The mitigation strategies are as follows:

- **Network segmentation:** Dividing the network into smaller, isolated segments can limit the spread of attacks and contain potential damage. Implementing **Virtual Local Area Networks** (**VLANs**) and using firewalls to control inter-segment traffic are effective segmentation strategies.

- **Intrusion Detection and Prevention Systems**: Intrusion Detection and Prevention Systems (**IDPS**) monitor network traffic for suspicious activity and can automatically block or alert administrators to potential threats. These systems use signature-based, anomaly-based, and heuristic-based detection methods to identify malicious activities.

- **Regular security audits:** Regular security audits and vulnerability assessments help identify and remediate weaknesses in the network infrastructure. Automated tools and manual reviews can uncover misconfigurations, outdated software, and other vulnerabilities.

- **Encryption:** Encrypting network traffic ensures that even if data is intercepted, it cannot be read or tampered with. Protocols like **Transport Layer Security (TLS)** for web traffic and IPsec for VPNs can protect data in transit.

Application-based attacks

Application-based attacks exploit vulnerabilities and misconfigurations in software applications to gain unauthorized access, manipulate data, or disrupt services. These attacks can target web applications, desktop software, and mobile apps. Understanding the methods and impacts of application-based attacks is crucial for developing secure software.

Types of application-based attacks

The types of application-based attacks are as follows:

- **SQL injection:** SQL injection involves inserting malicious SQL code into an application's database query. This can allow attackers to manipulate the database, retrieve sensitive information, or execute administrative operations. Proper input validation and the use of parameterized queries can mitigate SQL injection risks.

- **Cross-Site Scripting**: XSS attacks inject malicious scripts into web pages viewed by other users. These scripts can steal cookies, hijack sessions, or redirect users to malicious sites. Input validation and output encoding are critical defenses against XSS attacks.

- **Cross-Site Request Forgery:** CSRF attacks trick authenticated users into performing unwanted actions on a web application. Attackers exploit the user's session, making it appear as if the user has initiated the actions. Implementing anti-CSRF tokens and verifying the origin of requests can prevent CSRF attacks.

- **Remote Code Execution**: **Remote Code Execution (RCE)** vulnerabilities allow attackers to execute arbitrary code on a target system. This can result from flaws in the application code, such as buffer overflows or improper handling of user inputs. Regular code reviews, input validation, and keeping software up to date can reduce the risk of RCE.

Mitigation strategies

The mitigation strategies are as follows:

- **Secure coding practices:** Adopting secure coding practices helps prevent vulnerabilities from being introduced during the development process. This includes input validation, proper error handling, and using secure libraries and frameworks.

- **Regular patching and updates:** Keeping software and dependencies up to date ensures that known vulnerabilities are patched. Automated update systems and vulnerability management tools can help maintain an up-to-date software environment.

- **Application security testing:** Regular security testing, including static code analysis, dynamic analysis, and penetration testing, helps identify and remediate vulnerabilities. To catch issues early, security testing should be integrated into the development lifecycle (DevSecOps).

- **Access controls:** Implementing strict access controls ensures that users only have access to the resources necessary for their roles. **Role-based access control (RBAC)** and the principle of least privilege can minimize the impact of compromised accounts.

Human-based attacks

Human-based attacks exploit human behavior and psychology to gain unauthorized access to systems or sensitive information. These attacks rely on manipulation and deception rather than technical vulnerabilities, making them particularly challenging to defend against. This section explores standard human-based attack techniques and strategies to mitigate their impact.

Types of human-based attacks

The types of human-based attacks are as follows:

- **Phishing:** Phishing involves sending deceptive emails or messages to trick recipients into revealing sensitive information, such as passwords or credit card numbers. These messages often appear to come from legitimate sources and may contain urgent requests or enticing offers. Educating users about phishing and implementing email filters can help reduce the risk.

- **Social engineering:** Social engineering manipulates individuals into performing actions or divulging confidential information. Techniques include pretexting (creating a fabricated scenario), baiting (offering something enticing), and quid pro quo (exchanging services for information). Regular training and awareness programs can help employees recognize and resist social engineering attempts.

- **Spear phishing:** Spear phishing targets specific individuals or organizations with personalized messages that appear highly credible. Attackers gather information about the target to craft convincing emails or messages. Implementing **multi-factor authentication (MFA)** and verifying the authenticity of requests can mitigate spear phishing risks.

- **Baiting:** Baiting uses the promise of something desirable, such as free software or a USB drive labeled with enticing content, to lure victims into compromising their systems. The bait often contains malware or leads to phishing websites. Educating users about the risks and enforcing strict policies on unknown devices can prevent baiting attacks.

Mitigation strategies

The mitigation strategies are as follows:

- **Security awareness training:** Regular security awareness training helps employees recognize and respond to human-based attacks. Training should cover common tactics, red flags, and best practices for handling suspicious communications and requests.

- **Multi-factor authentication:** Implementing MFA adds an extra layer of security by requiring multiple verification forms. This makes it harder for attackers to gain access even if they obtain login credentials through phishing or social engineering.

- **Incident response plans:** A well-defined incident response plan ensures the organization can quickly and effectively respond to human-based attacks. This includes procedures for reporting, investigating, and mitigating the impact of attacks.

- **Email and communication filtering:** Advanced email and communication filtering technologies can help detect and block phishing attempts and other malicious messages. These filters can analyze content, sender reputation, and attachment safety to prevent harmful communications from reaching users.

Physical attacks

Physical attacks involve gaining unauthorized physical access to hardware and infrastructure to steal data, disrupt operations, or compromise systems. These attacks can bypass digital security measures and pose a significant risk to organizations. This section examines the methods and impact of physical attacks and strategies to secure physical assets.

Types of physical attacks

The types of physical attacks are as follows:

- **Theft of devices:** Stealing laptops, smartphones, and other portable devices can provide attackers direct access to sensitive data. Encrypting data on devices and implementing remote wipe capabilities can mitigate the impact of device theft.

- **Tampering with hardware:** Attackers may tamper with hardware components, such as inserting malicious devices into USB ports or installing hardware keyloggers. Regular physical inspections and using tamper-evident seals can help detect and prevent tampering.

- **Unauthorized access to facilities:** Gaining access to secure facilities, such as data centers or server rooms, allows attackers to manipulate or steal hardware, install malicious software, or disrupt operations. Strong access controls, such as biometric authentication and security personnel, can prevent unauthorized access.

- **Social engineering:** Social engineering techniques can also facilitate physical attacks. For example, attackers may pose as maintenance personnel or delivery workers to access secure areas. Training employees to verify identities and report suspicious behavior is essential.

Mitigation strategies

The mitigation strategies are as follows:

- **Access controls:** Implementing strict access controls, such as keycards, biometric scanners, and security personnel, ensures that only authorized individuals can access sensitive areas. Regularly reviewing and updating access permissions can prevent unauthorized access.

- **Physical security measures:** Installing surveillance cameras, alarm systems, and secure locks enhances physical security. Conducting regular security audits and drills helps identify vulnerabilities and improve response procedures.

- **Device encryption:** Encrypting data on devices ensures that the data remains protected even if a device is stolen. Full-disk encryption and secure boot processes can prevent unauthorized access to device data.

- **Secure disposal of hardware:** Properly disposing of hardware, such as using certified data destruction services or secure wiping methods, ensures that sensitive data cannot be recovered from discarded devices. Establishing clear disposal protocols can prevent data breaches.

Supply chain attacks

Supply chain attacks target third-party vendors and suppliers to compromise their clients' systems. These attacks exploit the trust and dependencies between organizations and their suppliers, often using the vendor as a conduit to infiltrate the target organization. This section explores the methods and impact of supply chain attacks and strategies to secure the supply chain.

Types of supply chain attacks

The types of supply chain attacks are as follows:

- **Software supply chain attacks:** Software supply chain attacks involve compromising software development or distribution processes to insert malicious code. This can occur through compromised source code repositories, build processes, or update mechanisms. Ensuring the integrity of software and implementing code-signing practices can mitigate these risks.

- **Hardware supply chain attacks:** Hardware supply chain attacks involve tampering with hardware components during manufacturing or distribution. This can include inserting malicious chips or altering firmware to create backdoors. Using trusted suppliers and conducting thorough inspections can help prevent hardware tampering.

- **Third-party service providers:** Attackers may target third-party service providers, such as cloud services or managed security providers, to gain access to their clients' systems. Establishing strong security requirements and regularly auditing third-party providers can mitigate these risks.

Mitigation strategies

The mitigation strategies are as follows:

- **Vendor risk management:** Implementing a robust vendor risk management program involves assessing the security practices of third-party vendors, establishing clear security requirements, and conducting regular audits. This ensures that vendors adhere to security standards and practices.

- **Supply chain transparency:** Maintaining transparency in the supply chain helps identify and address potential vulnerabilities. This includes tracking the origin and handling of components and software throughout the supply chain.

- **Secure development practices:** Adopting secure development practices, such as using version control, conducting code reviews, and implementing **continuous integration/continuous deployment** (**CI/CD**) pipelines with security checks, ensures the integrity of software throughout its lifecycle.

- **Incident response planning:** Developing and regularly updating incident response plans ensures that the organization can quickly and effectively respond to supply chain attacks. This includes procedures for identifying, containing, and mitigating the impact of compromised vendors.

Zero-day exploits

Zero-day exploits target undiscovered vulnerabilities in software and hardware before patches are available. These exploits pose a significant risk as they can bypass existing security measures and cause widespread damage. This section examines the nature of zero-day exploits, their impact, and strategies for defending against them.

Characteristics of zero-day exploits

The characteristics of zero-day exploits are as follows:

- **Unknown vulnerabilities:** Zero-day exploits leverage vulnerabilities unknown to the software vendor and the security community. These vulnerabilities remain unpatched and can be exploited until they are discovered and addressed.

- **High impact:** Zero-day exploits can have a high impact, leading to data breaches, system compromise, and disruption of services. The lack of available patches and mitigation strategies makes them particularly dangerous.

- **Advanced attack techniques:** Zero-day exploits often use advanced techniques to bypass security measures such as firewalls, intrusion detection systems, and antivirus software, making detection and prevention challenging.

Mitigation strategies

The mitigation strategies are as follows:

- **Threat intelligence:** Leveraging threat intelligence helps organizations stay informed about emerging threats and potential zero-day exploits. Subscribing to threat intelligence feeds and participating in information-sharing communities can provide early warnings.

- **Behavioral analysis:** Using behavioral analysis tools can help detect anomalies and suspicious activities that may indicate the presence of zero-day exploits. These tools analyze patterns and behaviors rather than relying on known signatures.

- **Regular software updates:** Keeping software up to date with the latest patches and updates reduces the attack surface for zero-day exploits. While zero-day vulnerabilities are unpatched, regular updates ensure that known vulnerabilities are addressed promptly.

- **Network segmentation:** Segmenting the network limits the spread of attacks and contains potential damage. Implementing micro-segmentation and using firewalls to control inter-segment traffic can enhance security.

- **Application whitelisting:** Application whitelisting ensures that only approved applications can run on the system. This can prevent unauthorized and potentially malicious software from executing, reducing the risk of zero-day exploits.

Conclusion

Understanding and defending against a wide range of cyber threats is essential for maintaining the security and integrity of information systems. Network-based attacks exploit weaknesses in network infrastructure, while application-based attacks target software vulnerabilities. Human-based attacks leverage psychology and deception, and physical attacks involve gaining unauthorized physical access to hardware. Supply chain attacks exploit dependencies on third-party vendors, and zero-day exploits target undiscovered vulnerabilities. By implementing robust security measures, conducting regular assessments, and fostering a culture of security awareness, organizations can mitigate the risks posed by these diverse threats.

Knowledge is our greatest weapon in the relentless pursuit of CyberSecurity. By comprehensively understanding the myriad cyber threats, from network and application attacks to human and physical threats, we arm ourselves with the insights needed to build resilient defenses. The future of CyberSecurity hinges on our ability to anticipate, adapt, and respond to these evolving challenges, ensuring a secure digital landscape for all.

By understanding and securing the myriad attack vectors, we can construct a multi-layered defense that stands resilient against the relentless tide of cyber threats.

Points to remember

- Early viruses and worms like Creeper and Morris Worm set the stage for modern CyberSecurity threats.

- The rise of malware, including Trojans, spyware, and ransomware, highlights the increasing sophistication and automation of cyber-attacks.

- APTs, often backed by nation-state actors, pose long-term espionage risks.

- Organized cybercrime groups execute targeted attacks and data breaches for financial gain.

- Phishing and social engineering exploit human behavior to extract sensitive information and manipulate individuals.

- DoS and DDoS attacks overwhelm systems, causing significant disruptions and financial losses.

Join our book's Discord space

Join the book's Discord Workspace for Latest updates, Offers, Tech happenings around the world, New Release and Sessions with the Authors:

https://discord.bpbonline.com

CHAPTER 3

Building a Secure Infrastructure

Introduction

In CyberSecurity, a robust infrastructure is your first line of defense. Building a secure infrastructure is not just about technology but about creating a resilient framework that protects your organization from the myriad threats of the digital age.

In today's digital age, the need for robust CyberSecurity measures has never been more critical. Organizations face growing threats that can compromise sensitive data, disrupt operations, and tarnish reputations. As we start *Chapter 3, Building a Secure Infrastructure*, we will explore the foundational elements for establishing a resilient CyberSecurity framework. This chapter will cover critical areas such as network security, endpoint security, firewalls, IDS and IPS, secure configuration practices, and deep and dark web security. These subchapters will provide valuable insights and practical guidance to fortify your organization's defenses against ever-evolving cyber threats. Some CyberSecurity measures are as shown in the following figure:

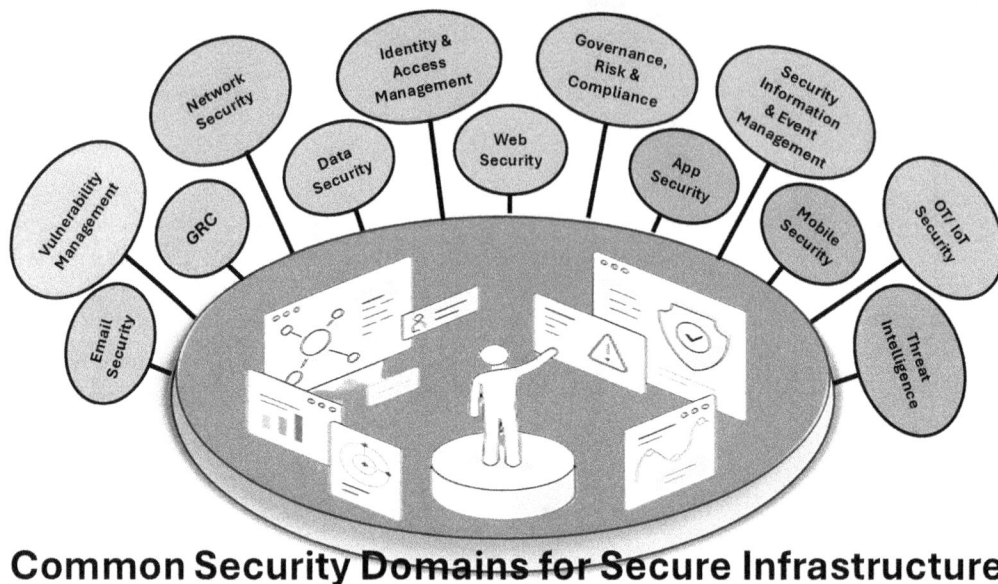

Common Security Domains for Secure Infrastructure

Figure 3.1: Common CyberSecurity controls for secure infrastructure

Structure

The chapter will cover the following sections:

- Network security
- Endpoint security
- Firewalls, IDS, and IPS
- Secure configuration practices
- Surface, deep, and dark web security

Objectives

By the end of this chapter, the readers should be able to gain essential knowledge and practical strategies for fortifying an organization's CyberSecurity defenses. It covers enhancing network security through robust architecture design, segmentation, and encryption protocols. The chapter addresses strengthening endpoint security with antivirus, EDR systems, and **mobile device management** (**MDM**). It also explores implementing and managing firewalls, IDS, and IPS. Secure configuration practices are emphasized, focusing on system hardening and applying security patches. Lastly, it examines deep and dark web security, discussing potential threats, monitoring tools, threat intelligence gathering, and legal and ethical considerations. This chapter equips readers with a solid foundation to mitigate cyber threats and protect organizational assets effectively.

Network security

Your network is the nervous system of your organization; its security is paramount to safeguarding your digital health.

Network security is the backbone of any secure infrastructure. It encompasses a range of technologies, devices, and practices designed to protect data integrity, confidentiality, and availability as it traverses your network. This section will examine the critical components of network security (*Figure 3.2*), including designing and implementing secure network architectures, deploying robust encryption protocols, and the importance of continuous monitoring and incident response.

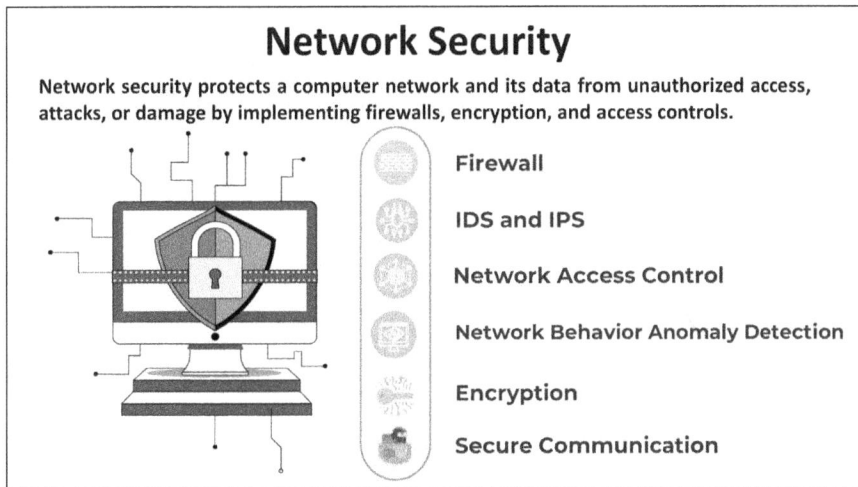

Network Security

Network security protects a computer network and its data from unauthorized access, attacks, or damage by implementing firewalls, encryption, and access controls.

- Firewall
- IDS and IPS
- Network Access Control
- Network Behavior Anomaly Detection
- Encryption
- Secure Communication

Figure 3.2: Key components of network security

Overview of network security

Network security refers to the strategies, policies, and technologies employed to protect a network's usability, integrity, safety, and data. This encompasses hardware and software technologies designed to respond to various threats and prevent unauthorized access, misuse, modification, or denial of a computer network and network-accessible resources. The primary goal is to create a secure environment for network users and to protect sensitive data.

The importance of network security cannot be overstated. With the proliferation of interconnected devices and the rise of the **Internet of Things (IoT)**, the potential attack surface for malicious actors has expanded dramatically. Adequate network security ensures business continuity by protecting against data breaches, maintaining data integrity, and ensuring critical services remain operational. It also helps in compliance with regulatory requirements and building customer trust by safeguarding sensitive information.

Threat landscape

The threat landscape for network security encompasses the array of potential dangers, vulnerabilities, and risks that can compromise the integrity, confidentiality, and availability of networked systems and data. This dynamic environment is shaped by various malicious actors, evolving attack methods, and emerging vulnerabilities. Understanding this landscape is vital for implementing effective network security measures and defending against cyber threats. Key threats in the network security landscape are as follows:

- **Malware:**
    - **Definition**: Malicious software designed to disrupt, damage, or gain unauthorized access to computer systems.
    - **Types**: Includes viruses, worms, ransomware, trojans, spyware, and adware.
    - **Impact**: Malware can steal sensitive data, disrupt operations, encrypt files for ransom, and create backdoors for further attacks.

- **Phishing:**
    - **Definition**: A form of social engineering where attackers deceive individuals into providing confidential information, often via email.
    - **Types**: Spear phishing (targeted attacks), whaling (targeting high-profile individuals), and clone phishing (replicating legitimate emails).
    - **Impact**: Phishing can lead to data breaches, financial loss, and unauthorized system access.

- **Distributed Denial of Service (DDoS) attacks:**
    - **Definition**: DDoS attacks overwhelm a network or service with excessive traffic, rendering it unusable.
    - **Methods**: Botnets (networks of compromised devices), amplification attacks, and volumetric attacks.
    - **Impact**: Causes service outages, disrupts business operations, and can be used as a smokescreen for other attacks.

- **Insider threats:**
    - **Definition**: Threats posed by individuals within the organization, such as employees, contractors, or business partners.
    - **Types**: Malicious insiders (intentional harm) and negligent insiders (unintentional harm).
    - **Impact**: Insider threats can result in data theft, sabotage, and unintentional exposure of sensitive information.

- **Zero-day exploits:**

  o **Definition**: Attacks that exploit previously unknown vulnerabilities in software or hardware.

  o **Characteristics**: Difficult to detect and defend against due to the lack of available patches.

  o **Impact**: Zero-day exploits can lead to significant breaches and are often used in targeted attacks.

- **Advanced Persistent Threats (APTs):**

  o **Definition**: Prolonged and targeted cyber-attacks aimed at stealing information or disrupting operations.

  o **Methods**: APTs typically involve sophisticated techniques, such as spear phishing, zero-day exploits, and custom malware.

  o **Impact**: APTs can result in significant data breaches, intellectual property theft, and long-term operational disruption.

- **Man-in-the-Middle (MitM) attacks:**

  o **Definition**: Attacks where the attacker intercepts and potentially alters communications between two parties.

  o **Methods**: Includes eavesdropping, session hijacking, and SSL stripping.

  o **Impact**: MitM attacks can lead to data theft, credential compromise, and manipulation of communications.

- **Supply chain attacks:**

  o **Definition**: Attacks that target an organization's supply chain to compromise its systems or data.

  o **Methods**: Includes compromising software updates, third-party service providers, and hardware components.

  o **Impact**: Supply chain attacks can introduce malware, create backdoors, and compromise the integrity of critical systems.

Designing secure network architectures

Network segmentation and zoning are crucial strategies for enhancing security within an organization's IT infrastructure. By dividing a network into smaller, isolated segments, these techniques limit access and reduce the potential impact of security breaches. This approach is instrumental in containing and controlling access to critical resources, thereby minimizing the risk of widespread compromise in the event of an attack.

Network segmentation

Network segmentation is the practice of dividing a larger network into smaller, isolated sub-networks or segments. Each segment operates independently, with its own set of security controls tailored to its specific needs and the risks it faces. This isolation is crucial for limiting the movement of malicious actors within the network, effectively containing any potential breaches and protecting sensitive information from unauthorized access. The key components of network segmentation are as follows:

- **Segment isolation**: The fundamental principle of network segmentation is the isolation of different segments. This isolation ensures that a compromise in one segment does not automatically lead to a compromise in another. For example, if a malware attack targets a less critical segment of the network, the segmentation prevents the malware from spreading to more sensitive segments, such as those containing customer data or financial records.

- **Granularity of segmentation**: The level of segmentation granularity can vary depending on the organization's specific security needs. Some networks might be divided into broad segments, such as separating the production environment from the development environment. Others might require more granular segmentation, where individual departments, applications, or even devices are segmented. The key is to strike a balance between security and manageability, ensuring that segmentation is both effective and practical.

- **Access control**: One of the primary benefits of network segmentation is the ability to implement strict access controls for each segment. Access to a particular segment is limited to only those users, devices, or systems that require it. This reduces the risk of unauthorized access and makes it more challenging for attackers to move laterally within the network. For instance, employees in the finance department might only have access to segments related to financial systems while being restricted from segments related to human resources or IT infrastructure.

- **Security policies and enforcement**: Each network segment can have its own tailored security policies. For example, a segment containing sensitive customer data might require encryption for all data in transit and at rest, while another segment used for general administrative tasks might not have such stringent requirements. By enforcing these policies at the segment level, organizations can ensure that security measures are appropriately applied based on the sensitivity and criticality of the data or systems within each segment.

- **Compliance and regulation**: Network segmentation is also a key strategy for meeting regulatory compliance requirements. Many regulations, such as the **Payment Card Industry Data Security Standard** (**PCI DSS**) or the **Health Insurance Portability and Accountability Act** (**HIPAA**), require sensitive data to be protected through robust security controls. Segmentation helps isolate and protect regulated data, making it easier for organizations to comply with these standards.

The key benefits of network segmentation are as mentioned here:

- **Enhanced security**: By isolating critical assets, network segmentation significantly enhances security. Even if one segment is compromised, the damage is contained, and the attacker's ability to access other parts of the network is severely limited.

- **Improved performance**: Segmentation can improve network performance by reducing congestion. Traffic within each segment is limited to relevant data, optimizing bandwidth usage.

- **Easier management**: Smaller segments are easier to monitor and manage. Security teams can focus on specific segments, ensuring more efficient incident response and threat management.

- **Regulatory compliance**: Many regulatory frameworks mandate segregating data and systems to protect sensitive information. Network segmentation helps organizations comply with these regulations.

Zoning in network security

Zoning is a concept that complements network segmentation by creating different areas within the network, each governed by specific security policies based on the level of trust required. The idea behind zoning is to establish different layers of security, where each zone has a distinct role and level of access control.

The key aspects of zoning are as follows:

- **Defining zones**: The first step in implementing zoning is to define the different zones within the network. Each zone is categorized based on its level of sensitivity, the type of data it handles, and the trust level of the entities accessing it. Common zones include the **demilitarized zone** (**DMZ**), internal zone, and external zone.

- **The demilitarized zone:** The DMZ is a critical component in the zoning strategy. It acts as a buffer between the internal network and external networks, such as the Internet. Public-facing services, such as web servers, email servers, and DNS servers, are typically hosted in the DMZ. The DMZ is designed to be highly secure, with strict access controls and monitoring in place to detect and mitigate any attacks. The goal is to protect the internal network from external threats while still allowing external users to access certain services.

- **Internal zone**: The internal zone encompasses the organization's core systems and data. This is where the most sensitive and critical information resides, such as customer data, financial records, and proprietary business information. Access to the internal zone is tightly controlled, with robust security measures to protect against unauthorized access. The internal zone is often segmented further to create isolated areas within it, ensuring that different departments or applications have their own secure environments.

- **External zone**: The external zone includes networks and systems that are outside the organization's control, such as the Internet or third-party service providers. Security measures in the external zone focus on detecting and mitigating threats before they reach the internal network. Firewalls, intrusion detection and prevention systems, and other perimeter security tools are commonly used to protect the external zone.

- **Access control in zoning**: Zoning allows for the implementation of strict access controls based on the level of trust required for each zone. For example, access to the internal zone might be restricted to only trusted devices and users, while the DMZ might allow limited access to external users for specific services. By enforcing access controls at the zone level, organizations can reduce the risk of unauthorized access and data breaches.

- **Security policies and monitoring**: Each zone can have its own set of security policies tailored to its specific needs. For example, the DMZ might have strict monitoring and logging requirements to detect any suspicious activity, while the internal zone might require encryptions-for all sensitive data. Continuous monitoring of each zone is essential to ensure that security policies are being enforced and to detect any potential threats.

The benefits of zoning are listed as follows:

- **Risk management**: Zoning helps organizations manage risk by categorizing different areas of the network based on their sensitivity and trust level. This allows implementing targeted security measures that are appropriate for the level of risk associated with each zone.

- **Access control**: By enforcing strict access controls for each zone, organizations can reduce the likelihood of unauthorized access. This is particularly important in protecting sensitive data and critical systems from external threats.

- **Incident containment**: In the event of a security breach, zoning helps contain the incident to a specific network area, preventing it from spreading and causing more extensive damage. This containment is crucial for minimizing the impact of the breach and ensuring a swift response.

- **Simplified compliance**: Zoning also simplifies compliance with regulatory requirements by isolating sensitive data and systems within specific zones. This makes it easier to demonstrate that the organization has taken appropriate steps to protect regulated data.

Implementing segmentation and zoning

Implementing segmentation and zoning requires careful planning and consideration of the organization's specific needs and risks. The following steps outline the process for effectively implementing these strategies:

1. **Identify critical assets and data**: The first step is to identify the organization's critical assets and data. This includes sensitive customer information, financial records, intellectual property, and critical business systems. Understanding where these assets are located and how they are accessed is essential for designing an effective segmentation and zoning strategy.

2. **Assess risks and threats**: Next, conduct a risk assessment to identify potential threats and vulnerabilities. This assessment should consider both internal and external threats, as well as the likelihood and impact of a potential breach. The results of the risk assessment will inform the design of the segmentation and zoning strategy.

3. **Design the segmentation and zoning strategy**: Based on the risk assessment, design a segmentation and zoning strategy that aligns with the organization's security objectives. This includes defining the different segments and zones, determining the level of isolation required for each, and establishing security policies and access controls.

4. **Implement security controls**: Once the strategy is designed, implement the necessary security controls for each segment and zone. This includes firewalls, intrusion detection and prevention systems, access control mechanisms, and monitoring tools. Ensure that security controls are appropriately configured and regularly updated to address emerging threats.

5. **Monitor and maintain**: Continuous monitoring is essential to ensure that the segmentation and zoning strategy is effective. Regularly review and update security policies, conduct audits, and perform vulnerability assessments to identify and address any weaknesses. Incident response plans should also be in place to address any security breaches.

6. **Review and improve**: Network segmentation and zoning are not one-time activities. Regularly review the strategy's effectiveness and make improvements as needed. As the organization's IT environment evolves, so should its segmentation and zoning strategy to address new risks and challenges.

Redundancy and failover mechanisms

Redundancy and failover mechanisms are vital components of a resilient network architecture. They ensure that network services remain available even during hardware failures, cyber-attacks, or other disruptions. These strategies are critical for maintaining business continuity, minimizing downtime, and protecting an organization's operations from unexpected events.

Understanding redundancy

Redundancy involves duplicating critical components or functions within a system to ensure availability during a failure. By having multiple instances of critical resources, organizations can quickly switch to a backup in case of a failure, ensuring uninterrupted operations.

The key aspects of redundancy are as follows:

- **Hardware redundancy**: Hardware redundancy involves duplicating physical components, such as servers, storage devices, and network equipment. For example, an organization might have multiple servers running the same applications, so if one server fails, another can take over without disrupting services.

- **Network path redundancy**: This involves creating multiple network paths to ensure that data can still flow between systems even if one path becomes unavailable. This is often achieved through techniques such as load balancing, where traffic is distributed across multiple paths, and failover routing, where traffic is automatically redirected to an alternate path in the event of a failure.

- **Data redundancy**: Data redundancy involves creating multiple copies of data to protect against loss. This can be done through techniques such as **Redundant Array of Independent Disks** (**RAID**) in storage systems, which duplicates data across multiple disks, or through regular backups stored in different locations.

- **Power redundancy**: Redundant power supplies and **uninterruptible power supplies** (**UPS**) ensure that critical systems remain operational during power outages. This is especially important in data centers, where even a brief power outage can result in significant downtime.

The benefits of redundancy are as follows:

- **High availability**: Redundancy ensures that critical systems and services remain available even during component failures, reducing the risk of downtime and maintaining business operations.

- **Improved reliability**: By duplicating critical resources, redundancy improves the reliability of systems, ensuring that failures do not lead to data loss or service interruptions.

- **Business continuity**: Redundancy is a key component of business continuity planning, ensuring that organizations can continue to operate in the face of unexpected events, such as hardware failures or cyber-attacks.

Understanding failover mechanisms

Failover mechanisms automatically transfer workloads to a standby system or component when the primary system fails. This helps maintain continuous operation and minimizes downtime. Failover mechanisms are often used in conjunction with redundancy to ensure that critical services remain available even during failures.

The key aspects of failover mechanisms are as follows:

- **Automatic failover**: Automatic failover involves seamlessly transferring workloads to a standby system without manual intervention. This is typically achieved through clustering, where multiple systems are connected and configured to take over if one fails. For example, in a database cluster, if the primary database server fails, another server in the cluster automatically takes over the processing.

- **Manual failover**: In some cases, failover may require manual intervention, where an administrator needs to activate the standby system. While this approach can be slower, it allows for more controlled and deliberate actions during a failure.

- **Cold, warm, and hot standby**: Failover systems can be configured as cold, warm, or hot standbys, depending on the level of readiness. Cold standby systems are powered off and require significant time to bring online, warm standby systems are running but not fully synchronized, and hot standby systems are fully synchronized and ready to take over instantly.

- **Testing and maintenance**: Regular testing and maintenance of failover mechanisms are crucial to ensure they function correctly when needed. This includes testing failover scenarios to identify any issues and performing routine maintenance to keep standby systems up-to-date.

The benefits of failover mechanisms are as follows:

- **Minimized downtime**: Failover mechanisms reduce downtime by ensuring that services can quickly switch to a standby system in the event of a failure, maintaining business continuity.

- **Seamless operations**: Automatic failover provides seamless transitions between systems, minimizing the impact on users and maintaining a consistent level of service.

- **Resilience**: Failover mechanisms enhance the overall resilience of an organization's IT infrastructure, ensuring that critical services remain operational even during failures.

Implementing redundancy and failover mechanisms

Implementing redundancy and failover mechanisms requires careful planning and a thorough understanding of an organization's critical systems and services. The following steps outline the process for effectively implementing these strategies:

1. **Identify critical systems and services**: Start by identifying the systems and services that are critical to the organization's operations. These components require redundancy and failover mechanisms to ensure continuous availability.

2. **Assess risks and failure points**: Conduct a risk assessment to identify potential failure points within the organization's IT infrastructure. This includes evaluating hardware, software, network paths, and data storage systems for vulnerabilities that could lead to downtime.

3. **Design redundancy and failover strategies**: Based on the risk assessment, design redundancy and failover strategies that address identified failure points. This includes determining the level of redundancy needed (for example, hardware, network paths, data), choosing the appropriate failover mechanisms (for example, automatic, manual, hot standby), and configuring systems accordingly.

4. **Implement and test**: Implement the redundancy and failover mechanisms according to the design plan. Once implemented, conduct thorough testing to ensure that the mechanisms function correctly and that systems can seamlessly switch to standby components in the event of a failure.

5. **Monitor and maintain**: Continuous monitoring is essential to ensure that redundancy and failover mechanisms remain operational. Review system performance regularly, test failover scenarios, and perform maintenance to address any issues that may arise.

6. **Review and update**: As with any security strategy, redundancy and failover mechanisms should be regularly reviewed and updated to address new risks and changes in the organization's IT environment. This includes revisiting the risk assessment, adjusting the level of redundancy, and ensuring that failover systems are kept up to date.

Encryption protocols

Encryption protocols are vital components of network security, ensuring that data transmitted across networks remains confidential and secure from unauthorized access. As cyber threats become increasingly sophisticated, encryption protocols have evolved to provide stronger, more reliable protection for sensitive information. This section delves into the principles of encryption, the various types of encryption protocols, and their applications in securing communications within a network.

Understanding encryption protocols

Encryption is the process of converting plain text data into an unreadable format, known as ciphertext, using an algorithm and an encryption key. The purpose of encryption is to protect data from unauthorized access, ensuring that only those with the correct decryption key can convert the ciphertext back into its original, readable form. Encryption protocols define the methods and processes used to secure data during transmission, making them an essential component of modern network security.

The key components of encryption protocols are as follows:

- **Algorithms**: Encryption protocols rely on mathematical algorithms to encrypt and decrypt data. These algorithms can vary in complexity and strength, with some designed for speed and efficiency, while others focus on providing robust security even against advanced cryptographic attacks.

- **Keys**: Encryption keys are critical to the encryption process. They are used to encode and decode the data, and the security of the encryption largely depends on the strength and secrecy of the keys. The length of the key (measured in bits) often determines the security level of the encryption, with longer keys providing stronger protection.

- **Modes of operation**: Encryption protocols often include different modes of operation, which define how data blocks are encrypted. Common modes include **Cipher Block Chaining (CBC)**, **Electronic Codebook (ECB)**, and **Counter (CTR)** modes, each with its own strengths and weaknesses depending on the application.

Encryption types

Encryption protocols can be broadly categorized into three types based on the nature of the keys used: symmetric, asymmetric, and hybrid encryption.

Symmetric encryption

Symmetric encryption, also known as private-key encryption, uses the same key for both encryption and decryption. This means that both the sender and receiver must have access to the same secret key. Symmetric encryption is known for its speed and efficiency, making it ideal for encrypting large volumes of data.

The key features of symmetric encryption are as follows:

- **Speed and efficiency**: Symmetric encryption algorithms are generally faster and more efficient than their asymmetric counterparts. This makes them suitable for encrypting large amounts of data, such as entire databases or large files.

- **Key management**: The primary challenge with symmetric encryption is key management. Since the same key is used for both encryption and decryption, securely distributing and managing the key among authorized users is crucial. If the key is compromised, the security of the encrypted data is at risk.

- **Common algorithms**: Some of the most widely used symmetric encryption algorithms include the **Advanced Encryption Standard (AES)**, **Data Encryption Standard (DES)**, and **Triple DES (3DES)**. AES, in particular, is highly regarded for its strength and efficiency and is commonly used in various security protocols.

The use cases are as follows:

- **Data-at-rest**: Symmetric encryption is often used to protect data-at-rest, such as files stored on a hard drive or backup tapes. Since the same key is used for encryption and decryption, it is efficient for securing large datasets.

- **Secure communications**: Symmetric encryption is also used in secure communications protocols like **Secure Sockets Layer (SSL)/Transport Layer Security (TLS)**, where it ensures the confidentiality of data transmitted over a network.

Asymmetric encryption

Asymmetric encryption, also known as public-key encryption, uses a pair of keys: a public key and a private key. The public key encrypts the data, while the private key decrypts it. This approach overcomes some of the key management challenges associated with symmetric encryption.

The key features of asymmetric encryption are as follows:

- **Public and private keys**: In asymmetric encryption, the public key can be freely distributed, while the private key remains confidential. Data encrypted with the public key can only be decrypted by the corresponding private key, ensuring secure communication even if the public key is known.

- **Security**: Asymmetric encryption is generally more secure than symmetric encryption because the private key is not shared. This makes it more difficult for attackers to compromise the encryption. However, asymmetric encryption is slower and less efficient than symmetric encryption, making it less suitable for encrypting large amounts of data.

- **Common algorithms**: Popular asymmetric encryption algorithms include **Rivest-Shamir-Adleman (RSA)**, Diffie-Hellman, and **Elliptic Curve Cryptography (ECC)**. RSA is one of the most widely used algorithms for secure data transmission and digital signatures.

The use cases are as follows:

- **Key exchange**: Asymmetric encryption is often used in key exchange protocols to securely share symmetric keys. Once the symmetric key is securely exchanged, it can be used for faster data encryption.

- **Digital signatures**: It is also used in digital signature schemes, where the private key is used to sign a message, and the public key is used to verify the signature's authenticity. This ensures data integrity and non-repudiation.

Hybrid encryption

Hybrid encryption combines the strengths of both symmetric and asymmetric encryption to create a more secure and efficient encryption protocol. In a typical hybrid encryption scheme, asymmetric encryption is used to exchange a symmetric key, which is then used to encrypt the actual data.

The key features of hybrid encryption are as follows:

- **Combination of strengths**: Hybrid encryption leverages the security of asymmetric encryption for key exchange and the efficiency of symmetric encryption for data encryption. This approach provides the best of both worlds: strong security without sacrificing performance.

- **Efficient key management**: Hybrid encryption simplifies key management and enhances security by using asymmetric encryption to exchange symmetric keys. Once the symmetric key is exchanged, the actual data can be encrypted and decrypted quickly using symmetric encryption.

- **Common implementations**: SSL/TLS is a prime example of a hybrid encryption protocol. During the SSL/TLS handshake, asymmetric encryption is used to exchange a symmetric session key, which is then used for encrypting the communication session.

The use cases are as follows:

- **Secure web communications**: Hybrid encryption is commonly used in securing web communications, such as HTTPS. The combination of asymmetric and symmetric encryption ensures that data transmitted between a web server and a client remains confidential and secure.

- **Email encryption**: Hybrid encryption is also used in email encryption systems, where the symmetric key encrypts the email content, and the asymmetric keys handle the key exchange.

Implementing encryption protocols in network security

Implementing encryption protocols in network security involves several critical steps, including selecting the appropriate encryption type, managing encryption keys, and integrating encryption into the organization's overall security architecture.

The steps to implement encryption protocols are as follows:

1. **Assess security requirements**: Start by assessing the organization's security requirements, including the sensitivity of the data being protected, the potential threats, and the regulatory compliance requirements. This assessment will guide the selection of the appropriate encryption protocols.

2. **Choose the right encryption protocol**: Based on the security assessment, select the encryption protocol that best meets the organization's needs. Consider factors such as the type of data being encrypted, the performance requirements, and the ease of key management.

3. **Implement key management**: Effective key management is crucial for securing encryption protocols. This includes generating strong keys, securely storing and distributing them, and regularly rotating keys to minimize the risk of compromise.

4. **Integrate encryption into the security architecture**: Encryption should be integrated into the organization's overall security architecture. This includes using encryption for data at rest, data in transit, and data in use and ensuring that encryption is applied consistently across all systems and applications.

5. **Monitor and maintain encryption systems**: Regularly monitor and maintain encryption systems to ensure they remain secure and effective. This includes updating encryption algorithms to address new vulnerabilities, regularly auditing key management practices, and ensuring compliance with relevant security standards.

6. **Educate and train employees**: Provide training and education to employees on the importance of encryption and best practices for handling sensitive data. This helps ensure that encryption protocols are used correctly and effectively across the organization.

Implementing VPNs and secure communications

In an increasingly connected world, the need to secure communications over public and private networks has never been more critical. **Virtual Private Networks** (**VPNs**) and secure communication protocols such as TLS and SSL play a vital role in ensuring that data transmitted between devices remains private, secure, and free from interception by unauthorized entities. This section explores the fundamentals of VPNs, their types and functions, and the key secure communication protocols that protect data in transit.

Understanding Virtual Private Networks

A VPN is a technology that creates a secure, encrypted connection over a less secure network, such as the Internet. This allows users to send and receive data as if their devices were directly connected to a private network, ensuring privacy and security even when using public Wi-Fi or other untrusted networks.

The key functions of VPNs are as follows:

- **Data encryption**: VPNs encrypt data before it is sent over the internet, making it unreadable to anyone who might intercept it. This ensures that sensitive information, such as login credentials, financial transactions, and personal communications, is protected from eavesdropping.

- **Anonymity and privacy**: VPNs help maintain online anonymity and protect users' privacy by masking their IP addresses and routing traffic through a secure server. This prevents websites, advertisers, and malicious actors from tracking users' online activities.

- **Bypassing geographical restrictions**: VPNs allow users to bypass geographical restrictions and access content that may be blocked or censored in their region. By connecting to a server in a different country, users can appear as though they are accessing the internet from that location.

- **Secure remote access**: VPNs enable secure remote access to a corporate network for employees working from home or on the go. This ensures that sensitive company data remains protected, even when accessed from outside the office.

- **Integrity and authentication**: VPNs ensure the integrity of the transmitted data by verifying that it has not been altered during transmission. Additionally, VPNs authenticate the identities of the communicating parties, ensuring that data is sent and received by authorized users.

The types of VPNs are as follows:

- **Remote access VPN**: This type of VPN allows individual users to connect to a private network remotely. It is commonly used by employees to access their organization's network from home or while traveling. Remote access VPNs provide secure, encrypted connections over the internet, ensuring that all data exchanged between the user's device and the corporate network is protected.

- **Site-to-site VPN**: Also known as a router-to-router VPN, this type of VPN connects entire networks. For example, a company with offices in multiple locations can use a site-to-site VPN to create a secure connection between each office's network. This allows resources to be shared securely across different locations as if they were on the same local network.

- **Client-to-Site VPN**: This is a variant of the site-to-site VPN, where individual clients connect to the organization's network. The client (user's device) communicates with a VPN gateway at the organization's network edge, providing secure access to network resources.

- **Layer 2 Tunneling Protocol (L2TP) VPN**: L2TP is a type of VPN that operates at the data link layer (Layer 2) of the OSI model. It is often combined with other encryption protocols, such as IPsec, to provide enhanced security. L2TP VPNs are commonly used for secure connections over the internet, especially when strong encryption is required.

- **IPsec VPN**: **Internet Protocol Security (IPsec)** is a suite of protocols used to secure internet communications by authenticating and encrypting each IP packet in a communication session. IPsec VPNs are widely used in site-to-site VPNs and remote access scenarios.

Secure communication protocols: TLS and SSL

Secure communication protocols are essential for protecting data transmitted over the Internet. TLS and SSL are two of the most widely used protocols for securing online communications. They ensure that data sent between a client (such as a web browser) and a server is encrypted and authenticated.

Secure Sockets Layer

SSL was the original protocol developed to secure communications over the internet. It provides a secure channel between two machines, typically a client and a server. SSL works by establishing an encrypted link that ensures all data passed between the web server and browsers remain private and integral.

The key features of SSL are as follows:

- **Encryption**: SSL uses encryption to protect data in transit, ensuring that any information sent over the internet cannot be read by unauthorized third parties. SSL encryption works by scrambling the data so that only the intended recipient, who has the correct decryption key, can read it.

- **Authentication**: SSL provides authentication by ensuring that the server a client is communicating with is the one it claims to be. This is done using digital certificates, which verify the server's identity.

- **Integrity**: SSL ensures data integrity by detecting any tampering with data during transmission. This is achieved using cryptographic hash functions, which create a unique checksum for each data packet sent.

- **Legacy Protocol**: While SSL was widely used in the past, it has been largely replaced by TLS due to several security vulnerabilities that were discovered over time. SSL is considered deprecated, and modern systems are advised to use TLS instead.

Transport Layer Security

TLS is the successor to SSL and is currently the most widely used protocol for securing Internet communications. TLS provides enhanced security features and addresses many vulnerabilities in SSL. It operates in a similar manner to SSL, establishing an encrypted connection between a client and a server to protect data in transit.

The key features of TLS are as follows:

- **Stronger encryption**: TLS uses stronger encryption algorithms than SSL, providing a higher level of security for data in transit. TLS supports a wide range of encryption methods, including AES and RSA.

- **Improved authentication**: TLS provides better authentication mechanisms, ensuring that the identities of both the client and server are verified before data is exchanged. This is typically done using digital certificates issued by trusted **Certificate Authorities (CAs)**.

- **Perfect Forward Secrecy (PFS):** TLS supports PFS, a feature that ensures that even if the session key is compromised, past communications remain secure. PFS achieves this by generating a unique session key for each communication session.

- **Backward compatibility**: While TLS is designed to replace SSL, it maintains backward compatibility with SSL, allowing systems that have not yet been upgraded to TLS to continue functioning securely.

- **Widespread adoption**: TLS is used in various applications, including secure web browsing (HTTPS), email encryption, and VPN connections. It is the standard protocol for securing internet communications today.

The types of secure communication protocols are as follows:

- **TLS:** As described above, TLS is the most widely used protocol for securing communications over the internet. It is the successor to SSL and provides robust encryption, authentication, and integrity checks to protect data in transit.

- **SSL:** Although SSL has largely been replaced by TLS, it is still important to understand SSL's role in developing secure communication protocols. SSL paved the way for secure online transactions and the widespread use of HTTPS.

- **IPsec:** IPsec is another critical protocol used for securing communications over the internet. It operates at the IP layer and is commonly used in VPNs to provide encrypted communication channels. IPsec offers several encryption and authentication options, making it versatile and secure for various applications.

- **SSH (Secure Shell):** SSH is a protocol used to securely access and manage remote systems over an unsecured network. It provides encrypted communication channels, ensuring that data exchanged between the client and the remote server is secure.

Implementing VPNs and secure communications

Implementing VPNs and secure communication protocols requires careful planning and consideration of the organization's security needs. The following steps outline a basic approach to implementing these technologies:

- **Assess security requirements**: Start by assessing the organization's security needs, including the types of data being transmitted, potential threats, and regulatory requirements. This assessment will guide the selection of the appropriate VPN and secure communication protocols.

- **Select the right VPN type**: Based on the security assessment, choose the one that best suits the organization's needs. For example, a remote access VPN may be ideal for employees working from home, while a site-to-site VPN might be better for connecting multiple office locations.

- **Deploy secure communication protocols**: Implement secure communication protocols like TLS and IPsec to protect data in transit. Ensure that all web servers, email servers, and VPN gateways are configured to use strong encryption and authentication methods.

- **Configure and manage VPNs**: Properly configure VPNs to ensure that they provide the desired level of security. This includes setting up strong encryption, authentication, and access control measures. Regularly review and update VPN configurations to address emerging threats.

- **Monitor and maintain security**: Continuously monitor VPN connections and secure communication channels for signs of unauthorized access or other security issues. Regularly update software and protocols to protect against new vulnerabilities.

- **Educate users**: Provide employees with training and education on the importance of using VPNs and secure communication protocols. This includes teaching users how to recognize phishing attempts and other social engineering attacks that could compromise security.

Continuous monitoring and incident response

In the ever-evolving landscape of CyberSecurity, continuous monitoring and incident response are fundamental components of a robust network security strategy. These practices ensure that organizations can detect, prevent, and respond to security threats in real-time, minimizing the potential impact of breaches and maintaining the integrity, confidentiality, and availability of critical assets. This section explores two key aspects of continuous monitoring and incident response: **Intrusion Detection and Prevention (IDS & IPS)** and real-time monitoring tools like **Security Information and Event Management (SIEM)**, **Network Traffic Analysis (NTA)**, and other advanced tools.

Intrusion detection and prevention

Intrusion Detection Systems (IDSs) and **Intrusion Prevention Systems (IPSs)** are integral parts of a network's defensive strategy, designed to identify and mitigate potential security threats before they can cause significant harm. While both IDS and IPS play crucial roles in network security, they serve slightly different purposes.

Intrusion Detection Systems

An IDS is a tool that monitors network traffic for suspicious activities and potential threats. It is primarily focused on detection rather than prevention, alerting administrators when it identifies potential security incidents. IDS can be deployed in two main forms:

- **Network-based IDS (NIDS):** NIDS monitors network traffic for entire network segments, analyzing packet data and identifying suspicious activities such as unauthorized access attempts, malware, and policy violations. NIDS is typically deployed at key network points, such as at the network perimeter or within critical internal segments, to provide broad coverage.

- **Host-based IDS (HIDS):** HIDS is installed on individual hosts (such as servers or workstations) and monitors the activities of that specific host. It can detect suspicious activities such as unauthorized file access, unexpected changes to system files, or unusual user behavior. HIDS provides a more granular level of monitoring compared to NIDS, offering insight into the activities occurring on individual devices.

The functionality of IDS is as follows:

- **Signature-based detection**: IDS uses predefined signatures to identify known threats. This method is highly effective at detecting established attack patterns but may struggle with new or unknown threats.

- **Anomaly-based detection**: IDS can also use anomaly-based detection, where it establishes a baseline of normal network behavior and flags any deviations from this baseline as potential threats. This method is useful for identifying zero-day attacks and other novel threats.

- **Alerting and reporting**: When a potential threat is detected, IDS generates alerts for network administrators, providing details about suspicious activity. This allows administrators to investigate the issue and take appropriate action.

Intrusion Prevention Systems

An IPS is an advanced version of IDS that detects potential threats and actively prevents them from compromising the network. IPS can block or reject malicious traffic in real-time, making it a proactive security measure. Like IDS, IPS can be deployed as either **network-based IPS (NIPS)** or **host-based IPS (HIPS)**.

The functionality of IPS is as follows:

- **Inline deployment**: Unlike IDS, which is often deployed in a passive mode, IPS is deployed inline, meaning it actively monitors and controls the traffic that passes through it. This allows IPS to block malicious traffic before it reaches its intended target.

- **Real-time threat prevention**: IPS can automatically act when it detects a threat, such as dropping malicious packets, terminating unauthorized connections, or blocking IP addresses. This real-time response helps prevent security incidents from escalating.

- **Threat intelligence integration**: Modern IPS solutions often integrate with threat intelligence feeds, which provide up-to-date information on emerging threats. This allows IPS to recognize and block new attack methods quickly.

- **Granular policy enforcement**: IPS can enforce security policies at a granular level, controlling which types of traffic are allowed or denied based on a wide range of criteria, such as IP addresses, ports, protocols, and content types.

Integration of IDS and IPS

Many security solutions combine IDS and IPS capabilities into a single system, often referred to as an **Intrusion Detection and Prevention System** (**IDPS**). This integration allows organizations to benefit from both detection and prevention in a unified platform, providing comprehensive protection against a wide range of threats.

Real-time monitoring tools

Real-time monitoring tools are essential for maintaining continuous visibility into network activities, detecting potential threats, and enabling rapid incident response. These tools collect, analyze, and correlate data from various sources across the network, providing actionable insights and alerts. Some of the key tools used in real-time monitoring include SIEM, NTA, and other advanced monitoring solutions.

Security Information and Event Management

SIEM is a centralized platform that aggregates and analyzes log data from various sources across the network, including firewalls, routers, servers, and endpoints. SIEM tools are designed to provide real-time insights into security events, helping organizations detect and respond to threats quickly.

The functionality of SIEM is as follows:

- **Log collection and aggregation**: SIEM collects log data from multiple sources, providing a centralized repository for security event data. This includes logs from firewalls, IDS/IPS, antivirus software, and other security devices.

- **Correlation and analysis**: SIEM analyzes the collected log data, looking for patterns or correlations that may indicate a security incident. For example, an SIEM tool might correlate multiple failed login attempts across different systems as an indicator of a brute-force attack.

- **Real-time alerting**: When SIEM identifies a potential threat, it generates real-time alerts, allowing security teams to respond quickly. Alerts are typically prioritized based on the severity of the threat.

- **Incident response support**: SIEM provides tools and dashboards that help security teams investigate and respond to incidents. This includes features like event timelines, forensic analysis tools, and integration with ticketing systems for incident management.

- **Compliance and reporting**: SIEM solutions often include reporting features that help organizations meet regulatory compliance requirements by providing detailed logs and audit trails of security events.

Network Traffic Analysis

NTA is a monitoring approach that focuses on analyzing network traffic to detect and respond to potential security threats. NTA tools provide deep visibility into the flow of data across the network, identifying anomalies and suspicious activities that may indicate a security breach.

The functionality of NTA is as follows:

- **Flow-based monitoring**: NTA tools analyze the flow of network traffic, examining aspects such as source and destination IP addresses, ports, protocols, and data volumes. This helps identify unusual traffic patterns that may suggest malicious activity, such as a DDoS attack or data exfiltration.

- **Anomaly detection**: NTA tools use baseline data to establish what constitutes normal network behavior. When deviations from this baseline are detected, NTA tools generate alerts for further investigation. This anomaly-based approach is effective at detecting new and unknown threats.

- **Encrypted traffic analysis**: Modern NTA tools are equipped to analyze encrypted traffic without decrypting it, using techniques such as machine learning to identify suspicious patterns within the encrypted data. This is crucial as more network traffic becomes encrypted, potentially hiding malicious activities.

- **Incident response integration**: NTA tools often integrate with SIEM and other security platforms, providing a broader context for detected threats. This allows for a more effective incident response by correlating network traffic data with other security event data.

Zero Trust Architecture (ZTA)

Zero Trust is a security model that fundamentally shifts the network security paradigm. Instead of assuming trust within the network perimeter, it operates under the principle of "**never trust, always verify**." This means that every user, device, and application, regardless of its location within or outside the network, is subject to strict authentication and authorization before accessing any resource.

Key principles

The key principles of the ZTA are explained as follows:

- **Continuous verification:** This is the cornerstone of Zero Trust. It mandates constant re-evaluation of trust. Every access request must be authenticated and authorized regardless of its origin (internal or external). This involves continuous checks on user identity, device health, and the request's legitimacy.

Example: **Multi-factor authentication (MFA)** is a prime example of continuous verification, requiring multiple forms of identification (e.g., password, biometrics, one-time code) to access resources.

- **Least privilege:** The **principle of least privilege (POLP)** dictates that users and devices should only have the absolute minimum access necessary to perform their required functions. This significantly limits the potential damage if an account is compromised.

  Example: A marketing employee might only need read-only access to customer data, while a system administrator might require elevated privileges for maintenance tasks.

- **Micro-segmentation:** This involves dividing the network into small, isolated segments. This limits the "**blast radius**" of a potential breach, confining the impact to a specific segment rather than allowing attackers to move laterally across the entire network.

  Example: Isolating sensitive databases or critical servers into highly secure segments within the network.

- **Data-centric security:** Zero Trust emphasizes protecting the data itself rather than solely relying on perimeter defenses. This involves implementing robust data encryption (both in transit and at rest) and strong **data loss prevention (DLP)** mechanisms.

  Types of Zero Trust implementations: There are two major types of Zero Trust implementation, which are explained here:

- **Zero Trust Network Access (ZTNA):** This model focuses on secure access to applications and data for remote users. It establishes secure connections between users and applications, regardless of their location or device.

- **Software-Defined Perimeter (SDP):** SDP creates a virtual perimeter around specific applications and data. Access to these resources is granted based on strict policies and continuous verification, regardless of the user's location within or outside the traditional network perimeter.

When effectively implemented, zero-trust principles can significantly enhance an organization's security posture. By continuously verifying every access request, enforcing the least privileged access, and segmenting the network, organizations can minimize the impact of potential breaches and improve their overall resilience against cyber threats.

Best practices for network security

Best practices and industry standards are essential for network security to ensure the confidentiality, integrity, and availability of data and resources. Implementing these practices helps organizations protect their networks against cyber threats and comply with regulatory requirements. The following are some of the key best practices and industry standards essential for network security:

- **Defense in depth**:

  o **Layered security approach**: Implement multiple layers of security controls, such as firewalls, IDS/IPS, antivirus software, and encryption, to protect against various types of threats. Each layer acts as a barrier that an attacker must breach, making it more difficult for them to access critical systems.

  o **Segmentation and zoning**: Divide the network into different segments or zones, each with its security controls and access policies. This limits the spread of threats and restricts access to sensitive areas.

- **Regular security audits and vulnerability assessments:**

  o **Conduct regular audit**s: Perform security audits to review and evaluate the effectiveness of security controls, identify potential weaknesses, and ensure compliance with security policies and regulations.

  o **Vulnerability assessments and penetration testing**: Regularly assess the network for vulnerabilities and conduct penetration testing to simulate attacks and identify exploitable weaknesses.

- **Access control and identity management:**

  o **Implement the POLP:** Ensure that users and systems have only the minimum level of access necessary to perform their functions. This reduces the risk of unauthorized access to sensitive information.

  o **Multi-factor authentication**: Require MFA for accessing critical systems and sensitive data. MFA adds an additional layer of security by requiring users to provide multiple forms of verification before granting access.

- **Encryption and data protection:**

  o **Encrypt sensitive data**: Use strong encryption protocols to protect data at rest, in transit, and in use. Encryption ensures that even if data is intercepted, it remains unreadable without the appropriate decryption keys.

  o **Implement secure communication protocols**: Use secure communication protocols, such as SSL/TLS, to protect data transmitted over the network. These protocols provide encryption and authentication to secure data exchanges between systems.

- **Continuous monitoring and incident response:**

  - **Deploy Intrusion Detection and Prevention Systems:** Monitor network traffic for suspicious activity and implement measures to detect and prevent intrusions. IDS/IPS solutions help identify and respond to threats in real-time.

  - **Establish an incident response plan**: Develop and regularly update an incident response plan that outlines procedures for detecting, responding to, and recovering from security incidents. The plan should include roles and responsibilities, communication protocols, and post-incident analysis.

- **Network security standards and compliance:**

  - **Adopt industry standards**: Implement recognized network security standards, such as ISO/IEC 27001, NIST CyberSecurity Framework, and CIS Controls, to guide the development and management of security practices.

  - **Compliance with regulations**: Ensure that network security practices comply with relevant regulations, such as GDPR, HIPAA, and PCI DSS. Compliance with these regulations is essential for protecting sensitive data and avoiding legal and financial penalties.

- **Patch management and system updates:**

  - **Regularly apply security patches**: Ensure that all systems and software are regularly updated with the latest security patches. Patch management helps protect against known vulnerabilities that could be exploited by attackers.

  - **Automate patch deployment:** Use automated tools to streamline patch deployment across the network. This reduces the risk of human error and ensures that all systems are consistently updated.

- **Employee training and awareness:**

  - **Conduct security training**: Provide regular training to employees on security best practices, including recognizing phishing attacks, using strong passwords, and reporting suspicious activities. Well-informed employees are a critical line of defense against cyber threats.

  - **Create a security culture**: Foster a culture of security awareness within the organization by encouraging employees to take an active role in protecting the network and data. Regularly communicate security policies and procedures to keep security at the top of mind.

- **Secure configuration management:**

  - **Implement secure configuration baselines**: Establish and enforce secure configuration baselines for all systems and devices. This includes disabling unnecessary services, changing default passwords, and configuring firewalls and access controls.

- o **Automate configuration management**: Use configuration management tools to automate the deployment and enforcement of security configurations across the network. This helps ensure consistency and reduces the risk of misconfigurations.

- **Backup and disaster recovery:**

  - o **Regular backups**: Perform regular backups of critical data and systems. Ensure that backups are stored securely and can be quickly restored in the event of a disaster or ransomware attack.

  - o **Develop a disaster recovery plan**: Create and regularly test a disaster recovery plan that outlines procedures for restoring systems and data in case of a security breach or other disaster. The plan should prioritize the recovery of essential services and data.

Endpoint security

Each endpoint is a gateway to your network; securing them is crucial to preventing unauthorized access and data breaches.

Endpoint security refers to the process of securing end-user devices such as desktops, laptops, smartphones, tablets, and other devices that connect to a network. Securing these endpoints is essential to protect sensitive data and maintain network security. This section will cover various strategies and technologies to enhance endpoint security, such as antivirus solutions, **endpoint detection and response** (**EDR**) systems, and MDM practices. The key components of endpoint security are shown in the following figure:

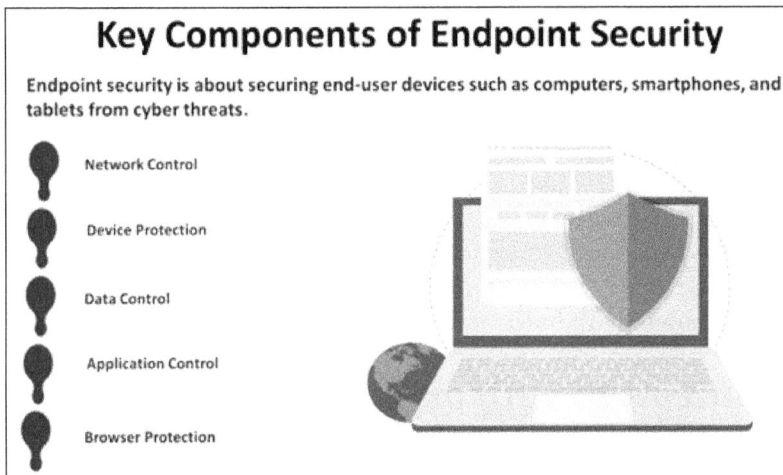

Figure 3.3: Key components of endpoint security

Introduction to endpoint security

Endpoints are devices that connect to your network and allow users to access, process, and store information. These include desktops, laptops, smartphones, tablets, and IoT devices. Endpoint security is vital because it is the first defense against cyber threats. Since endpoints are distributed across various locations and often connect from outside traditional network boundaries, they are particularly vulnerable to attacks.

Importance of endpoint security

Endpoints serve as gateways to a network, and if compromised, they can provide attackers with direct access to sensitive data and critical systems. The importance of endpoint security cannot be overstated, as a single compromised device can lead to a full-scale network breach, resulting in data loss, financial damage, and reputational harm.

The key reasons why endpoint security is crucial are as follows:

- **Protection against evolving threats**: Cyber threats constantly evolve, with attackers developing new methods to infiltrate systems. Effective endpoint security provides a first line of defense against these threats, ensuring that devices are protected against malware, ransomware, phishing attacks, and other forms of cyberattacks.

- **Compliance with regulations**: Many industries are subject to strict regulatory requirements concerning data security. Endpoint security measures help organizations comply with these regulations by ensuring that data on end-user devices is adequately protected.

- **Support for remote workforces**: With the rise of remote work, endpoint security has become even more critical. Remote employees often connect to corporate networks using personal devices or through unsecured networks, increasing the risk of cyberattacks. Endpoint security solutions ensure that remote devices are secure, even when operating outside the traditional network perimeter.

- **Data protection**: Endpoints are repositories of valuable data, including sensitive personal information, intellectual property, and financial records. Protecting this data from unauthorized access and breaches is a key objective of endpoint security.

- **Incident response and mitigation**: In the event of a security incident, endpoint security tools can detect, respond to, and mitigate the impact of the attack. This minimizes potential damage and speeds up the recovery process.

Common threats to endpoints

Endpoints are exposed to a wide range of cyber threats, varying in complexity and severity. Understanding the following common threats is essential for developing effective endpoint security strategies:

- **Malware**: Malicious software, or malware, is one of the most prevalent threats to endpoints. Malware includes viruses, worms, Trojans, ransomware, spyware, and other malicious code designed to damage, steal, or manipulate data.

- **Phishing attacks**: Phishing is a social engineering tactic where attackers trick users into revealing sensitive information, such as passwords or credit card numbers, by posing as a trustworthy entity. Phishing attacks often target endpoints through email, messaging apps, or malicious websites.

- **Ransomware**: Ransomware is a type of malware that encrypts the data on an endpoint and demands payment, usually in cryptocurrency, for the decryption key. Ransomware attacks can cripple an organization by locking down critical data and systems.

- **Zero-day exploits**: Zero-day vulnerabilities are previously unknown software flaws that attackers exploit before they are patched by the software vendor. These exploits can be particularly dangerous because they are difficult to detect and defend against without specific knowledge of the vulnerability.

- **Insider threats**: Not all threats originate from external attackers. Insider threats involve employees, contractors, or other trusted individuals who misuse their access to company data and systems for malicious purposes. This can include data theft, sabotage, or unintentional security breaches.

- **Device theft or loss**: Physical theft or loss of an endpoint device can lead to unauthorized access to sensitive data, especially if the device is not encrypted or adequately secured.

Antivirus and anti-malware solutions

Antivirus software is a fundamental component of endpoint security, designed to detect, prevent, and remove malware. There are several types of antivirus solutions, each with distinct features:

- **Signature-based antivirus**: This traditional type of antivirus software relies on known signatures of malware to detect and remove threats. It compares the code of files on a device against a database of known malware signatures. While effective against known threats, signature-based antivirus may struggle to detect new or unknown malware.

- **Heuristic-based antivirus**: Heuristic-based antivirus software uses algorithms to analyze the behavior of programs and files to identify suspicious activities that may indicate malware. This approach can detect new or modified malware that does not have a known signature.

- **Behavioral-based antivirus**: This type of antivirus focuses on monitoring the behavior of software in real-time. It identifies anomalies or behaviors that are indicative of malware, such as unauthorized access to sensitive data or attempts to modify critical system files.

- **Cloud-based antivirus**: Cloud-based antivirus solutions offload much of the processing required for threat detection to the cloud rather than relying solely on the local device. This allows for more efficient scanning, reduced resource usage on the endpoint, and access to up-to-date threat intelligence.

Deployment and management

Deploying and managing antivirus and anti-malware solutions is a critical aspect of endpoint security. Effective deployment ensures that all endpoints within an organization are adequately protected, while proper management ensures that the solutions remain effective over time.

The deployment strategies are as follows:

- **Centralized deployment:** Organizations typically deploy antivirus software through a centralized management console, which allows IT administrators to distribute the software across multiple endpoints, enforce security policies, and monitor the status of all protected devices.

- **Automated updates:** Antivirus software must be regularly updated to protect against the latest threats. Automated updates ensure that all endpoints receive the latest virus definitions and security patches without requiring manual intervention.

- **Real-time scanning:** Antivirus solutions should be configured to perform real-time scanning of all files and programs as they are accessed or executed. This helps prevent malware from infecting the device before being detected during scheduled scans.

The management practices are as follows:

- **Policy enforcement:** IT administrators should enforce security policies that dictate how antivirus software is configured, ensuring that settings such as real-time protection, scheduled scanning, and automatic updates are enabled.

- **Monitoring and reporting:** Continuous monitoring of antivirus activity is essential to detect any issues or outbreaks. Reporting tools provide visibility into the security status of all endpoints, allowing administrators to take corrective action if necessary.

- **Incident response:** In the event of a malware infection, antivirus solutions should facilitate rapid incident response, including quarantine or removal of infected files, system restoration, and root cause analysis.

Endpoint detection and response

EDR is a CyberSecurity tool that provides advanced capabilities for detecting and responding to endpoint security incidents. It monitors endpoints for suspicious activity and gathers data to identify and take remediation measures in real-time. This can include logging processes, services, and programs that are run and files that are accessed. The key features and benefits include the following:

- **Real-time monitoring**: EDR solutions continuously monitor endpoint activities, capturing detailed data on processes, file changes, network connections, and user behavior. This real-time visibility allows for the early detection of threats that may bypass traditional antivirus software.

- **Threat hunting**: EDR enables proactive threat hunting, where security teams actively search for signs of compromise across endpoints. This is particularly useful for detecting APTs and other stealthy attacks that may not trigger conventional alerts.

- **Incident response**: EDR solutions provide tools for rapid incident response, including the ability to isolate infected devices, terminate malicious processes, and roll back malicious changes. This helps contain and mitigate the impact of a security incident.

- **Forensic analysis**: EDR captures and stores detailed endpoint data, which can be used for forensic analysis during and after a security incident. This data helps security teams understand the scope of the attack, identify the entry point, and develop strategies to prevent future incidents.

- **Integration with SIEM**: EDR solutions often integrate with SIEM systems, providing a comprehensive view of security events across the organization. This integration enhances threat detection and correlation by combining endpoint data with network and application logs.

Implementation strategies

Implementing EDR solutions requires careful planning to ensure they are effective and do not disrupt business operations:

- **Scalability**: Ensure the EDR solution can scale to cover all endpoints across the organization, including remote and mobile devices. Cloud-based EDR solutions can offer greater scalability and flexibility.

- **Policy configuration**: Define and enforce security policies through the EDR platform, such as rules for detecting and responding to specific threats and thresholds for generating alerts.

- **Automation**: Leverage automation capabilities in EDR to reduce the workload on security teams. Automated responses to detected threats can help contain incidents quickly without waiting for manual intervention.

- **Training and awareness**: Train security teams on how to use the EDR platform effectively, including threat-hunting techniques, incident response procedures, and forensic analysis.

Mobile device management

With the increasing use of mobile devices in the workplace, securing these endpoints is essential. MDM refers to an organization's comprehensive suite of technologies, policies, and processes for managing, securing, and monitoring mobile devices such as smartphones, tablets, and laptops. MDM aims to optimize the functionality and security of mobile devices within an enterprise while protecting the corporate network and data.

Securing mobile endpoints

Securing mobile endpoints presents unique challenges due to their portability, frequent use outside of secure environments, and the diversity of devices and operating systems. MDM solutions address these challenges by providing the following security capabilities:

- **Device enrollment and authentication**: MDM solutions enable the secure enrollment of devices into the corporate network, often requiring strong authentication methods such as MFA to verify the user's identity.

- **Data encryption**: MDM solutions enforce encryption of data stored on mobile devices, ensuring that sensitive information remains protected even if the device is lost or stolen.

- **Remote wipe and lock**: In case a device is lost or stolen, MDM solutions allow administrators to wipe it remotely to prevent unauthorized access to corporate data. Additionally, remote lock features can be used to disable the device.

- **App management**: MDM solutions allow administrators to control which applications can be installed or used on mobile devices. This helps prevent the use of unauthorized or potentially harmful apps that could introduce security risks.

- **Secure access to corporate resources**: MDM solutions provide secure access to corporate resources, such as email, intranets, and file servers, by enforcing VPN connections or secure containers for business data.

Policies and best practices

Effective MDM requires the implementation of robust policies and adherence to best practices:

- **Device compliance**: Establish policies that define the minimum security requirements for devices, such as mandatory encryption, regular updates, and the use of secure apps.

- **Access control**: Implement role-based access controls to ensure that users only have access to the resources they need for their job functions. This limits the potential exposure of sensitive data.

- **User training**: Educate users on the importance of mobile security, including safe usage practices, recognizing phishing attempts, and the risks associated with unsecured public Wi-Fi networks.

- **Regular audits and monitoring**: Conduct regular audits to ensure compliance with MDM policies and continuously monitor mobile devices for signs of unauthorized access or policy violations.

- **Incident response**: Developing and implementing an incident response plan for mobile security breaches, including remote wiping and data recovery procedures.

Endpoint security best practices

User awareness and training are crucial components of endpoint security. Educating users on security best practices helps prevent many common threats:

- **Security training programs**: Develop and implement comprehensive security training programs that educate employees on endpoint security threats, safe computing practices, and the importance of following security policies.

- **Phishing simulations**: Conduct regular phishing simulations to test employees' ability to recognize and respond to phishing attempts. Use the results to identify areas for improvement and provide targeted training.

- **Encourage strong passwords**: Enforce the use of strong, unique passwords for all endpoint devices and applications. Implement password management tools to help users create and store complex passwords securely.

Regular updates and patches that need to be done are as follows:

- **Automated patch management**: Implement automated patch management systems to ensure that all endpoints receive security patches and updates as soon as they are released. This reduces the window of vulnerability for newly discovered threats.

- **Software and firmware updates**: Regularly update both the software and firmware on endpoint devices to protect against vulnerabilities that could be exploited by attackers.

- **End-of-life management**: Replace or decommission devices and software that are no longer supported by the vendor, as they may no longer receive critical security updates.

Securing endpoints is like fortifying the gates of a fortress; it is a crucial defense against intruders.

Firewalls, IDS, and IPS

Firewalls, IDS, and IPS are your frontline defenders; they form the shield that guards your digital fortress.

Firewalls, IDSs, and IPSs are essential components of a secure network infrastructure. These technologies work together to prevent unauthorized access, detect suspicious activities, and block potential threats. This section will examine the functionalities, deployment strategies, and best practices for firewalls, IDS, and IPS to protect your network. The functions of a firewall are as follows:

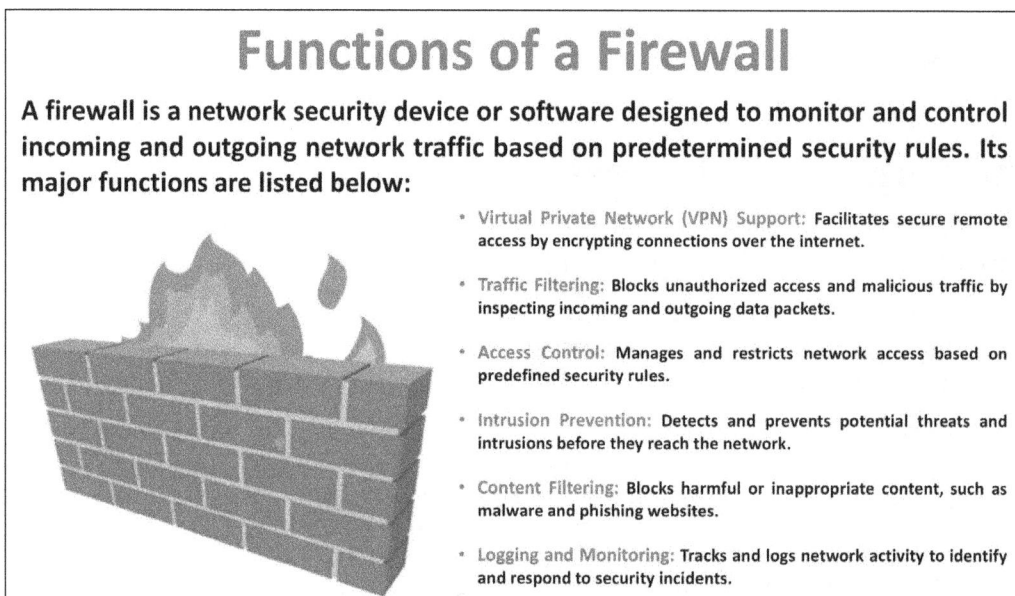

Functions of a Firewall

A firewall is a network security device or software designed to monitor and control incoming and outgoing network traffic based on predetermined security rules. Its major functions are listed below:

- Virtual Private Network (VPN) Support: **Facilitates secure remote access by encrypting connections over the internet.**

- Traffic Filtering: **Blocks unauthorized access and malicious traffic by inspecting incoming and outgoing data packets.**

- Access Control: **Manages and restricts network access based on predefined security rules.**

- Intrusion Prevention: **Detects and prevents potential threats and intrusions before they reach the network.**

- Content Filtering: **Blocks harmful or inappropriate content, such as malware and phishing websites.**

- Logging and Monitoring: **Tracks and logs network activity to identify and respond to security incidents.**

Figure 3.4: Functions of a firewall

Understanding firewalls

A **firewall** is a critical network security device or software that monitors, controls, and filters incoming and outgoing network traffic based on predetermined security rules. Its primary function is to establish a barrier between a trusted internal network and untrusted external networks, such as the Internet, to prevent unauthorized access and potential threats. There are several types of firewalls, each suited to different network environments and security needs:

- **Packet-filtering firewalls**: The most basic type of firewall, packet-filtering firewalls inspect data packets and allow or block them based on source and destination IP addresses, port numbers, and protocols. They operate at the OSI model's network layer (Layer 3) and the transport layer (Layer 4).

- **Stateful inspection firewalls**: These firewalls maintain a state table to track the state of active connections and make decisions based on the context of the traffic. By considering the connection state in addition to IP addresses and port numbers, they offer more robust security than packet-filtering firewalls.

- **Proxy firewalls**: Proxy firewalls, also known as application-layer firewalls, act as intermediaries between users and the services they access. They inspect packets at the OSI model's application layer (Layer 7), providing detailed inspection of web, email, and other application traffic. This type of firewall can filter content and enforce policies based on the application data.

- **Next-Generation Firewalls (NGFWs):** NGFWs combine traditional firewall capabilities with advanced features such as intrusion prevention, deep packet inspection, application awareness, and identity-based access control. They provide comprehensive protection by integrating multiple security functions into a single device.

Configuration and management

Effective firewall configuration and management are crucial for maintaining network security. The key points to keep in mind are as follows:

- **Define security policies**: Establish clear security policies that outline the rules for allowing or blocking traffic based on the organization's security requirements.

- **Rule creation and optimization**: Create firewall rules that align with the security policies. Optimize rules to minimize complexity and reduce the risk of misconfigurations. Regularly review and update rules to address emerging threats and changes in the network environment.

- **Network segmentation**: Use firewalls to segment the network into smaller zones with varying levels of trust. Implementing network segmentation helps contain potential breaches and limits the spread of malware.

- **Monitoring and logging**: Enable logging and monitoring features to track firewall activity and detect any anomalies or suspicious behavior. Analyze logs regularly to identify potential security incidents.

- **Regular updates and patching**: Keep firewall software and firmware up to date with the latest patches and updates. This helps address known vulnerabilities and ensures the firewall remains effective against new threats.

Intrusion Detection Systems

An IDS is a security solution designed to monitor network or system activities for malicious activities, policy violations, or anomalies that may indicate a security breach or intrusion.

The primary goal of an IDS is to detect and alert administrators to potential threats so that appropriate actions can be taken to mitigate risks and respond to security incidents. There are two main types of IDS:

- **Network-based IDS (NIDS):** NIDS monitors network traffic for suspicious activity. It is typically deployed at strategic points within the network, such as at the perimeter or in front of critical servers. NIDS analyzes packets for known attack patterns and anomalies, providing alerts when potential threats are detected.

- **Host-based IDS (HIDS):** HIDS operates on individual hosts or devices, monitoring system logs, file integrity, and process activity for signs of compromise. HIDS can provide detailed insights into the behavior of specific systems and detect threats that may bypass network-level defenses.

Monitoring and alerting

Effective IDS monitoring and alerting are essential for timely detection and response to security incidents:

- **Signature-based detection**: This IDS uses a database of known attack signatures to identify malicious activity. It can quickly detect known threats but may struggle with new or unknown attacks.

- **Anomaly-based detection**: Establishes a baseline of normal network behavior and flags deviations from this baseline as potential threats. Anomaly-based IDS can detect novel attacks but may generate false positives if normal behavior is not well-defined.

- **Behavioral analysis**: Monitors network traffic and system activity behavior to identify unusual patterns that may indicate a threat. Behavioral analysis can detect sophisticated attacks that do not match known signatures.

- **Alert management**: Configure the IDS to generate alerts for significant events and potential threats. Prioritize alerts based on severity and potential impact to ensure that critical incidents receive prompt attention.

Intrusion Prevention Systems

An IPS is a real-time network security technology designed to detect, prevent, and respond to potential threats and malicious activities. Unlike an IDS, which primarily focuses on identifying and alerting about potential threats, an IPS takes proactive measures to block or mitigate these threats automatically. Its primary goal is to protect networks and systems by preventing intrusions before they can cause damage or compromise security. Key functionalities and benefits of IPS include:

- **Real-time threat prevention**: IPS can immediately block or mitigate threats, preventing them from reaching their targets. This includes dropping malicious packets, resetting connections, and blocking IP addresses.

- **Comprehensive security coverage**: IPS integrates multiple security functions, including deep packet inspection, protocol analysis, and application layer filtering. This provides robust protection against a wide range of threats.

- **Automated response**: IPS automates the response to detected threats, reducing the need for manual intervention and enabling faster attack mitigation.

- **Reduced false positives**: Advanced IPS solutions use machine learning and behavioral analysis to reduce false positives, ensuring that legitimate traffic is not mistakenly blocked.

Deployment considerations

Deploying an IPS requires careful planning to ensure optimal performance and security:

- **Network placement**: Position the IPS at crucial points within the network where it can effectively monitor and protect critical assets. Common deployment locations include the network perimeter, data centers, and in front of high-value servers.

- **Performance impact**: Consider the potential impact of IPS on network performance. High-throughput environments may require dedicated hardware or optimized configurations to handle the inspection and processing of large traffic volumes.

- **Integration with existing security tools**: Ensure the IPS integrates seamlessly with other security solutions, such as firewalls, SIEM systems, and network monitoring tools. This enhances the overall security posture and enables a coordinated response to threats.

- **Policy tuning**: Configure IPS policies to balance security and usability. Fine-tune detection and prevention rules to minimize false positives and avoid disrupting legitimate network activities.

Integration and management

Effective integration and coordination of firewalls, IDS, and IPS are essential for comprehensive network security. The points to keep in mind are as follows:

- **Unified security policies**: Develop unified security policies that govern the behavior of firewalls, IDS, and IPS. This ensures consistency and coherence in the overall security strategy.

- **Centralized management**: Use centralized management platforms to configure, monitor, and update firewalls, IDS, and IPS from a single interface. This simplifies administration and improves visibility into the security environment.

- **Event correlation**: Correlate events and alerts from firewalls, IDS, and IPS to gain a holistic view of security incidents. This enables more accurate threat detection and response.

- **Collaborative response**: Implement automated workflows and playbooks coordinating firewall, IDS, and IPS response actions. This will enhance the efficiency and effectiveness of incident response.

Centralized management tools

Centralized management tools provide a unified platform for managing and monitoring security devices:

- **SIEM:** SIEM systems aggregate and analyze security data from multiple sources, providing real-time insights and alerts. They facilitate event correlation, threat hunting, and compliance reporting.

- **NMS:** NMS tools monitor network devices, including firewalls, IDS, and IPS, for performance and availability. They provide visibility into network health and help identify potential issues.

- **UTM:** UTM solutions consolidate multiple security functions, such as firewall, IDS, IPS, and antivirus, into a single device. This simplifies management and provides comprehensive protection.

Best practices

Implementing effective deployment strategies ensures the success of firewalls, IDS, and IPS:

- **Risk assessment**: Conduct a thorough risk assessment to identify critical assets, potential threats, and vulnerabilities. Use this information to guide the deployment of security devices.

- **Layered security**: Adopt a layered security approach that combines multiple defenses, including firewalls, IDS, and IPS, to provide comprehensive protection.

- **Regular updates**: To protect against emerging threats, keep security devices updated with the latest signatures, patches, and firmware.

- **Continuous monitoring**: Implement continuous monitoring and logging to detect and respond to real-time security incidents.

When firewalls, IDS, and IPS work together, they create an unbreakable shield that safeguards your network from relentless cyber threats. By understanding the functionalities, deployment considerations, and best practices for firewalls, IDS, and IPS, organizations can build a resilient security infrastructure that effectively protects against a wide range of cyber threats.

Secure configuration practices

A secure system starts with the right configuration; improper settings can leave the doors wide open for attackers.

Secure configuration is a critical aspect of CyberSecurity that involves setting up systems, applications, and networks to minimize vulnerabilities and protect against threats. This chapter will explore the importance of proper configuration, system hardening techniques, secure software development practices, and the role of audits and assessments in maintaining security. Additionally, we will discuss configuration management tools that help automate and ensure continuous compliance.

Importance of proper configuration

Proper configuration is foundational to maintaining a secure IT environment. Misconfigurations can lead to vulnerabilities that attackers exploit, potentially causing data breaches, service disruptions, and financial loss. Ensuring that systems are configured securely involves setting appropriate access controls, applying necessary security patches, and disabling unnecessary services.

- **Prevent unauthorized access**: Proper configuration helps enforce access controls, ensuring that only authorized users and processes can access sensitive information and resources.

- **Reduce vulnerabilities**: Correctly configured systems are less likely to have exploitable weaknesses that attackers can use to gain a foothold in the network.

- **Compliance**: Many regulatory frameworks require organizations to follow specific configuration standards to protect sensitive data. Proper configuration ensures compliance with these standards.

- **Operational efficiency**: Secure configuration contributes to system stability and performance, reducing downtime caused by security incidents.

Common misconfigurations

Misconfigurations are a common cause of security breaches. Some of the most frequent misconfigurations include:

- **Default credentials**: Failure to change default usernames and passwords can allow attackers to access systems easily.

- **Exposed services**: Leaving unnecessary services and ports open increases the attack surface, providing more entry points for attackers.

- **Weak password policies**: Inadequate password policies, such as allowing weak or easily guessable passwords, can compromise security.

- **Insecure permissions**: Incorrectly set permissions can grant users or applications more access than needed, leading to potential abuse or data leakage.

- **Unpatched systems**: Failing to apply security patches promptly leaves systems vulnerable to known exploits.

System hardening

System hardening involves securing systems by reducing their attack surfaces and minimizing how an attacker can access or exploit a system. Key techniques include:

- **Disabling unnecessary services**: Turn off services not required for the system's operation to eliminate potential entry points for attackers and reduce the number of potential vulnerabilities that can be exploited.

- **Least privilege principle**: Grant users and applications the minimum level of access necessary to perform their functions, reducing the risk of privilege escalation. Implement **role-based access controls** (**RBAC**) to manage permissions effectively.

- **Secure configurations**: Apply secure baseline configurations that adhere to best practices and industry standards, such as the CIS Benchmarks. These configurations should be regularly reviewed and updated to address new vulnerabilities.

- **Remove unnecessary software**: Uninstall unnecessary software, as it can introduce vulnerabilities. This reduces the attack surface and simplifies the management of security patches.

Applying security patches

Regularly applying security patches is crucial for maintaining the security of systems. Patches address vulnerabilities that attackers could exploit. Effective patch management involves the following:

- **Patch management policy**: Develop and implement a patch management policy that outlines the procedures for identifying, testing, and applying patches. This policy should include timelines for patch deployment based on the severity of the vulnerabilities.

- **Regular updates**: Schedule regular updates to ensure all systems are patched promptly. Automated tools can help streamline the patch management process.

- **Testing patches**: Test patches in a controlled environment before applying them to production systems to avoid compatibility issues and ensure stability. This helps prevent disruptions to business operations.

- **Prioritizing patches**: Patches should be prioritized based on the severity of the vulnerabilities they address and the criticality of the systems they affect. High-severity vulnerabilities should be addressed first to minimize the risk of exploitation.

Secure software development

Secure software development involves integrating security practices throughout the software development lifecycle to protect applications from threats and vulnerabilities. This includes activities like threat modeling, secure coding, code reviews, and security testing.

It ensures the software is resilient against attacks, safeguarding sensitive data and maintaining user trust. Addressing security early on reduces the risk of breaches, lowers costs associated with fixing vulnerabilities post-deployment, and complies with regulatory requirements. Ultimately, it helps in delivering robust, reliable, and secure software solutions.

Secure coding practices

Secure coding practices refer to guidelines, principles, and techniques to create software that is resistant to security vulnerabilities and attacks (*Figure 3.5*). These practices are integrated throughout the software development lifecycle to ensure the code is robust, reliable, and can defend against potential threats. Secure coding is essential for protecting applications from various cyberattacks, such as SQL injection, **cross-site scripting (XSS)**, and buffer overflows, etc. Secure coding practices involve the following:

- **Input validation**: Validate all input data to ensure it is correct, complete, and not malicious. Input validation helps prevent attacks such as SQL injection and XSS.

- **Output encoding**: Encode output data to prevent attacks like SQL injection and XSS. Proper encoding ensures that data is rendered safely in the intended context.

- **Error handling**: Implement proper error handling to prevent the disclosure of sensitive information through error messages. Use generic error messages to avoid revealing details about the system's internals.

- **Authentication and authorization**: Ensure robust authentication and authorization mechanisms to control access to resources and data. Using MFA to enhance security and enforce strong password policies.

- **Secure data storage**: Strong encryption algorithms should be used to encrypt sensitive data both in transit and at rest. Avoid storing sensitive information, such as passwords or personal data, in plain text. Secure methods should also be used to manage encryption keys and credentials.

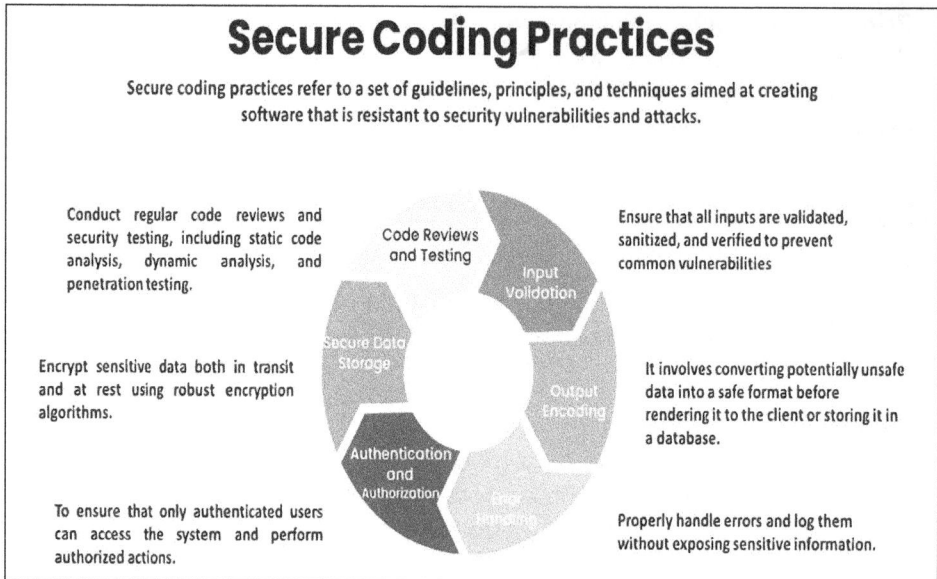

Secure Coding Practices

Secure coding practices refer to a set of guidelines, principles, and techniques aimed at creating software that is resistant to security vulnerabilities and attacks.

Conduct regular code reviews and security testing, including static code analysis, dynamic analysis, and penetration testing.

Code Reviews and Testing

Ensure that all inputs are validated, sanitized, and verified to prevent common vulnerabilities

Input Validation

Encrypt sensitive data both in transit and at rest using robust encryption algorithms.

Secure Data Storage

Output Encoding

It involves converting potentially unsafe data into a safe format before rendering it to the client or storing it in a database.

Authentication and Authorization

Error Handling

To ensure that only authenticated users can access the system and perform authorized actions.

Properly handle errors and log them without exposing sensitive information.

Figure 3.5: Secure coding practices

Code review and testing

Regular code reviews and testing are vital for identifying and fixing security issues before the software is deployed:

- **Peer reviews**: Conduct peer reviews to ensure the code meets security standards and best practices. Peer reviews provide an additional layer of scrutiny and help identify potential security flaws.

- **Static analysis**: Use static analysis tools to detect vulnerabilities in source code without executing it. Static analysis can identify issues such as buffer overflows, SQL injection, and hard-coded credentials.

- **Dynamic analysis**: Perform dynamic analysis to test the behavior of running applications and identify runtime vulnerabilities. Dynamic analysis can uncover issues that are not detectable through static analysis alone.

- **Penetration testing**: Conduct penetration testing to simulate attacks and identify security weaknesses that could be exploited. Penetration testing provides a realistic assessment of the application's security posture.

Audits and assessments

Security audits are systematic evaluations of an organization's security policies, practices, controls, and systems to assess their effectiveness in protecting against threats and vulnerabilities. A security audit aims to identify weaknesses, ensure compliance with security standards and regulations, and provide recommendations for improving overall security posture. Critical stages in conducting security audits include:

- **Define scope**: Clearly define the scope of the audit, including the systems, applications, and data to be reviewed. This helps focus the audit on critical areas and ensures comprehensive coverage.

- **Review policies and procedures**: Assess the organization's security policies, procedures, and controls to ensure they are adequate and effective. Identify any gaps or weaknesses in the existing security framework.

- **Examine configurations**: Check the configurations of systems and applications to identify deviations from security baselines and verify that they align with best practices and industry standards.

- **Analyze logs**: Review system and application logs to detect unusual or suspicious activities. Log analysis helps identify potential security incidents and provides insights into the effectiveness of security controls.

Vulnerability assessments

A vulnerability assessment systematically identifies, evaluates, and prioritizes security vulnerabilities within an organization's systems, applications, and network infrastructure. The primary goal of a vulnerability assessment is to uncover weaknesses that attackers could potentially exploit and to provide recommendations for mitigating these vulnerabilities to enhance overall security. The key components are as follows:

- **Automated scanning**: Automated tools scan for known vulnerabilities and misconfigurations, providing a comprehensive overview of the organization's security posture.

- **Manual testing**: Complement automated scanning with manual testing to identify complex vulnerabilities that tools might miss. Manual testing allows for a more in-depth analysis of potential security issues.

- **Risk assessment**: Evaluate the potential impact and likelihood of exploiting vulnerabilities to prioritize remediation efforts. Risk assessment helps organizations allocate resources effectively to address the most critical vulnerabilities.

- **Remediation planning**: Develop and implement a plan to address identified vulnerabilities, including patching, configuration changes, and other mitigations. Remediation planning ensures that vulnerabilities are addressed in a timely and systematic manner.

Configuration management tools

Configuration management tools are designed to automate the management of system configurations, ensuring that systems are correctly configured, consistent, and compliant with organizational policies and standards. These tools' primary purposes are to streamline infrastructure management, reduce manual errors, and enhance overall efficiency and security. The key benefits of using these tools are as follows:

- **Consistency**: Ensure all systems are configured consistently according to predefined security policies and standards. Consistent configurations reduce the risk of misconfigurations and security breaches.

- **Efficiency**: Automate repetitive tasks, reducing the time and effort required for manual configuration and management. Automation improves operational efficiency and frees up resources for other security tasks.

- **Scalability**: Easily manage configurations across large and complex environments, ensuring that security policies are applied uniformly. Scalability is essential for maintaining security in growing and dynamic environments.

- **Auditability:** Maintain detailed records of configuration changes for auditing and compliance purposes. Configuration management tools provide a clear audit trail, making it easier to demonstrate compliance with regulatory requirements.

Continuous compliance monitoring

Continuous compliance monitoring ensures systems remain compliant with security policies and regulatory requirements over time. Key practices include:

- **Real-time monitoring**: Continuously monitor systems for configuration changes and security violations. Real-time monitoring helps detect and respond to potential security issues promptly.

- **Automated remediation**: Automatically correct non-compliant configurations to maintain security and compliance. Automated remediation reduces the risk of human error and ensures that configurations remain secure.

- **Policy enforcement**: Enforce security policies consistently across all systems, applications, and networks. Policy enforcement ensures that security controls are applied uniformly and effectively.

- **Reporting and alerts**: Generate reports and alerts to inform stakeholders of compliance status and any issues needing attention. Reporting and alerts provide visibility into the organization's security posture and help drive continuous improvement.

Secure configuration is not a one-time task; it is an ongoing process that fortifies your defenses against evolving threats. By following secure configuration practices, organizations can significantly reduce their attack surfaces, mitigate vulnerabilities, and ensure their systems are resilient against cyber threats.

Surface, deep, and dark web security

Navigating the shadows of the internet requires vigilance and insight; understanding the deep and dark web is crucial for fortifying your CyberSecurity defenses.

The deep web and dark web represent significant internet areas that traditional search engines do not index. While the deep web comprises unindexed, legitimate content, the dark web is often associated with illicit activities. This chapter delves into the definitions, risks, monitoring strategies, and ethical considerations surrounding the deep and dark web. Understanding these elements is essential for building a robust CyberSecurity infrastructure capable of addressing threats from these obscure parts of the internet. The following table illustrates the differences between surface, deep, and dark web:

Aspect	Surface web	Deep web	Dark web
Definition	The part of the internet accessible via search engines	Parts of the internet not indexed by search engines	Subset of the deep web accessible only via special tools
Access	Accessible through standard browsers	Requires authentication or specific permissions	Requires specialized software like Tor
Content	Publicly available information and websites	Private databases, academic journals, subscription sites	Illicit marketplaces, forums for illegal activities
Examples	News websites, blogs, social media	Online banking, medical records, subscription-based content	Darknet marketplaces, illegal forums, whistleblowing sites
Use cases	Information sharing, e-commerce, social networking	Confidential information, proprietary research	Anonymity for illegal activities, private communications
Visibility	Indexed and searchable by traditional search engines	Not indexed by search engines	Not indexed and designed to be hidden

Table 3.1: Differentiation between surface, deep, and dark web

Introduction to the surface, deep, and dark web

The **surface web** is the part of the Internet accessible to the general public through search engines and standard web browsers. Examples of the surface web include search engine results and websites that do not require a particular configuration to access. The **deep web** refers to parts of the Internet not indexed by standard search engines. This includes private databases, academic journals, and subscription-based services. The **dark web**, a subset of the deep web, requires specific software like **The Onion Router** (**Tor**) to access and is often associated with illegal activities such as drug trafficking, arms dealing, and cybercrime.

The different types of webs (*Figure 3.6*) are as follows:

- **Surface web**: The Surface Web, accessible via standard search engines, only makes up a small portion of the Internet. It is sometimes called the **'public web'** because it is accessible to anyone with an internet connection.

- **Deep web**: It encompasses a vast array of content that remains hidden from traditional search engines, including medical records, financial data, and proprietary research. Accessing these areas usually requires authentication and authorization.

- **Dark web**: Accessible only through specialized software, the dark web hosts marketplaces for illegal goods and services, forums for cybercriminals, and other hidden services. It operates on anonymity networks, making tracing users' identities and activities difficult.

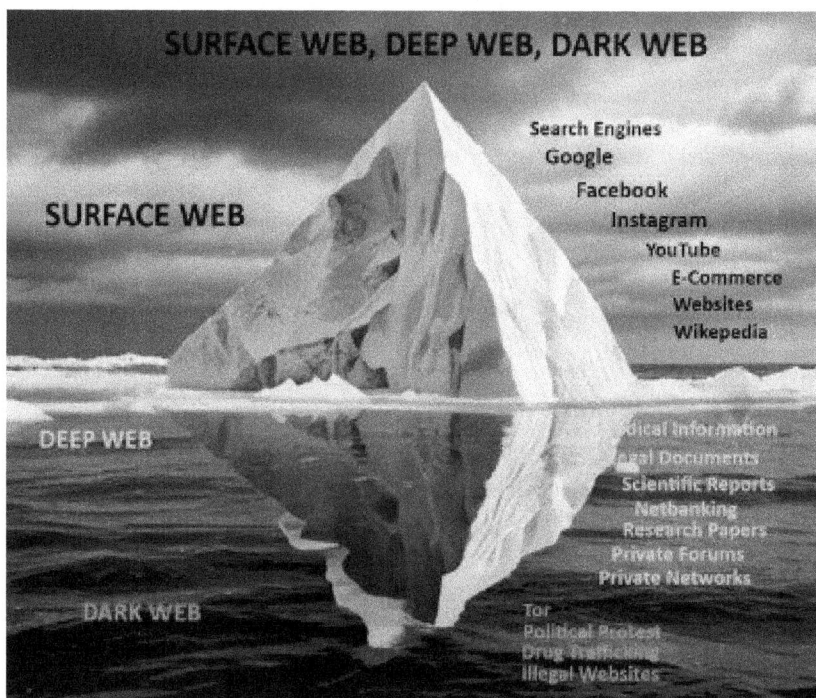

Figure 3.6: Surface web, deep web, and dark web

Common misconceptions

There are several misconceptions about the deep and dark web that need clarification:

- **Equating deep web with dark web**: Many people mistakenly believe the terms are interchangeable. The deep web is largely benign and necessary for privacy and security, while the dark web is a small portion of it used for illicit activities.

- **All activities on the dark web are illegal**: While much of it is associated with illegal activities, it hosts whistleblowing sites, privacy-focused communication tools, and other legitimate services.

- **Impossibility of monitoring**: Despite the anonymity of the dark web, law enforcement and CyberSecurity professionals have developed methods to monitor and track illegal activities and actors.

Risks and threats

The dark web poses several risks and threats to individuals, organizations, and governments:

- **Data breaches**: Stolen data, including personal information, financial records, and intellectual property, is often sold on the dark web. This data can be used for identity theft, fraud, and other malicious purposes.

- **Cybercrime services**: The dark web offers services for hire, such as DDoS attacks, hacking tools, and malware. Cybercriminals can purchase these services to launch attacks against organizations.

- **Illicit goods and services**: Marketplaces on the dark web facilitate the sale of illegal drugs, weapons, counterfeit currency, and more. These activities contribute to real-world crime and societal harm.

- **Emerging threats**: New threats continually emerge from the dark web, including advanced ransomware schemes, cyber-espionage operations, and coordinated disinformation campaigns.

Dark web-related incidents

Several high-profile incidents highlight the risks posed by the dark web:

- **Silk Road**: One of the most infamous dark web marketplaces, Silk Road, facilitated the sale of illegal drugs and other contraband. Its shutdown by law enforcement highlighted the dark web's role in global illicit trade.

- **Ashley Madison breach**: Personal data from the Ashley Madison dating site was leaked and sold on the dark web, leading to widespread blackmail and extortion attempts.

- **Equifax data breach**: Stolen data from the Equifax breach, including sensitive personal information, appeared on the dark web, exacerbating the breach's impact and enabling further criminal activity.

Monitoring the deep and dark web

Monitoring the deep and dark web is a critical component of modern CyberSecurity strategies. This activity involves searching for potential threats, such as stolen data, cybercriminal communications, and emerging attack vectors that could target an organization. The following tools and techniques are commonly used for this purpose:

- **Dark web crawlers:** Dark web crawlers are specialized automated tools designed to navigate and index dark web content, like how traditional search engines crawl the surface web. These crawlers are essential for systematically discovering and collecting data from hidden services and dark web sites, many of which are accessible only through anonymity networks like Tor.

  o **Functionality:** Dark web crawlers automatically search for and retrieve content from dark web forums, marketplaces, and other hidden services. They are configured to follow specific patterns and can be tailored to identify certain types of information, such as stolen credentials, credit card numbers, or mentions of specific organizations.

  o **Advantages:** Crawlers provide broad coverage and can continuously monitor large sections of the dark web for relevant data. They allow CyberSecurity teams to keep track of new threats, leaked data, and ongoing discussions among cybercriminals.

  o **Challenges:** Dark web sites are often designed to resist crawling efforts by limiting access, using CAPTCHAs, or changing URLs frequently. Effective crawlers must be adaptable and capable of overcoming these barriers without alerting site administrators.

- **Threat intelligence platforms: Threat intelligence platforms (TIPs)** aggregate, analyze, and distribute threat data from various sources, including the deep and dark web. These platforms are vital for contextualizing the data collected and turning it into actionable intelligence that can be used to bolster an organization's security posture.

  o **Functionality:** TIPs combines data from dark web crawlers, **open-source intelligence (OSINT)**, security feeds, and other sources. They process this information to identify emerging threats, track the activities of known threat actors, and provide insights into potential vulnerabilities.

  o **Advantages:** TIPs integrate data from multiple sources to provide a comprehensive view of the threat landscape. They often include features like automated alerting, reporting, and integration with other security tools, such as SIEM systems.

- **Challenges:** The effectiveness of a TIP depends on the quality and relevance of the data it aggregates. Additionally, organizations must have skilled analysts who can interpret the intelligence and apply it to their specific context.

- **Human intelligence (HUMINT):** Human intelligence involves leveraging human interactions and social engineering techniques to gather information directly from individuals within dark web communities. This approach can uncover valuable insights that automated tools may miss, particularly when it comes to understanding the intent and capabilities of threat actors.

  - **Functionality:** HUMINT activities include engaging in dark web forums, participating in discussions, and establishing relationships with insiders. This allows security professionals to gather firsthand information about upcoming attacks, new vulnerabilities, or emerging tools used by cybercriminals.

  - **Advantages:** HUMINT provides deep, nuanced insights beyond what can be captured by automated tools. It allows for real-time intelligence gathering and can reveal the intentions, plans, and strategies of threat actors that might not be evident from data alone.

  - **Challenges:** Engaging in dark web communities requires significant expertise and caution to avoid exposure or legal issues. Security professionals must maintain anonymity and ensure that their activities do not inadvertently support illegal activities or violate ethical guidelines.

- **Real-time monitoring tools:** Real-time monitoring tools are essential for continuously observing the dark web and responding quickly to potential threats. These tools often combine elements of crawling, threat intelligence, and automated analysis to provide up-to-the-minute data on emerging risks.

  - **Functionality:** These tools monitor specific dark web sites, forums, and communication channels in real-time, looking for **indicators of compromise (IoCs)**, mentions of an organization, or other relevant signals. They often include alert mechanisms that notify security teams when a potential threat is detected.

  - **Advantages:** The primary benefit of real-time monitoring is the ability to respond quickly to new threats, reducing the window of vulnerability. These tools help ensure that organizations are aware of developments as they happen, allowing for swift action to mitigate risks.

  - **Challenges:** Real-time monitoring requires continuous attention and the ability to filter out noise from genuinely actionable threats. It also demands a robust infrastructure to handle the volume of data being collected and analyzed.

- **Data analytics and correlation tools:** These tools are crucial for making sense of the vast amounts of data collected from the dark web. They use advanced algorithms, machine learning, and big data techniques to identify patterns, correlations, and anomalies that might indicate a threat.

    o **Functionality:** Data analytics tools process large datasets from various sources, including the dark web, to identify trends, predict future attacks, and uncover hidden connections between different pieces of intelligence. These tools often employ machine learning to improve their accuracy over time.

    o **Advantages:** These tools help security teams proactively defend against threats by uncovering patterns that might not be immediately obvious. They enable more informed decision-making and help prioritize responses to the most significant risks.

    o **Challenges:** The effectiveness of data analytics tools depends on the quality of the input data and the sophistication of the algorithms used. False positives can be a concern, and organizations need skilled data scientists to interpret the results accurately.

- **Legal and ethical compliance tools:** Given the sensitive nature of dark web monitoring, it is essential to use tools that ensure compliance with legal and ethical standards. These tools help organizations navigate the complex landscape of privacy laws and regulations while conducting their monitoring activities.

    o **Functionality:** Legal and ethical compliance tools include features that anonymize data, ensure that monitoring activities do not violate laws, and provide documentation to demonstrate compliance with regulatory requirements. They may also include audit trails and reporting capabilities to support transparency.

    o **Advantages:** These tools help protect organizations from legal repercussions and ensure that their dark web monitoring activities are conducted ethically. They are critical for maintaining trust with customers, stakeholders, and regulatory bodies.

    o **Challenges:** Compliance requirements can vary significantly between jurisdictions, making it challenging to ensure that all monitoring activities are legal. Organizations must stay up-to-date with the latest regulations and adjust their monitoring practices accordingly.

The techniques for monitoring the deep and dark web are as follows:

- **Surface web reconnaissance:**

    o Begin by gathering information from surface web sources, such as social media, forums, and news outlets, to identify trends and threats that may originate from the deep or dark web.

- o Use OSINT techniques to collect and analyze data from public sources, providing context for dark web monitoring activities.

- **Dark web access and anonymity:**

  - o Use Tor or other anonymizing networks to access the dark web safely. Maintaining anonymity is essential to avoid detection by cybercriminals and protect the security team from potential retaliation.

  - o Employ VPNs and secure operating systems, such as Tails, to enhance security and anonymity while browsing the dark web.

- **Automated monitoring and alerts:**

  - o Set up automated monitoring tools and alerts that continuously scan dark web sites, forums, and marketplaces for specific keywords, such as the organization's name, employee credentials, or sensitive data.

  - o Use machine learning algorithms to analyze patterns and detect anomalies in dark web activities, allowing for more efficient threat detection.

- **Threat actor profiling:**

  - o Monitor known threat actors' activities and communications on dark web forums and marketplaces to develop profiles. Understanding their tactics, TTPs can help predict future attacks.

  - o Track the movements and behavior of these threat actors across different dark web platforms to identify potential risks before they materialize.

- **HUMINT:**

  - o Leverage human intelligence by engaging with sources within the dark web community. This can involve infiltrating forums or establishing trusted relationships with individuals who have access to valuable information.

  - o Use social engineering techniques to gather intelligence from dark web users without revealing the security team's true identity or intentions.

- **Data correlation and analysis:**

  - o Correlate data collected from the dark web with other sources of threat intelligence, such as SIEM systems, firewall logs, and endpoint detection platforms, to gain a comprehensive understanding of potential threats.

  - o Use advanced analytics and visualization tools to identify patterns and trends in dark web activities, enabling proactive threat mitigation.

- **Best practices for monitoring the deep and dark web:**
  - o **Legal and ethical considerations:** Ensure that all monitoring activities comply with legal and ethical guidelines. This includes avoiding participation in illegal activities and respecting privacy rights.

  - o **Use of trained professionals:** Engage trained CyberSecurity professionals who have experience navigating the deep and dark web. Their expertise is crucial for safely and effectively conducting monitoring activities.

  - o **Data handling and privacy:** Implement strict protocols for handling sensitive data discovered on the dark web. This includes secure storage, controlled access, and proper disposal of data that is no longer needed.

  - o **Continuous monitoring:** Regularly update monitoring tools and techniques to adapt to the ever-changing landscape of the dark web. Continuous monitoring is essential for staying ahead of emerging threats.

  - o **Incident response integration:** Integrate dark web monitoring with the organization's incident response plan to ensure that any threats identified can be quickly addressed and mitigated.

  - o **Collaboration with law enforcement:** Establish relationships with law enforcement agencies to report illegal activities discovered on the dark web. Collaboration can help dismantle criminal networks and protect the organization from future attacks.

Mitigation strategies

Proactive measures are essential for defending against threats originating from the deep and dark web:

- **Network segmentation**: It refers to the Isolation of critical systems and data to limit the impact of a breach. This helps contain threats and prevent lateral movement within the network.

- **Advanced threat detection**: Implementing advanced detection systems, such as AI-powered anomaly detection, to identify and respond to unusual activities that may indicate a threat.

- **Employee training**: Regularly training employees on security best practices, including recognizing phishing attempts and avoiding risky online behavior. Informed employees are a critical line of defense.

Incident response planning

A robust incident response plan ensures preparedness for dark web-related threats:

- **Preparation**: Developing and regularly updating incident response plans that outline roles, responsibilities, and procedures for addressing security incidents.

- **Detection and analysis**: Establishing mechanisms to detect incidents early and analyze their nature and impact. This involves real-time monitoring, forensic analysis, and threat intelligence integration.

- **Containment, eradication, and recovery**: Implementing strategies to contain the threat, eradicate malicious actors and their tools, and recover affected systems and data. This ensures minimal disruption to business operations.

Compliance with laws and regulations

Monitoring the dark web and responding to related threats must comply with relevant laws and regulations:

- **Data privacy laws**: Ensuring compliance with data privacy laws, such as GDPR and CCPA, when collecting and processing personal data from the dark web.

- **Law enforcement collaboration**: Working with law enforcement agencies to share intelligence and coordinate efforts in addressing dark web-related crimes helps ensure the legal and ethical handling of evidence and suspects.

- **Regulatory requirements**: Adhering to industry-specific regulations, such as PCI-DSS for financial institutions, ensures that security measures meet legal standards.

Ethical issues in monitoring

Monitoring the dark web raises several ethical issues that must be carefully considered:

- **Privacy concerns**: Balancing the need for security concerning individual privacy, avoiding unnecessary surveillance, and ensuring data collection is proportionate and justified.

- **Use of deception**: Ethically, deception, such as creating fake personas, must be employed to gather intelligence. It should be limited to preventing harm and conducted transparently within the organization.

- **Accountability and transparency**: Ensuring transparency in monitoring practices and maintaining accountability for actions taken based on dark web intelligence. Organizations should have clear policies and oversight mechanisms.

Understanding and monitoring the deep and dark web is vital to modern CyberSecurity. It provides insights that fortify defenses and mitigate emerging threats.

Conclusion

Chapter 3, Building a Secure Infrastructure, aims to provide readers with the essential knowledge and practical strategies to fortify an organization's CyberSecurity defenses. This chapter begins by enhancing network security by designing robust network architectures, implementing segmentation, zoning, redundancy, and failover mechanisms, and utilizing encryption protocols to protect data in transit. It then delves into strengthening endpoint security by offering guidance on deploying and managing antivirus and anti-malware solutions, implementing EDR systems, and securing mobile devices through MDM.

The chapter also covers the implementation and management of firewalls, IDSs, and IPSs, educating readers on their types, configuration, functionality, and benefits. Secure configuration practices are emphasized, discussing the importance of proper system configuration, reducing attack surfaces through system hardening, applying security patches, and following secure software development practices. Lastly, the chapter addresses deep and dark web security, providing an understanding of these hidden areas of the internet, identifying potential threats, and discussing monitoring tools, threat intelligence gathering, proactive defense measures, and legal and ethical considerations. The readers will have a solid foundation in building and maintaining a secure infrastructure to mitigate cyber threats and protect organizational assets effectively.

Points to remember

- **Comprehensive network security**: Design secure network architectures with segmentation, zoning, and encryption to protect data in transit.

- **Robust endpoint security**: Use antivirus solutions, EDR systems, and MDM practices to secure all endpoints, including mobile devices.

- **Effective use of firewalls, IDS, and IPS**: Configure and manage firewalls, IDS, and IPS to detect and prevent threats in real-time.

- **Secure configuration practices**: Apply proper system configurations, reduce attack surfaces, apply security patches, follow secure coding practices, and conduct regular security audits and vulnerability assessments.

- **Deep and dark web security**: Understand the risks from the deep and dark web, use monitoring tools and techniques, and consider legal and ethical implications for proactive defense measures.

- **Continuous monitoring and incident response**: Implement continuous monitoring with real-time tools and develop effective incident response strategies, adhering to industry standards and best practices.

CHAPTER 4
Defending Data Strategies

Introduction

In the digital age, safeguarding data is not just an obligation but a strategic necessity. Our comprehensive guide empowers you, the reader, to build impenetrable defenses and resilient protection strategies for your greatest asset. It instills confidence in your ability to navigate the complexities of data security and protection.

In today's digital age, data is the lifeblood of any organization. Protecting this asset is paramount to maintaining trust, ensuring compliance, and safeguarding against financial loss. *Chapter 4, Defending Data Strategies,* details the comprehensive strategies that leave no stone unturned. These strategies are essential for securing data at every stage of its lifecycle, providing a sense of reassurance and security. In the new era, data powers decision-making, innovation, and growth like fuel-driving machines, as depicted in *Figure 4.1.* Organizations leverage data insights to optimize operations, understand customer behavior, and gain competitive advantages, making it a critical asset in modern business strategies.

Figure 4.1: Data is the new fuel of business

Structure

The following sections will be covered:

- Data classification and sensitivity

- Encryption and secure communication

- Access control and authentication

- Data Loss Prevention

- Data breach management

Objectives

By the end of this chapter, readers will have a comprehensive understanding of the essential techniques and best practices for safeguarding organizational data. The chapter emphasizes the importance of identifying and categorizing data based on its sensitivity to ensure appropriate protection measures are applied. By exploring encryption technologies and secure communication protocols, the chapter highlights the significance of converting data into unreadable formats to protect it from unauthorized access at rest and in transit.

The chapter also explores access control and authentication mechanisms, demonstrating how these tools restrict data access to authorized individuals, thereby minimizing risks. It addresses **Data Loss Prevention** (DLP) technologies, which are crucial for detecting and preventing unauthorized data access, use, or transmission. Additionally, the chapter prepares organizations to effectively manage data breaches by outlining immediate response actions, communication strategies, and long-term remediation efforts, emphasizing the need for a proactive approach and a robust **incident response plan** (IRP).

Data classification and sensitivity

Understanding the value and sensitivity of your data is the first step in protecting it.

In the digital age, data is an organization's most valuable asset. It drives decision-making, fuels innovation, and enables service delivery. However, as data grows exponentially in volume and complexity, so do the risks associated with managing it. Cyber threats, regulatory requirements, and the increasing expectations of customers and stakeholders demand that organizations not only protect their data but also manage it effectively.

Data classification is the process of organizing data into categories based on its sensitivity, value, and importance to the organization. This foundational practice is the cornerstone of any effective data security strategy. By classifying data, organizations can determine which data needs the most protection and allocate resources accordingly. Without proper classification, organizations run the risk of under or over-protecting their data, leading to increased vulnerabilities, inefficiencies, and potential non-compliance with regulatory requirements.

At its core, data classification involves assigning a label to data that reflects its level of sensitivity. This label determines the security measures and access controls that must be applied to the data. For example, public data might require minimal protection, while sensitive or confidential data might require encryption, access restrictions, and regular monitoring. Data classification also plays a critical role in compliance, as many regulations require organizations to demonstrate that they have appropriately classified and protected sensitive data.

The benefits of data classification extend beyond security. Properly classified data enables organizations to make more informed decisions about how data is used, shared, and retained. It also facilitates better data governance, as organizations can more easily track and manage data throughout its lifecycle. In short, data classification is not just about protecting data; it is about empowering organizations to manage their data more effectively and responsibly.

This chapter will explore the principles of data classification, the various models and frameworks available, and the best practices for implementing a classification scheme that aligns with organizational goals and regulatory requirements. We will also examine the challenges and considerations organizations must address when classifying data and provide practical examples and case studies to illustrate how effective data classification can enhance security and business operations.

Importance of data sensitivity

The concept of data sensitivity lies at the heart of data classification. Sensitivity refers to the potential impact on the organization if the data were exposed, altered, or destroyed without authorization. Understanding data sensitivity is crucial because it directly influences the level of protection that needs to be applied to the data. In essence, the more sensitive the data, the more stringent the security measures required to safeguard it.

Defining data sensitivity

Data sensitivity is typically defined by several factors, including the content of the data, its context, and the potential consequences of its exposure. These factors help organizations assess the risk associated with the data and determine the appropriate classification level. Common factors that contribute to data sensitivity include the following:

- **Confidentiality requirements**: Data that contains confidential information, such as **personally identifiable information (PII)**, financial records, or trade secrets, is considered highly sensitive. Unauthorized access to this data could result in legal penalties, economic loss, and damage to reputation.

- **Integrity requirements**: Data that must remain accurate and unaltered is also considered sensitive. For example, healthcare records or financial transactions must be protected to ensure they are not tampered with, as any alteration could have serious consequences.

- **Availability requirements**: Data that must be readily accessible at all times, such as data critical to business operations, is sensitive regarding availability. Any disruption to access could result in operational downtime, lost revenue, and customer dissatisfaction.

- **Regulatory and compliance obligations:** Many industries are subject to regulations that dictate how certain types of data must be handled. Data subject to these regulations, such as healthcare records under HIPAA or financial data under GDPR, is inherently sensitive and requires appropriate classification and protection.

Impact of data sensitivity on security measures

Data sensitivity directly influences the security measures that must be implemented to protect it. For example, susceptible data may require rest and transit encryption, **multi-factor authentication (MFA)**, and strict monitoring and logging of all access and activity. In contrast, less sensitive data may require only basic access controls and monitoring.

When determining data sensitivity, organizations must also consider the potential consequences of a data breach. Exposing sensitive customer data could result in significant financial penalties, legal action, and loss of customer trust. In such cases, organizations must implement the highest levels of protection to prevent unauthorized access.

Data sensitivity also influences data retention policies. Susceptible data may need to be retained for extended periods to comply with regulatory requirements, while less sensitive data can be safely deleted after a shorter retention period. Proper classification helps organizations manage data retention effectively, ensuring that sensitive data is retained and protected for the required duration.

Challenges in assessing data sensitivity

Assessing data sensitivity is not without its challenges. One of the primary challenges is the sheer volume of data that organizations must classify. With data being generated at unprecedented rates, identifying and classifying all sensitive data can be difficult. Additionally, data sensitivity can change over time as the context in which the data is used changes. For example, previously considered low-sensitivity data may become highly sensitive if combined with other data or used in a new context.

Another challenge is ensuring consistency in data classification. Different teams or individuals within an organization may interpret what constitutes sensitive data differently, leading to inconsistent classification and protection measures. To address this challenge, organizations must establish clear classification criteria and provide training to ensure that all employees understand the importance of data sensitivity and how to assess it.

Despite these challenges, assessing data sensitivity is critical in data classification. By understanding the sensitivity of their data, organizations can implement the appropriate security measures to protect it, ensuring that they meet both their security and compliance obligations.

Classification models and frameworks

Several data classification models and frameworks exist that organizations can use to classify their data based on sensitivity. These models provide a structured approach to data classification, helping organizations categorize their data to align with their security goals and regulatory requirements.

Traditional data classification models

Traditional data classification models are based on a tiered system, categorizing data into limited sensitivity levels. These models are straightforward to implement, making them popular for many organizations.

Three-level model

The three-level model is one of the most used data classification models. It categorizes data into three levels of sensitivity, listed as follows:

- **Public:** Data that is intended for public consumption and does not require any special protection. Examples include press releases, marketing materials, and publicly available reports.

- **Private**: Data intended for internal use should not be shared with the public. This data may include internal communications, employee records, and non-sensitive business plans.

- **Confidential**: Data that is highly sensitive and requires the highest level of protection. Examples include trade secrets, intellectual property, financial records, and customer information.

The three-level model is easy to understand and implement, making it suitable for organizations with relatively simple data environments. However, its simplicity can also be a limitation, as it may not provide enough granularity to address the specific security needs of more complex data environments.

Four-level model

The four-level model expands on the three-level model by adding a level of sensitivity. The explanation is as follows:

- **Public**: Data that can be freely shared with the public.

- **Internal**: Data intended for internal use but not considered highly sensitive. Examples include internal reports, meeting notes, and project plans.

- **Confidential**: Data that is sensitive and requires protection, such as customer information, financial records, and intellectual property.

- **Highly confidential/restricted**: Data that is extremely sensitive and requires the highest level of protection. Examples include trade secrets, classified government information, and other data that, if exposed, could have severe consequences.

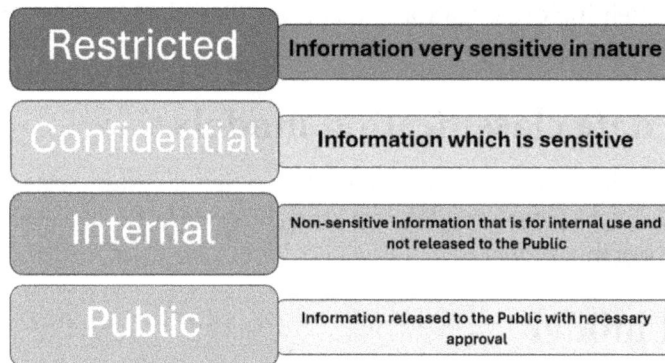

Restricted	Information very sensitive in nature
Confidential	Information which is sensitive
Internal	Non-sensitive information that is for internal use and not released to the Public
Public	Information released to the Public with necessary approval

Data Classification

Figure 4.2: Data classification

The four-level data classification model (*Figure 4.2*) provides more granularity than the three-level model, making it better suited for organizations with more complex data environments. It allows organizations to apply different levels of protection based on the data's specific sensitivity, ensuring that susceptible data receives the highest level of security.

Advanced classification frameworks

In addition to traditional models, more advanced classification frameworks provide greater flexibility and granularity in data classification. These frameworks are often used by organizations with complex data environments or those subject to strict regulatory requirements. The models are listed as follows:

- **Data-centric security model:**

    o The data-centric security model focuses on protecting the data rather than the environment in which it resides. This model classifies data based on its content, context, and potential impact of exposure, regardless of where it is stored or processed.

    o The data-centric security model is instrumental in cloud and multi-cloud environments, where data may be stored and processed in different locations. By focusing on the data, organizations can ensure that sensitive data is protected, no matter where it resides. This model also supports using data-centric security technologies like encryption, tokenization, and data masking. These technologies protect data by rendering it unreadable or unusable to unauthorized users. These technologies can be applied based on the classification level, ensuring that sensitive data is always protected.

- **Risk-based classification framework:**

    o The risk-based classification framework takes a dynamic approach by categorizing data based on the potential risks associated with its exposure. This framework considers factors such as the likelihood of a data breach, the potential impact of exposure, and the regulatory requirements that apply to the data. In a risk-based classification framework, data that poses a higher risk to the organization is classified at a higher sensitivity level and receives more protection. For example, data that is subject to strict regulatory requirements or that could cause significant financial or reputational damage if exposed would be classified as highly sensitive. The risk-based classification framework is well-suited for organizations operating in high-risk environments or complying with stringent regulations. It allows organizations to prioritize their data protection efforts based on the specific risks they face, ensuring that the most critical data is protected.

Automated classification tools and technologies

As data volumes continue to grow, manual classification processes become increasingly impractical. Many organizations are turning to automated classification tools and technologies that can analyze and categorize data based on predefined criteria to address this challenge. Some classification tools are listed as follows:

- **Machine learning and artificial intelligence (AI):** Machine learning and AI are transforming the way organizations classify data. These technologies can analyze large volumes of data, identify patterns, and categorize data based on its content and context. For example, AI algorithms can automatically identify and classify sensitive information, such as PII, based on keywords, patterns, and other indicators. AI and machine learning can also adapt to changing data environments by continuously learning from new data and updating classification rules. This dynamic approach allows organizations to keep pace with the ever-changing nature of their data, ensuring that classification remains accurate and relevant.

- **Data tagging and metadata:** Automated classification tools often rely on data tagging and metadata to classify data. Tags and metadata are labels or attributes attached to data, providing information about its content, sensitivity, and other characteristics. For example, a tag might indicate that a document contains confidential information or an email contains PII. These tags can be applied automatically based on predefined rules or criteria, making it easier for organizations to classify and manage large volumes of data. Metadata can also enforce classification policies, ensuring that sensitive data is protected according to its classification level.

Challenges in choosing a classification model

Choosing a suitable data classification model or framework is critical to the success of an organization's data security strategy. However, organizations must address several challenges and considerations when selecting a classification model. The challenges are as follows:

- **Complexity of the data environment:** The complexity of an organization's data environment is critical in determining which classification model is most appropriate. Organizations with relatively simple data environments may find that traditional models, such as the three-level or four-level model, are sufficient. However, organizations with more complex data environments, such as those operating in cloud or multi-cloud environments, may require more advanced frameworks, such as the data-centric security model or risk-based classification framework.

- **Regulatory requirements:** Regulatory requirements significantly determine how data should be classified and protected. Organizations must consider the specific regulations that apply to their industry and geography when choosing a classification model. For example, organizations subject to the **General Data Protection Regulation** (**GDPR**) must classify and protect personal data according to the regulation's requirements, while those subject to **HIPAA** must classify and protect healthcare information.

  Organizations must also ensure their classification model aligns with industry-specific standards or best practices. For example, financial institutions may need to follow the guidelines set forth by the **Financial Industry Regulatory Authority (FINRA)** or the **Payment Card Industry Data Security Standard (PCI DSS).**

- **Scalability and flexibility:** As organizations grow and evolve, their data environments will also change. The classification model or framework must be scalable and flexible enough to accommodate these changes. For example, as an organization expands into new markets or adopts new technologies, its data environment may become more complex, requiring a more sophisticated classification model.

  Organizations must also consider the scalability of their classification tools and technologies. Automated classification tools must be able to handle large volumes of data and adapt to changing data environments. This scalability is essential for ensuring that classification remains accurate and effective as the organization grows.

- **Balancing security and accessibility:** One of the primary challenges in data classification is balancing the need for security with accessibility. While susceptible data must be protected with stringent security measures, it must also be accessible to authorized users who need it to perform their jobs. Overly restrictive classification can hinder productivity and create friction within the organization.

  To address this challenge, organizations must establish clear classification criteria that consider security and accessibility. For example, data classified as confidential may be encrypted and restricted to authorized users, but it should also be accessible to those who need it to perform critical business functions.

- **Integration with existing security infrastructure**: Organizations must consider how their chosen classification model or framework will integrate with their existing security infrastructure. The classification model must be compatible with the organization's security tools, technologies, and processes. For example, if the organization uses DLP tools, the classification model must work seamlessly with these tools to enforce classification policies.

  Organizations must also ensure that their classification model aligns with their broader security strategy. For example, if the organization follows a zero-trust security model, the classification model must support the principles of zero trust, such as least privilege access and continuous monitoring.

Implementing data classification in organizations

Implementing data classification in an organization is a multi-step process that involves careful planning, execution, and ongoing management. The success of the implementation depends on the organization's ability to align its classification scheme with its business goals, regulatory requirements, and security objectives. The step-by-step process to implement Data classification is explained as follows:

1. **Define classification criteria:** The first step in implementing data classification is defining the criteria for categorizing data. These criteria should be based on the organization's specific needs, including the types of data it handles, the regulatory requirements it must comply with, and the potential risks associated with data exposure.

   a. **Identify data types**: Organizations must begin by identifying the data types they handle. This includes structured data, such as databases and spreadsheets, and unstructured data, such as emails, documents, and multimedia files. By identifying all data types, organizations can ensure that their classification scheme covers all aspects of their data environment.

   b. **Establish sensitivity levels**: Organizations must establish sensitivity levels that reflect the value and importance of the data. These levels should be clearly defined and consistent across the organization. For example, an organization might establish four sensitivity levels: public, internal, confidential, and highly confidential. When establishing sensitivity levels, organizations should consider the potential impact of data exposure, the regulatory requirements that apply to the data, and the business value of the data. This will help ensure the classification scheme accurately reflects the organization's security needs.

   c. **Develop classification rules**: Once the sensitivity levels have been established, organizations must develop classification rules that determine how data will be categorized. These rules should be based on the classification criteria and consistently applied across the organization. For example, a classification rule might specify that all customer information is confidential while all marketing materials are public. The rules should also specify the security measures that must be applied to each classification level, such as encryption, access controls, and monitoring.

2. **Develop a classification policy:** The next step in implementing data classification is to develop a classification policy that formalizes the scheme and provides guidance to employees. The policy should outline the classification criteria, sensitivity levels, and rules, as well as the roles and responsibilities of employees in the classification process.

   a. **Policy creation**: Creating a classification policy requires input from vital organizational stakeholders, including IT, legal, compliance, and business units. This ensures that the policy aligns with the organization's goals and objectives. The policy should also include guidelines for handling classified data, such as how to label and store data, share data securely, and handle data breaches. These guidelines help ensure that employees understand their responsibilities and know how to protect sensitive data.

b. **Training and awareness**: To ensure the successful implementation of the classification policy, organizations must provide training and awareness programs for employees. These programs should educate employees about the importance of data classification, how to apply classification rules, and how to handle classified data. Training and awareness programs should be tailored to the needs of different employee groups. For example, IT staff may require more technical training on using classification tools, while business units may require training on identifying and classifying sensitive data.

3. **Classification process implementation:** With the classification criteria and policy in place, the next step is implementing the classification process across the organization. This involves categorizing all data according to the established classification rules and applying the appropriate security measures.

a. **Manual vs. automated classification:** Organizations must decide whether to use a manual, automated, or hybrid approach to data classification. Manual classification involves employees categorizing data based on the criteria, while automated classification uses tools and technologies to analyze and categorize data automatically. Manual classification is often used for small datasets or susceptible data that require careful handling. However, it can be time-consuming and prone to human error. Automated classification is more efficient and scalable, making it suitable for organizations with large volumes of data. A hybrid approach combines manual and automated classification, allowing organizations to leverage the benefits of both methods.

b. **Classification tools and technologies**: Organizations should implement classification tools and technologies that can analyze and categorize data based on predefined criteria to support the classification process. These tools may include data discovery tools, DLP systems, and encryption solutions. Data discovery tools help organizations identify and locate sensitive data across their environment. DLP systems enforce classification policies by preventing unauthorized access to or sharing classified data. Encryption solutions protect classified data by rendering it unreadable to unauthorized users.

4. **Monitoring and reviewing classifications:** Data classification is not a one-time process. Organizations must continuously monitor and review classifications to ensure they remain accurate and relevant as data changes or new data is created.

a. **Ongoing monitoring**: Ongoing monitoring involves regularly reviewing classified data to ensure it is handled according to its classification level. This includes monitoring access controls, encryption, and other security measures to ensure they are applied correctly. Organizations should also monitor for changes in data sensitivity. For example, previously considered low-sensitivity data may become highly sensitive if combined with other data or used in a new context. Regular monitoring helps organizations identify and address these changes in sensitivity.

b. **Review and update classification criteria**: As the organization's data environment evolves, the classification criteria may need to be updated. This could be due to changes in regulatory requirements, the introduction of new technologies, or shifts in business priorities. Organizations should regularly review their classification criteria to ensure they continue aligning with their goals and objectives. Any changes to the requirements should be reflected in the classification policy and communicated to employees.

5. **Reporting and auditing:** Organizations must implement reporting and auditing processes to track the effectiveness of their data classification efforts. These processes help organizations identify gaps or weaknesses in their classification scheme and take corrective action.

a. **Reporting on classification compliance**: Reporting involves tracking critical metrics related to data classification, such as the percentage of data classified, the number of classification errors, and the effectiveness of classification tools. These metrics can be used to assess the classification process's overall success and identify areas for improvement. Reports should be generated regularly and shared with key stakeholders, including IT, legal, compliance, and executive leadership. This helps ensure all stakeholders know the organization's classification efforts and can provide input on necessary changes.

b. **Conducting audits**: Audits are an essential part of the data classification process, as they provide an independent assessment of the organization's compliance with its classification policy. Audits can be conducted internally by the organization's audit team or externally by third-party auditors. The audit process involves reviewing classified data, criteria, and tools to ensure they align with the organization's policy and regulatory requirements. Auditors may also interview employees to assess their understanding of the classification process and adherence to classification guidelines. Any issues identified during the audit should be documented and addressed through corrective action plans. Regular audits help organizations maintain the integrity of their classification scheme and ensure compliance with regulatory requirements.

Regulatory and compliance considerations

Data classification is critical in helping organizations meet their regulatory and compliance obligations. Many regulations require organizations to classify and protect sensitive data according to specific criteria, and failure to comply can result in significant penalties.

Key regulations impacting data classification

Several key regulations impact data classification, depending on the organization's industry and geography. Some of the most notable regulations are as follows:

- **GDPR:** GDPR is a European regulation that requires organizations to classify and protect personal data, including PII. Organizations must implement appropriate security measures based on the sensitivity of the data and report any data breaches to the relevant authorities.

- **Health Insurance Portability and Accountability Act (HIPAA):** HIPAA is a U.S. regulation that requires healthcare organizations to classify and protect **patient health information (PHI)**. Organizations must implement safeguards to ensure PHI's confidentiality, integrity, and availability.

- **Payment Card Industry Data Security Standard:** PCI DSS is a global standard that requires organizations to classify and protect payment card information. Organizations must implement security measures such as encryption and access controls to protect cardholder data.

- **Sarbanes-Oxley Act (SOX): SOX** is a U.S. regulation that requires publicly traded companies to classify and protect financial data. Organizations must implement internal controls and procedures to ensure the accuracy and security of financial information.

Aligning classification with regulatory requirements

To comply with regulatory requirements, organizations must align their data classification scheme with the specific criteria set forth by the regulations. This may involve categorizing data according to the types of information specified in the rules, such as PII, PHI, or financial data.

Organizations must also ensure that the security measures applied to classified data meet the standards required by the regulations. For example, GDPR requires organizations to implement encryption and access controls for personal data, while HIPAA requires audit trails and risk assessments for PHI.

Compliance with regulatory requirements also involves ongoing monitoring and reporting. Organizations must regularly review their classification scheme to ensure they remain aligned with the regulations and update them as necessary. They must also generate reports demonstrating compliance with regulatory requirements, such as **data protection impact assessments (DPIAs)** under GDPR.

Challenges in meeting compliance requirements

Meeting compliance requirements can be challenging, particularly for organizations that operate in multiple jurisdictions or industries. Each regulation may have data classification and protection criteria, making it difficult to develop a single classification scheme that meets all requirements.

To address these challenges, organizations should take a risk-based approach to compliance, focusing on the regulations that pose the most significant risk to their business. They should also work closely with legal and compliance teams to ensure their classification scheme meets all applicable regulations.

In addition, organizations should consider using automated tools and technologies to support compliance efforts. For example, data discovery tools can help organizations identify and classify regulated data, while DLP systems can enforce classification policies and prevent unauthorized access to sensitive data.

Case studies and practical examples

This section will present case studies and practical examples of data classification to illustrate its importance and impact on an organization's security posture.

The case studies are as follows:

- **Case study: Financial institution:**
    - A large financial institution implemented a data classification scheme to comply with PCI DSS and SOX regulations. The institution classified all payment card information as highly confidential and applied encryption, access controls, and monitoring to protect the data. The institution also classified financial data as confidential and implemented internal controls to ensure its accuracy and integrity. By aligning its classification scheme with regulatory requirements, the institution was able to meet its compliance obligations and reduce the risk of data breaches.

- **Case study: Healthcare organization:**
    - A healthcare organization implemented a data classification scheme to comply with HIPAA regulations. The organization classified PHI as highly confidential and applied encryption, audit trails, and access controls to protect the data. The organization also conducted regular risk assessments and audits to ensure its classification scheme met HIPAA requirements. By implementing a robust classification scheme, the organization was able to protect patient privacy and avoid costly penalties for non-compliance.

- **Case study 3: Global corporation:**

  o   A global corporation operating in multiple jurisdictions implemented a data classification scheme to comply with GDPR and other international regulations. The corporation classified personal data according to GDPR criteria and applied encryption, access controls, and breach reporting procedures to protect the data. The corporation also classified other types of sensitive data, such as intellectual property and trade secrets, according to their value and importance to the business. By taking a risk-based approach to data classification, the corporation could meet its compliance obligations and protect its most valuable assets.

Practical example

Implementing automated classification: A technology company implemented an automated classification tool to classify data based on predefined criteria. The tool used machine learning algorithms to analyze data and assign classification labels based on content and context.

The company also used data tagging and metadata to enforce classification policies, ensuring that sensitive data was protected according to its classification level. By automating the classification process, the company could scale its classification efforts and reduce the risk of human error.

Lessons learned

These case studies and practical examples demonstrate the importance of data classification in protecting sensitive data and meeting regulatory requirements. They also highlight the benefits of using automated tools and technologies to support classification efforts.

Organizations that implement effective data classification schemes can enhance their security posture, reduce the risk of data breaches, and ensure compliance with regulatory requirements. By taking a structured and strategic approach to data classification and enabling informed decision-making, organizations can protect their most valuable assets.

Remember, *Effective data classification is not just about security—it is about enabling informed decision-making and compliance.*

In conclusion, data classification is a critical component of any data security strategy. By understanding the value and sensitivity of their data, organizations can implement the appropriate security measures to protect it, ensuring that they meet both their security and compliance obligations. Effective data classification empowers organizations to manage their data more effectively, enabling informed decision-making and responsible data governance.

This section has explored the principles of data classification, the various models and frameworks available, and the best practices for implementing a classification scheme.

It has also examined the challenges and considerations organizations must address when classifying data and provided practical examples and case studies to illustrate the importance of data classification in action.

Effective data classification will become more critical as data grows in volume and complexity. Organizations prioritizing data classification will be better equipped to protect their data, meet regulatory requirements, and drive business success in the digital age.

Encryption and secure communication

Encryption transforms data into a formidable fortress, impenetrable by unauthorized entities.

Encryption has become an indispensable pillar of data security in the digital age, where cyber threats are constantly evolving and the value of sensitive information continues to rise. Encryption ensures that even if data is intercepted or accessed without authorization, it remains useless to unauthorized users by converting readable data into an unreadable format. This section looks at the intricate world of encryption, exploring the different types of encryption technologies, comparing symmetric and asymmetric encryption, highlighting key management practices, and examining secure communication protocols. Furthermore, it outlines practical strategies for implementing encryption effectively and provides real-world examples and case studies to illustrate its critical role in modern CyberSecurity.

Overview of encryption technologies

Encryption technologies have evolved significantly since their inception, adapting to meet the growing demands for data security in an increasingly interconnected world. The essence of encryption lies in its ability to convert plaintext (readable data) into ciphertext (encoded data) using cryptographic algorithms, making the information unreadable to anyone who does not possess the corresponding decryption key. This section provides a comprehensive overview of encryption technologies, exploring their historical development, fundamental principles, and the various encryption algorithms used in modern CyberSecurity.

The earliest forms of encryption date back to ancient civilizations, where ciphers protected military communications and sensitive information. Today, encryption has become far more sophisticated, utilizing complex mathematical algorithms and cryptographic keys that are virtually impossible to crack using brute force. Modern encryption algorithms can be broadly categorized into two main types: symmetric encryption, where the same key is used for encryption and decryption, and asymmetric encryption, which uses a pair of related keys (public and private) for the encryption and decryption process.

Encryption plays a crucial role in protecting data at rest, data in transit, and data being processed, ensuring that sensitive information remains secure across all stages of its lifecycle. This includes securing communications between users and systems, protecting stored data from unauthorized access, and safeguarding data transmitted over networks.

Key components of encryption technologies include cryptographic algorithms, such as **Advanced Encryption Standard (AES), Rivest-Shamir-Adleman (RSA),** and **Elliptic Curve Cryptography (ECC)**, as well as cryptographic keys, which are the secret values used to encrypt and decrypt data.

The effectiveness of encryption relies on the algorithm's strength, the encryption key's length, and the proper management of cryptographic keys. Encryption algorithms are designed to provide a high level of security while maintaining efficient performance, with longer keys offering greater security but requiring more computational power. As cyber threats continue to evolve, encryption technologies must also adapt, with ongoing research focused on developing new algorithms that can withstand emerging threats, such as quantum computing, which has the potential to break current encryption methods.

In summary, encryption technologies form the backbone of modern data security, providing a powerful tool for protecting sensitive information from unauthorized access. By understanding the principles and mechanisms behind encryption, organizations can implement robust security measures that safeguard their data against a wide range of cyber threats.

Symmetric vs. asymmetric encryption

Encryption methods can be broadly categorized into two main types: symmetric and asymmetric encryption. Each type has its unique characteristics, strengths, and use cases, making it suitable for different applications within data security. This section provides an in-depth comparison of symmetric and asymmetric encryption, examining how each method works, its advantages and disadvantages, and the scenarios in which it is most effectively used.

Symmetric encryption

Symmetric encryption, also known as secret-key encryption, is the oldest and most straightforward form. In symmetric encryption, the same key is used for both encrypting and decrypting data, which means that both the sender and receiver must have access to the shared key. This fast and efficient method makes it ideal for encrypting large volumes of data in real-time. Symmetric encryption algorithms, such as AES, **Data Encryption Standard (DES)**, and Triple DES, are widely used to secure data at rest and in transit. *Figure 4.3* demonstrates how a symmetric encryption functions:

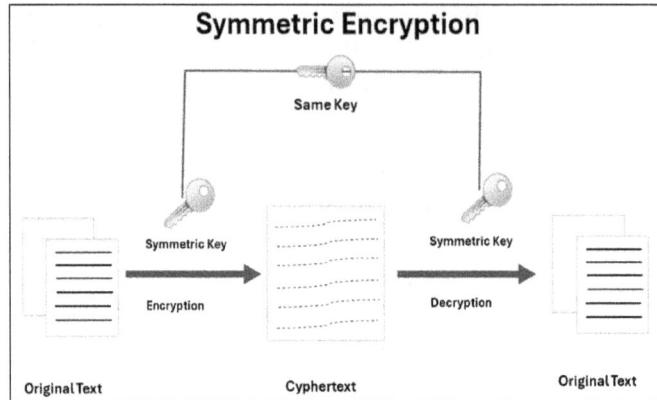

Figure 4.3: How symmetric encryption works

One of the primary advantages of symmetric encryption is its speed and efficiency, as the same key is used for both encryption and decryption, reducing the computational overhead. However, this also presents a significant challenge in terms of key management. The shared key must be kept secret and securely transmitted between the sender and receiver, which can be challenging to manage, especially in large or distributed environments. If the key is compromised, all encrypted data can be easily decrypted, posing a significant security risk.

Asymmetric encryption

Asymmetric encryption, also known as public-key encryption, addresses some of the critical management challenges associated with symmetric encryption by using a pair of mathematically related keys: public and private. The public key encrypts data, while the private key decrypts it. Since the public key can be shared openly without compromising security, asymmetric encryption eliminates the need for secure key distribution between parties. *Figure 4.4* demonstrates how a symmetric encryption functions:

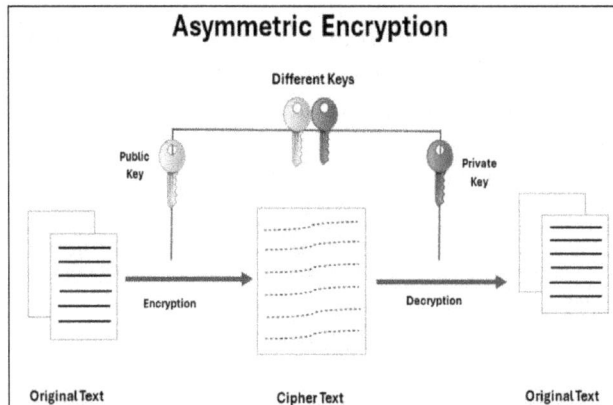

Figure 4.4: How asymmetric encryption works

Asymmetric encryption algorithms, such as RSA, ECC, and **Digital Signature Algorithm** (**DSA**), provide higher security than symmetric encryption, as the decryption key (private key) remains confidential and never needs to be shared. However, asymmetric encryption is slower and more computationally intensive than symmetric encryption, making it less suitable for encrypting large amounts of data. Instead, asymmetric encryption is often used for secure key exchange, digital signatures, and encrypting small amounts of sensitive information, such as authentication credentials.

Hybrid encryption systems

In practice, many secure communication protocols, such as SSL/TLS, use a combination of symmetric and asymmetric encryption in a hybrid encryption system. In these systems, asymmetric encryption is used to exchange a symmetric session key securely, which is then used to encrypt the bulk of the data. This approach combines the speed and efficiency of symmetric encryption with the security and critical management benefits of asymmetric encryption, providing a balanced solution for secure data transmission.

Understanding the differences between symmetric and asymmetric encryption is crucial for selecting the correct encryption method for a given application. Symmetric encryption offers speed and efficiency but requires careful key management, while asymmetric encryption provides enhanced security at the cost of increased computational complexity. By leveraging the strengths of both methods in hybrid encryption systems, organizations can achieve a robust and secure approach to data encryption.

Key management practices

Key management is one of the most critical aspects of effectively implementing encryption. Cryptographic keys are the foundation of all encryption processes, and their security directly impacts the overall effectiveness of the encryption. Poor key management practices can lead to key compromise, rendering the encryption useless and exposing sensitive data to unauthorized access. This section explores the best practices for managing cryptographic keys. The aspects of managing cryptographic keys are as follows:

- **Key generation**: Securing cryptographic keys is the first step in key management. Keys should be generated using a reliable and secure **random number generator** (**RNG**) to ensure they are truly random and unpredictable. The strength of the key depends on its length and the algorithm used; for example, AES keys are typically 128, 192, or 256 bits in size, with longer keys providing greater security. It is essential to follow industry standards and best practices when generating keys, as weak or improperly generated keys can compromise the security of the entire encryption system.

- **Key distribution**: Distributing cryptographic keys securely is one of the most challenging aspects of key management. In symmetric encryption, the shared key must be securely transmitted between the sender and receiver without being intercepted by unauthorized parties. This can be achieved through secure channels, such as physical transfer, encrypted communication links, or asymmetric encryption to protect the symmetric key during transmission. Asymmetric encryption simplifies key distribution, as the public key can be shared openly. However, care must still be taken to ensure the authenticity of the public key, often using digital certificates and trusted certificate authorities.

- **Key storage:** Storing cryptographic keys securely is crucial to preventing unauthorized access. Keys should never be stored in plain text and should always be protected using encryption, access controls, and **hardware security modules (HSMs)**. HSMs are specialized devices designed to generate, store, and manage cryptographic keys securely, offering physical and logical protections that make key compromise significantly more difficult. For software-based key storage, secure enclaves and **key management services (KMS)** offered by cloud providers can provide secure environments for key storage and management.

- **Key rotation and expiry**: Regularly rotating cryptographic keys is a best practice that helps minimize the risk of key compromise. Key rotation involves generating new keys periodically and updating systems to use the new keys while securely retiring the old ones. This process ensures that the exposure window is limited even if a key is compromised. Keys should also have defined lifespans, with policies for crucial expiry and replacement, to ensure that outdated or vulnerable keys are not used in encryption processes.

- **Key disposal**: When cryptographic keys are no longer needed, they must be securely disposed of to prevent unauthorized access. This involves securely deleting the key material from all systems and devices, ensuring that it cannot be recovered. Keys stored in HSMs can often be securely destroyed using built-in mechanisms, while software-stored keys should be overwritten multiple times to prevent recovery.

- **Key management policies and auditing**: Establishing comprehensive key management policies and regularly auditing key management practices are essential for maintaining a secure encryption environment. Key management policies should define roles and responsibilities, key usage guidelines, and key generation, distribution, storage, rotation, and disposal procedures, as well as mechanisms for responding to key compromise incidents. Regular audits help ensure policy compliance, identify potential vulnerabilities, and provide opportunities for continuous improvement.

Effective key management is vital to the success of any encryption strategy. By implementing best practices for key generation, distribution, storage, rotation, and disposal, organizations can significantly enhance the security of their cryptographic keys and, by extension, their encryption systems. Robust key management policies and regular audits help maintain the integrity and security of keys, ensuring that encrypted data remains protected against unauthorized access.

Secure communication protocols

Secure communication protocols protect data as it travels across networks, safeguarding it from interception, tampering, and unauthorized access. Protocols such as **Secure Sockets Layer (SSL)**, **Transport Layer Security (TLS)**, and **Virtual Private Networks (VPNs)** use encryption to secure data in transit, providing a safe environment for online communications, remote access, and data exchange. This section explores the most widely used secure communication protocols, underlying mechanisms, and applications in modern CyberSecurity:

- **SSL and TLS:** SSL and its successor, TLS, are cryptographic protocols designed to communicate securely over a computer network. SSL/TLS is widely used to secure web traffic, ensuring that data transmitted between a client (such as a web browser) and a server remains confidential and tamper-proof. These protocols use asymmetric and symmetric encryption to establish a secure connection, authenticate the server (and, optionally, the client), and protect the data transmitted between the two parties.

  The SSL/TLS handshake process involves several steps, including exchanging cryptographic keys, negotiating encryption algorithms, and establishing a secure session key. Once the handshake is complete, data is encrypted using symmetric encryption, providing security and performance. SSL/TLS certificates, issued by trusted **certificate authorities (CAs)**, verify the server's identity, helping prevent man-in-the-middle attacks. The major differences between SSL and TLS are tabulated:

SSL	TLS
SSL stands for Secure Socket Layer.	TLS stands for Transport Layer Security.
SSL supports the Fortezza algorithm.	TLS does not support the Fortezza algorithm.
SSL 3.0 is the latest SSL protocol.	TLS 1.3 is the latest TLS protocol.
In SSL, The Message Authentication Code (MAC) protocol is used.	In TLS, The **Hashed Message Authentication Code (HMAC)** protocol is used.
In SSL, the message digest is used to create a master secret.	In TLS, a Pseudo-random function is used to create a master secret.
SSL is more complex than TLS.	TLS is simpler than SSL.
SSL is less reliable and slower.	TLS is highly reliable and faster. It provides less latency.
SSL uses the port to set up the explicit connection.	TLS uses the protocol to set up implicit connections.
SSL has been depreciated (Jun 2015).	TLS is still widely used.

Table 4.1: Comparison between SSL and TLS

- **VPNs:** VPNs are another critical tool for secure communication, providing a secure and encrypted tunnel through which data can travel. VPNs are commonly used to enable remote access to corporate networks, protect online privacy, and secure data transmission over public networks, such as the Internet. VPNs protect against eavesdropping, data interception, and unauthorized access by encrypting all data sent and received. The illustration in *Figure 4.5* demonstrates the importance of a VPN:

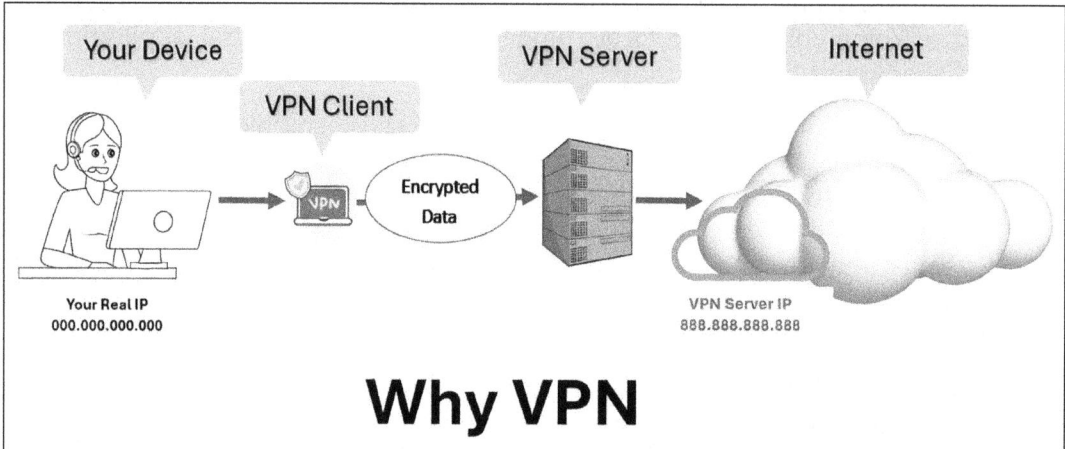

Figure 4.5: VPN

VPNs create a secure connection between a user's device and a remote server, encrypting all data that passes through the connection. This not only ensures the privacy of the data but also masks the user's IP address, providing anonymity and protecting against tracking and surveillance. VPNs are widely used in personal and corporate settings, providing a reliable method for securing remote communications.

- **Email security protocols:** Email remains one of the most widely used forms of communication, making it a prime target for cyberattacks. Protocols such as **Pretty Good Privacy (PGP)** and **Secure/Multipurpose Internet Mail Extensions (S/MIME)** encrypt email messages, ensuring that only the intended recipient can read the content. PGP and S/MIME use symmetric and asymmetric encryption and digital signatures to protect the confidentiality and integrity of email communications.

- **End-to-end encryption:** End-to-end encryption (E2EE) is a secure communication method that encrypts data on the sender's device and keeps it encrypted until it reaches the recipient's device. This approach ensures that no third party, including service providers, can access the encrypted data. E2EE is commonly used in messaging apps, video calls, and file-sharing services, providing a high level of privacy and security for users.

Secure communication protocols are essential for protecting data in transit, ensuring that sensitive information remains confidential and secure as it travels across networks. By using protocols such as SSL/TLS, VPNs, and email encryption, organizations can safeguard their communications against interception, tampering, and unauthorized access, providing a secure environment for data exchange.

Encryption implementation strategies

Implementing encryption effectively requires a strategic approach that considers the organization's specific needs, regulatory requirements, and threat landscape. This section explores various encryption implementation strategies, offering practical guidance on selecting the right encryption methods, integrating encryption into existing systems, and ensuring ongoing compliance with industry standards and best practices. The major factors in implementing encryption in any organization are mentioned as follows:

- **Choosing the right encryption algorithms:** Selecting the appropriate encryption algorithm is critical in the implementation process. Factors to consider include the level of security required, the performance impact, and the specific use case. For example, AES is commonly used for securing data at rest due to its high security and efficiency. In contrast, RSA is often used to ensure key exchanges in communication protocols. It is essential to use algorithms widely recognized and approved by industry standards bodies, such as the **National Institute of Standards and Technology** (**NIST**).

- **Integrating encryption into systems and applications:** Encryption should be integrated into systems and applications to minimize disruption while maximizing security. This involves identifying data that needs to be encrypted, selecting the appropriate encryption method, and implementing encryption at multiple layers, including application, file, and disk-level encryption. Application-level encryption provides the highest level of security by encrypting data before it is written to disk, ensuring that data remains protected even if the underlying storage is compromised.

- **Compliance with regulatory requirements:** Many industries are subject to regulatory requirements that mandate encryption to protect sensitive data. Regulations such as the GDPR, HIPAA, and PCI DSS require organizations to implement encryption in their overall security strategy. It is essential to stay informed about the latest regulatory updates and ensure that encryption practices are aligned with compliance requirements.

- **Performance considerations:** While encryption provides high security, it can also introduce performance overhead, mainly when dealing with large volumes of data or high-frequency transactions. To mitigate performance impacts, organizations can optimize encryption processes by using hardware acceleration, selecting efficient encryption algorithms, and implementing encryption selectively, focusing on the most sensitive data.

- **Testing and validation:** Thorough testing and validation are essential to ensure that encryption is implemented correctly and functions as intended. This includes testing encryption and decryption processes, validating key management procedures, and conducting regular security assessments to identify and address potential vulnerabilities. Penetration testing and vulnerability assessments can help identify weaknesses in encryption implementations, allowing organizations to make necessary adjustments to improve security.

Implementing encryption effectively requires careful planning, strategic decision-making, and a commitment to ongoing evaluation and improvement. By selecting the right encryption methods, integrating encryption into systems, and ensuring compliance with regulatory requirements, organizations can build a robust encryption strategy that protects their data against a wide range of cyber threats.

Real-world applications and case studies

Encryption is not just a theoretical concept; it plays a crucial role in real-world applications, protecting sensitive information across various industries and use cases. This section highlights practical examples and case studies that illustrate the importance of encryption in everyday scenarios, demonstrating how organizations can effectively implement encryption to safeguard their data.

The case studies are as follows:

- **Case study 1: Financial services and data encryption:**
    - The financial services industry handles vast amounts of sensitive data, including personal information, financial transactions, and account details. Encryption is a fundamental component of the industry's security strategy, protecting data at rest in databases, data in transit between financial institutions, and data being processed by payment systems. One notable example is the widespread use of encryption in ATMs, where PINs and transaction data are encrypted to prevent theft and fraud.

- **Case study 2: Healthcare and patient data protection:**
    - In the healthcare sector, protecting patient data is not only a legal requirement but also a moral obligation. Encryption is used extensively to secure **electronic health records (EHRs)**, medical devices, and communications between healthcare providers. For example, hospitals use encryption to protect patient data stored in databases, transmitted over networks, and shared between medical devices, ensuring that sensitive information remains confidential and secure.

- **Case study 3: E-commerce and secure transactions:**
    - E-commerce platforms use encryption to secure online transactions, protect customer information, and build user trust. SSL/TLS encryption is used to

secure data exchange between customers and websites, including payment details, personal information, and order data. By implementing robust encryption measures, e-commerce companies can reduce the risk of data breaches and protect their customers from fraud.

Encryption in IoT and Cloud computing

As technology evolves, encryption finds new applications in emerging fields such as the **Internet of Things (IoT)** and cloud computing. IoT devices often transmit sensitive data over networks, making encryption essential for protecting information from interception and tampering. Similarly, cloud providers offer encryption services to protect data stored in the cloud, ensuring that customers' information remains secure even in shared environments.

These real-world examples underscore encryption's critical role in protecting sensitive information across various industries. By implementing encryption effectively, organizations can safeguard their data, comply with regulatory requirements, and build trust with their customers and partners.

Access control and authentication

Who can access your data is just as critical as how it is protected.

In CyberSecurity, securing sensitive information goes beyond simply protecting the data; it also involves ensuring that access to this data is strictly controlled and limited to authorized individuals only. Access controls and authentication mechanisms form the first line of defense, acting as gatekeepers that regulate who can view, modify, or interact with data and systems. This section comprehensively explores access control models and authentication techniques, highlighting their critical role in safeguarding digital assets.

Access controls determine the conditions under which users can access resources, while authentication verifies the identity of users attempting to access those resources. Together, they create a layered security approach that prevents unauthorized access and ensures accountability through user identification and activity tracking. In this chapter, we delve into various access control models, such as **Discretionary Access Control (DAC), Mandatory Access Control (MAC)**, and **Role-Based Access Control (RBAC)**. We will also explore modern authentication techniques, including MFA, biometrics, and **Identity and Access Management (IAM)** systems, which are crucial for creating robust, secure, and adaptable access control environments.

Introduction to access control models

Access control models are the backbone of a robust CyberSecurity strategy, serving as the first line of defense in protecting sensitive data and resources from unauthorized access. The primary objective of access control is to manage who has access to what information and under what conditions. Organizations employ different access control models tailored to their specific security needs and operational environments to achieve this. Understanding the fundamental access control models is essential for implementing effective security measures.

Access control models determine the framework through which access permissions are granted, managed, and enforced. Each model has unique principles, advantages, and limitations, making it suitable for organizations and security environments. This section will explore the nuances of DAC, MAC, and RBAC and how they contribute to a secure information system. The access control models are as follows:

- **Discretionary Access Control:** DAC is one of the most flexible and commonly used access control models. Under DAC, the data owner or creator has complete authority to define who can access their resources and to what extent. Permissions are usually granted based on user identity and group membership, allowing data owners to exercise granular control over access rights. However, while DAC offers flexibility, it can also introduce security risks due to the potential for unauthorized permission changes and the spread of access rights, making it less suitable for environments that require stringent security controls.

- **Mandatory Access Control:** MAC is a more rigid access control model that enforces security policies centrally and non-discretionarily. Under MAC, access rights are determined by a system administrator based on predefined classifications of data and user clearance levels. This model is widely used in high-security environments, such as government and military settings, where data sensitivity and strict compliance are critical. MAC's strength lies in its ability to prevent unauthorized access by strictly controlling how data is accessed and by whom. Still, it can also be cumbersome to manage due to its complexity and inflexibility.

- **Role-Based Access Control:** RBAC is a widely adopted model that assigns access permissions based on the user's organizational role. Roles are defined according to job functions, each granting specific access rights to resources necessary to perform assigned tasks. RBAC simplifies access management by grouping users based on their roles, reducing the administrative burden of managing individual permissions. It is particularly effective in large organizations with well-defined structures, as it aligns access rights with the organizational hierarchy, enhancing security and efficiency.

Authentication techniques and technologies

Authentication is the process of verifying the identity of a user, device, or system before granting access to resources. It is a fundamental aspect of access control, ensuring that only authorized entities can access sensitive data. Authentication techniques have evolved significantly, incorporating various technologies that enhance security and improve user experience.

The primary goal of authentication is to ensure that the entity requesting access is who or what it claims to be. Authentication methods can be broadly categorized into three factors: something you know (knowledge), something you have (possession), and something you are (biometrics). These factors can be used individually or in combination to create MFA systems that provide higher security. Various types of authentication techniques are mentioned as follows:

- **Password-based authentication:** To enhance the security of password-based authentication, organizations can implement best practices such as enforcing strong password policies, requiring regular password changes, and using password managers to generate and store complex passwords. Additionally, incorporating MFA can mitigate the risks associated with password compromises.

- **Token-based authentication:** Token-based authentication uses physical or digital tokens to verify a user's identity. Tokens can be hardware devices, such as smart cards or USB security keys, or software-based, such as **time-based one-time passwords (TOTP)** generated by authentication apps. Tokens provide an additional layer of security by requiring possession of the token and knowledge of a password.

- **Biometric authentication:** Biometric authentication verifies identity-based on unique biological characteristics, such as fingerprints, facial recognition, iris scans, or voice patterns. Biometrics offer high security because they are difficult to replicate and cannot be easily stolen or forgotten. Biometric authentication is increasingly popular in consumer devices, such as smartphones, and is also used in secure access control systems, such as biometric door locks.

Data Loss Prevention

Preventing data loss is not just about security—it is about preserving trust and integrity.

Data is critical for organizations in the digital era, driving decision-making, innovation, and competitive advantage. However, the value of data also makes it a prime target for theft, loss, and unauthorized access. DLP technologies are designed to safeguard sensitive information by detecting, preventing, and responding to potential data breaches and leaks. Effective DLP is essential for maintaining security and preserving trust and integrity with clients, partners, and stakeholders.

DLP solutions are complex systems that integrate policies, technologies, and processes to ensure that sensitive data remains protected throughout its lifecycle, whether it is in transit, at rest, or in use. This section explores the various types of DLP solutions, their deployment strategies, and the policies and procedures required for successful implementation. Additionally, it addresses common challenges faced in DLP and provides practical insights through case studies and best practices.

Definition and purpose

DLP refers to a set of technologies and practices designed to prevent the unauthorized transmission, access, or loss of sensitive data. The primary purpose of DLP is to protect data from being inadvertently or maliciously exposed or removed from an organization. By implementing DLP measures, organizations can reduce the risk of data breaches, comply with regulatory requirements, and maintain their data's confidentiality, integrity, and availability.

The key objectives of DLP are as follows:

- **Protection of sensitive data**: DLP aims to safeguard sensitive information such as **personal identifiable information** (**PII**), financial data, intellectual property, and trade secrets from unauthorized access or disclosure.

- **Compliance with regulations**: Many industries are subject to strict data protection regulations, such as GDPR, HIPAA, and PCI-DSS. DLP helps organizations adhere to these regulations by enforcing data protection policies and providing audit trails.

- **Mitigation of insider threats**: DLP solutions can detect and prevent malicious or negligent actions by insiders who may attempt to leak or misuse sensitive data.

- **Preventing data exfiltration**: DLP technologies help prevent unauthorized data transfers, whether they are through email, cloud services, or removable media.

- **Maintaining data integrity**: A critical objective of DLP is to ensure that data is not tampered with or corrupted by external attackers or internal errors.

The components of DLP solutions are as follows:

- **Data discovery:** The first step in implementing effective DLP is identifying where sensitive data resides within the organization. Data discovery tools scan databases, file systems, and cloud storage to locate and classify sensitive information.

- **Data classification:** Once sensitive data is discovered, it must be classified according to its sensitivity level. Classification helps determine the appropriate protection measures and access controls required.

- **Policy enforcement:** DLP solutions use predefined policies to monitor and control data usage. These policies define data access, transmission, and storage rules, ensuring that sensitive data is handled according to organizational standards.

- **Monitoring and detection:** Continuous data activity monitoring helps detect potential threats or policy violations. DLP systems use various methods, such as content inspection and contextual analysis, to identify unauthorized access or transmission attempts.

- **Incident response:** When a DLP system detects a potential data loss event, it triggers an alert or response action. This can include blocking the transmission, notifying administrators, or initiating a forensic investigation.

- **Reporting and auditing:** DLP solutions provide detailed logs and reports on data activity, policy violations, and incident responses. These reports are essential for compliance auditing and security analysis.

The following is a depiction of DLP's anatomy:

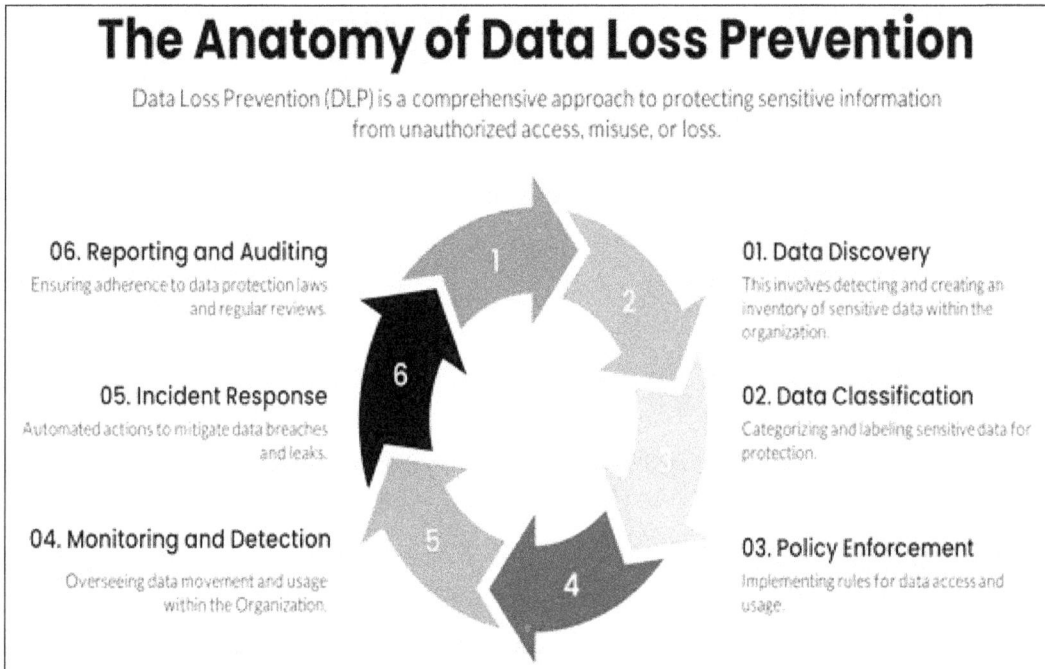

The Anatomy of Data Loss Prevention

Data Loss Prevention (DLP) is a comprehensive approach to protecting sensitive information from unauthorized access, misuse, or loss.

06. Reporting and Auditing
Ensuring adherence to data protection laws and regular reviews.

05. Incident Response
Automated actions to mitigate data breaches and leaks.

04. Monitoring and Detection
Overseeing data movement and usage within the Organization.

01. Data Discovery
This involves detecting and creating an inventory of sensitive data within the organization.

02. Data Classification
Categorizing and labeling sensitive data for protection.

03. Policy Enforcement
Implementing rules for data access and usage.

Figure 4.6: The anatomy of DLP

Types of DLP solutions

DLP solutions can be categorized based on deployment methods, focus areas, and functionalities. Understanding these types helps organizations choose the right solution for their specific needs.

Network-based DLP

Network-based DLP solutions are deployed at network boundaries to monitor and control data traffic. These solutions inspect data as it moves across the network, including email, web traffic, and file transfers.

The key features are as follows:

- **Traffic inspection**: Analyses network traffic for sensitive data patterns and content.
- **Policy enforcement**: Enforces data protection policies by blocking or encrypting sensitive data in transit.
- **Alerts and reporting**: Provides real-time alerts and detailed reports on data transmission activities.

The pros are:

- **Comprehensive coverage:** Monitors all data traffic entering and leaving the network.
- **Real-time protection:** Detects and responds to data loss incidents as they occur.

The cons are:

- **Complex deployment:** Requires integration with network infrastructure and may impact network performance.
- **Limited visibility:** This may not cover data stored on endpoints or cloud services.

Endpoint-based DLP

Endpoint-based DLP solutions are installed on laptops, desktops, and mobile devices. These solutions focus on monitoring and controlling data activities at the endpoint level.

The key features are as follows:

- **Local monitoring**: Tracks and controls data access and usage on endpoints.
- **Policy enforcement**: Prevents unauthorized data transfers to removable media or external devices.
- **Encryption:** Encrypts sensitive data stored on endpoints to protect against theft.

The pros are:

- **Granular control:** Provides detailed visibility and control over data activities on individual devices.
- **Protection against insider threats:** Helps prevent data loss caused by internal users.

The cons are:

- **Resource intensive:** May require significant resources to deploy and manage on all endpoints.
- **Limited network visibility:** Does not provide visibility into data transmitted over the network.

Cloud-based DLP

Cloud-based DLP solutions focus on protecting data stored and accessed through cloud services. These solutions integrate with cloud platforms to monitor and secure data in cloud environments.

The key features are as follows:

- **Cloud integration**: Connects with cloud storage and application services to monitor data usage.
- **Policy enforcement**: Applies data protection policies to cloud-based data and applications.
- **Access controls**: Manages permissions and access to cloud-stored sensitive data.

The pros are:

- **Scalability**: Easily scales with the growth of cloud services and storage.
- **Comprehensive coverage**: Protects data across multiple cloud platforms and services.

The cons are:

- **Integration complexity**: Requires integration with various cloud services and platforms.
- **Visibility challenges**: We may face challenges monitoring data across different cloud environments.

Content-based DLP

Content-based DLP solutions analyze data content to identify and protect sensitive information. These solutions use pattern matching, keyword searches, and content inspection techniques.

The key features are as follows:

- **Content inspection:** Analyses data content for patterns, keywords, and sensitive information.
- **Policy application:** Applies policies based on the content and context of the data.
- **Detection techniques:** Utilizes various methods to detect and classify sensitive data.

The pros are:

- **Precise detection:** Accurately identifies sensitive data based on content analysis.
- **Customizable policies:** Allows for creating custom policies based on content types.

The cons are:

- **Performance impact:** Content inspection can be resource-intensive and impact system performance.

- **False positives:** This may generate false positives if the content analysis is not finely tuned.

Context-based DLP

Context-based DLP solutions consider the context in which data is accessed or transmitted. These solutions analyze factors such as user roles, data types, and access locations to make data protection decisions.

The key features are as follows:

- **Contextual analysis:** Assesses the context of data usage to determine risk levels.

- **Adaptive policies:** Adjusts data protection policies based on contextual factors.

- **Dynamic enforcement:** Applies policies dynamically based on data access context.

The pros are:

- **Flexible protection:** Adapts policies based on the context of data usage, providing more nuanced protection.

- **Risk-based approach:** Focuses on high-risk scenarios based on context analysis.

The cons are:

- **Complex configuration:** Requires detailed configuration to assess context accurately.

- **Potential for misconfiguration:** Risk of misconfiguration leading to insufficient protection.

Deployment Strategies for DLP

Implementing DLP solutions effectively requires careful planning and execution. The following deployment strategies can help organizations maximize the benefits of DLP:

- **Assess organizational needs**: Before deploying DLP solutions, thoroughly assess the organization's data protection needs. Identify the types of sensitive data, data storage locations, and potential threats. This assessment will inform the selection and configuration of DLP solutions.

- **Define data protection policies:** Establish clear policies outlining how sensitive data should be handled, stored, and transmitted. Define policies for data classification, access controls, and incident response. Ensure that these policies align with regulatory requirements and organizational goals.

- **Select the right DLP solution:** Choose a DLP solution that best fits the organization's needs, considering data types, deployment environment, and integration requirements. Evaluate different DLP solutions based on their features, scalability, and compatibility with existing systems.

- **Implement a phased approach**: Deploy DLP solutions in phases to minimize disruption and ensure a smooth implementation. Start with a pilot deployment to test the solution's effectiveness and make necessary adjustments. Gradually roll out the solution across the organization, addressing any issues.

- **Integrate with existing security systems:** Integrate DLP solutions with other security systems, such as SIEM and IAM systems. Integration enhances visibility, enables centralized management, and improves incident response capabilities.

- **Train and educate users:** Educate employees about data protection policies and the importance of DLP. Provide training on how to recognize and report potential data loss incidents. User awareness is crucial for the success of DLP efforts, as employees play a key role in preventing data breaches.

- **Monitor and fine-tune DLP settings:** Continuously monitor DLP activities to enforce policies effectively. Analyze alerts and reports to identify patterns, potential issues, and areas for improvement; fine-tune DLP settings and policies based on real-world data and feedback.

- **Conduct regular audits and reviews:** Perform regular audits and reviews of DLP implementation to assess its effectiveness and policy compliance. Identify any gaps or weaknesses and make necessary adjustments to enhance data protection measures.

- **Prepare for incident response**: Develop and implement an IRP for handling data loss events. Ensure that the plan includes procedures for investigating incidents, mitigating damage, and communicating with stakeholders. Regularly test and update the plan to ensure its effectiveness.

DLP policies and procedures

Effective DLP implementation requires well-defined policies and procedures that guide how sensitive data is protected. The following elements are essential for developing and maintaining robust DLP policies and procedures:

- **Data classification:** Establish a data classification scheme that categorizes data based on sensitivity level. Classification should include criteria for identifying confidential, restricted, and public data. Use this classification to determine the appropriate level of protection for each data category.

- **Access control policies:** Define access control policies that specify who can access sensitive data and under what conditions. Implement role-based or attribute-based access controls to enforce these policies. Ensure that access permissions are reviewed and updated regularly.

- **Data handling and transmission:** Create policies for handling and transmitting sensitive data. Specify requirements for encryption, secure data transfer methods, and secure storage. Ensure that data handling procedures align with regulatory requirements and organizational standards.

- **Incident detection and response:** Develop procedures for detecting and responding to data loss incidents. Define how incidents should be reported, investigated, and mitigated. Establish communication protocols for informing stakeholders and regulatory bodies if necessary.

- **Monitoring and reporting:** Implement monitoring and reporting procedures to track data activity and detect potential policy violations. Define how alerts should be generated, escalated, and addressed. Ensure that reports provide actionable insights for improving data protection.

- **Training and awareness:** Create training programs to educate employees about data protection policies and DLP procedures. Regularly update training materials to reflect changes in policies and emerging threats. Foster a culture of data security awareness within the organization.

- **Policy review and updates:** Regularly review and update DLP policies and procedures to ensure they remain practical and relevant. Conduct policy reviews in response to regulations, business operations, and technology changes. Incorporate feedback from audits and incident investigations to improve policies.

Overcoming common DLP challenges

Implementing and maintaining DLP solutions can present various challenges. Proactively addressing the following challenges can help ensure the effectiveness of DLP efforts:

- **Complexity of deployment:** DLP solutions can be complex to deploy, particularly in large and diverse environments. To address this, use a phased deployment approach and seek guidance from vendors or consultants with expertise in DLP implementation.

- **Balancing security and usability:** Overly strict DLP policies can impact user productivity and lead to resistance. Strive to balance security with usability by fine-tuning policies to minimize disruptions while still providing effective protection.

- **Integration with existing systems:** Integrating DLP solutions with existing security and IT systems can be challenging. Work closely with vendors and IT teams to ensure seamless integration and compatibility with existing infrastructure.

- **Managing false positives and negatives:** DLP systems may generate false positives (innocent activities flagged as threats) or false negatives (actual threats missed). Continuously monitor and adjust DLP settings to reduce false positives and negatives and refine detection techniques.

- **Ensuring user compliance:** Employees may inadvertently or intentionally bypass DLP measures. Implement training programs to educate users about data protection policies and the consequences of non-compliance. Regularly communicate the importance of DLP and involve users in the protection process.

- **Addressing evolving threats:** Cyber threats constantly evolve, and DLP solutions must adapt to address new risks. Stay informed about emerging threats and update DLP policies and technologies to maintain effective protection.

Case studies and best practices

Case studies are beneficial in data security and loss prevention because they provide real-world examples of data breaches, illustrating how attacks occur and what vulnerabilities are exploited. They offer valuable lessons from past incidents, helping organizations avoid similar mistakes and improve their security measures. Additionally, case studies highlight effective strategies and solutions that have been successfully implemented, serving as a guide for others. They also aid in understanding potential risks and impacts, enabling better vulnerability assessment. Furthermore, case studies are useful educational tools for training employees and raising awareness about data security. Lastly, they allow organizations to benchmark their security practices against industry standards and peers, identifying areas for improvement. For the maximum benefit of readers, a few relevant case studies are mentioned as follows:

Financial institution enhancing data protection

A large financial institution faced challenges protecting sensitive customer data across its network, endpoints, and cloud services. The organization implemented a comprehensive DLP strategy that included network-based and cloud-based DLP solutions. By integrating DLP with its existing SIEM system, the institution gained visibility into data activities and improved its incident response capabilities. The deployment of content-based and context-based DLP measures helped detect and prevent data loss incidents, while regular training and policy updates ensured ongoing effectiveness.

The best practices are as follows:

- Conduct thorough data discovery and classification before deploying DLP solutions.

- Integrate DLP with SIEM and IAM systems for enhanced visibility and control.

- Use a combination of DLP solutions (network, endpoint, cloud) to cover all data protection needs.

Regularly review and update DLP policies and technologies to address emerging threats.

Healthcare provider securing patient data

A healthcare provider needs to protect patient data in compliance with HIPAA regulations. The organization implemented endpoint-based and network-based DLP solutions to monitor and control data access and transmission. The provider successfully mitigated the risk of data breaches by enforcing encryption and access controls. Regular audits and training programs ensured that employees understood their role in data protection. The DLP implementation contributed to compliance with regulatory requirements and improved overall data security.

The best practices are as follows:

- Implement DLP solutions that are compliant with industry regulations (for example, HIPAA).

- Enforce encryption for sensitive data both in transit and at rest.

- Conduct regular audits and training to ensure compliance and effectiveness.

- Leverage DLP solutions that offer integration with other security and compliance tools.

Technology company preventing intellectual property theft

A technology company sought to prevent the theft of intellectual property by insiders. To this end, it deployed content-based and context-based DLP solutions to monitor data access and usage. The company effectively prevented unauthorized data transfers by defining and enforcing access policies based on user roles and data sensitivity. Implementing MFA and regular security training further strengthened data protection measures.

The best practices are as follows:

- Define and enforce access policies based on data sensitivity and user roles.

- Implement MFA to enhance authentication security.

- Regularly review and update DLP policies to address evolving risks.

- Educate employees on the importance of protecting intellectual property.

DLP is a critical aspect of any comprehensive data security strategy. By understanding the different types of DLP solutions, implementing effective deployment strategies, and addressing common challenges, organizations can enhance their ability to protect sensitive data and prevent data loss incidents. DLP safeguards valuable information and helps preserve trust and integrity with clients, partners, and stakeholders. Through diligent policy enforcement, continuous monitoring, and adherence to best practices, organizations can achieve robust data protection and maintain a strong security posture in an increasingly complex digital landscape.

Data breach management

It is not a matter of if, but when—being prepared for a data breach is essential.

In today's digital landscape, data breaches are an unfortunate reality that organizations must confront. Despite robust security measures, no system is entirely impervious to attack. How an organization manages a data breach can greatly influence the fallout, affecting everything from regulatory compliance to public perception. Effective data breach management involves a proactive approach, well-defined processes, and swift action to mitigate damage and recover effectively.

This section explores the comprehensive strategies and procedures necessary for managing data breaches. It covers immediate response actions, communication strategies, legal and regulatory considerations, long-term remediation, and the importance of a well-defined IRP. By understanding and implementing these practices, organizations can better navigate the complexities of a data breach and minimize its impact.

Definition and importance: Data breach management refers to an organization's systematic approach to addressing and mitigating the impact of unauthorized access to its sensitive data. This involves a series of coordinated actions aimed at minimizing damage, communicating with stakeholders, and ensuring compliance with legal and regulatory requirements.

The significance of data breach management lies in its ability to do the following:

- **Minimize damage:** Effective breach management helps contain and limit the extent of the breach, reducing potential harm to the organization and its stakeholders.

- **Protect reputation:** A well-handled breach response can help preserve the organization's reputation, demonstrating its commitment to security and transparency.

- **Ensure compliance:** Adhering to legal and regulatory requirements during a breach is crucial for avoiding penalties and legal consequences.

- **Facilitate recovery:** A structured approach to breach management enables organizations to recover more quickly and resume normal operations.

The key elements of data breach management are as follows:

- **Incident response plan:** A documented strategy outlining how the organization will respond to data breaches. This plan should include roles, responsibilities, and procedures for managing breaches.

- **Communication strategy:** A communication plan with internal and external stakeholders, including customers, regulators, and the media.

- **Legal and regulatory compliance:** Understanding and adhering to applicable laws and regulations related to data breaches.

- **Remediation and recovery:** Steps to address vulnerabilities, restore affected systems, and implement measures to prevent future breaches.

Importance of preparedness

Preparation is critical in managing data breaches effectively. Organizations should regularly update their IRPs, conduct training exercises, and stay informed about evolving threats. Preparedness helps ensure that the organization can respond swiftly and efficiently when a breach occurs.

The immediate response actions are as follows:

- **Detection and identification:** The first step in managing a data breach is detecting and identifying it. This involves:

  - **Monitoring systems:** Use SIEM systems, **intrusion detection systems (IDS)**, and other monitoring tools to detect unusual activity or unauthorized access.

  - **Incident triage**: Assess the severity of the incident and determine its impact on data security. Identify the affected systems, data, and users.

- **Containment:** Once a breach is detected, immediate containment is essential to prevent further damage:

  - **Isolate affected systems:** Disconnect compromised systems from the network to stop the spread of the breach.

  - **Control access:** Restrict access to sensitive data and systems to prevent additional unauthorized activity.

  - **Preserve evidence:** Document and preserve evidence related to the breach for investigation and legal purposes.

- **Eradication:** After containment, focus on eradicating the root cause of the breach:

  - **Remove threats:** Eliminate malware, vulnerabilities, or other threats contributing to the breach.

  - **Patch vulnerabilities:** Apply security patches and updates to address any weaknesses exploited during the breach.

- **Recovery**: Restoring normal operations is a crucial phase:

  - **Restore systems:** Rebuild and restore affected systems from clean backups.

  - **Verify integrity:** Ensure systems and data are secure and intact before returning them online.

  - **Monitor for residual threats:** Monitor for any signs of residual threats or additional attacks.

- **Documentation and reporting**: Document every step taken during the response:

  o **Incident log:** Maintain a detailed action log, including detection, containment, eradication, and recovery efforts.

  o **Internal reporting**: Report the incident to senior management and relevant internal teams.

  o **External reporting:** Prepare to report the breach to regulatory authorities and affected individuals as required.

The communication and notification strategies are as follows:

- **Internal communication**: Effective internal communication ensures that all relevant personnel are informed and aligned:

  o **Notifying key stakeholders:** Inform senior management, IT teams, and other relevant departments about the breach.

  o **Coordination:** Establish a communication team to manage internal updates and coordinate the response efforts.

- **External communication**: Communicating with external stakeholders is crucial for maintaining trust and transparency:

  o **Customer notification:** Notify affected customers about the breach, providing details about the impact and steps being taken to address it.

  o **Regulatory notification:** Report the breach to regulatory authorities by legal requirements. Ensure timely and accurate reporting to avoid penalties.

  o **Media management:** Prepare public statements and engage with the media to manage the narrative and provide updates. Address media inquiries promptly and accurately.

- **Message content and timing:** Ensure that messages are clear, accurate, and timely:

  o **Clarity**: Provide clear information about what happened, the impact, and the steps to address the breach.

  o **Transparency**: Be transparent about the extent of the breach and the potential risks to affected individuals.

  o **Timeliness**: Communicate promptly to keep stakeholders informed and minimize speculation.

- **Addressing concerns**: Be prepared to address concerns from affected individuals and stakeholders:

  o **Customer support:** Offer support and resources to affected customers, including guidance on protecting themselves.

- o **FAQs and updates:** Regularly update and answer frequently asked questions to address common concerns.

The legal and regulatory considerations are as follows:

- **Understanding legal obligations:** Data breaches often trigger legal and regulatory requirements, including:

  - o **Data protection laws:** Familiarize yourself with data protection laws, such as GDPR, HIPAA, and CCPA, which mandate specific breach notification and response procedures.

  - o **Regulatory reporting:** Ensure compliance with reporting requirements for data breaches, including timelines and content.

- **Notification requirements:** Different jurisdictions have varying notification requirements:

  - o **Timeliness**: Many regulations require notification within a specific timeframe (for example, 72 hours under GDPR).

  - o **Content:** Notifications should include details about the breach, the types of data affected, and the steps to address the issue.

  - o **Affected individuals:** Notify individuals whose data has been compromised and guide how they can protect themselves.

- **Legal counsel and representation:** Engage legal counsel to navigate the complexities of breach management:

  - o **Legal advice:** Obtain legal advice on compliance with regulations, potential liabilities, and breach response strategies.

  - o **Representation:** Work with legal representatives to handle investigations, negotiations, and potential legal actions.

- **Regulatory investigations and penalties:** Prepare for potential regulatory investigations and penalties:

  - o **Cooperation**: Cooperate with regulatory investigations and provide requested documentation and evidence.

  - o **Penalties**: Be aware of potential penalties and fines for non-compliance and take steps to mitigate their impact.

The actions for long-term remediation and recovery are as follows:

- **Post-breach analysis:** Conduct a thorough post-breach analysis to understand the root cause and impact:

- o **Root cause analysis:** Identify the underlying causes of the breach and any vulnerabilities exploited.

- o **Impact assessment:** Assess the impact on data, systems, and stakeholders.

- **Strengthening security posture:** Implement measures to prevent future breaches:

- o **Security enhancements:** Strengthen security controls, such as updating firewalls, implementing advanced threat detection, and enhancing encryption.

- o **Policy updates:** Review and update data protection policies and procedures based on lessons learned from the breach.

- **Continuous monitoring and improvement:** Establish ongoing monitoring and improvement processes:

- o **Regular audits:** Conduct security audits and vulnerability assessments to identify and address potential weaknesses.

- o **Training and awareness:** Provide ongoing training for employees on data security best practices and emerging threats.

- **Restoring stakeholder trust**: Rebuild trust with affected stakeholders through transparency and accountability.

- o **Communication:** Communicate openly about the steps taken to address the breach and prevent future incidents.

- o **Support:** Offer support and resources to affected individuals and stakeholders to help them recover.

Developing an incident response plan

An IRP is essential for managing data breaches effectively. It provides a structured approach to detecting, responding to, and recovering from security incidents.

The key components of an IRP are as follows:

- **Roles and responsibilities:** Define roles and responsibilities for the incident response team, including key stakeholders and decision-makers.

- **Incident detection and reporting**: Establish procedures for detecting and reporting security incidents.

- **Response procedures**: Outline the steps for containing, eradicating, and recovering from a breach.

- **Communication plan:** Develop a communication strategy for internal and external stakeholders.

- **Documentation and reporting**: Specify how incidents should be documented and reported.

- **Training and testing:** Include regular training and testing of the IRP to ensure readiness.

- **Regular review and updates:** Regularly review and update the IRP to ensure its effectiveness:

    o **Plan updates:** Update the plan based on organizational, technological, and threat landscape changes.

    o **Lessons learned:** Incorporate lessons from previous incidents and exercises to improve the plan.

Effective data breach management is crucial for minimizing the impact of security incidents and preserving organizational integrity. By understanding and implementing the steps outlined in this section, organizations can better prepare for and respond to data breaches. Preparedness, clear communication, legal compliance, and continuous improvement are key to managing breaches successfully and maintaining trust with stakeholders. Organizations can navigate the complexities of data breach management through a proactive approach and well-defined processes and strengthen their overall security posture.

Conclusion

The chapter underscores the critical importance of a comprehensive and proactive approach to data security. By systematically classifying data based on sensitivity, organizations can apply tailored protection measures that align with their security priorities and regulatory requirements. Encryption and secure communication protocols are emphasized as essential defenses, ensuring that data remains safe even if intercepted by unauthorized entities.

The chapter also highlights the significance of access controls and authentication, which act as gatekeepers of sensitive information, allowing only authorized individuals to access data. DLP strategies enhance security by monitoring and controlling data flow, preventing accidental or malicious leaks.

Finally, the chapter addresses the inevitability of data breaches, stressing that preparedness through robust IRPs and effective breach management is crucial for minimizing impact. By integrating these strategies, organizations can build a resilient data security framework that protects sensitive information and enhances business integrity, compliance, and stakeholder trust. The comprehensive approach outlined in this chapter is a vital guide for organizations seeking to strengthen their defenses in an increasingly complex and threat-laden digital landscape.

Points to remember

- **Data classification is essential for tailored security**: Understanding the sensitivity and value of data through proper classification allows organizations to apply appropriate security measures, ensuring that critical information receives the protection it needs.

- **Encryption is the backbone of data security**: By converting data into unreadable formats, encryption protects information at rest and in transit, making it indecipherable to unauthorized entities and significantly reducing the risk of data breaches.

- **Access controls and authentication safeguard data access**: Implementing strong access control models and authentication techniques, such as MFA and identity management, ensure that only authorized users can access sensitive data.

- **DLP prevents unauthorized data movement**: DLP technologies detect and prevent unauthorized access, use, or transmission of sensitive data, effectively controlling data flow within and outside the organization.

- **Proactive breach management minimizes impact**: Preparing for data breaches with well-defined IRPs, including immediate actions, communication strategies, and compliance measures, is critical for mitigating damage and maintaining trust.

- **A comprehensive security framework enhances trust and compliance**: By integrating data classification, encryption, access control, DLP, and breach management strategies, organizations can create a robust security posture that safeguards data integrity and complies with regulatory standards.

Join our book's Discord space

Join the book's Discord Workspace for Latest updates, Offers, Tech happenings around the world, New Release and Sessions with the Authors:

https://discord.bpbonline.com

CHAPTER 5

Identity and Access Management

Introduction

In the digital realm, your identity is your most valuable asset. Protecting it is not just a necessity but a critical defense line in the ever-evolving world of CyberSecurity.

Identity and Access Management (**IAM**) is the backbone of any robust CyberSecurity strategy. As organizations embrace digital transformation, safeguarding user identities and managing access permissions has never been more critical. IAM ensures that the right individuals have the appropriate access to technology resources, mitigating risks of unauthorized access and data breaches.

This chapter looks at the essential components of IAM, exploring authentication methods, authorization protocols, and advanced security measures such as **Single Sign-On** (**SSO**) and **Multi-Factor Authentication** (**MFA**). Organizations can enhance security, streamline access, and foster a resilient digital environment by mastering IAM.

Structure

The following sections will be covered:

- Identity and Access Management
- Authentication methods

- Authorization and Role-Based Access Control
- SSO and MFA

Objectives

This chapter on IAM equips readers with a comprehensive understanding of the critical elements forming modern CyberSecurity's foundation. It begins by differentiating between authentication and authorization, explaining their essential roles in securing digital environments. Through exploring various authentication methods, from traditional passwords to advanced biometrics and token-based systems, readers gain insight into how to implement these technologies effectively in an enterprise setting. The chapter underscores the importance of selecting methods that balance security and usability, addressing the complexities of large-scale environments. Additionally, the **Role-Based Access Control (RBAC)** section highlights how permissions are managed efficiently based on user roles, ensuring that access is granted only to those requiring it. Advanced models like **Attribute-Based Access Control (ABAC)** and **Policy-Based Access Control (PBAC)** are also discussed to give readers a broader view of evolving authorization frameworks.

The chapter further delves into SSO and MFA, two essential technologies that have reshaped access management. SSO simplifies the user experience by enabling access to multiple systems with a single set of credentials, reducing administrative burdens and password fatigue. Meanwhile, MFA strengthens security by requiring numerous verification factors, significantly reducing the risk of unauthorized access. The integration of SSO and MFA demonstrates how these technologies can work in tandem to improve both security and user convenience. By the end of the chapter, readers will have developed a holistic understanding of IAM, equipping them to make informed decisions about implementing authentication and authorization systems that protect organizational assets while maintaining a seamless user experience.

Identity and Access Management

In the digital age, managing who you are and what you can do is the keystone of CyberSecurity.

IAM is critical to modern CyberSecurity strategies. It focuses on ensuring that the right individuals access the right resources at the correct times for the right reasons. IAM systems are designed to secure digital identities, streamline access permissions, and enhance organizations' overall security posture by mitigating unauthorized access risks. As businesses expand their digital footprint, the complexity of managing user identities and permissions grows, making IAM a foundational element of an effective access control strategy.

IAM is more than just a set of technologies; it is a comprehensive framework that combines policies, processes, and technologies to manage digital identities and control access to organizational resources. Effective IAM helps organizations enforce security policies, comply with regulatory requirements, and enhance operational efficiency by automating access control tasks. In this section, we will explore the critical components of IAM, its significance in CyberSecurity, various IAM models, best practices, and how IAM can be implemented to safeguard organizational assets. *Figure 5.1* illustrates multiple factors contributing to IAM:

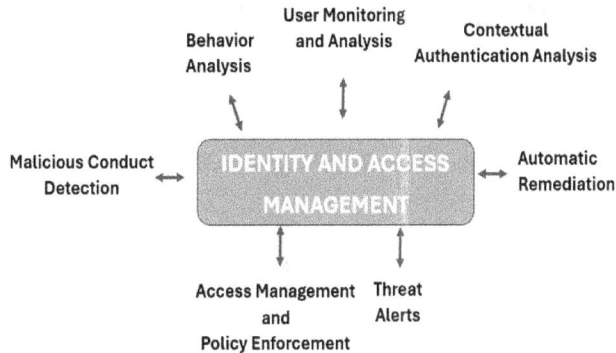

Figure 5.1: *Factors contributing to IAM*

Core components of IAM

IAM systems consist of several core components that work together to manage identities and control access. They are as follows:

- **Identity management**: Identity management involves creating, maintaining, and managing digital identities for an organization's users, devices, applications, and services. It ensures that each entity has a unique and verifiable identity, which forms the basis for access decisions.

- **Access management:** Access management focuses on enforcing access controls based on the organization's policies. This includes defining who can access resources under what conditions and monitoring how access is used.

- **Authentication:** Authentication is verifying an individual's identity before granting access. Standard authentication methods include passwords, biometrics, smart cards, and MFA, which combine multiple verification methods to enhance security.

- **Authorization:** Once authenticated, authorization determines what actions the user can perform within the system. This is managed through access control policies that define permissions based on roles, attributes, or rules.

- **User provisioning and de-provisioning:** User provisioning involves creating user accounts, assigning permissions, and granting access to resources based on job roles. De-provisioning removes access when users change roles or leave the organization, ensuring access is continuously aligned with the user's status.

- **Single Sign-On:** SSO allows users to authenticate once and gain access to multiple applications without needing to log in separately. SSO simplifies the user experience and reduces the number of credentials that need to be managed.

- **Federated Identity Management (FIM):** FIM enables users to access resources across multiple domains or organizations using a single set of credentials. This is particularly useful in **business-to-business (B2B)** scenarios where users need seamless access to external systems.

- **Audit and compliance management:** IAM systems include monitoring and auditing capabilities that track user activities, access requests, and policy changes. These logs are essential for compliance reporting, security analysis, and identifying potential security incidents.

Significance of IAM in CyberSecurity

IAM is pivotal in ensuring that digital identities are adequately managed and that access to critical resources is tightly controlled. As cyber threats continue to evolve, IAM plays a crucial role in the following:

- **Reducing the risk of data breaches:** By enforcing strict access controls, IAM minimizes the risk of unauthorized access to sensitive information, reducing the likelihood of data breaches.

- **Ensuring regulatory compliance:** Many industries are subject to regulations that mandate specific access control measures. IAM helps organizations meet compliance requirements by providing audit trails, enforcing access policies, and managing user identities in line with regulatory standards.

- **Enhancing operational efficiency:** Automated IAM processes reduce the manual effort required to manage user accounts and permissions, freeing up IT resources and speeding up access provisioning.

- **Supporting zero-trust security models:** IAM is integral to Zero-Trust architectures, which operate on the principle of *never trust, always verify*. In a Zero-Trust model, IAM continuously verifies identities and enforces access policies regardless of the user's location or network.

IAM models and approaches

IAM can be implemented through various models, each catering to specific organizational needs, listed as follows:

- **Role-Based Access Control (RBAC):** RBAC assigns access permissions based on user roles within the organization. Roles are defined according to job functions, and users are granted permissions that align with their roles. RBAC simplifies access management by grouping permissions into roles, making it easier to enforce consistent access policies.

- **Attribute-Based Access Control (ABAC):** ABAC uses attributes of the user, resource, or environment to make access decisions. For example, access can be granted based on a user's location, time of access, or the sensitivity level of the data. ABAC offers greater flexibility and granularity than RBAC but can be more complex to implement.

- **Policy-Based Access Control (PBAC):** PBAC leverages predefined policies to control access decisions. Policies can be based on various criteria, including roles, attributes, and contextual factors. PBAC is often used in dynamic environments where access requirements frequently change.

- **Identity-Based Access Control (IBAC):** IBAC focuses on the user's identity and assigns permissions directly to that identity. This model is often used when specific users need unique access rights not shared with others.

- **Least privilege access:** This approach ensures that users have the minimum access necessary to perform their job functions. By restricting access to only what is needed, the least privilege reduces the potential attack surface and limits the damage that can occur if an account is compromised.

Best practices for implementing IAM

Implementing IAM effectively requires careful planning, robust policies, and a commitment to continuous improvement. The following best practices can help organizations maximize the benefits of their IAM systems:

- **Develop a comprehensive IAM strategy**: Start with a clear IAM strategy that aligns with the organization's security goals, compliance requirements, and business objectives. Define the scope of IAM, identify key stakeholders, and establish governance frameworks to oversee its implementation and ongoing management.

- **Adopt Multi-Factor Authentication (MFA):** Enhance security by implementing MFA, which requires users to provide multiple verification forms before accessing resources. MFA significantly reduces the risk of unauthorized access, even if user credentials are compromised.

- **Implement strong password policies:** Ensure password policies enforce strong, unique passwords requiring regular updates. Password management tools can help users maintain secure credentials without sacrificing convenience.

- **Automate user provisioning and de-provisioning:** Automate the provisioning and de-provisioning of user accounts. This reduces errors, speeds up access management, and ensures that permissions align with the user's current role.

- **Leverage SSO and federated identity management:** Implement SSO and FIM to simplify the user experience. These solutions reduce the number of credentials users need to manage and provide seamless access to multiple systems.

- **Regularly audit access rights**: Conduct periodic audits of access rights to ensure that permissions are appropriate and in line with organizational policies. Regular audits help identify orphaned accounts, outdated permissions, and potential security gaps.

- **Monitor and analyze access logs:** Use IAM's logging and monitoring capabilities to track user activities, identify unusual behavior, and respond to potential security incidents. Access logs provide valuable insights into how resources are used and can be instrumental in detecting malicious activities.

- **Educate users on IAM policies:** User awareness is critical to IAM success. Educate users about IAM policies, the importance of protecting their credentials, and their role in maintaining a secure environment.

- **Plan for scalability and future growth:** Design IAM solutions that can be scaled to accommodate future growth and changing business needs. Scalable IAM systems ensure that IAM can keep pace as the organization expands without compromising security.

- **Integrate IAM with other security systems:** IAM should be integrated with other security systems, such as **Security Information and Event Management (SIEM)** solutions, to provide a holistic view of the security landscape and enhance incident response capabilities.

Implementing robust IAM systems

Implementing IAM requires a strategic approach considering technology, people, and processes. Organizations should begin by thoroughly assessing their current access control practices and identifying gaps that must be addressed. This assessment will inform the design of the IAM solution, which should be tailored to the organization's specific needs. Key steps in implementing an effective IAM system are mentioned as follows:

- **Define IAM policies and procedures:** Establish clear policies that define how identities are managed, how access is granted, and the criteria for revoking access. Policies should cover all aspects of IAM, including authentication requirements, password management, and access review procedures.

- **Select the right IAM tools and technologies**: Choose IAM tools that align with your organization's requirements. Key factors include scalability, integration capabilities, user experience, and support for advanced security features like MFA and SSO.

- **Involve stakeholders in IAM planning**: Successful IAM implementation requires input from stakeholders, including IT, security, HR, and compliance teams. Collaboration ensures that the IAM system meets the needs of all departments and supports the organization's overall security strategy.

- **Deploy IAM in phases**: Rather than implementing IAM all at once, consider a phased approach that prioritizes high-risk areas first. This allows for gradual adoption, minimizes disruptions, and provides opportunities to refine the system based on feedback.

- **Test and validate IAM controls**: Before full deployment, thoroughly test IAM controls to ensure they function as intended. Validation should include testing for security vulnerabilities, verifying that access controls are properly enforced, and ensuring that user experiences are intuitive and efficient.

  Continuously monitor and improve: IAM is not a one-time project but an ongoing process that requires continuous monitoring and improvement. Regularly review IAM policies, update access controls as needed, and stay informed about emerging threats that could impact IAM security.

IAM is a cornerstone of CyberSecurity, providing the framework for managing digital identities and controlling access to critical resources. By implementing robust IAM systems, organizations can enhance their security posture, reduce the risk of unauthorized access, and ensure compliance with regulatory requirements. Effective IAM goes beyond technology; it requires a strategic approach integrating policies, processes, and people to create a secure and efficient access management environment. As cyber threats continue to evolve, the importance of IAM will only grow, making it an essential component of any comprehensive CyberSecurity strategy.

Authentication methods

Authentication is the digital handshake between the user and the system. A secure handshake ensures you interact with the right person, device, or service.

Authentication is the first step in securing access to systems and data. It confirms the identity of users, devices, and services, forming the frontline defense against unauthorized access. This subchapter explores traditional and modern authentication methods, including passwords, biometric authentication, token-based systems, and emerging technologies like behavioral biometrics. We will examine their strengths, vulnerabilities, and best practices for implementation in an enterprise environment.

Role of authentication

Authentication is a cornerstone of CyberSecurity, serving as the first line of defense against unauthorized access to systems, applications, and data. It is the process of verifying the identity of a user, device, or service before granting access to resources. In an increasingly interconnected digital landscape, where sensitive information is constantly at risk, robust authentication methods are critical for maintaining security and trust.

Historically, authentication was a straightforward process involving simple passwords and **personal identification numbers (PINs)**. However, as cyber threats have evolved, so have the methods and technologies used to authenticate identities. Today, the landscape includes a wide array of authentication mechanisms ranging from traditional methods, such as passwords and security questions, to advanced technologies like biometric authentication, token-based systems, and adaptive authentication techniques.

The effectiveness of an authentication system hinges on two primary factors: security and usability. Security ensures that unauthorized users cannot gain access, while usability ensures that legitimate users can easily authenticate themselves without excessive friction. Striking the right balance between these two factors is essential for implementing a successful authentication strategy that protects assets without hindering productivity. The following figure illustrates that authentication is a must to access resources:

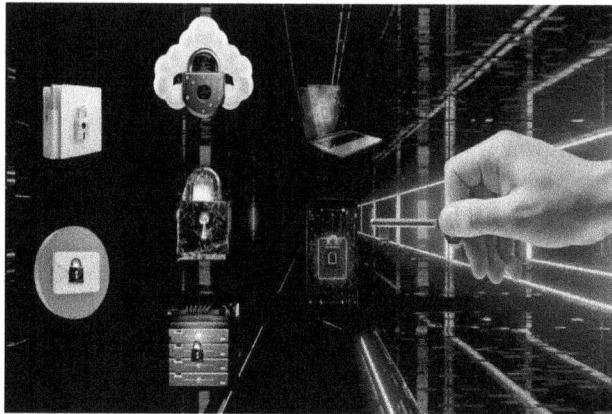

Figure 5.2: Authentication is the key

Traditional authentication methods

Traditional authentication methods in CyberSecurity primarily rely on something the user knows, such as passwords or security questions. These methods have been the cornerstone of digital security for decades due to their simplicity and ease of implementation. However, they come with significant vulnerabilities, including susceptibility to brute force attacks, phishing, and social engineering. Passwords can be easily guessed or stolen, especially if users employ weak or reused passwords across multiple sites. Despite these drawbacks, traditional authentication remains widely used, often supplemented by additional layers of security like **two-factor authentication (2FA)** to enhance protection against unauthorized access.

Password-based authentication

Password-based authentication is one of the oldest and most widely used methods for verifying user identities. A password is a secret string of characters known only to the user, which is used to prove their identity. Despite its prevalence, password-based authentication is fraught with security challenges.

Its strengths are as follows:

- **Simplicity:** Easy to implement and understand.

- **Ubiquity:** Supported by virtually all systems and applications.

- **Low Cost:** Requires minimal investment in infrastructure.

The vulnerabilities are as follows:

- **Weak passwords:** Users often choose simple, easily guessable passwords due to convenience, increasing the risk of brute-force attacks.

- **Password reuse:** Reusing the same password across multiple accounts exposes users to credential stuffing attacks, where attackers use stolen credentials to gain unauthorized access.

- **Phishing and social engineering:** Attackers frequently exploit human weaknesses by tricking users into revealing their passwords through phishing emails or deceptive websites.

- **Password databases:** If password databases are not adequately protected, they become lucrative targets for cybercriminals. Even hashed passwords can be cracked if weak hashing algorithms are used.

The best practices are as follows:

- Encourage the use of strong, unique passwords by implementing password policies that mandate complexity (for example, a mix of upper and lower case letters, numbers, and special characters).

- Utilize password managers to generate and store complex passwords securely.

- Enforce periodic password changes and prevent the reuse of old passwords.

- Implement account lockout mechanisms after a set number of failed login attempts to deter brute-force attacks.

Security questions

Security questions are used as an additional layer of authentication, often as a fallback when a user forgets their password. Users answer pre-selected questions, such as their mother's maiden name or the name of their first pet, to prove their identity.

The strengths are as follows:

- **Accessibility:** Provides an alternative method for users to regain access to their accounts.

- **Ease of use:** Familiar to most users and easy to set up.

The vulnerabilities are as follows:

- **Predictability:** Many security questions have predictable answers that can be easily guessed or found on social media profiles.

- **Inconsistent answers:** Users may need to remember their answers or provide consistent responses, leading to access issues.

- **Social engineering:** Answers to security questions can be exploited through social engineering techniques, where attackers gather personal information to bypass authentication.

The best practices are as follows:

- Use more obscure or less guessable security questions.

- Avoid questions that can be easily answered with publicly available information.

- Regularly review and update security questions to reflect changes in a user's personal information.

Biometric authentication

Biometric authentication leverages unique biological traits to verify a user's identity. Unlike passwords or security questions, biometric data is inherently linked to the individual, making it a powerful tool for enhancing security. Standard biometric methods include fingerprints, facial recognition, voice recognition, and behavioral biometrics.

Fingerprint authentication

Fingerprint authentication analyzes the unique patterns of ridges and valleys on a user's fingertip. This method is widely used in mobile devices, laptops, and access control systems.

The strengths are as follows:

- **High accuracy:** Fingerprints are unique to each individual, providing a high level of security.

- **Convenience:** Quick and easy to use, reducing authentication time.

- **Low risk of duplication:** Difficult to replicate without sophisticated tools.

The vulnerabilities are as follows:

- **Spoofing:** Attackers can use lifted fingerprints to create molds and bypass fingerprint scanners.

- **Sensor issues:** Dirty or damaged sensors can lead to false rejections.

- **Data breach risks:** If biometric data is stolen, it cannot be reset like a password, posing a long-term security risk.

The best practices are as follows:

- Use anti-spoofing technologies, such as liveness detection, to prevent unauthorized access.

- Encrypt stored biometric data to protect against breaches.

- Regularly update fingerprint scanners to maintain accuracy and security.

Facial recognition

Facial recognition uses algorithms to analyze facial features and match them against a stored template. It is commonly used to unlock smartphones, access secure areas, and verify identities in banking apps.

The strengths are as follows:

- **Hands-free authentication:** Requires no physical contact, enhancing user convenience.

- **Fast and intuitive:** Provides rapid authentication with minimal user input.

- **Adaptive learning:** Modern systems can adapt to changes in appearance, such as facial hair or glasses.

The vulnerabilities are as follows:

- **Spoofing with photos or masks:** Some facial recognition systems can be tricked with photos, masks, or deepfake technology.

- **Lighting conditions:** Poor lighting or extreme angles can affect the accuracy of facial recognition.

- **Privacy concerns:** The collection and storage of facial data raise significant privacy and regulatory concerns.

The best practices are as follows:

- Implement MFA to complement facial recognition.

- Use 3D mapping and liveness detection to prevent spoofing.

- Ensure compliance with privacy regulations regarding the use of facial data.

Voice recognition

Voice recognition analyzes the unique patterns in a person's voice, including pitch, tone, and cadence. It is often used in call centers, virtual assistants, and secure access systems.

The strengths are as follows:

- **Natural and user-friendly:** Voice recognition provides a hands-free and seamless authentication experience.

- **Personalization:** Can be combined with voice commands to enhance user interactions.

The vulnerabilities are as follows:

- **Background noise:** Environmental noise can interfere with voice recognition accuracy.

- **Voice mimicry:** Advanced attackers can mimic a user's voice or use recorded samples to bypass authentication.

- **Throat illnesses:** Temporary changes in voice due to illness can lead to false rejections.

The best practices are as follows:

- Combine voice recognition with other authentication factors, such as a PIN or facial recognition.

- Anti-spoofing techniques like liveness detection are used to verify the authenticity of the voice sample.

- Continuously train voice recognition systems to improve accuracy and adapt to variations.

Behavioral biometrics

Behavioral biometrics analyze patterns in user behavior, such as typing speed, mouse movements, and even how a user holds their smartphone. This method provides continuous authentication without interrupting the user experience.

The strengths are as follows:

- **Continuous monitoring:** Provides ongoing authentication, detecting anomalies in real-time.

- **Difficult to replicate:** Behavioral patterns are unique and challenging for attackers to mimic.

- **Seamless integration:** Operates in the background without requiring additional input from the user.

The vulnerabilities are as follows:

- **Variability in behavior:** Stress, fatigue, or changes in environment can affect behavioral patterns, leading to false positives.

- **Privacy concerns:** Continuous monitoring of user behavior can raise privacy issues if not handled transparently.

The best practices are as follows:

- Use behavioral biometrics as an additional layer of security rather than a standalone method.

- Implement transparent privacy policies and ensure users are aware of the data being collected.

- Continuously refine behavioral models to minimize false positives and improve accuracy.

Retina authentication

Retina authentication is a biometric authentication method that uses the unique patterns of a person's retina to verify identity. The retina at the back of the eye contains a complex network of blood vessels unique to everyone, making it an ideal marker for secure identification. Specialized scanners analyze the retina's pattern by shining a low-intensity light into the eye, capturing a unique image for authentication.

The strengths are as follows:

- **High accuracy:** Retina patterns are complicated to replicate, offering one of the highest levels of accuracy among biometric methods. The uniqueness of retinal patterns, even between identical twins, makes this an effective security measure.

- **Low false-positive rate**: Due to the retina's complexity and minimal external exposure, the rate of false positives (unauthorized users being allowed access) is minimal.

- **Secure against spoofing**: Since the retina is an internal organ, it is highly resistant to tampering or spoofing compared to a fingerprint or facial recognition, which may be susceptible to replication through images or models.

The vulnerabilities are as follows:

- **Expensive equipment:** Retina scanners are typically costly and require sophisticated hardware for precise retina mapping, making them less accessible for widespread use.

- **User inconvenience**: Retina scanning can be uncomfortable as users need to position their eyes close to a scanning device. This can hinder user experience, especially compared to less invasive methods like fingerprint or facial recognition.

- **Health and accessibility concerns**: Certain medical conditions, such as cataracts or retinal diseases, may affect the accuracy of the scan. Users with impaired vision might find retina scanners challenging to use effectively.

- **Privacy concerns**: Retina scans are highly personal and invasive, so concerns about privacy and data misuse can arise if biometric data is improperly handled or stored.

The best practices are as follows:

- While retina authentication is highly secure, it is best used as a MFA system, especially in high-security environments. This can add additional layers of verification, such as requiring a password or token.

- Due to the precision required for retina scanning, the equipment must be regularly maintained and calibrated to ensure consistent accuracy.

- The biometric data generated from retina scans should be encrypted and stored securely, complying with GDPR to protect user privacy and prevent unauthorized access to sensitive information.

- Guidance on correctly using retina scanners and accessibility for those with eye conditions can improve user experience and reduce the risk of authentication failures.

Token-based authentication

Token-based authentication uses physical or digital tokens to verify a user's identity. These tokens are typically generated for a specific session or transaction, adding an extra layer of security.

One-Time Passwords

One-Time Passwords (OTPs)are temporary codes generated for a single use, usually sent via SMS, email, or generated by an authenticator app. They are widely used in banking, online transactions, and 2FA.

The strengths are as follows:

- **Time-limited:** OTPs expire after a short period, reducing the window of opportunity for attackers.

- **Two-factor authentication:** Often used as a second factor in combination with passwords, enhancing security.

The vulnerabilities are as follows:

- **Phishing and man-in-the-middle attacks:** OTPs can be intercepted by attackers through phishing or session hijacking.

- **SIM swapping:** Attackers can gain control of a user's phone number to receive OTPs meant for the victim.

The best practices are as follows:

- Use app-based OTP generators instead of SMS-based OTPs to mitigate SIM swapping risks.

- Educate users about phishing risks and encourage them not to share OTPs.

- Implement transaction monitoring to detect suspicious use of OTPs.

Smart cards and security tokens

Smart cards and security tokens store encrypted authentication credentials, often used in high-security environments such as government and corporate settings. They require physical possession, adding a layer of *something you have* to the authentication process.

The strengths are as follows:

- **High security:** Smart cards and tokens are difficult to clone or forge.

- **Integration with physical access control:** Used in conjunction with physical access systems, such as door locks and secure areas.

The vulnerabilities are as follows:

- **Loss or theft:** Physical tokens can be lost or stolen, compromising security.

- **Compatibility issues:** Not all systems support smart cards or security tokens, limiting their usability.

The best practices are as follows:

- Use tokens with built-in PIN protection to prevent unauthorized use if they are lost.

- Regularly update token firmware to maintain security standards.

- Implement token lifecycle management to track and revoke lost or stolen tokens.

Hardware tokens

Hardware tokens, such as USB keys (for example, YubiKey), provide an extra layer of security by requiring the user to connect the token to their device during authentication physically. These tokens often use cryptographic protocols like **Fast Identity Online (FIDO)** for secure communication.

The strengths are as follows:

- **Resilient to phishing:** Hardware tokens provide strong protection against phishing attacks, as they require a physical presence.

- **No passwords needed:** Many hardware tokens eliminate the need for passwords, relying on public key cryptography for authentication.

The vulnerabilities are as follows:

- **Physical damage:** Hardware tokens can be damaged or become inoperable over time.

- **Loss of tokens:** As with other physical tokens, losing the device can result in a loss of access.

The best practices are as follows:

- Enforce the use of PINs or biometric verification in conjunction with hardware tokens.

- Maintain spare tokens and a secure recovery process for lost or damaged tokens.

- Regularly test and validate the tokens to ensure their functionality.

Emerging authentication trends

As cyber threats evolve, so too must authentication methods. Emerging trends like adaptive authentication and context-aware authentication are transforming how we approach identity verification, making the process more dynamic and intelligent.

Adaptive authentication

Adaptive authentication uses real-time data to assess the risk of an authentication attempt. It evaluates factors such as user location, device type, time of access, and behavior patterns to determine the appropriate level of authentication required. If an anomaly is detected, such as an attempt to log in from an unusual location, the system may request additional verification steps, such as MFA.

The strengths are as follows:

- **Dynamic security:** Adapts to changing risk levels, providing a flexible security posture.

- **Minimizes user friction:** Only prompts for additional authentication when necessary, balancing security with convenience.

The vulnerabilities are as follows:

- **Privacy concerns:** Collecting contextual data, such as location, may raise privacy issues.

- **False positives:** Misinterpretation of normal behavior as anomalous can lead to unnecessary authentication challenges.

The best practices are as follows:

- Communicate data collection practices to users to mitigate privacy concerns.

- Continuously refine algorithms to reduce false positives and improve accuracy.

- Combine adaptive authentication with other security measures, such as user behavior analytics.

Context-aware authentication

Context-aware authentication goes beyond adaptive methods by incorporating environmental and situational data into the authentication decision-making. It assesses not just the user's identity but also the broader context of the interaction, such as the device's security posture, the network being used, and the time of day.

The strengths are as follows:

- **Holistic approach:** Provides a comprehensive assessment of authentication attempts, reducing the likelihood of unauthorized access.

- **Enhanced user experience:** Reduces the need for frequent logins and authentication challenges when the context is deemed low risk.

The vulnerabilities are as follows:

- **Complex implementation:** Context-aware systems require advanced analytics and integration with various data sources.

- **Potential for over-reliance:** Sole reliance on contextual data can be risky if not combined with other authentication factors.

The best practices are as follows:

- Integrate context-aware authentication with MFA to provide layered security.

- Regularly audit the data sources used for context evaluation to ensure their reliability and security.

- Use machine learning to refine context assessments and improve system accuracy over time.

The authentication landscape is continuously evolving, driven by technological advancements and the ever-present threat of cyberattacks. From traditional methods like passwords to cutting-edge techniques such as behavioral biometrics and adaptive authentication, each approach brings strengths and challenges. By understanding these methods and implementing best practices, organizations can build a resilient authentication strategy that protects against unauthorized access and enhances the overall user experience. In CyberSecurity, the correct authentication methods are not just about preventing breaches—they are about establishing trust, maintaining control, and ensuring that every digital handshake is secure.

Authorization and Role-Based Access Control

Access without control is a risk waiting to happen. Role-Based Access Control puts power in the hands of those who need it—no more, no less.

While authentication identifies a user, authorization determines what that user can do within a system. RBAC is a pivotal strategy for managing user permissions based on roles, ensuring that individuals have access only to the resources necessary for their job functions. This subchapter covers the principles of RBAC, its implementation in diverse environments, and how it enhances security and operational efficiency.

Introduction to authorization

While authentication verifies a user's identity, authorization determines what that authenticated user is allowed to do within a system. This distinction is fundamental in CyberSecurity: authentication asks, *Who are you?* while authorization asks, *What can you do?* Together, they form the backbone of access management, but they serve distinct and complementary purposes.

Authorization is a critical component of CyberSecurity that enforces policies defining access rights, ensuring users can only access data and perform actions necessary for their roles. This control mechanism prevents unauthorized access to sensitive information, minimizes potential damage from security breaches, and supports compliance with GDPR, HIPAA, and PCI-DSS regulations.

At the heart of authorization lies the concept of least privilege, a security principle that dictates users should have the minimum access necessary to perform their job functions. Implementing adequate authorization controls protects resources and reduces the attack surface, making systems more resilient against insider threats and external attacks.

RBAC is one of the most widely used authorization models, particularly in enterprise environments. By assigning permissions based on predefined roles rather than individual users, RBAC simplifies access rights management, enhances security, and improves organizational efficiency.

Principles of RBAC

RBAC is a policy-neutral access control mechanism defined around roles and permissions. It is designed to manage access rights by associating roles with users and linking them to the permissions required to perform specific tasks. This model streamlines granting and revoking access, making it easier to maintain consistent security policies across an organization. *Figure 5.3* indicates the functioning of role-based access assignments through administrators:

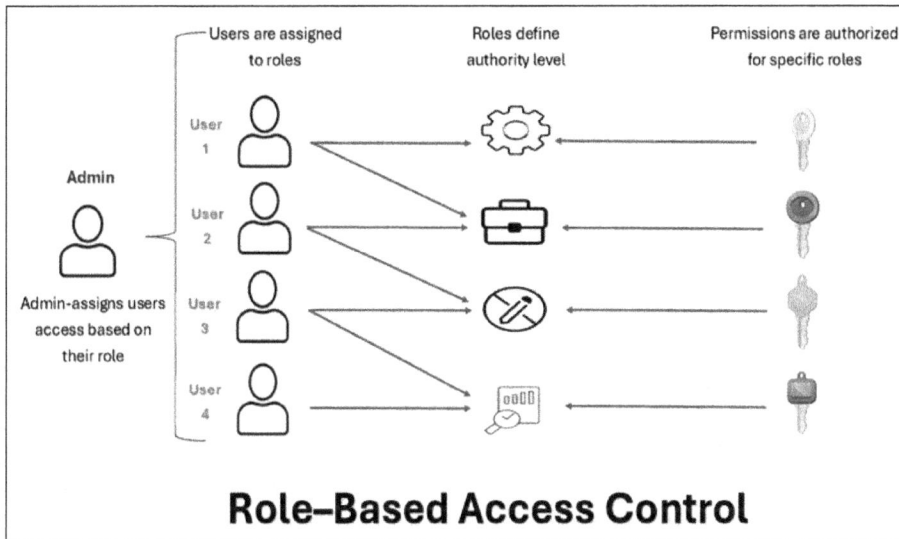

Figure 5.3: Role-Based Access Control

Core concepts of RBAC

RBAC operates on three key concepts: roles, permissions, and users. Understanding these elements is essential for implementing RBAC effectively:

- **Roles**: A role represents a set of access rights grouped to match the responsibilities of a job function. For example, an **Admin** role might have permissions to manage user accounts, configure system settings, and access all data, while a **User** role might only have permissions to view specific data and perform routine tasks.

- **Permissions**: Permissions are the specific actions that can be performed on a resource, such as read, write, execute, or delete. Permissions are assigned to roles rather than individual users, creating a layer of abstraction that simplifies access management.

- **Users**: Users are the individuals or entities needing access to system resources. Users are assigned roles based on their job responsibilities, which in turn grants them the permissions associated with those roles.

- **Sessions**: A session is a user accessing the system under a specific role. Sessions can be dynamic, allowing users to activate or deactivate roles based on their current tasks, thereby adhering to the principle of least privilege.

Types of RBAC models

RBAC is not a one-size-fits-all solution; it has several variations to suit different organizational needs. They are as follows:

- **Flat RBAC**: In this basic model, roles are defined without any hierarchical relationship. Users can be assigned multiple roles, but there is no concept of role inheritance.

- **Hierarchical RBAC**: This model introduces role hierarchies, allowing roles to inherit permissions from other roles. For example, a **Manager** role can inherit all permissions from a **Staff** role, plus additional permissions unique to management responsibilities.

- **Constrained RBAC (separation of duties):** This model enforces separation of duties by preventing users from activating roles that could lead to conflicts of interest. For example, a user with the **Accounts Payable** role might be restricted from also having the **Accounts Receivable** role to prevent fraud.

- **Dynamic RBAC**: Dynamic RBAC allows for real-time changes in role assignments based on context, such as time of day or location. This flexibility is beneficial in environments that require adaptive security measures.

Advantages of RBAC

RBAC offers several benefits that make it a preferred choice for access control in complex environments:

- **Scalability**: RBAC scales easily as organizations grow, allowing administrators to manage access rights efficiently without individually configuring each user.

- **Consistency**: By standardizing access rights across roles, RBAC ensures consistent enforcement of security policies, reducing the risk of accidental over-permission.

- **Reduced administrative overhead**: RBAC simplifies the process of managing user permissions, especially during onboarding, role changes, or offboarding.

- **Improved compliance**: RBAC supports compliance with regulatory requirements by providing a clear, auditable trail of access rights and user actions.

Common challenges in RBAC implementation

Despite its advantages, RBAC implementation can present several challenges mentioned as follows:

- **Role explosion**: Organizations may create an excessive number of roles to accommodate varying permissions, leading to "role explosion." This makes management difficult and defeats the purpose of simplification.

- **Role conflicts**: In complex environments, overlapping roles may lead to conflicts where users inadvertently receive more access than intended.

- **Maintenance**: Keeping roles and permissions updated with changing job functions requires ongoing maintenance, which can become resource-intensive.

Implementing RBAC

Implementing RBAC involves careful planning, execution, and maintenance. Best practices can help organizations avoid common pitfalls and achieve a secure, efficient access control environment.

Best practices for RBAC implementation

The best practices for RBAC implementation are as follows:

- **Conduct a role audit**: Before implementing RBAC, conduct a comprehensive audit of existing roles, permissions, and user access patterns. This audit helps identify unnecessary permissions and roles that must be consolidated or eliminated.

- **Define clear roles and responsibilities**: Clearly define roles based on job functions and responsibilities. Each role should be directly tied to specific tasks, minimizing the permissions overlap between roles.

- **Follow the principle of least privilege:** Ensure that each role provides only the permissions necessary for the job function. Regularly review and adjust roles to prevent permission creep, where users accumulate access rights over time.

- **Implement Separation of Duties (SoD):** Enforce SoD policies to prevent conflicts of interest and reduce the risk of fraud. Use constrained RBAC models to restrict role combinations that could lead to security risks.

- **Automate role assignment and de-provisioning**: Automate assigning and revoking roles to streamline user lifecycle management. This reduces human error risk and ensures access rights are promptly updated when job roles change.

- **Monitor and review access regularly**: Regularly review role assignments and permissions to ensure that they remain aligned with job functions. Implement logging and auditing to track access patterns and detect anomalies.

- **Involve stakeholders in role design**: Engage various stakeholders, including IT, HR, and department managers, in the role design process. This collaboration ensures that roles accurately reflect business needs and security requirements.

Common pitfalls in RBAC implementation

The common pitfalls in RBAC implementation are as follows:

- **Overcomplicating roles**: Creating too many granular roles can complicate management and lead to confusion. Aim for a balance between specificity and simplicity.

- **Inadequate role documentation**: Poor documentation of roles and permissions can hinder maintenance and troubleshooting. Maintain detailed records of role definitions, permissions, and their purpose.

- **Ignoring role inheritance**: Neglecting hierarchical roles can lead to redundancy and inefficiency. Use inheritance to streamline roles and reduce duplication.

- **Lack of ongoing maintenance**: Failing to update roles and permissions regularly can lead to security gaps. Treat RBAC as an evolving process that requires continuous monitoring and adjustment.

Case studies in RBAC implementation

The following are some case studies:

- **Case study 1: Financial institution:**

  - A large financial institution implemented RBAC to manage access across multiple departments. By defining roles such as **Teller**, **Loan Officer**, and **Branch Manager**, the institution reduced unauthorized access incidents by 40% and streamlined compliance reporting, saving thousands of hours annually in audit preparation.

- **Case study 2: Healthcare organization:**

  - A healthcare provider used RBAC to secure patient data and comply with HIPAA regulations. Roles were defined based on job functions such as **Doctor**, **Nurse**, and **Admin Staff**, each with specific access to patient records. This approach minimized data breaches and ensured only authorized personnel could access sensitive information.

- **Case study 3: Manufacturing company:**

  - A manufacturing company faced challenges with role sprawl due to overlapping job functions. After implementing a hierarchical RBAC model, the company consolidated roles and reduced the total number by 60%. This simplified access management and enhanced operational efficiency by reducing the time spent on access requests and approvals.

Advanced authorization models

As organizations grow more complex, traditional RBAC may only sometimes meet the nuanced needs of access management. Advanced models such as ABAC and PBAC offer more dynamic and context-aware approaches to authorization.

Attribute-Based Access Control

ABAC uses attributes, characteristics of users, resources, and the environment to make authorization decisions. Unlike RBAC, where permissions are tied to roles, ABAC dynamically evaluates access requests based on multiple factors, such as the user's department, the sensitivity of the resource, and the time of access.

The strengths are as follows:

- **Granular control**: ABAC provides fine-grained access control by considering multiple attributes, offering more flexibility than role-based models.

- **Context-aware decisions**: ABAC can adapt to changing contexts, such as granting access only during business hours or restricting access based on location.

The challenges are as follows:

- **Complexity**: ABAC requires sophisticated rule engines and attribute management, making it more complex to implement and maintain.

- **Policy management**: Managing and updating policies can be challenging, especially as the number of attributes grows.

The best practices are as follows:

- Start with a pilot project to refine attribute definitions and access policies.

- Use automated tools to manage attributes and monitor policy effectiveness.

- Involve key stakeholders in defining and validating attribute-based rules.

Policy-Based Access Control

PBAC, also known as Rule-Based Access Control, uses predefined policies to make authorization decisions. These policies are rules defining which users can perform specific actions under certain conditions.

The strengths are as follows:

- **Automated decision-making**: PBAC automates access decisions, reducing the need for manual approvals and minimizing delays.

- **Scalable**: PBAC scales easily as new policies can be added without restructuring existing roles or permissions.

The challenges are as follows:

- **Policy conflicts**: Overlapping policies can lead to conflicts, resulting in unintended access grants or denials.

- **High maintenance**: PBAC requires regular updates to policies to keep pace with evolving business needs and security threats.

The best practices are as follows:

- Implement a centralized policy management system to streamline the creation, modification, and enforcement of policies.

- Regularly test and validate policies to ensure they align with organizational goals and security requirements.

- Use logging and analytics to monitor policy effectiveness and identify areas for improvement.

Future of access control

Automation, artificial intelligence, and machine learning are increasingly driving the future of authorization and access control. These technologies transform how organizations manage access, moving beyond static roles and rules to more adaptive and intelligent systems.

Automated access management

Automation streamlines access management by using predefined workflows and triggers to grant or revoke access without manual intervention. This approach reduces administrative overhead and minimizes the risk of human error.

The benefits are as follows:

- **Speed**: Automated systems can process access requests instantly, reducing delays and improving productivity.

- **Accuracy**: Automation reduces the likelihood of mistakes in assigning permissions, ensuring that access rights are always up to date.

The challenges are as follows:

- **Dependency on technology**: Automated systems depend on robust, well-maintained software, and any failure can disrupt access management.

- **Initial setup**: The initial configuration of automated workflows can be complex and resource-intensive.

AI-driven access management

AI and machine learning are introducing predictive and adaptive elements to access control. These technologies can analyze user behavior patterns to detect anomalies, predict access needs, and adjust permissions in real-time.

The benefits are as follows:

- **Proactive security**: AI can detect unusual access patterns indicative of a potential breach, triggering automated responses to mitigate risk.

- **Personalized access**: AI-driven systems can tailor access rights based on individual user behavior, reducing friction while maintaining security.

The challenges are as follows:

- **Data privacy**: AI-driven access management relies on vast amounts of data, raising privacy concerns that must be managed carefully.

Bias in decision-making: AI models can inadvertently introduce bias into access decisions if not properly trained and monitored.

The best practices are as follows:

- Use AI to complement, not replace, existing access control models.

- Continuously validate AI models to ensure accuracy and fairness in access decisions.

  Implement robust data governance policies to protect user privacy and comply with regulations.

Authorization is more than just a security measure; it is a fundamental component of effective governance and risk management. RBAC provides a structured, role-based approach that balances security with operational efficiency, while advanced models like ABAC and PBAC offer dynamic, context-aware alternatives for more complex environments. Organizations can build a robust access control framework that protects their assets and empowers their workforce by adopting best practices, avoiding common pitfalls, and embracing emerging technologies. As the CyberSecurity landscape continues to evolve, so must our approach to managing access and adapting to new challenges with intelligence, agility, and precision.

SSO and MFA

Simplify access, amplify security—SSO and MFA are the dual pillars that support seamless user experiences and robust protection.

In the evolving landscape of CyberSecurity, managing user access to systems and applications is more critical than ever. SSO and MFA are two transformative technologies that enhance IAM by balancing security and convenience. SSO simplifies access by allowing users to log in once and gain access to multiple applications, while MFA strengthens security by requiring multiple forms of verification. Together, they form the foundation of a zero-trust security model, which assumes no trust between any user, device, or application until verified. This chapter explores the principles, benefits, and best practices for implementing SSO and MFA in modern enterprise environments.

Introduction to SSO

SSO is an authentication process that allows users to access multiple applications or services with one login credential. Rather than requiring users to remember and manage multiple usernames and passwords for different systems, SSO centralizes authentication into a single access point, significantly improving the user experience. Once authenticated, the user can access connected applications without logging in again until the session expires.

SSO typically relies on trusted **identity providers (IdPs)** that authenticate users on behalf of multiple **service providers** (SPs). This is achieved through standardized protocols such as OAuth, **Security Assertion Markup Language (SAML)**, and OpenID Connect, which facilitate secure token exchange between the IdP and SPs, validating the user's identity across different applications.

The role of SSO in CyberSecurity

SSO plays a crucial role in modern CyberSecurity strategies by reducing the attack surface associated with password fatigue. When users are overwhelmed by the need to remember multiple credentials, they often resort to insecure practices such as reusing passwords or writing them down. SSO addresses these issues by limiting the required credentials, thereby improving security and reducing the administrative burden on IT departments.

The key components of SSO systems are as follows:

- **Identity Provider (IdP):** The entity responsible for authenticating the user and issuing tokens to access various service providers.

- **Service Providers (SPs):** Applications or services that accept authentication tokens from the IdP to grant access to users.

- **Authentication protocols:** SSO systems use protocols like SAML, OAuth, and OpenID Connect to facilitate secure token exchanges between IdPs and SPs.

- **Security tokens:** Temporary digital credentials issued by the IdP that confirm the user's identity to the SP.

Benefits of SSO

SSO offers many benefits that make it an attractive solution for organizations seeking to improve security and user experience. Here, we look at its core advantages and how it supports organizational goals:

- **Improved user experience:** One of SSO's most significant benefits is its seamless user experience. By enabling users to access multiple applications with a single login, SSO reduces friction for users, enhancing productivity and satisfaction. Employees spend less time managing passwords and more time focusing on their work, which translates to improved efficiency and morale.

- **Reduced IT overhead:** SSO significantly reduces the workload on IT support teams by minimizing the number of password-related issues they have to handle. Password resets are among the most common helpdesk requests, often accounting for a substantial portion of IT support costs. SSO minimizes these requests, allowing IT teams to focus on more strategic initiatives.

- **Enhanced security:** While SSO consolidates access points, it also improves security by enforcing more robust, centralized authentication policies. It enables the consistent application of password policies, such as complexity requirements and expiration schedules, across all connected applications. Additionally, SSO often integrates seamlessly with MFA, adding an extra layer of security.

- **Streamlined compliance:** For organizations bound by regulatory requirements, SSO simplifies compliance by providing a centralized audit trail of user access. This makes monitoring and reporting on who has access to what systems easier, ensuring that access controls align with regulatory standards.

- **Centralized access control:** SSO provides administrators with a single point of control to manage user access. This centralization simplifies onboarding and offboarding processes, ensuring access rights are promptly updated in response to changes in an employee's role or employment status. It also allows for rapid response in case of security incidents, such as immediately revoking access for a compromised account.

MFA defined

MFA is a security mechanism that requires users to present two or more verification factors to authenticate themselves. This approach significantly reduces the risk of unauthorized access, adding layers of protection that are difficult for attackers to bypass. Unlike single-factor authentication, which relies solely on a password, MFA combines something the user knows (password), something the user has (a device), and something the user is (biometric data).

The core authentication factors are as follows:

- **Something you know:** This factor involves information known to the user, such as passwords, PINs, or answers to security questions. It is the most traditional form of authentication but also the most vulnerable to phishing, social engineering, and brute-force attacks.

- **Something you have:** This factor involves physical items or digital tokens that the user possesses. Examples include smartphones (for receiving OTPs or push notifications), smart cards, hardware tokens, and software tokens generated by authentication apps like Google Authenticator.

- **Something you are:** This factor relies on biometric data unique to the individual, such as fingerprints, facial recognition, voice patterns, or iris scans. Biometrics provide a high level of security, as they are difficult to replicate, but they also raise privacy concerns and require careful implementation to avoid false positives or negatives.

- **Something you do:** This emerging factor focuses on behavioral biometrics, such as typing speed, mouse movements, or how a user interacts with their device. These patterns are intricate to imitate, adding a dynamic layer of security to the authentication process.

By requiring multiple factors, MFA adds layers of verification that significantly reduce the likelihood of unauthorized access. For example, even if a password is compromised, an attacker must possess the user's smartphone or biometric data to authenticate successfully. *Figure 5.4* highlights how access can be validated and made more secure by including MFA:

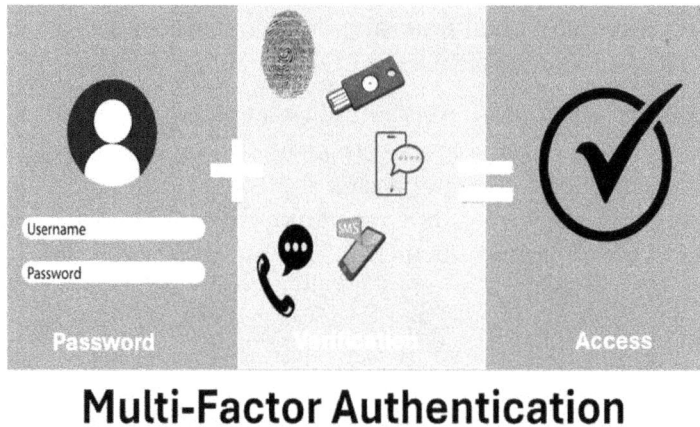

Multi-Factor Authentication

Figure 5.4: MFA makes access much more secure

MFA in action

Implementing MFA involves configuring multiple layers of verification during the login process. For example, after entering a password, a user might be required to approve a push notification sent to their registered mobile device. Alternatively, they might need to provide a fingerprint scan to complete the login.

The common MFA methods are as follows:

- **SMS-based verification:** Users receive a one-time code via SMS that they must enter to complete the authentication process. While easy to implement, SMS-based MFA is vulnerable to SIM-swapping and other attacks that can compromise the security of the second factor.

- **Authenticator apps:** Apps such as Google Authenticator, Microsoft Authenticator, and Authy generate **time-based one-time passwords** (**TOTPs**) that provide a more secure second factor than SMS. These apps work offline, resist interception, and can be used across multiple services.

- **Hardware security keys:** Physical security keys, such as YubiKey or Google Titan, use protocols like FIDO **Universal 2nd Factor** (**U2F**) to provide a decisive, phishing-resistant second factor. Users authenticate by inserting the key into their device or tapping it when prompted.

- **Biometrics:** MFA implementations may include biometric factors such as fingerprint scans or facial recognition, adding a unique, hard-to-replicate layer of authentication.

The benefits of MFA are as follows:

- **Mitigates credential-based attacks:** MFA drastically reduces the effectiveness of credential theft techniques such as phishing, keylogging, and brute force attacks. Even if an attacker obtains the user's password, they still need the second or third authentication factor to gain access.

- **Supports zero-trust security models:** Zero-trust models assume no implicit trust between users and systems. MFA aligns with this approach by continuously verifying user identities at every access point, ensuring that only authorized individuals gain access to resources.

- **Enhanced security for remote workforces:** As remote work becomes more prevalent, MFA provides an essential layer of security for employees accessing corporate resources from outside the traditional office environment. It ensures that even compromised credentials do not result in unauthorized access.

- **Improved compliance with regulatory standards:** Many industry regulations, such as PCI-DSS, GDPR, and HIPAA, mandate the use of MFA for sensitive data access. Implementing MFA helps organizations comply with these standards, reducing legal and financial risks associated with data breaches.

Despite its advantages, implementing MFA can present challenges, including the following:

- **User resistance:** Users may resist MFA due to perceived inconvenience or lack of familiarity with the technology.

- **Integration issues:** Integrating MFA into existing systems and applications may require significant effort, particularly for legacy systems not designed with MFA in mind.

- **Backup and recovery:** Organizations must have backup and recovery options for users who lose access to their second factor, such as account recovery procedures or alternative authentication methods.

MFA is a powerful tool for enhancing security and reducing the risk of unauthorized access. By incorporating multiple layers of verification, MFA provides robust protection for accounts and sensitive information. Adopting MFA will be critical in strengthening organizational security as threats evolve.

Combining SSO and MFA

SSO and MFA are often deployed together to maximize security without compromising user convenience. While SSO streamlines access by reducing the required logins, MFA compensates by adding robust security layers to the initial authentication. This combination allows organizations to simplify the login process while maintaining high protection against unauthorized access. Some major benefits are mentioned as follows:

- **Enhancing security without sacrificing user experience**: Deploying SSO with MFA provides a balanced approach: SSO reduces login fatigue, and MFA ensures that access is verified through multiple factors. For example, a user might log in once using their SSO credentials, but MFA is triggered when accessing particularly sensitive applications or data.

- **Implementing conditional access**: Conditional access policies enable organizations to tailor the application of SSO and MFA based on risk factors such as user location, device type, or access time. For instance, if a user logs in from a trusted device within the corporate network, they might only need SSO. However, MFA would be required to ensure security if the login occurs from an unrecognized device or an unusual location.

- **Role of adaptive authentication**: Adaptive authentication uses AI and machine learning to analyze user behavior and adjust authentication requirements in real-time. For example, if a user's login behavior deviates from the norm, adaptive systems can prompt for additional verification steps, such as biometric confirmation, ensuring that access is always contextually secure.

The best practices for combining SSO and MFA are as follows:

- **Prioritize high-risk access points:** Apply MFA to critical systems and data even when SSO is in use, ensuring that additional verification is required for the most sensitive access points.

- **Educate users:** Training employees on the importance of MFA and how to use it effectively helps increase adoption and reduce resistance.

- **Monitor and adjust policies:** Review authentication logs regularly to identify potential security gaps and adjust SSO and MFA policies accordingly.

The challenges in SSO implementation are as follows:

- **Single point of failure:** If the SSO system is compromised, it can expose access to multiple connected applications. Implementing redundant and highly available SSO infrastructures, coupled with rigorous security protocols, is essential.

- **Integration complexity:** Integrating SSO with legacy systems and diverse applications requires thorough planning and execution. Organizations should prioritize compatibility with modern authentication standards and work closely with vendors to ensure smooth integration.

- **User resistance:** Changes in how users access systems might make SSO more challenging. Clear communication, training, and a phased implementation approach can help ease this transition.

The challenges in MFA implementation are as follows:

- **User convenience vs. security balance:** Striking the right balance between robust security and user convenience can be challenging. Overly stringent MFA policies may lead to frustration, while lenient configurations might expose vulnerabilities.

- **Technical difficulties:** Users might experience issues with receiving OTPs, or biometric readers may fail. Providing multiple MFA options and offering user support for technical issues are vital to maintaining a positive experience.

- **Privacy concerns:** Biometric data raises privacy concerns, and organizations must ensure that such data is stored and processed securely. Compliance with privacy regulations and transparent communication about data use are crucial.

The best practices for SSO and MFA implementation are as follows:

- **Start small, scale gradually:** Begin with a pilot program to test SSO and MFA in a controlled environment. Gather feedback, make necessary adjustments, and gradually expand the rollout across the organization.

- **Utilize user-friendly MFA methods:** Offer a range of MFA options, such as push notifications, hardware tokens, or biometric authentication, to accommodate user preferences and minimize disruptions.

- **Continuously monitor and improve:** Regularly audit authentication logs, conduct security assessments, and update SSO and MFA configurations to address emerging threats and vulnerabilities.

- **Leverage AI and machine learning:** Use AI-driven adaptive authentication to analyze user behavior patterns and dynamically adjust authentication requirements, balancing security with convenience.

*In a world where security and convenience often clash, **SSO and MFA** bring harmony. Together, they streamline access and fortify defenses, making secure, seamless authentication a reality.*

SSO and MFA represent the convergence of user convenience and security in IAM. By centralizing authentication and introducing multiple verification factors, these technologies help organizations minimize risks associated with credential theft, reduce IT overhead, and improve user satisfaction. As threats continue to evolve, integrating SSO and MFA into a comprehensive, adaptive security strategy is no longer a luxury; it is a necessity. By adopting these technologies thoughtfully, businesses can protect their assets, empower their employees, and build a resilient digital environment that stands firm against today's CyberSecurity landscape challenges.

Conclusion

The chapter highlights IAM's essential role in securing digital systems by effectively managing authentication and authorization processes. By understanding and implementing robust authentication methods, such as biometrics and token-based systems, alongside authorization frameworks like RBAC, organizations can ensure that users have secure and appropriate access to resources. The chapter also emphasizes the significance of combining SSO with MFA to balance security with user convenience. Ultimately, integrating these technologies strengthens organizational security while simplifying access management, fostering a resilient and user-friendly digital environment.

Points to remember

- **Authentication vs. authorization**: Authentication verifies a user's identity, while authorization determines what resources the user can access after authentication is complete.

- **Role-Based Access Control**: RBAC assigns permissions based on predefined user roles, ensuring users only access what they need to perform their jobs.

- **Single Sign-On (SSO)**: SSO simplifies user access by allowing one set of credentials to be used across multiple systems, reducing password fatigue and administrative burden.

- **Multi-Factor Authentication (MFA)**: MFA adds extra security by requiring multiple forms of verification, making it harder for unauthorized users to gain access to sensitive systems.

- **Balancing security and usability:** Effective IAM strategies must balance stringent security measures with user convenience, ensuring seamless, secure access without compromising system protection.

- **IAM in modern CyberSecurity**: A well-implemented IAM strategy is essential to protecting digital assets and ensuring proper user access in an increasingly complex CyberSecurity landscape.

CHAPTER 6
Security Policies and Procedures

Introduction

Strong security policies are the foundation of digital resilience; without them, even the most advanced defenses will crumble.

Well-defined security policies and procedures are the foundation of any robust CyberSecurity program. Without them, even the most advanced technology and tools would fail to protect an organization's critical assets. Security policies are the **rulebooks** that define how an organization governs its digital assets, establishes control, and ensures compliance. Security policies are designed to protect the confidentiality, integrity, and availability of business data, systems, and networks. Adhering to these policies ensures that business operations remain secure and compliant with all relevant regulations. The procedures are the **actionable steps** that bring these policies to life. They shape the culture of security, drive compliance, and form the bedrock of any secure enterprise.

The importance of having clear, comprehensive, and enforceable security policies cannot be overstated. They serve as a lighthouse, guiding organizations through the turbulent waters of cyber threats, regulatory obligations, and ever-evolving risks. However, what makes a security policy effective? What are the elements that differentiate a generic checkbox-compliance document from a robust, enforceable, and practical set of guidelines? This chapter will address the answers to these questions.

Structure

The following sections will be covered:

- Security policy framework
- Compliance and regulatory considerations
- Security awareness and training

Objectives

This chapter focuses on building a comprehensive security policy framework that supports an organization's CyberSecurity strategy. It emphasizes the importance of aligning security policies with business objectives to protect digital assets and meet regulatory requirements, such as GDPR, HIPAA, and PCI-DSS. The chapter outlines the core components of a practical security framework, including acceptable use policies, access control measures, data classification, incident response protocols, and third-party risk management. Tailoring security policies to fit specific business needs and operational efficiency is a key theme, ensuring that policies are scalable as the organization grows.

This chapter also stresses the critical role of employee security awareness and training, highlighting the human factor as both a vulnerability and a strength in CyberSecurity. Organizations are guided through developing effective training programs, using methods like phishing simulations and role-based training to engage employees at all levels. Governance mechanisms are explored to ensure policy enforcement, including automation, audits, and feedback loops. Finally, the chapter emphasizes the importance of aligning security policies with globally recognized frameworks such as NIST and ISO 27001, helping organizations strengthen their defenses while adapting to an ever-evolving threat landscape. The following figure depicts the outline of the **Policy**, **Procedure**, and **Guidelines**:

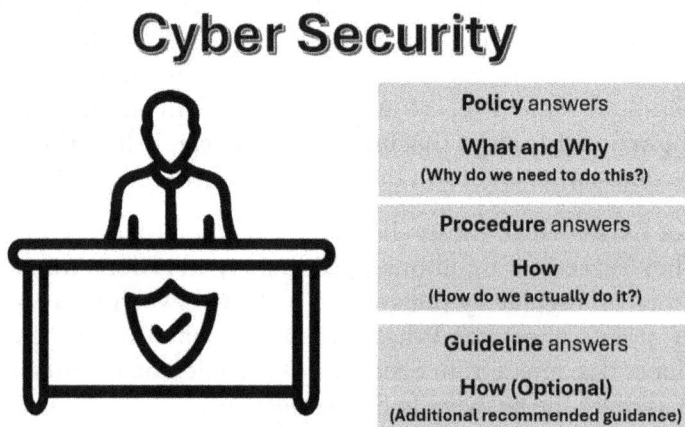

Figure 6.1: Policy, Procedure and Guideline

Security policy framework

A robust security policy framework is the skeleton of your organization's CyberSecurity body—it supports, strengthens, and protects every aspect of your digital defense.

In the rapidly evolving world of CyberSecurity, where digital threats grow in sophistication and frequency, a robust security policy framework forms the backbone of an organization's defense strategy. **Security policy frameworks** provide a structured set of principles, rules, and guidelines that define how an organization manages and protects its digital assets. These frameworks help establish clear boundaries for how data, networks, and systems should be accessed, monitored, and used, ensuring consistency in security practices across the enterprise.

The importance of a security policy framework is multifold. It creates an organized foundation that aligns security initiatives with business objectives, ensuring that security measures protect assets and enable the organization to meet its strategic goals. In addition, a strong framework enables organizations to comply with various regulatory requirements, minimizes the risk of data breaches, and prepares the business to respond effectively to cyber incidents.

At the most basic level, a security policy framework is essential for any organization to manage CyberSecurity risks, adhere to compliance with laws and regulations, and protect its assets. It serves as a **guiding force** for how employees interact with systems, ensures that security responsibilities are clear, and facilitates the enforcement of policies and procedures.

Aligning security policies with organizational objectives

The most effective security policies are not developed in isolation from the organization's strategic objectives. They must be designed to support the overall business goals while mitigating risks. This alignment ensures that security is not viewed as a roadblock to innovation but rather as a **key enabler** for the organization to achieve its objectives safely and efficiently.

Organizations that fail to align their security policies with business goals often encounter inefficiencies, such as unnecessary bureaucratic hurdles, delayed project timelines, and strained relationships between IT/security teams and the rest of the organization. Misalignment can also lead to gaps in coverage, leaving critical systems and processes vulnerable to attack.

To ensure alignment, it is critical to involve **top management** and **key stakeholders** from different departments, such as legal, operations, and executive management, in the policy development process. This ensures that security policies address CyberSecurity risks and consider the organization's broader mission, culture, and operational requirements.

When policies are developed with input from all relevant areas, they are more likely to be followed and integrated into day-to-day operations.

Role of policies, procedures, and guidelines

Policies, procedures, and guidelines are at the core of a security policy framework. Each plays a unique role in shaping the organization's overall security posture. The same is explained as follows:

- **Policy**: A **policy** is a formal, high-level document that defines an organization's security posture and the principles that govern its approach to protecting information and systems. It establishes the **what** and **why** behind security measures, creating a clear framework for decision-making, behavior, and responsibilities across the organization.

  CyberSecurity policies are designed to ensure that all employees and stakeholders understand the organization's expectations when it comes to securing its data and infrastructure. These policies typically outline the scope, objectives, and roles related to CyberSecurity. For instance, a **data privacy policy** may specify that personal information must be encrypted, defining how data should be handled to prevent unauthorized access, but it will not necessarily give a step-by-step process. A **password policy** might require complex passwords and regular updates to minimize the risk of unauthorized logins.

  Policies are enforceable and mandatory, meaning that all employees, contractors, and vendors who interact with the organization's data or systems must comply with the defined rules. Depending on the policy in question, non-compliance can lead to disciplinary action, security breaches, or legal penalties.

  Security policies are usually reviewed periodically to ensure they align with **organizational objectives** and **regulatory requirements**, such as GDPR, HIPAA, PCI DSS etc. They are typically written in a high-level, rigid manner to provide clarity, consistency, and standardization across all departments. By setting the overarching principles, CyberSecurity policies create the foundation for developing detailed procedures and guidelines. In essence, a CyberSecurity policy is an organization's formal commitment to safeguarding its digital assets, outlining the fundamental "**rules of the game**."

- **Procedure**: A **procedure** in CyberSecurity is a detailed, step-by-step set of instructions that outlines **how** to implement and comply with a specific policy. While policies provide high-level rules, procedures focus on the **how**; they describe the exact processes to follow to ensure that CyberSecurity measures are applied correctly and consistently across the organization.

  Procedures are designed to standardize complex tasks, making it easier for employees to perform actions that align with the organization's security policies.

For example, a **Data Backup Procedure** might outline how often data backups should occur, which systems to back up, where to store the backups, and how to recover data in the event of a system failure. Another example is an **Incident Response Procedure**, which details the steps to follow when a security breach is detected, from notifying the right personnel to isolating affected systems and reporting the incident to authorities if required.

Procedures are critical because they help eliminate ambiguity when implementing security measures. They provide clarity and consistency, reducing the likelihood of human error, a common cause of data breaches. Since these documents are prescriptive, employees can rely on them to carry out tasks without extensive CyberSecurity expertise.

CyberSecurity procedures, like policies, are typically mandatory and often audited to ensure adherence. They may be updated more frequently than policies to reflect technological changes, threat landscapes, or organizational processes. While policies define **what** needs to be done, procedures outline **how** to do it, ensuring that security goals are effectively and efficiently met.

- **Guidelines**: Guidelines are recommended practices or suggestions to help employees and teams implement security policies and procedures more effectively. Unlike policies and procedures, guidelines are **optional** and provide **flexibility**, allowing individuals to apply their judgment based on specific situations or organizational needs.

   Guidelines typically offer advice on **best practices** for maintaining security but do not carry a policy or procedure's mandatory or enforceable weight. For example, a **Password Management Guideline** might recommend using a password manager to generate and store complex passwords, but employees are not strictly required to follow this advice. Similarly, a **Remote Work Security Guideline** could suggest using **virtual private networks** (**VPNs**) and secure Wi-Fi connections when working remotely, offering employees a range of options to secure their devices and data.

   While guidelines are not enforceable, they are essential in fostering a culture of security awareness and best practices within an organization. They offer valuable flexibility when strict compliance with policies or procedures may not be practical or necessary. For instance, guidelines may vary depending on an employee's role, the sensitivity of the data they handle, or the specific threats they face.

   Guidelines are often used in dynamic and rapidly changing areas of CyberSecurity where new threats or technologies emerge regularly. They allow organizations to recommend proactive measures without the need for frequent updates to rigid policies or procedures. While **optional**, adhering to security guidelines can significantly enhance an organization's overall CyberSecurity posture by promoting responsible behavior and decision-making at all levels.

Table 6.1 highlights the key differences between **Policy**, **Procedure**, and **Guidelines** in the context of CyberSecurity:

Aspect	Policy	Procedure	Guideline
Definition	A formal, high-level statement outlining an organization's principles and rules for decision-making regarding security.	Step-by-step instructions detailing how to carry out specific tasks or processes to comply with the policy.	Recommendations or best practices that provide flexibility on how to implement security measures.
Purpose	To establish **what** and **why** of an organization's security stance and set expectations for behavior.	To describe **how** specific actions should be taken to achieve compliance with the policy.	To offer **suggestions** and advice on how to meet the policy objectives effectively.
Enforceability	Mandatory for all employees; compliance is required and typically enforceable.	Mandatory; non-compliance may lead to corrective actions or disciplinary measures.	Optional; employees may follow them but are not strictly required to.
Flexibility	Rigid and broad, providing little room for interpretation.	More specific but still requires adherence to prescribed steps.	Flexible and adaptable to various situations, allowing discretion.
Level of detail	High-level, focused on the **goals** and overall approach.	Detailed, focusing on the specific **tasks** and **steps**.	Less detailed, offering broad guidance on how to act.
Time frame	Long-term, reviewed periodically to ensure alignment with the organization's goals and external regulations.	It can be frequently updated to reflect operational changes or process improvements.	Informal and updated as needed based on emerging best practices or lessons learned.
Examples	Data Privacy Policy, Acceptable Use Policy.	Incident Response Procedure, Data Backup Procedure.	Password Management Guidelines, Remote Work Security Guidelines.

Table 6.1: Key difference between Policy, Procedure, and Guideline

Core components of a security policy

The **core components of any security policy** are the fundamental elements that help define how an organization protects its information, systems, and assets. These components ensure that security policies are comprehensive, enforceable, and aligned with the organization's objectives and regulatory requirements. All policies must be version-controlled and approved by management to ensure consistency, accountability, and compliance across the organization.

The following are the key core components of any security policy:

- **Purpose and scope:**

    o **Purpose**: Clearly defines why the security policy is being implemented and what it aims to achieve, such as protecting sensitive information, ensuring compliance, or maintaining business continuity.

    o **Scope**: Outlines the policy's boundaries, including which systems, data, employees, departments, and third parties it applies to. It establishes the areas of operation the policy will govern, ensuring coverage of all critical assets.

- **Roles and responsibilities:**

    o **Responsibilities**: This section specifies the roles of various stakeholders (employees, management, IT staff, and third-party service providers) in implementing and complying with the policy. For instance, it outlines who is responsible for incident response, who enforces access control measures, and who manages system audits.

    o **Ownership**: Establishes policy ownership, assigning responsibility to a security or risk management team to ensure continuous enforcement, review, and updates.

- **Security controls and measures:** This section defines specific controls and measures to protect assets, prevent unauthorized access, and mitigate security risks. These controls may include:

    o **Access controls**: Rules for who can access systems and data based on **role-based access control (RBAC)**, least privilege, or **multi-factor authentication (MFA)**.

    o **Encryption**: Encryption standards for protecting data at rest and in transit.

    o **Data backup and recovery**: Procedures for data backup, disaster recovery, and business continuity.

    o **Network security**: Guidelines for securing the organization's network through firewalls, **intrusion detection systems (IDS)**, and VPNs.

- **Acceptable Use Policy (AUP):** It outlines acceptable and unacceptable use of organizational resources such as IT systems, internet, email, and data. It includes:

    o **Employee behavior**: Defines acceptable behaviors regarding data access, software installation, and online activities.

- o **Prohibited activities**: Lists activities like unauthorized software installation, misuse of corporate email, or accessing inappropriate content.

- **Incident response and reporting:**

  - o **Incident response plan**: Provides a structured approach to detecting, responding to, and recovering from security incidents such as breaches, malware infections, or insider threats.

  - o **Reporting mechanism**: Describes how employees should report suspicious activities or security breaches and who should be notified.

  - o **Incident escalation**: Specifies how incidents are escalated, managed, and resolved within the organization.

- **Data classification and handling:** It establishes a framework for classifying and handling data based on sensitivity, confidentiality, and risk:

  - o **Data classification**: Categorizes data into levels such as public, confidential, restricted, and highly sensitive.

  - o **Handling requirements**: Defines how each classification of data should be handled, protected, and shared, both within and outside the organization.

  - o **Retention and disposal**: Specifies how long data should be retained and the proper methods for securely disposing of data when it is no longer needed.

- **Compliance and regulatory requirements:** It ensures that the policy aligns with relevant **industry standards** and **regulatory frameworks** (for example, GDPR, HIPAA, PCI-DSS, ISO 27001). This includes:

  - o **Regulatory compliance**: Outlines specific compliance obligations based on the organization's industry and the regions where it operates.

  - o **Legal obligations**: Details how the organization will comply with data protection laws and contractual security requirements.

- **Audit and monitoring:** It establishes processes for regularly auditing and monitoring security controls to ensure compliance with the policy:

  - o **Log management**: Describes how network and system logs should be collected, retained unaltered, monitored, and analyzed to detect potential security incidents.

  - o **Audit frequency**: Specifies the frequency of internal and external audits to evaluate the effectiveness of the security controls.

  - o **Metrics and reporting**: Defines **key performance indicators (KPIs)** and metrics to monitor policy compliance and security performance.

- **Policy enforcement and disciplinary actions:** The organization must disseminate the policy enforcement and disciplinary actions to all employees to ensure everyone understands the consequences of non-compliance and the importance of adhering to established procedures:

- o **Enforcement mechanisms**: Describes tools, technologies, and processes used to ensure compliance, such as automated access controls and logging.

- o **Disciplinary actions**: Lists potential disciplinary measures for violations of the policy, ranging from warnings to termination of employment or legal action.

- **Training and awareness:** This ensures that employees are trained and made aware of their responsibilities under the policy:

- o **Security awareness program**: Regularly educates employees on key CyberSecurity principles and their roles in maintaining security.

- o **Role-specific training**: Provides specialized training for staff in high-risk roles (for example, IT, security operations, or data handlers).

- o **Phishing simulations**: Includes simulated phishing campaigns and other exercises to reinforce employee vigilance against threats.

- **Policy review and updates:** This portion explains how often the security policy will be reviewed and updated to ensure it remains relevant and effective:

- o **Review cycle**: Specifies the time intervals (for example, annually or semi-annually) for reviewing the policy.

- o **Change management**: Describes the process for updating the policy in response to changes in the threat landscape, technological advancements, or regulatory updates.

- o **Approval process**: Details who is responsible for reviewing, approving, and disseminating policy changes.

Frameworks/standards for security policy development

In today's complex CyberSecurity landscape, frameworks and standards are pivotal in guiding organizations toward effective security policy development. They provide a structured, consistent approach to managing and mitigating risks, ensuring that security measures are aligned with best practices, legal requirements, and industry benchmarks. By adhering to established frameworks such as NIST, ISO/IEC 27001, and CIS Controls, organizations can build robust security policies that safeguard their digital assets and foster trust among stakeholders. This section explores the leading frameworks and standards, offering insights into how they can be adapted to meet an organization's unique security needs.

Overview of NIST CyberSecurity framework

The **NIST CyberSecurity framework** is one of the most widely used frameworks for managing CyberSecurity risks. Developed by the U.S. **National Institute of Standards and Technology (NIST)**, the framework provides a structured approach to managing CyberSecurity through five core functions:

- **Identify**: Understand the organization's risk environment and identify critical assets and vulnerabilities.

- **Protect**: Implement security controls to safeguard critical assets from cyber threats.

- **Detect**: Develop processes for monitoring and detecting potential security incidents.

- **Respond**: Establish procedures for responding to security incidents.

- **Recover**: Develop plans for restoring normal operations following a security incident.

Figure 6.2 shows the CSF functions as a wheel because all of the unctions relate to one another:

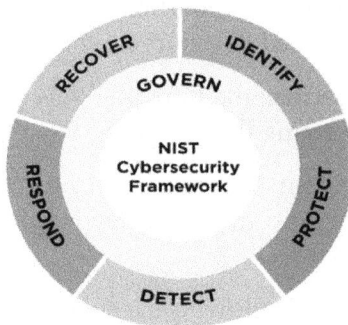

Figure 6.2: NIST CSF 2.0[1]

The NIST CyberSecurity framework is designed to be flexible and scalable, making it suitable for organizations of all sizes and industries. It provides a common language for managing CyberSecurity risks and helps organizations prioritize their security efforts based on their unique risk profile.

ISO/IEC 27001 standards

ISO/IEC 27001 is an internationally recognized **information security management system (ISMS)** standard. It provides a framework for establishing, implementing, maintaining, and continually improving an ISMS to ensure information confidentiality, integrity, and availability.

---

1. **https://nvlpubs.nist.gov/nistpubs/CSWP/NIST.CSWP.29.pdf**

The ISO/IEC 27001 standard is structured around the **Plan-Do-Check-Act (PDCA)** cycle, which promotes a continuous improvement approach to information security. The standard includes requirements for conducting risk assessments, implementing security controls, and regularly reviewing and updating security policies and procedures.

ISO/IEC 27001 is particularly valuable for organizations that must demonstrate their commitment to information security to external stakeholders, such as customers, regulators, and business partners.

Center for Internet Security controls

The **Center for Internet Security (CIS) controls** are a set of best practices for CyberSecurity designed to help organizations protect themselves against the most common cyber threats. The CIS Controls are divided into three categories:

- **Basic controls**: These controls focus on establishing a strong security foundation, such as inventorying and controlling hardware and software assets, securing network devices, and managing administrative privileges.

- **Foundational controls**: These controls focus on managing security risks through vulnerability management, email and web browser protections, and malware defenses.

- **Organizational controls**: These controls focus on security governance and include incident response, penetration testing, and security awareness training policies.

The CIS controls are widely regarded as a practical and actionable set of guidelines that can help organizations improve their CyberSecurity posture without the need for extensive resources.

Choosing the right framework for your organization

Choosing the right security policy framework depends on several factors, including the organization's size, industry, regulatory requirements, and risk appetite. Some organizations may adopt a single framework, such as NIST or ISO/IEC 27001, while others may combine elements from multiple frameworks to create a hybrid approach.

When evaluating different frameworks, organizations should consider the following:

Compliance requirements: Does the framework align with regulatory requirements in your industry or region?

- **Risk management capabilities**: Does the framework provide a comprehensive approach to identifying and managing CyberSecurity risks?

- **Scalability**: Can the framework be adapted as the organization grows and its risk landscape evolves?

- **Ease of implementation**: How complex and resource-intensive is the framework to implement?

Ultimately, the goal is to select a framework that aligns with the organization's business objectives, risk profile, and resource constraints.

Customizing security policies for business needs

While many security policies are universal, different industries face unique security challenges and regulatory requirements that must be addressed through **industry-specific policies**. For example:

- **Healthcare organizations**: It must comply with regulations like the **Health Insurance Portability and Accountability Act (HIPAA)** and **Health Information Technology for Economic and Clinical Health (HITECH),** which require stringent controls for protecting patient data and ensuring privacy.

- **Financial institutions**: They must adhere to regulations such as the **Gramm-Leach-Bliley Act (GLBA)** and **Payment Card Industry Data Security Standard (PCI-DSS)**, which mandate specific controls for securing financial data and preventing fraud.

- **Manufacturing companies**: They face unique challenges related to securing **operational technology (OT)** and **industrial control systems (ICS)**, which are often critical to the production process but may lack robust security protections.

Customizing security policies to address industry-specific risks ensures organizations can protect their critical assets effectively and comply with relevant regulations.

Balancing security and operational efficiency

One of the biggest challenges in designing security policies is finding the right balance between **security and operational efficiency**. Too many security controls can create bottlenecks, slow down business processes, and frustrate employees. On the other hand, insufficient security measures can leave the organization vulnerable to attack.

To strike the right balance, organizations should take a **risk-based approach** to security. This involves evaluating the potential impact of a security breach on the organization and prioritizing security measures that address the highest risks. By focusing on the most critical threats, organizations can implement effective security controls without unnecessarily hindering operations.

It is also important to involve **key stakeholders** from different departments in the policy development process. This ensures that security policies are aligned with the organization's operational needs and that any potential trade-offs between security and efficiency are carefully considered.

Creating scalable policies for growing organizations

As organizations grow and evolve, their security needs become more complex. Policies that work well for a small business may no longer be effective as the organization expands into new markets, adopts new technologies, or faces new regulatory requirements. Therefore, it is essential to design **scalable security policies** that can adapt to the changing needs of the organization.

Scalable policies should be flexible enough to accommodate changes in the organization's structure, technology stack, and risk profile. For example, as an organization grows, it may need to expand its **access control policies** to account for new user roles, or it may need to update its **data classification policies** to reflect the introduction of new types of data.

Regular reviews and updates to security policies are critical for ensuring that they remain effective as the organization grows.

Policy governance and enforcement mechanisms

For security policies to be effective, it is essential to establish clear **ownership and responsibility** for their development, implementation, and enforcement. Security policies may be ignored or inconsistently applied without clear ownership, leaving the organization vulnerable to attack.

Ownership of security policies should be assigned to specific individuals or teams who are responsible for:

- **Developing and updating policies**: This includes researching best practices, consulting with stakeholders, and ensuring that policies align with the organization's risk management strategy.

- **Implementing policies**: This involves working with IT, security, and operations teams to ensure that the necessary technical controls and processes are in place to enforce the policies.

- **Monitoring compliance**: This involves regularly auditing the organization's systems, networks, and processes to ensure that security policies are followed.

In larger organizations, ownership of security policies may be shared across multiple teams, such as IT, legal, and compliance. In these cases, it is essential to establish clear lines of communication and collaboration between teams to ensure that policies are implemented consistently.

Policy approval, distribution, and revision processes

Once security policies have been developed, they must be **approved, distributed, and regularly revised** to ensure their effectiveness. The approval process typically involves **executive leadership** or a **governance board** that reviews the policies to ensure they align with the organization's strategic goals and risk management strategy.

After approval, policies should be distributed to all employees, contractors, and third parties who are expected to follow them. This can be done through email, intranet portals, or training sessions. It is essential that all employees know the policies and understand their responsibilities for complying with them.

Finally, security policies should be **regularly reviewed and updated** to reflect changes in the organization's risk landscape, technology stack, or regulatory environment. This process should involve **cross-functional collaboration** between IT, security, legal, and compliance teams to ensure policies remain relevant and practical.

Automated enforcement through tools and technology

In today's complex security landscape, manually enforcing security policies is often impractical. To ensure policies are consistently applied across the organization, many companies rely on **automated enforcement mechanisms** that use tools and technology to enforce policies in real-time.

Some examples of automated enforcement tools include:

- **Identity and access management (IAM) systems**: These systems automatically enforce **access control policies** by ensuring users can only access the systems and data they are authorized to use.

- **Data loss prevention (DLP) tools**: DLP tools help enforce **data classification and handling policies** by monitoring the organization's networks for unauthorized data transfers and blocking them when necessary.

- **Security information and event management (SIEM) systems**: SIEM systems help enforce **incident response policies** by automatically detecting and responding to security incidents in real-time.

Automated enforcement mechanisms help reduce the burden on IT and security teams by consistently applying security policies across the organization.

Evaluating the security policy framework

Security policies should be subject to **regular audits** to ensure that they remain effective and are being followed by employees. Policy audits typically involve:

- **Reviewing the organization's systems and networks** to ensure that they comply with security policies

- **Interviewing employees and stakeholders** to assess their understanding of and compliance with security policies

- **Identifying gaps or weaknesses** in the organization's security policies and controls

Policy audits can be conducted by internal teams, such as IT or security, or by **third-party auditors** who bring an outside perspective. Audit results should be used to update and improve security policies.

Incorporating lessons learned from incidents

Every security incident presents an opportunity to improve the organization's security policies and procedures. After a security incident, it is essential to conduct a **post-incident review** to identify the root cause and determine whether existing security policies were adequate to prevent or mitigate the impact of the incident.

If gaps or weaknesses are identified, the organization should update its security policies to address the incident's root cause. This may involve implementing new controls, revising existing policies, or providing additional training to employees.

Adapting policies to evolving threats and technologies

The threat landscape is constantly evolving, and new technologies are emerging continually. Organizations must regularly **update their security policies** to address new threats and take advantage of new technologies to stay ahead of the curve.

For example, organizations adopting **cloud computing** may need to update their **data classification and handling policies** to address the unique challenges of securing data in the cloud. Similarly, as new **cyber threats** emerge, organizations may need to update their **incident response policies** to ensure that they can effectively respond to new types of attacks.

By regularly reviewing and updating their security policies, organizations can stay ahead of evolving threats and ensure that their security controls remain effective.

Compliance and regulatory considerations

In an era where regulatory fines can cripple organizations, CyberSecurity compliance is not just about protection—it's about survival.

In today's hyperconnected digital landscape, where data breaches and cyber attacks have the potential to cause catastrophic damage, regulatory compliance has become a cornerstone of CyberSecurity. Governments and regulatory bodies worldwide have recognized the importance of protecting sensitive information, leading to the establishment of stringent regulations designed to ensure that organizations implement effective CyberSecurity measures. Compliance is no longer a mere checkbox activity; it is a business imperative that safeguards sensitive data and ensures business continuity and reputation.

The stakes are high. Non-compliance with regulations can result in severe financial penalties, legal repercussions, and lasting reputational damage. As regulatory frameworks continue to evolve, organizations must stay informed and agile in their approach to compliance. This chapter will explore the various CyberSecurity compliance frameworks and regulations organizations must adhere to, how to integrate compliance into security policies, and strategies to mitigate non-compliance risks.

Overview of CyberSecurity regulations

CyberSecurity regulations have become fundamental in the global effort to protect sensitive information and maintain digital trust. These regulations are designed to mitigate the risks posed by data breaches, cyber attacks, and other security incidents by setting stringent requirements for how organizations collect, store, process, and secure data. Some of the most notable CyberSecurity regulations include the European Union's **General Data Protection Regulation (GDPR)**, which governs data protection and privacy for all individuals within the EU; the HIPAA in the U.S., which ensures the safety of healthcare data; and the PCI-DSS, which safeguards payment card information globally. These regulations often require organizations to implement technical controls, conduct risk assessments, ensure data encryption, and maintain detailed records of data handling activities. Non-compliance with these CyberSecurity regulations can lead to severe financial penalties, legal consequences, and loss of consumer trust. As cyber threats grow in complexity, governments continue to introduce new laws and updates to existing frameworks, such as India's **Digital Personal Data Protection Act (DPDPA)**, emphasizing the importance of global CyberSecurity alignment and cross-border data management.

The growing importance of data protection laws

The growing importance of data protection laws cannot be overstated in today's digitally driven world. As businesses increasingly rely on data to fuel their operations, the volume of personal and sensitive information being collected, stored, and processed has skyrocketed. This surge in data usage, coupled with the rising cyber crime threats, has made data protection laws a critical necessity for safeguarding privacy and maintaining public trust. These laws provide a legal framework to ensure that organizations handle personal data responsibly, maintaining confidentiality, integrity, and transparency.

Data breaches and cyber attacks targeting sensitive information, whether personal, financial, or healthcare-related, can have catastrophic consequences, including identity theft, financial loss, and reputational damage for individuals and organizations alike. To mitigate these risks, governments across the globe have implemented stringent data protection regulations, setting guidelines for how organizations must collect, process, store, and secure data. At the heart of these laws is the recognition that individuals have a fundamental right to control their personal data and to be informed about how it is being used.

One of the most influential regulations in this area is the GDPR in the European Union, which has set the standard for data protection worldwide. GDPR emphasizes the principles of **data minimization, transparency, and accountability**, requiring organizations to obtain clear consent before processing personal data and to provide mechanisms for individuals to access, correct, or delete their information. The hefty penalties for non-compliance have underscored the importance of robust data protection measures, prompting businesses to prioritize CyberSecurity and data privacy like never before.

In the United States, sector-specific laws such as the HIPAA and the **California Consumer Privacy Act** (**CCPA**) have provided further regulation in areas like healthcare and consumer rights. These laws are designed to protect sensitive data and give individuals more control over their information, setting precedents that influence global data privacy practices.

In India, the growing reliance on digital platforms for commerce, communication, and governance has led to the development of the **DPDPA**. Enacted in 2023, this legislation is India's response to the increasing need for comprehensive data protection. The DPDPA lays out the framework for processing personal data and grants individuals rights concerning their personal information. It mandates that businesses obtain explicit consent for data collection and ensures that data is processed for specific, lawful purposes. One of the act's key features is its emphasis on data localization, requiring certain types of data to be stored within India, which enhances national security and data sovereignty.

The DPDPA also introduces accountability measures for organizations, requiring them to implement strong data security practices and appoint **data protection officers** (**DPOs**) to oversee compliance. The act applies to businesses that process the personal data of Indian citizens, regardless of where the company is located, demonstrating India's commitment to protecting the privacy of its citizens in the global digital economy. Non-compliance with the DPDPA can lead to significant fines, placing it in line with other stringent global data protection laws.

As data plays a pivotal role in shaping economies and societies, the significance of data protection laws will only grow. These regulations are not just about compliance; they are about building a safer digital ecosystem where trust is paramount. For organizations, adhering to data protection laws is now an essential part of their risk management and governance strategies, ensuring they can safeguard personal information while fostering innovation and growth in the digital age.

Compliance and regulatory challenges

In an increasingly connected and data-driven world, compliance and regulatory challenges have become critical aspects of organizational governance, particularly in the realm of CyberSecurity. With the rise in sophisticated cyber attacks, governments and regulatory bodies across the globe have implemented a wide range of laws and standards to protect personal data, ensure the integrity of information systems, and promote the responsible handling of digital assets. Skilled resources are essential to manage and address CyberSecurity compliance and non-compliance issues effectively.

For organizations, navigating these complex regulatory landscapes can be daunting. They must meet industry-specific requirements and adapt to the evolving nature of data privacy laws across jurisdictions. Compliance is no longer just a matter of securing systems but also proving, through documentation and audits, that security measures are in place and consistently enforced. Balancing the need for security while meeting regulatory obligations, particularly in highly regulated industries such as finance, healthcare, and technology, can be challenging. Organizations must adopt robust **governance, risk, and compliance** (**GRC**) strategies to stay ahead of emerging regulations and avoid penalties, ensuring long-term business sustainability and operational continuity.

Impact of non-compliance on businesses

Non-compliance with CyberSecurity regulations can devastate businesses, extending far beyond legal fines. Failing to adhere to CyberSecurity and data protection laws can lead to financial, operational, and reputational damage in an era where data is an asset. Financial penalties imposed by regulators can be steep, with organizations facing multi-million-dollar fines for significant breaches of regulations such as GDPR, HIPAA, or PCI-DSS. However, the costs extend beyond fines; non-compliance often results in operational disruptions, mainly when businesses must halt operations to address security incidents or implement corrective measures. Additionally, reputational damage can be even more costly. Breaches of trust resulting from non-compliance erode customer loyalty and may lead to a loss of business. Publicized data breaches or incidents of non-compliance often trigger lawsuits, resulting in further legal and financial repercussions. Beyond the immediate impact, non-compliance can also prevent a business from forming strategic partnerships or entering new markets, where adherence to CyberSecurity regulations is a prerequisite. In this environment, compliance costs are always far less than the potential consequences of non-compliance, making CyberSecurity governance a critical business priority.

Key compliance frameworks and regulatory standards

Several key regulatory frameworks govern CyberSecurity across different sectors, each with specific requirements to protect sensitive information. Some of the most influential frameworks include the GDPR, HIPAA, PCI-DSS, and CCPA. In this section, we will delve into the core components of these regulations and their impact on businesses.

General Data Protection Regulation

The GDPR, which came into effect in May 2018, is a comprehensive data protection regulation that applies to all organizations processing personal data of **European Union** (**EU**) residents, regardless of the organization's location. Its primary focus is to give individuals greater control over their data and to impose stringent requirements on organizations that collect, process, or store such data.

The GDPR is built around several key principles that organizations must adhere to, including:

- **Lawfulness, fairness, and transparency**: Organizations must process personal data lawfully and transparently.

- **Purpose limitation**: Data should be collected for specific, legitimate purposes and not processed in an incompatible manner.

- **Data minimization**: Organizations must collect only the necessary data for the intended purpose.

- **Accuracy**: Personal data must be kept accurate and up to date.

- **Storage limitation**: Data should be stored only for as long as necessary.

- **Integrity and confidentiality**: Organizations must ensure the security of personal data through appropriate technical and organizational measures.

GDPR also mandates that organizations implement mechanisms to secure personal data, such as **encryption, anonymization**, and **pseudonymization**. Furthermore, organizations must conduct regular **Data Protection Impact Assessments (DPIAs)** and appoint a **Data Protection Officer (DPO)** if they engage in large-scale processing of personal data.

Consequences of non-compliance: Non-compliance with GDPR can result in hefty fines, with penalties reaching up to €20 million or 4% of an organization's global annual revenue, whichever is higher. The regulation's enforcement mechanisms are stringent, with supervisory authorities across the EU empowered to investigate and impose penalties for violations.

Health Insurance Portability and Accountability Act

HIPAA, established in 1996, is a U.S. regulation designed to protect the privacy and security of healthcare information. It applies to **covered entities** (such as healthcare providers, health plans, and healthcare clearinghouses) and **business associates** that handle **protected health information (PHI)** on behalf of covered entities.

Security and privacy rules: HIPAA is composed of two primary rules that govern the protection of healthcare information:

- **The privacy rule**: Establishes standards for protecting PHI and grants individuals rights over their health information, including the right to access their data.

- **The security rule**: Specifies the administrative, physical, and technical safeguards covered entities and business associates must implement to ensure the confidentiality, integrity, and availability of **electronic PHI (ePHI)**. These include:

  o **Administrative safeguards**: Risk analysis, workforce training, and access controls.

- Physical safeguards: Facility access controls, workstation security, and device management.

- Technical safeguards: Encryption, audit controls, and integrity controls.

Consequences of non-compliance: HIPAA violations can result in civil and criminal penalties, with fines ranging from $100 to $50,000 per violation, depending on the severity and intent of the breach. Criminal charges can lead to imprisonment for up to 10 years in cases of willful neglect.

Payment Card Industry Data Security Standard

PCI-DSS is a set of security standards designed to protect cardholder data and reduce fraud in the payment card industry. The standard applies to organizations that process, store, or transmit payment card data.

Safeguarding payment card information: PCI-DSS includes 12 core requirements, which are organized into six control objectives:

- **Build and maintain a secure network**: Install and maintain a firewall configuration and avoid using vendor-supplied defaults.

- **Protect cardholder data**: Use encryption to protect data at rest and in transit.

- **Maintain a vulnerability management program**: Implement anti-virus programs and develop secure systems and applications.

- **Implement strong access control measures**: Restrict access to cardholder data only to those needing it.

- **Monitor and test networks**: Track and monitor all access to network resources and cardholder data.

- **Maintain an information security policy**: Develop and maintain one that addresses information security.

Consequences of non-compliance: Non-compliance with PCI-DSS can result in significant fines from payment card brands, the termination of the organization's ability to process card payments, and an increased risk of data breaches.

California Consumer Privacy Act

The CCPA, which went into effect in January 2020, grants California residents significant privacy rights over their personal information. The law applies to organizations that collect personal data from California residents and meet specific revenue or data processing thresholds.

Data rights for consumers: The CCPA provides California residents with the following rights:

- **The right to know** what personal information is collected, used, or shared.

- **The right to access** their personal information.

- **The right to request deletion** of their data.

- **The right to opt out** of the sale of personal information.

Consequences of non-compliance: Violations of the CCPA can lead to civil penalties of up to $7,500 per intentional violation, and individuals have the right to sue for data breaches under certain conditions.

Table 6.2 provides vital information on various compliance and regulatory standards:

Framework/ standard	Primary focus	Industry/application	Key requirements
GDPR	Protects personal data of EU citizens and regulates data processing, collection, and transfer.	All organizations handling EU citizens' data.	Consent-based data collection, right to access/erasure, data breach notification.
HIPAA	Protects sensitive patient health information in the healthcare industry.	Healthcare providers, insurers, and related entities.	Safeguards for data security and privacy, breach notification, and audits.
PCI-DSS	Ensures secure handling of payment card information to prevent fraud and breaches.	Organizations that store, process, or transmit payment card data, including credit and debit cards	Encryption of cardholder data, secure network requirements, regular monitoring.
CCPA	Grants California consumers rights to control how businesses handle their personal information.	Any business operating in California handling consumer data.	Opt-out provisions, data transparency, and access requests.
ISO/IEC 270001	International standard for information security management, focusing on establishing, implementing, and maintaining ISMS.	Organizations of all sizes and industries.	Risk management, documentation of controls, continual improvement processes.

Table 6.2: Key details on global compliance standards

Integrating compliance into security policies

Organizations must develop security policies incorporating specific regulatory requirements to comply with global and regulatory frameworks. This involves mapping regulatory mandates to security controls and ensuring that policies are comprehensive, up-to-date, and enforceable. Organizations should also develop policies for log and data retention, audit trails, encryption, and access management **to meet regulatory requirements**.

Mapping regulatory requirements to security controls

One of the most effective ways to ensure compliance is by mapping regulatory requirements to specific security controls. This process involves analyzing the requirements of relevant regulations and determining which security controls are necessary to achieve compliance.

For example:

- GDPR requires that organizations implement encryption for personal data. This can be mapped to specific encryption policies within the organization.

- HIPAA mandates access controls for ePHI. This can be mapped to RBAC policies that limit access to sensitive healthcare data.

Organizations can create a clear and actionable roadmap for achieving compliance by mapping regulatory requirements to security controls.

Developing policies to ensure compliance

Compliance-focused security policies should address critical areas such as **data retention**, **encryption**, and **access management**. These policies should be aligned with regulatory requirements and integrated into the organization's security strategy.

- **Data retention policies**: These policies define how long data should be retained and when it should be deleted. Regulatory requirements may dictate specific retention periods for certain types of data, such as digital identity data and security logs

- **Encryption policies**: Encryption policies ensure that sensitive data is encrypted at rest and in transit, as required by regulations like GDPR and PCI-DSS.

- **Access management policies**: Access management policies define how access to sensitive data is controlled, including using RBAC, MFA, the need-to-know, and least privilege principles.

Tools and technologies to support regulatory compliance

Compliance can be complex and resource-intensive, but **tools and technologies** can help streamline the process. Organizations should consider leveraging technologies such as:

- **Governance, Risk, and Compliance (GRC)**: GRC tools help organizations manage governance, risk management, and compliance processes in a centralized platform. They streamline policy management, risk assessment, regulatory compliance tracking, control testing, and audit management. By integrating these functions, GRC tools enhance organizational efficiency, reduce risks, and ensure adherence to legal and regulatory standards. They provide near real-time visibility into compliance status, enabling informed decision-making and reducing the risk of fines and penalties.

- **Data loss prevention (DLP)**: DLP solutions are designed to detect and prevent data breaches by monitoring, detecting, and blocking sensitive data while in use, in motion, and at rest. They help organizations comply with data protection regulations by ensuring that sensitive information is not shared outside the corporate network. DLP tools can identify and classify sensitive data, enforce encryption, and apply policies to prevent unauthorized access or transmission. This helps protect intellectual property and maintain regulatory compliance.

- **Security Information and Event Management (SIEM)**: SIEM tools collect and analyze security-related data across an organization's IT infrastructure. They provide real-time monitoring, threat detection, and incident response capabilities. SIEM solutions aggregate logs and events from various sources, correlate them to identify potential security incidents, and generate alerts for security teams to investigate. SIEM tools help organizations meet regulatory requirements for monitoring and reporting security incidents by offering comprehensive visibility into security events.

- **Encryption solutions**: Encryption tools protect data by converting it into a secure format that authorized parties can only read. They are essential for ensuring data confidentiality and integrity in transit and at rest. Encryption helps organizations comply with regulations that mandate the protection of sensitive information, such as financial data, **personal identifiable information** (PII), and PHI. By using robust encryption algorithms and critical management practices, organizations can safeguard data against unauthorized access and breaches.

- **Identity and access management:** IAM solutions manage user identities and control access to critical systems and data. They ensure that only authorized users can access specific resources based on their roles and responsibilities. IAM tools include **single sign-on** (SSO), MFA, and access governance. IAM solutions help organizations comply with regulatory requirements for data protection and access management by enforcing strict access controls and monitoring user activities.

- **Endpoint Detection and Response (EDR):** EDR tools provide continuous monitoring and response capabilities for endpoint devices such as laptops, desktops, and servers. They detect and investigate suspicious activities, provide real-time threat intelligence, and automate response actions to mitigate threats. EDR solutions help organizations comply with regulations that require proactive threat detection and incident response. By protecting endpoints, EDR tools enhance overall security posture and reduce the risk of data breaches.

- **Vulnerability management:** Vulnerability management tools identify, assess, and prioritize vulnerabilities in an organization's IT environment. They scan systems, applications, and networks for known vulnerabilities and provide recommendations for remediation. By regularly assessing and addressing vulnerabilities, organizations can reduce their attack surface and comply with regulatory requirements for vulnerability management. These tools also help maintain up-to-date security patches and configurations.

By leveraging these tools, organizations can automate many aspects of compliance and reduce the risk of human error.

Global compliance considerations

Organizations that operate in multiple jurisdictions must navigate the complexities of complying with different regulations across borders. This section explores the challenges of managing compliance globally and provides strategies for aligning with emerging global standards:

- **Managing compliance across multiple jurisdictions:** Different countries and regions have regulatory frameworks for data protection, and organizations must ensure they comply with all applicable regulations. This can be particularly challenging when dealing with **international data transfers** and **cross-border compliance**. The GDPR, for example, places strict limitations on transferring personal data outside the EU, while the CCPA imposes its requirements for protecting the data of California residents.

  Organizations must be prepared to implement different compliance strategies depending on the jurisdiction in which they operate.

- **Understanding international data transfer rules:** One of the most significant challenges for global organizations is complying with international data transfer rules. GDPR, for instance, requires that personal data be transferred only to countries that provide adequate data protection or through mechanisms like **Standard Contractual Clauses** (**SCCs**) or **Binding Corporate Rules** (**BCRs**).

- **Aligning with emerging global standards:** In addition to established regulations like GDPR and HIPAA, new data protection laws are emerging worldwide. One notable example is India's DPDPA, which imposes data protection requirements similar to GDPR requirements. As new regulations emerge, organizations must stay informed and adjust their compliance strategies accordingly.

Mitigating risks and penalties for non-compliance

Non-compliance with regulatory requirements can result in significant financial and legal penalties. In this section, we explore the potential consequences of non-compliance and provide strategies for mitigating the associated risks:

- **Financial and legal consequences of non-compliance:** Non-compliance with regulations can result in **financial penalties**, **legal actions**, and **reputational damage**. In addition to fines, organizations may face lawsuits from affected individuals or regulatory authorities. In some cases, non-compliance can also result in the suspension of business operations.

- **Real-world case studies of compliance failures:** Examining real-world examples of compliance failures can provide valuable insights into non-compliance risks. For example:

  o **British Airways:** In 2018, British Airways was fined £20 million under GDPR for failing to prevent a data breach that compromised the personal data of over 400,000 customers.

  o **Target:** In 2013, Target suffered a data breach that exposed the credit card information of 40 million customers. The company ultimately paid $18.5 million in fines and settlements.

- **Strategies for responding to non-compliance incidents:**

  o Responding to non-compliant CyberSecurity incidents requires a structured, proactive approach to mitigate risks, prevent further damage, and maintain regulatory adherence. First, organizations should establish a well-defined incident response plan, ensuring that every stakeholder knows their role in the event of a breach or non-compliance issue. This includes setting up a dedicated incident response team capable of quickly identifying, containing, and remedying the problem.

  o Next, timely communication is crucial. Affected parties, including customers, regulatory bodies, and business partners, must be informed promptly to minimize service disruptions, damage to reputation, and legal exposure. Transparency ensures regulatory compliance and demonstrates a responsible approach to data protection.

  o Forensic investigation is crucial in identifying the incident's root cause and understanding how the non-compliance occurred. This helps not only resolve the immediate issue but also prevent similar incidents in the future.

  o Finally, organizations should implement corrective actions and preventive measures, such as policy adjustments, security enhancements, and additional staff training, to address the vulnerabilities that led to the incident. Regular audits and continuous monitoring should be followed to maintain compliance in the future. Lessons learned from security incidents are crucial for improving an organization's CyberSecurity posture.

Building a culture of compliance

Achieving long-term compliance requires more than just implementing security controls; it requires building a **culture of compliance** throughout the organization. This section explores how to foster a compliance-first mindset at all levels of the organization.

- **Establishing accountability for compliance:** To build a culture of compliance, organizations must establish clear accountability at every level. This includes appointing a **Chief Compliance Officer (CCO)** or similar role to oversee compliance efforts and ensure policies are followed.

- **Continuous monitoring and updating of compliance-related policies:** Compliance is not a one-time effort; it requires continuous monitoring and updating of policies to keep up with changing regulations and emerging threats. Regular audits and assessments should be conducted to ensure that the organization complies with relevant regulations.

- **Employee training on compliance and ethical responsibilities:** Training employees on compliance and ethical responsibilities is essential for building a culture of compliance. Employees should be regularly educated on the importance of data protection, non-compliance risks, and their role in maintaining compliance.

    In an increasingly regulated digital landscape, CyberSecurity compliance is not optional; it is essential for the survival of any organization. From GDPR to HIPAA, organizations must navigate a complex web of regulatory frameworks to protect sensitive data and avoid severe penalties. By integrating compliance into security policies, leveraging the right tools and technologies, and fostering a culture of compliance, organizations can meet regulatory requirements and strengthen their overall CyberSecurity posture.

Security awareness and training

The weakest link in any CyberSecurity system is often the human factor; a well-trained workforce can transform a vulnerability into your greatest defense.

In today's digital age, organizations face an ever-growing number of cyber threats, and even the most advanced security technologies can be rendered ineffective if employees are not adequately trained to recognize and respond to these risks. The human factor remains one of the most significant vulnerabilities in any CyberSecurity system, and many cyber attacks succeed not due to weaknesses in technical infrastructure but because of human error. Social engineering attacks like phishing exploit employees' lack of awareness, making them an attractive target for attackers.

Importance of security awareness training

A comprehensive **security awareness and training program** serves as the **first line of defense** against such threats. These programs educate employees on security policies, raise awareness of potential threats, and equip them with the tools and knowledge to protect the organization from cyber attacks. However, to be effective, security awareness must go beyond basic training; it needs to be a continuous effort engaging and relevant to the organization's evolving security landscape.

In this section, we will explore building and maintaining adequate security awareness programs using a combination of training methods tailored to various organizational roles. We will discuss how to make training engaging, assess its effectiveness, and address the challenges organizations often face in implementing these programs.

Role of employees in CyberSecurity defense

Employees play a **pivotal** role in CyberSecurity defense as they are often the first line of defense against attacks. Hackers and cyber criminals frequently target employees through phishing, social engineering, and malicious email attachments. These methods rely on exploiting human error rather than technical vulnerabilities. For this reason, a well-informed and vigilant workforce can prevent many cyber incidents from occurring in the first place. When employees are trained to recognize phishing emails, dubious links, or suspicious requests for information, they can help stop attacks before they penetrate the organization's network.

Each employee, regardless of their department or seniority, holds responsibility for maintaining CyberSecurity. For example, IT staff are trained to protect infrastructure and respond to technical incidents. At the same time, employees in non-technical roles must understand how to handle sensitive information, follow access control policies, and use secure communication channels. When employees know their specific role in the security landscape, they can make informed decisions that reduce the risk of human error. They can also assist in detecting anomalies or unusual activity, contributing to an organization-wide defense strategy.

Additionally, a culture of shared responsibility in CyberSecurity makes employees feel accountable and engaged in protecting the company. This also fosters better collaboration between technical and non-technical teams, making CyberSecurity a collective effort. Ultimately, an organization that empowers its employees to be proactive in defense has a more robust and resilient security posture.

Common security risks tied to human error

Human error remains one of the leading causes of CyberSecurity breaches, accounting for a significant percentage of incidents worldwide. Even the most well-secured systems can be compromised due to mistakes employees make, often unknowingly. Common security risks tied to human error include weak passwords, improper handling of sensitive data, falling victim to phishing attacks, and failing to adhere to security protocols.

Weak passwords are a frequent vulnerability. Many employees use simple, easily guessable passwords or reuse the same passwords across multiple accounts, making it easier for cyber criminals to gain access to critical systems. Another common mistake is mishandling sensitive information by sending confidential data via unsecured channels, leaving devices unattended, or sharing sensitive documents without encryption. These actions expose the organization to data breaches and identity theft.

Phishing attacks are among the most prevalent methods cyber criminals use to exploit human error. These attacks involve tricking employees into clicking malicious links or providing confidential information under false pretenses. Employees who are not adequately trained in recognizing these scams can inadvertently allow attackers to access the organization's network.

Moreover, failing to follow security protocols can have serious consequences. This includes neglecting to apply software updates or using unauthorized devices and applications that may not meet the organization's security standards. Human error can also manifest more subtly, such as not reporting suspicious activity and allowing threats to go undetected for extended periods. Therefore, addressing these risks through targeted security awareness training is crucial to reducing human-related vulnerabilities.

Security awareness is a continuous effort

CyberSecurity is an ever-evolving field, with new threats emerging constantly. As attackers become more sophisticated, organizations must ensure their security awareness efforts keep pace. This is why security awareness must be a continuous, ongoing effort rather than a one-time training event. Regular, updated training programs help employees stay informed about the latest threats, emerging attack methods, and the best practices to defend against them.

A continuous security awareness effort ensures that employees retain critical security knowledge and develop the instincts to recognize and respond to security risks. Over time, regular training and simulations help embed CyberSecurity principles into the organizational culture, making security a natural part of employees' day-to-day activities. Continuous education also provides opportunities to update employees on any changes to company policies, legal regulations, and industry standards. For example, new data privacy laws or emerging phishing techniques may require adjustments in how employees manage sensitive information.

Frequent training also helps to keep CyberSecurity at the forefront of employees' minds. Without regular reminders, security practices can become lax, and employees may revert to unsafe behaviors. By incorporating a continuous cycle of learning, testing (such as phishing simulations), and feedback, organizations can identify gaps in their security posture and address them before they result in security incidents.

Continuous security awareness creates an environment of vigilance and accountability, where employees feel empowered to report potential threats and security concerns. This collaborative approach enhances the organization's overall resilience to attacks. Security awareness is critical to maintaining a solid and adaptive defense in a world where the threat landscape constantly shifts.

Building an effective security awareness program

Building an effective security awareness program is a multi-faceted task. The key to success lies in designing a program relevant to the employees' day-to-day activities, addressing real-world threats, and providing practical guidance on mitigating risks. Major factors contributing to identifying suitable Security awareness programs are as follows:

- **Identifying key areas for training:** Every security awareness program should identify the key areas where employees are most vulnerable. **Phishing** is the most common attack vector, making phishing awareness and detection skills crucial. Other important areas include the following:

    o **Social engineering**: Employees should understand how attackers use psychological manipulation to gain sensitive information.

    o **Password management**: Weak and reused passwords are a common vulnerability. Training should cover the importance of strong passwords, password management tools, and MFA.

    o **Physical security**: Employees must be trained to secure physical assets, such as laptops and smartphones, and ensure that confidential information is not left in unsecured locations.

    o **Data protection**: It is essential to understand how to handle sensitive data, especially personal and financial information, in accordance with regulatory requirements (for example, GDPR or HIPAA).

- **Establishing a baseline understanding of security across the workforce:** Before launching a full-scale security awareness program, it is crucial to assess the organization's current security knowledge level. This baseline will help identify gaps in understanding and target training efforts more effectively. Organizations can use surveys, quizzes, and focus groups to assess employees' awareness of security issues and their ability to identify and mitigate threats.

- **Tailoring programs for different roles and departments:** Not all employees face the same security risks. For example, those in finance or HR departments may deal with sensitive personal or financial data. At the same time, IT staff must be trained on secure system configurations and managing privileged access. By tailoring security awareness programs to the specific roles and responsibilities of employees, organizations can ensure that training is both relevant and practical. Additionally, creating customized programs for different departments or teams will make employees more engaged, as they will see the direct impact of the training on their daily activities.

Engaging training methods

Traditional security awareness training programs often fail because they are dull and repetitive and do not engage employees. A successful program must captivate employees and make learning an interactive and enjoyable experience. Some methods are as follows:

- **Gamification and interactive learning:** One effective method to engage employees is through **gamification**, the use of game-like elements in training. This could include leaderboards, rewards for completing security challenges, or simulations that put employees in real-world scenarios where they must make security decisions. Gamification encourages competition and participation, transforming what might otherwise be a dry subject into an engaging and enjoyable experience.

- **Phishing simulations and their effectiveness:** Phishing simulations are an increasingly popular tool in security awareness programs. These simulations involve sending fake phishing emails to employees to see how they respond. The results can help assess how well employees can identify phishing attempts and provide insight into which areas of the organization are most vulnerable. Additionally, phishing simulations offer a **teachable moment**—if an employee falls for a simulated phishing email, immediate feedback can be given to reinforce the correct behavior.

- **Role-playing incident response scenarios:** Another effective teaching method is role-playing exercises, where employees act out different roles in a simulated security incident. For example, an incident response scenario could involve a ransomware attack where employees must decide how to respond, whom to notify, and what steps to take to contain the breach. These exercises not only build knowledge but also improve collaboration and communication skills in the event of an actual incident.

- **Security posters and screensavers:** Physical security awareness posters and security screensavers are potent tools for reinforcing CyberSecurity messages within an organization. These posters are strategically placed in high-traffic areas such as break rooms, hallways, and near elevators, ensuring maximum visibility. They serve as constant reminders of crucial security practices and policies, helping to keep CyberSecurity at the top of employees' minds. Effective security posters are visually appealing and convey clear, concise messages. They often use bold graphics and simple language to highlight essential security tips, such as strong passwords, recognizing phishing attempts, and safeguarding sensitive information. By regularly updating the content of these posters, organizations can address emerging threats and keep the information relevant.

- **Incorporating real-life breach case studies:** Another way to make training more engaging is by incorporating real-life case studies of well-known data breaches.

By examining the causes and consequences of these breaches, employees can better understand the impact of security failures and the importance of following security best practices.

Table 6.3 provides information regarding various training methods that can be opted by organizations:

Training methods	Description	Benefits	Example
Gamification	Incorporates game-like elements, such as challenges and leaderboards, into the training to increase engagement.	Boosts participation, makes learning fun and encourages friendly competition.	A leaderboard for employees who report the most phishing emails correctly.
Phishing simulations	Sends simulated phishing emails to employees to test their ability to recognize and avoid phishing attacks.	Provides real-world practice and immediate feedback to improve phishing detection skills.	Monthly fake phishing email tests, with post-simulation results sent to employees.
Role-playing scenarios	Simulates a real-world incident, allowing employees to act out their roles in response to a security breach.	Enhances readiness by practicing incident response protocols in a controlled environment.	A tabletop exercise simulating a ransomware attack.
Security posters and screensavers	It creates a multi-faceted approach to CyberSecurity awareness.	Employees are consistently reminded of security best practices.	Posters in office high-traffic areas and screensaver on Laptops
Case studies of breaches	Analyses well-known security breaches to illustrate the consequences of poor security practices.	Demonstrates the real-world impact of security failures and reinforces the importance of best practices.	A case study on the Equifax breach, highlighting lessons on patch management and data protection.

Table 6.3: Various security awareness and training methods

Measuring training effectiveness

An essential part of any security awareness program is the ability to measure its effectiveness. Without clear metrics, it is impossible to know whether the program works or if employees retain the information. The importance of metrics is as outlined:

- **Metrics to assess behavioral change and risk reduction:** Security awareness training aims to reduce risk by changing employee behavior. Metrics such as the click rate on phishing simulations, the number of security incidents reported by employees, and the time taken to report incidents can all be used to measure the program's effectiveness. Over time, organizations should see a decline in risky behaviors and an increase in proactive security measures.

- **Tools to monitor training completion and engagement: Learning management systems (LMS)** are commonly used to track training completion rates and engagement. These systems can provide data on which employees have completed the training, how well they performed on quizzes or assessments, and how engaged they were during the sessions. This data can be used to identify areas where additional training may be needed or to reward employees who consistently demonstrate good security practices.

- **Continuous assessment through surveys and feedback loops:** Security awareness training should not be a one-time event; it should be continuously assessed and improved. Regular surveys and feedback loops allow employees to share their experiences with the training program, identify areas for improvement, and suggest new topics for future training sessions. Additionally, security teams can use feedback to refine the content and delivery methods to make the training more effective. The following table provides key metrics by which security training effectiveness can be measured:

Metric	Description	Purpose	Example
Phishing simulation click rate	The percentage of employees who clicked on phishing simulation emails.	Measures employee susceptibility to phishing attacks and the effectiveness of phishing awareness training.	After a phishing simulation, 20% of employees clicked on the malicious link.
Training completion rate	The percentage of employees who have completed assigned security awareness training modules.	Tracks participation and ensures employees are compliant with training requirements.	95% of employees completed the mandatory annual security awareness training.
Incident reporting rate	The number of potential security incidents reported by employees.	Encourages proactive behavior and helps measure how aware employees are of security threats in real-time.	A rise in the number of reported phishing attempts following a phishing awareness campaign.
Behavioral change metrics	Tracks changes in employee behavior over time, such as improved password management practices or reduced risky behavior.	Evaluates the long-term impact of security training on actual behavior in day-to-day tasks.	75% of employees now use multifactor authentication for system access, up from 50% before training.

Table 6.4: Key metrics for evaluating the effectiveness of security awareness training

Specialized training for key roles

While all employees should receive general security awareness training, specific organizational roles require specialized training. The recommended trainings for dedicated Organization segments are mentioned here:

- **Executive and management training on CyberSecurity risks and responsibilities:** Executives and senior managers need a clear understanding of their responsibilities regarding CyberSecurity. Their decisions often have significant security implications, and they must be aware of the potential risks associated with strategic decisions, such as adopting new technologies or entering new markets. The importance of this training lies in its ability to enhance decision-making, ensure regulatory compliance, and foster a proactive approach to risk management. Well-informed executives can lead practical incident response efforts, make strategic decisions that balance business objectives with security needs, and set a tone for a culture of security awareness throughout the organization. This comprehensive approach helps build a resilient organization capable of withstanding and quickly recovering from cyber threats. Specialized training for executives should focus on:

  o Cyber risk management

  o Regulatory compliance

  o Incident response decision-making

  o Business continuity planning

  o Fostering a security culture

- **Role-based training for IT, security, and data handling staff:** Role-based training is essential for ensuring that employees in specific roles understand the unique CyberSecurity risks and responsibilities associated with their positions. This targeted approach enhances the organization's overall security posture by providing relevant and practical knowledge. Their training should cover:

  o Secure system configurations

  o Vulnerability management

  o Data encryption

  o Identity and access management

  o Incident detection and response

  Role-based training ensures that key personnel have the technical skills to implement and manage the organization's security infrastructure.

- **Developing security champions across departments:** A **security champion** is an employee who advocates for security within their department and helps raise awareness among their colleagues. Security champions can act as the first line of defense, promoting best practices and encouraging others to follow security protocols. By identifying and training security champions in each department, organizations can create a distributed network of security advocates who contribute to a culture of security awareness.

Sustaining a culture of security awareness

Creating a culture of security awareness requires ongoing effort. Organizations must continuously update their training programs, encourage employees to report potential security incidents, and celebrate security achievements to maintain engagement. The awareness culture can be achieved by following these recommendations:

- **Regular updates to training based on evolving threats:** CyberSecurity threats are constantly evolving, and so should security awareness programs. New training modules should be introduced regularly to address emerging threats, such as new phishing tactics or the rise of ransomware. By keeping the content fresh and relevant, organizations can ensure that employees remain vigilant and informed.

- **Encouraging a reporting culture for potential security incidents:** Employees should feel comfortable reporting potential security incidents without fear of punishment. Encouraging a reporting culture helps detect and respond to threats more quickly and reinforces the importance of security throughout the organization. Employees should be reminded that reporting suspicious activity is key to maintaining the organization's security.

- **Celebrating security milestones and fostering positive reinforcement:** Celebrating security achievements, such as reaching a milestone of zero phishing incidents or completing a significant security training initiative, can help foster a positive security culture. Recognizing and rewarding employees who consistently demonstrate sound security practices encourages others to follow suit. Positive reinforcement effectively motivates employees and builds a sense of ownership in the organization's security efforts.

Challenges and solutions in security training

Implementing an effective security awareness program is not without its challenges. Organizations often face resistance from employees, difficulty catering to diverse learning needs, and the logistical challenges of training a remote or hybrid workforce. The significant challenges and solutions faced by the information security team are mentioned here:

- **Overcoming employee resistance and fatigue:** Employees may resist security training because they view it as time-consuming or irrelevant to their role. Organizations should communicate the importance of security awareness and tie training directly to the employee's day-to-day activities to overcome this resistance. Additionally, engaging and interactive training can help reduce fatigue and motivate employees to learn.

- **Addressing diverse learning needs and levels of technical understanding:** Not all employees have the same technical expertise, and security training must be tailored to address these differences. Offering multiple formats, such as video tutorials, interactive simulations, and written guides, ensures that employees with varying learning preferences and technical abilities can engage with the content effectively.

- **Ensuring remote and hybrid workforce participation in training programs:** With more employees working remotely or in hybrid environments, ensuring everyone participates in security training can be challenging. Virtual training platforms, webinars, and online simulations allow remote employees to participate in the same training as their in-office counterparts. It is also essential to address the unique security challenges of remote work, such as securing home networks and managing devices in multiple locations.

Security awareness and training are essential components of any organization's CyberSecurity strategy. By building a comprehensive and engaging security awareness program, tailoring training to different roles, and continuously assessing its effectiveness, organizations can significantly reduce the risk of human error and strengthen their overall security posture. In a world where cyber threats constantly evolve, the human factor remains the most unpredictable and potentially most dangerous element of the security landscape. However, with the proper training and awareness programs, employees can transform from a weak link into one of the most robust defenses against cyber attacks.

Role of Information Security team

The **information security (Infosec)** team is critical in preparing and implementing any organization's policies, procedures, and guidelines. Their expertise ensures that security frameworks are aligned with industry standards, regulatory requirements, and the business's unique needs. The Infosec team is responsible for developing and enforcing security policies that govern access control, data protection, incident response, and third-party risk management. They also ensure that procedures are documented and scalable to address evolving threats and organizational growth. Beyond policy development, the Infosec team is crucial in driving security awareness training programs and helping embed a CyberSecurity vigilance culture throughout the organization. By continuously educating employees on best practices, common risks like phishing and social engineering, and their responsibilities, the Infosec team transforms the workforce into active participants in the defense of the organization's information assets. Their efforts safeguard critical data and help reduce the risk of human error, ensuring that the security posture remains robust and adaptive in the face of emerging cyber threats.

Conclusion

The chapter underscores the foundational role of security policy frameworks in safeguarding an organization's digital assets. Policies, procedures, and guidelines create a structured approach to managing risks, ensuring regulatory compliance, and aligning security efforts with business goals. Additionally, the chapter highlights the necessity of security awareness programs to counter human error, which often poses the most significant CyberSecurity risk. Organizations can fortify their defenses by promoting continuous education and vigilance among employees. The information security team is central to developing, implementing, and monitoring these policies and training programs, ensuring a proactive security culture that evolves with emerging threats.

Points to remember

- **Security policy framework:** A well-defined security policy framework is crucial for managing risks and aligning CyberSecurity measures with organizational goals.

- **Regulatory compliance**: Compliance with GDPR, HIPAA, and DPDPA regulations is essential to avoid legal and financial repercussions and ensure data protection and privacy.

- **Regular updates:** Security policies must be regularly reviewed and updated to adapt to evolving cyber threats, emerging technologies, and new regulatory requirements.

- **Human factor:** Security awareness programs are essential in minimizing human error, one of the most common causes of CyberSecurity breaches.

- **Security awareness and training:** Security awareness programs help reduce risks caused by human error, a leading CyberSecurity threat. Tailored training ensures different organizational roles are adequately prepared for specific security challenges.

- **Information security team**: The Infosec team plays a pivotal role in developing, enforcing, and updating policies and promoting continuous security awareness across the organization.

CHAPTER 7
Incident Response

Introduction

Incident response is not just about managing crises; it is the art of anticipation, coordination, and strategic recovery that defines the resilience of any organization.

Incident response is a critical function in CyberSecurity that ensures organizations effectively deal with security breaches and minimize damage. A well-structured **incident response** (**IR**) process can significantly reduce recovery time and associated costs while preventing future attacks. With the growing complexity of threats, organizations need to be agile and adaptable, employing a combination of detection, response, and recovery strategies. This chapter focuses on the critical aspects of incident response, offering technical and managerial insights into creating robust defense mechanisms against cyberattacks. The following figure is a symbolic image of a security professional handling an incident:

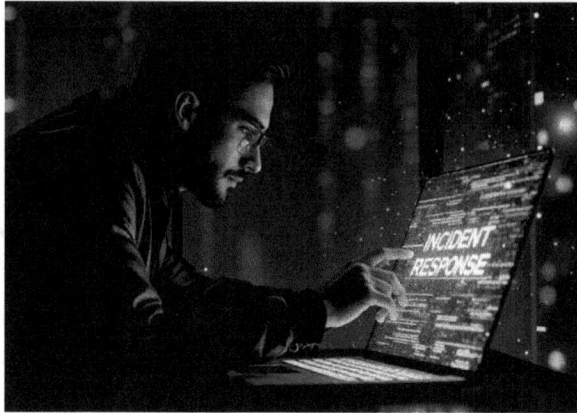

Figure 7.1 *Incident response*

Structure

The following sections will be covered:

- Threat hunting and intelligence
- Establishing an incident response team
- Incident identification and classification
- Containment and eradication
- Recovery and lessons learned
- Testing and training for effective incident response

Objectives

This chapter, *incident response,* provides a holistic view of the entire IR lifecycle, emphasizing both proactive and reactive strategies. It begins by exploring how threat hunting and CTI contribute to anticipating and mitigating risks before incidents occur. Establishing an **incident response team** (**IRT**) with clear roles and responsibilities is critical for a coordinated defense. The chapter also covers incident identification and classification, highlighting the need for rapid detection and accurate categorization to ensure an appropriate response. Containment and eradication steps are discussed in detail, focusing on limiting damage and removing environmental threats. Recovery processes, including system restoration and **post-incident analysis** (**PIA**), are essential to resume normal operations and identify lessons learned for future prevention. Lastly, the chapter underscores the importance of regular testing, simulations, and training to maintain a state of readiness. By the end of this chapter, readers will understand how to create, manage, and optimize an effective IR strategy, ensuring organizational resilience in the face of evolving CyberSecurity threats.

Threat hunting and intelligence

Intelligence-driven defense can be the difference between a controlled event and a crippling breach.

As cyberattacks grow in sophistication, traditional reactive approaches to CyberSecurity are no longer sufficient to defend modern enterprises. Waiting for an attack to happen and responding is often too late, especially when dealing with **advanced persistent threats (APTs)**, zero-day exploits, and stealthy malware. Proactivity is essential, where **threat hunting** and **cyber threat intelligence (CTI)** are critical.

Threat hunting is a proactive CyberSecurity practice that involves actively searching for signs of compromise or malicious activity that may have evaded traditional security defenses. Instead of relying solely on automated alerts or pre-configured rules, skilled CyberSecurity professionals utilize a mix of human expertise and advanced tools to uncover hidden threats that can bypass traditional defenses.

On the other hand, threat intelligence provides critical context about adversaries, attack techniques, and vulnerabilities. It is about identifying threats, predicting future attacks, and preparing defenses accordingly. This intelligence-driven approach allows organizations to anticipate attacks and act before damage occurs. By integrating threat hunting with CTI, organizations can create a powerful, unified defense that can detect and mitigate even the most advanced cyber threats before they cause harm.

In this section, we will study the concept of threat hunting, explore the different categories of CTI, and examine how these elements come together to form an integrated defense strategy. We will also review the tools, techniques, and skills that CyberSecurity professionals use to stay ahead of attackers.

Threat hunting concept and its importance

Threat hunting is the active search for potential threats or abnormal activities within an organization's network that might indicate a breach. Unlike traditional automated security solutions that rely on rule-based detection mechanisms such as firewalls, **intrusion detection systems (IDS)**, and **security information and event management (SIEM)** systems, threat hunting emphasizes manual or semi-automated investigations driven by hypothesis-based explorations.

The goal of threat hunting is not only to detect known threats but also to discover unknown threats, like *living off the land* attacks, where attackers use legitimate tools and software to carry out their actions. These threats can bypass signature-based systems because they do not match known malware or attack patterns.

Proactive vs. reactive security

Traditional CyberSecurity models focus on reactive measures, waiting for an attack to be detected and then responding. This works well for known threats, but as attackers become more sophisticated, they are increasingly able to bypass traditional security controls.

Threat hunting fills this gap by adopting a proactive approach. Hunters do not wait for alerts to trigger their investigations; they actively seek anomalies, unusual behaviors, and potential breaches. This proactive stance is essential because it gives organizations the ability to detect stealthy attacks, APTs, and insider threats before they cause significant damage.

The importance of threat hunting is because of the following:

- **Detection of advanced threats**: Modern attackers often use tactics designed to bypass traditional detection mechanisms. Threat hunters seek out these advanced threats that automated systems might miss.

- **Improved incident response**: Threat hunting helps organizations identify the presence of an attack earlier, which allows for quicker and more effective incident response. The sooner a threat is detected, the less damage it can cause.

- **Reduced dwell time**: One of the key metrics in CyberSecurity is **dwell time**, which refers to the amount of time an attacker is present in the network before being detected. Threat hunting reduces dwell time by actively looking for threats instead of waiting for alerts.

- **Continuous learning and adaptation**: Threat hunting helps CyberSecurity teams learn more about emerging threats and adversary tactics. This knowledge allows them to refine their defenses, making future attacks harder to execute successfully.

- **Enhanced visibility**: Threat hunters explore parts of the network that may not be regularly monitored by automated tools, providing a clearer picture of the entire organizational ecosystem and identifying blind spots.

Understanding cyber threat intelligence

Cyber threat intelligence (CTI) refers to the information organizations gather about cyber threats, which helps them make informed decisions about defending against those threats. CTI provides context, mechanisms, indicators, implications, and actionable insights regarding current and emerging threats. Instead of focusing purely on the technical aspects of an attack, CTI offers a broader perspective on the threat landscape, including information on adversary motives, tactics, and plans.

Threat intelligence helps organizations transition from reactive defense to proactive strategies, allowing them to anticipate attacks, mitigate risks, and adjust defenses before exploitation. CTI is typically categorized into three levels: **strategic, operational, and tactical,** explained as follows:

- **Strategic threat intelligence:** Strategic intelligence offers a high-level view of the threat landscape and focuses on long-term trends, including adversary motives, geopolitical conditions, and emerging risks. It is typically used by senior management and decision-makers to guide CyberSecurity strategies, investments, and policy development.

Strategic intelligence is less focused on the technical specifics of individual attacks and more on understanding the broader context of cyber risks. For example, it may include reports on nation-state actors or evolving attack vectors that are relevant to a specific industry or sector.

- **Operational threat intelligence:** Operational intelligence is more specific than strategic intelligence and is focused on known threats, ongoing campaigns, and adversary tactics. It is designed to help incident responders and security teams understand the nature of threats actively targeting the organization or industry. Operational intelligence typically includes details about specific threat actors, their **tools, techniques, and procedures** (**TTPs**), and attack timelines.

  For example, operational intelligence might include information about a new ransomware campaign targeting a particular type of vulnerability in widely used software. This intelligence helps security teams prepare defenses or update IR plans accordingly.

- **Tactical threat intelligence:** Tactical intelligence is the most technical and granular form of CTI, focused on the **indicators of compromise** (**IOCs**), such as IP addresses, file hashes, domain names, and malware signatures. It is typically used by network defenders, SOC analysts, and threat hunters to identify and neutralize specific attacks directly.

  Tactical intelligence feeds into the threat-hunting process by providing data points that can be used to detect malicious activity. For example, if CTI reveals a specific domain used in phishing attacks, threat hunters can search for any traces of that domain in their organization's network traffic.

Integration with incident response

Threat hunting and threat intelligence largely contribute to the broader IR process in many ways, mentioned as follows:

- **Role of threat hunting and intelligence in incident response:** Both threat hunting and CTI play critical roles in enhancing the IR process. While IR is typically considered a reactive activity, dealing with incidents after they occur, threat hunting and intelligence bring a proactive element to the process by identifying potential threats before they escalate into full-blown incidents.

- **Proactive incident detection:** Threat hunting can help organizations detect an incident earlier in its lifecycle, allowing for faster containment and remediation. For instance, a threat hunter might discover a previously undetected breach by noticing suspicious behavior on a server or endpoint. This early detection can significantly reduce the impact of the incident by preventing data exfiltration or lateral movement within the network.

- **Informed decision-making with CTI:** Threat intelligence enriches the IR process by providing context about the nature of the threat. During an active incident, operational and tactical threat intelligence can help the IRT understand what kind of attack they are dealing with, which threat actor is likely behind it, and what defensive measures are most effective. This can speed up incident triage, reduce false positives, and ensure that the right resources are allocated to address the threat.

- **Reducing recovery time:** By integrating threat hunting and intelligence into the IR process, organizations can reduce the time required to recover from incidents. For example, if threat hunters can identify the tactics or tools being used in an attack, they can quickly develop specific containment strategies, thus minimizing the threat's ability to propagate further.

- **Continuous feedback loop:** Threat hunting and intelligence create a feedback loop that contributes to the continuous improvement of incident response. After an incident is resolved, the intelligence gathered is used to refine detection mechanisms, update threat-hunting techniques, and enhance response protocols. This learning process ensures that the organization is better prepared for future threats.

Tools and techniques for threat hunting

The effectiveness of threat hunting depends heavily on the tools and techniques used to gather, analyze, and interpret data. Various specialized tools, both commercial and open source, are available to aid threat hunters in their quest to identify potential threats. These tools typically fall into several categories, described as follows:

- **Endpoint Detection and Response (EDR):** EDR platforms are crucial tools for threat hunters. They provide visibility into endpoint activities and enable rapid detection of suspicious behavior. EDR solutions monitor endpoint processes, network connections, and file system changes, allowing threat hunters to detect malware, lateral movement, and other malicious activity. Popular EDR tools include **SentinelOne, CrowdStrike Falcon**, and **Microsoft Defender for Endpoint**.

- **Security information and event management (SIEM):** SIEM systems aggregate logs from various sources (such as firewalls, servers, and applications) and use predefined rules to detect anomalies and generate alerts. While SIEM platforms are often used for automated threat detection, they also play a critical role in threat hunting by providing a centralized repository of historical data that can be queried to identify patterns of suspicious activity. **LogRhythm, IBM QRadar**, and **Elastic Security** are well-known SIEM platforms.

- **Network traffic analysis (NTA):** Network traffic analysis tools monitor traffic across the organization's network and help identify anomalous patterns, such as unusual communication between internal systems and external IPs. NTA tools are particularly useful for identifying **command-and-control** (**C2**) communications, lateral movement, and data exfiltration. Popular NTA solutions include **Zscaler**, **Darktrace**, **Corelight**, and **Zeek** (formerly known as Bro).

- **Threat intelligence platforms (TIPs):** Threat intelligence platforms help collect, process, and analyze threat data from various sources. These platforms integrate external threat feeds with internal logs and data to provide a comprehensive view of the threat landscape. Threat hunters use TIPs to correlate known IOCs with observed activities in the network. Notable TIPs include **Cyble**, **ThreatConnect**, **Anomali**, and **Malware Information Sharing Platform** (**MISP**).

- **Forensic tools:** Forensic analysis is an integral part of threat hunting, especially in cases where threat hunters need to investigate suspicious files, logs, or endpoint artifacts. Tools such as **Autopsy**, **FTK (Forensic Toolkit)**, and **SIFT (SANS Investigative Forensics Toolkit)** allow threat hunters to conduct deep-dive investigations into potential security incidents.

Hunting techniques

There are various techniques that threat hunters employ to detect threats that have evaded traditional security controls. Some of the most used techniques include:

- **Hypothesis-driven hunting**: Threat hunters develop hypotheses based on observed behaviors, current intelligence, or past incidents. They then test these hypotheses by searching for evidence of malicious activity. For example, a hypothesis might be that a new zero-day vulnerability is being exploited in the wild, leading the hunter to search for specific IOCs related to the vulnerability.

- **TTP-based hunting**: Threat hunters focus on the TTPs of known adversaries. They use frameworks like **MITRE ATT&CK** to identify common patterns of attack and proactively search for signs that these TTPs are being used in their network.

- **Behavioral analysis**: Threat hunters look for unusual behaviors that could indicate malicious activity. This could include abnormal login patterns, unexpected file system changes, or unusual network traffic. Behavioral analysis is instrumental in identifying insider threats or attacks that use legitimate credentials to evade detection.

- **Anomaly detection**: Threat hunters use machine learning and statistical analysis to identify deviations from normal behavior patterns. For example, if a system that typically generates 10MB of outbound traffic per day suddenly generates 1GB of traffic, this could indicate data exfiltration. Anomaly detection tools can help identify such irregularities.

Human intelligence and skill

While tools and automation are essential components of modern CyberSecurity, they are not a substitute for human expertise. Threat hunting relies on the skill, intuition, and creativity of experienced CyberSecurity professionals who can interpret data, identify anomalies, and develop hypotheses about potential threats. These professionals bring unique skills, including deep technical knowledge, an understanding of the broader threat landscape, and the ability to think like an attacker.

The key skills for threat hunters are as follows:

- **Technical proficiency**: Threat hunters need a deep understanding of networking, operating systems, endpoint security, and malware analysis. They must use tools like SIEMs, EDRs, and forensic analysis platforms to gather and analyze data.

- **Adversarial thinking**: Effective threat hunters need to think like attackers. This means understanding cybercriminals' tactics, techniques, and procedures and anticipating their next move. Adversarial thinking is crucial for developing hypotheses and identifying weaknesses in the organization's defenses.

- **Problem-solving skills**: Threat hunters must be able to analyze complex data sets, identify patterns, and draw logical conclusions. They must approach each investigation methodically and think critically about the evidence they uncover.

- **Collaboration and communication**: Threat hunting is often a team effort, requiring close collaboration with other members of the security team, including incident responders, SOC analysts, and threat intelligence analysts. Effective communication ensures that discoveries made during threat-hunting are appropriately acted upon.

- **Adaptability and continuous learning**: The threat landscape is constantly evolving, and threat hunters need to stay updated with the latest threats, tools, and techniques. This requires continuous learning, attending security conferences, participating in online forums, and staying current with threat intelligence feeds.

Establishing an incident response team

The strength of an incident response is not just in the tools but in the people behind them.

The right tools and technologies are essential in the face of increasing cyber attacks. Still, the true backbone of any effective IR strategy lies in the people managing the incidents, the incident response team (IRT. Establishing a skilled and well-organized IRT can make the difference between successfully mitigating a security event and facing disastrous consequences, such as prolonged downtime, data loss, or damage to an organization's reputation.

This section focuses on building a competent IRT, detailing the essential roles, skills, and responsibilities required to address security breaches efficiently and minimize damage.

We will examine the critical importance of cross-functional expertise, covering various disciplines such as CyberSecurity, network administration, and legal advisement. Additionally, effective communication protocols are explored, emphasizing how internal and external communications during an incident can determine the overall success of a response effort. A well-coordinated IRT is the backbone of any IR effort. A symbolic image of the IRT is as follows:

Figure 7.2: Incident response team

We will also discuss the necessity of clear leadership within the IRT to ensure coordinated actions and decisive decision-making amid a crisis. Finally, this section highlights the importance of continuous training and development to ensure the team is prepared to handle standard and advanced cyber threats. By the end of this section, readers will understand how to build, manage, and optimize an IRT that is both technically proficient and capable of navigating the complexities of modern CyberSecurity threats.

Building the IRT

Cyber incidents come in many forms, from malware infections and phishing attacks to insider threats and full-scale data breaches. To effectively manage these diverse threats, organizations must have a well-structured IRT composed of individuals with specialized skills. The roles within an IRT must be clearly defined, and each team member should understand their responsibilities during an incident to ensure an organized and effective response.

Core roles in an IRT

The process of building an IRT begins with identifying the key roles that are necessary to manage different aspects of incident response. While the exact structure of an IRT can vary depending on the size and complexity of the organization, several core roles should be considered, as elaborated here:

- **Incident Response Manager (IRM):** The IRM oversees the entire response process, ensures that incidents are handled efficiently, and coordinates communication between team members. They make critical decisions regarding containment, mitigation, and recovery efforts. The IRM must deeply understand the organization's CyberSecurity policies, risk management protocols, and the operational impact of security incidents. This role requires strong leadership skills, the ability to make high-stakes decisions, and the capacity to manage team dynamics under pressure.

- **Security analysts:** Security analysts play a central role in identifying, analyzing, and mitigating threats. They monitor alerts, examine logs, and investigate unusual activity to determine whether a security event has occured. Security analysts are also responsible for performing forensics, collecting evidence, and assessing the scope of an incident. Depending on the organization, the IRT might have multiple security analysts specializing in different areas, such as network security, endpoint security, or malware analysis.

- **Network administrators:** Network administrators ensure the organization's network infrastructure is secure and functioning correctly. During incidents, they are often called upon to monitor network traffic, identify anomalies, and implement defensive measures, such as blocking malicious IP addresses or isolating compromised systems. Network administrators also work closely with security analysts to mitigate threats and restore affected network services.

- **System administrators:** System administrators are responsible for maintaining and securing the organization's IT infrastructure, including servers, applications, and databases. During an incident, they are tasked with identifying vulnerabilities, patching systems, and ensuring that compromised systems are restored and configured securely. System administrators also manage access controls and ensure that sensitive data is adequately protected.

- **Digital forensics experts:** Forensic experts are critical for investigating incidents involving data breaches or insider threats. They collect and analyze digital evidence to determine how an attack occurred, which systems were compromised, and what data may have been exfiltrated. Forensic experts also work to preserve evidence for legal or regulatory purposes.

- **Legal advisors:** Cyber incidents can have significant legal implications, especially if they involve customer data breaches, intellectual property theft, or violations of data protection laws. Legal advisors ensure that the organization complies with relevant regulations, such as the **General Data Protection Regulation (GDPR)** or the **Health Insurance Portability and Accountability Act (HIPAA)**. They also assist with reporting requirements, comply with regulatory timelines, and help prepare for any legal actions resulting from the incident.

- **Public Relations (PR) or communications specialists:** Effective communication during a cyber incident is essential to maintaining public trust and mitigating reputational damage. PR or communications specialists are responsible for crafting internal and external messages about the incident. This includes communicating with employees, customers, stakeholders, and the media, ensuring that messaging is clear, accurate, and aligned with the organization's response strategy.

- **Risk and compliance officers:** Risk and compliance officers ensure the organization adheres to its risk management policies and regulatory requirements. They assess incidents' potential business impact, evaluate the effectiveness of response efforts, and recommend improvements to security controls. Risk officers also manage relationships with external auditors or regulatory bodies.

Cross-functional expertise

An effective IRT must possess many skills to handle the diverse challenges that cyber incidents pose. This cross-functional expertise ensures the team can manage an incident's technical, legal, operational, and reputational aspects. It also allows the team to respond holistically to ensure that no critical aspect is overlooked.

While technical skills are critical for incident response, the value of having non-technical experts on the IRT cannot be overstated. For example, legal advisors ensure compliance with regulations, while communications specialists manage the flow of information to key stakeholders. This diverse skill set enables the IRT to address all aspects of an incident, from identifying and containing the threat to handling legal liabilities and maintaining the organization's public image. The critical benefits of cross-functional teams are as follows:

- **Holistic incident management:** Incidents affect multiple areas of an organization, from IT infrastructure to legal and public relations concerns. Experts from different fields ensure that the IRT can manage incidents from every angle.

- **Improved decision-making:** Cross-functional teams bring different perspectives to the table, which helps the team make more informed and well-rounded decisions. Technical experts can advise on the best containment strategies while legal advisors ensure compliance with data breach reporting laws.

- **Faster recovery:** Having a team with diverse skill sets allows the IRT to tackle multiple aspects of the incident simultaneously, resulting in a quicker and more effective response. For example, while security analysts mitigate the threat, PR specialists can communicate with stakeholders, and legal advisors can manage regulatory reporting.

Communication protocols

Effective communication is a cornerstone of successful incident response. A well-coordinated communication strategy ensures that all internal and external stakeholders are informed and that the response effort is aligned. Failure to communicate effectively can lead to confusion, delays, and even more significant damage to the organization.

Communication protocols are broadly segregated into internal and external communication protocols, explained as follows:

- **Internal communication protocols:** Within the organization, communication during an incident must be structured and efficient. Each member of the IRT needs to be informed of their specific role, and information about the incident must be disseminated quickly and accurately. Some key internal communication practices include:

  o **Incident updates:** All relevant stakeholders, including IT teams, senior leadership, and business units affected by the incident, should receive regular updates. These updates should include details about the incident's status, the steps being taken to contain it, and any additional actions required from specific teams.

  o **Escalation procedures:** Clear escalation procedures must be in place if an incident escalates beyond the IRT's initial scope or requires executive-level decision-making. This ensures that critical decisions, such as taking systems offline or notifying external stakeholders, are made quickly and with appropriate authority.

  o **Secure communication channels:** Secure communication channels are essential during an incident to prevent attackers from intercepting or disrupting internal communications. Tools such as encrypted messaging platforms, secure email, and virtual war rooms can help the IRT coordinate efforts while maintaining confidentiality.

- **External communication protocols:** External communication is equally important and must be handled carefully to avoid reputational damage or legal repercussions. External stakeholders typically include customers, partners, regulators, and the media. Some key external communication practices include:

  o **Customer communication:** Prompt and transparent communication is essential if a cyber incident involves customer data. Customers should be informed of the nature of the breach, what data was compromised, and what steps they should take to protect themselves (such as changing passwords or monitoring suspicious activity). The timing of these communications is critical to maintaining customer trust.

  o **Media and public relations:** PR teams are responsible for managing communications with the media and the public. Providing accurate and consistent information is essential to prevent speculation or misinformation. Preapproved media statements can help ensure that messaging is controlled and aligned with the organization's overall response strategy.

  o **Regulatory and legal communications:** Many industries are subject to data breach notification laws that require organizations to report incidents to regulatory bodies within specific timeframes. Legal advisors must work closely with the IRT to ensure compliance with these regulations and prepare the necessary documentation.

IR team leadership

Effective leadership is essential in any crisis to guide the team through high-pressure situations and ensure that responses are well-coordinated and timely. In the context of incident response, leadership becomes even more crucial as cyber incidents can escalate quickly, affecting multiple areas of an organization. The IRM, acting as the central leader of the team, is responsible for steering the course of action, making rapid decisions, and ensuring that all team members perform their roles effectively.

Leadership during IR is not just about directing the team but also about fostering a collaborative environment where information flows freely and actions are aligned with the overall strategy. The IRM must be able to motivate the team, maintain morale under stressful conditions, and ensure that all stakeholders are kept informed of developments. This involves balancing technical decision-making and interpersonal skills to handle the pressure and complexities of an evolving threat landscape. The key responsibilities of the IRM are as follows:

- **Decision-making authority:** The IRM has the ultimate authority to respond to an incident. Whether it is containing the threat, shutting down systems, or communicating with external parties, the IRM must make quick, informed decisions based on the available data. Delays in decision-making can result in increased damage and longer recovery times, so the IRM must have the confidence and knowledge to act decisively.

- **Coordination and communication:** A vital part of the IRM's role is coordinating the activities of different team members and ensuring that everyone is working towards the same goal. This requires clear communication within the IRT and with other departments, such as IT, legal, and public relations. The IRM must also manage communication with senior leadership and ensure that executive-level decision-makers are kept in the loop.

- **Maintaining focus:** During an incident, teams can quickly become overwhelmed by the sheer volume of tasks and data. The IRM must help the team focus by prioritizing actions, managing time effectively, and preventing distractions. This includes setting clear objectives for each response phase and ensuring the team adheres to the **incident response plan (IRP)**.

- **Risk management:** Every decision made during IR carries an element of risk. The IRM must balance the need for rapid containment with the potential impact of those decisions on business operations. For example, shutting down critical systems may prevent further damage, but it could also result in significant downtime that affects business continuity. The IRM must evaluate these risks and make decisions that align with the organization's broader risk management strategy.

- **Post-incident review and accountability:** After the incident is resolved, the IRM is responsible for leading a post-incident review to assess what went well and what did not and how the team can improve for future incidents. This review should include input from all members of the IRT and other stakeholders involved in the response. The IRM must document and integrate any lessons learned into the organization's IRP to improve future responses.

Training and development

Cyber threats constantly evolve, with new attack vectors and advanced techniques emerging regularly. As a result, an IRT must continuously hone its skills and stay up to date with the latest trends in CyberSecurity. Training and development are critical components of building an effective IRT to respond to various incidents with agility and confidence.

Regular training, simulations, and tabletop exercises ensure the team can execute the IRP effectively. These exercises enhance technical skills and improve team coordination, decision-making, and communication under pressure. Continuous training also helps identify gaps in the team's knowledge and areas where additional resources or skills may be needed. The critical components of an effective training program are as follows:

- **Tabletop exercises:** Tabletop exercises are discussion-based simulations that allow the IRT to walk through different incident scenarios without the pressure of real-time response. These exercises help team members understand their roles, identify potential weaknesses in the IRP, and improve collaboration. Tabletop exercises can be conducted for various scenarios, from phishing attacks to ransomware outbreaks.

- **Red team/blue team exercises:** Red team/blue team exercises involve simulated attacks (red team) and defenses (blue team) to test the organization's IR capabilities in a more hands-on manner. These exercises efficiently identify vulnerabilities, test detection and response capabilities, and sharpen the team's ability to handle real-world attacks. Red team/blue team exercises often reveal areas where improvements to both technology and processes are needed.

- **CyberSecurity drills and simulations:** Full-scale CyberSecurity simulations are a more immersive form of training where the IRT is presented with a simulated attack and must respond as if it were an actual incident. These drills are valuable for testing the team's ability to manage stress, make decisions under pressure, and follow the IRP. They also help build muscle memory for incident response, ensuring the team is prepared to act quickly when an incident occurs.

- **On-the-job training and certifications:** Ongoing education is crucial for individual team members to stay current with industry standards and best practices.

Encouraging team members to pursue certifications such as **Certified Incident Handler (CIH)**, **Certified Information Systems Security Professional (CISSP)**, and **Certified Ethical Hacker (CEH)** can enhance their skills and provide formal recognition of their expertise. Additionally, sending team members to industry conferences and training sessions can provide valuable networking opportunities and insights into emerging threats.

*   **Cross-training and knowledge sharing:** Cross-training ensures that all team members are familiar with different roles and responsibilities within the IRT. This is particularly important for smaller organizations where team members may need to perform multiple functions during an incident. Cross-training also fosters collaboration and knowledge sharing, enabling the team to respond more effectively to incidents that require a multidisciplinary approach.

In addition to formal training exercises, regular debriefs after actual incidents are essential for reinforcing lessons learned and continuously improving the incident response process. These debriefs should be conducted constructively, focusing on identifying opportunities for improvement rather than assigning blame.

The strength of an incident response effort depends on the technologies and tools an organization has available and the people behind them. Establishing an effective IRT requires careful planning, the right mix of skills, and strong leadership. By building a multidisciplinary team, defining clear roles and responsibilities, and fostering cross-functional collaboration, organizations can ensure that their response to cyber incidents is swift and coordinated.

Incident identification and classification

The quicker you identify, the faster you can neutralize.

In CyberSecurity, time is of the essence. The faster a threat is identified, the more influential the response can limit damage. Incident identification and classification are the cornerstones of an efficient incident response strategy. This subchapter dives deep into how organizations can detect potential security incidents early and accurately and how to classify them according to their severity, scope, and potential impact. Early detection, followed by proper classification, enables security teams to allocate resources appropriately, take action swiftly, and prevent minor incidents from escalating into full-blown crises.

The identification process is closely tied to advanced detection techniques, including SIEM systems, IDS, and anomaly detection tools. However, it is not just about detection; it is equally essential to classify incidents based on their risk, impact, and urgency. Effective classification allows teams to prioritize responses and manage resources efficiently, ensuring that the most critical threats are addressed first. This section explores tools, techniques, and frameworks that help organizations detect and classify incidents effectively:

- **Importance of early detection:** In CyberSecurity, the time between initiating and detecting an attack is critical. Attackers can often infiltrate systems and remain undetected for weeks or even months. According to recent studies, the average time to detect a breach can exceed 200 days. During this time, attackers can exfiltrate data, compromise additional systems, and cause significant damage. This is why incident detection techniques are vital—they provide the first line of defense in recognizing malicious activity before it can wreak havoc.

- **Using SIEM systems for centralized event management:** One of the most potent tools for incident detection is an SIEM system. SIEM systems provide real-time analysis of security alerts generated by network hardware and applications. They aggregate data from various sources—such as firewalls, antivirus programs, and IDS—and use this data to identify suspicious patterns or behaviors. SIEM systems are particularly useful because they correlate events across multiple systems, providing a holistic view of the organization's security posture. Key benefits of SIEM systems include:

  - **Centralized monitoring:** SIEM systems provide a single platform for viewing security events across an entire network.

  - **Real-time detection:** SIEM systems can detect potential incidents in real-time, allowing for faster response.

  - **Automated alerts:** SIEM systems can automatically trigger alerts when suspicious activity is detected, reducing the burden on security teams.

- **Intrusion Detection Systems (IDS and Intrusion Prevention Systems (IPS):** IDS and IPS are other crucial components of an organization's detection strategy. IDS are designed to monitor network traffic for signs of malicious activity, while IPS goes a step further by detecting and preventing real-time threats. IDS and IPS technologies come in two primary forms:

  - **Network-based IDS/IPS:** These monitor all network traffic and are typically placed at critical points in the network infrastructure.

  - **Host-based IDS/IPS:** These monitor the activity of individual devices (hosts) and are typically installed on critical servers or endpoints.

IDS and IPS work with other detection tools like firewalls and SIEM systems to provide layered security. They use signature-based detection (where known patterns of malicious activity are detected) and anomaly-based detection (where deviations from normal behavior are flagged) to identify potential threats.

- **Anomaly detection tools:** Anomaly detection tools use machine learning and statistical models to identify abnormal patterns of behavior that may indicate a security incident. These tools effectively detect sophisticated or previously unknown threats that traditional signature-based detection systems might miss. Critical features of anomaly detection tools include:

o **Machine learning algorithms** enable the system to learn what "normal" looks like for a given environment and identify deviations.

o **Behavioral analysis**: Anomaly detection tools analyze the behavior of users, devices, and applications to detect unusual patterns.

o **Adaptability**: As threat landscapes evolve, anomaly detection systems can continuously learn and adapt to new normal behaviors, making them more effective.

While anomaly detection tools can be handy, they are also prone to generating false positives, which can overwhelm security teams. For this reason, it is essential to fine-tune these tools and integrate them into a broader detection and response strategy.

• **A structured approach to incident classification:** Once an incident has been detected, the next step is to classify it. Classification is crucial because it helps security teams prioritize their responses based on the severity and potential impact of the incident. Organizations risk underestimating or overestimating threats without a structured classification system, leading to inefficient resource use. A well-defined classification framework allows teams to:

o Quickly determine the severity of the incident.

o Assign the appropriate level of resources for investigation and mitigation.

o Escalate incidents to higher levels of management if necessary.

Developing a classification matrix

A practical incident classification framework often includes a classification matrix. This matrix is typically based on factors such as the type of attack, the systems affected, and the potential impact on business operations. A simple example of a classification matrix might look like this:

Severity level	Description	Examples	Required actions
Low	Minor incidents with limited impact	Phishing email, unsuccessful login attempts	Monitor, no immediate action is needed
Medium	Incidents with moderate impact on operations	Malware infection on a non-critical system	Investigate, mitigate, and prevent further spread
High	Incidents that significantly disrupt business	Ransomware infection on critical systems	Immediate response, escalate to senior management
Critical	Incidents with severe impact on multiple systems	Data breach, widespread DDoS attack	Full incident response activation, executive involvement

Table 7.1: Sample of classification matrix for incident classification

This classification matrix can be tailored to an organization's needs and risk tolerance.

Criteria for classification

When classifying incidents, organizations should consider the following criteria:

- **Scope**: How many systems or users are affected? Is the incident confined to a single device, or does it affect the entire network?

- **Severity**: How critical are the systems or data affected by the incident? Does the incident impact mission-critical services?

- **Duration**: How long has the incident occurred, and will it persist without intervention?

- **Data Sensitivity**: Is sensitive data compromised, such as **personally identifiable information (PII)** or financial data?

- **Legal and regulatory impact**: Does the incident trigger legal or regulatory requirements, such as breach notification laws?

By applying these criteria, teams can more accurately classify incidents and allocate resources accordingly.

Severity and risk analysis

Risk analysis plays a central role in determining the severity of an incident. When an incident is detected, security teams must assess the potential risks associated with the threat. This involves evaluating the likelihood of the incident causing harm and the possible impact on the organization. Risk analysis typically involves two key components:

1. **Likelihood**: How likely is it that the incident will result in a successful attack or data breach?

2. **Impact**: What potential damage could result from the incident? This includes financial losses, reputational harm, legal liabilities, and operational disruption.

Categorizing incidents based on risk

A common approach to risk analysis is to categorize incidents into one of three risk levels:

- **Low risk**: Incidents that are unlikely to cause significant harm to the organization. These might include minor phishing attempts or isolated malware infections that can be easily contained.

- **Medium risk**: Incidents that pose a moderate threat to business operations. These could involve compromised credentials, malware infections on non-critical systems, or limited data exposure.

- **High risk**: Incidents that have the potential to cause significant disruption or damage. Examples include ransomware infections on critical systems, widespread data breaches, or attacks targeting sensitive intellectual property.

By categorizing incidents in this way, organizations can prioritize their responses and ensure that high-risk incidents are addressed immediately.

Escalation protocols

In some cases, incidents require immediate action and higher-level decision-making. Escalation protocols define when and how incidents should be escalated to senior management or external stakeholders, such as legal counsel or law enforcement.

Without clear escalation procedures, incidents may be mishandled or delayed, resulting in more significant damage to the organization. Escalation protocols help ensure that the right people are involved at the right time and that the incident is managed by the organization's risk tolerance and legal obligations.

Incidents should be escalated based on several factors, including:

- **Severity of the incident**: High-severity incidents that threaten critical systems or sensitive data should be escalated immediately.

- **Business impact**: The incident should be escalated if it is likely to cause significant operational disruption, financial loss, or reputational damage.

- **Legal and regulatory requirements**: Incidents that involve the loss of sensitive data or potential regulatory violations should be escalated to legal and compliance teams.

- **Public relations concerns**: If the incident can become public or cause reputational harm, it should be escalated to the communications and PR teams.

Establishing an escalation chain

An effective escalation protocol includes a clearly defined escalation chain that specifies who should be notified at each severity level. This might include:

- **Low-severity incidents**: Handled by the IRT without the need for escalation.

- **Medium severity incidents**: Escalated to IT managers or department heads for additional support.

- **High-severity incidents**: Escalated to senior leadership, legal teams, and external partners as necessary.

Containment and eradication

Control the chaos before it controls you.

Once an incident is identified and classified, the next steps in the incident response process are containment and eradication. These phases are critical to limiting the impact of the incident and ensuring that the threat is fully neutralized. Containment involves isolating the affected systems to prevent further damage and spread, while eradication is focused on removing the malicious presence entirely and restoring the environment to a secure state. Both phases require careful planning, coordination, and execution to minimize downtime and business disruption while maximizing recovery effectiveness.

Containment and eradication are not isolated actions; they must be embedded in a broader incident response framework that includes real-time communication with stakeholders, forensic analysis to understand the nature and scope of the attack, and preventive measures to avoid recurrence. This subchapter will explore these aspects in depth, offering actionable strategies for managing these phases and ensuring that organizations emerge more robust and more resilient from incidents.

Importance of containment

When a security incident occurs, containment is the first line of defense to prevent the situation from escalating. The goal of containment is to isolate the affected systems quickly, minimize damage, and buy time for a deeper investigation and eradication process. Failing to contain an incident promptly can spread malicious activity across the network, causing more significant data loss, financial damage, and reputational harm.

Short-term containment strategies: Short-term containment refers to the immediate actions taken once an incident is detected. The focus here is on limiting the spread of the threat without necessarily eliminating it altogether. The goal is to create a temporary boundary around the affected systems for further analysis and remediation.

Key short-term containment strategies include:

- **Network segmentation:** Isolating compromised segments of the network to prevent lateral movement of attackers. This can involve disconnecting infected systems from the internet or internal networks while maintaining critical services.

- **Quarantining systems:** To contain the threat, affected endpoints or servers are placed in quarantine. This prevents the malware or attacker from interacting with other systems.

- **Disabling user accounts:** If user accounts have been compromised, temporarily disabling them can prevent attackers from escalating privileges or accessing additional systems.

- **Blocking IPs or domains:** If the attack is externally driven (such as via C2 servers), blocking the associated IP addresses or domains can limit the attacker's ability to communicate with compromised systems.

Long-term containment strategies

While short-term containment buys time, long-term containment focuses on developing a more permanent solution that mitigates the risk of the threat re-emerging after remediation. Long-term containment may involve more systemic changes and ongoing monitoring.

Examples of long-term containment strategies include:

- **Patching vulnerabilities:** Identifying and applying security patches to the compromised systems and to similar systems that may be vulnerable to the same exploit.

- **Implementing firewall rules:** Updating firewall rules to restrict unauthorized access and prevent lateral movement in the future.

- **Rebuilding affected systems:** In some cases, the best approach may be to rebuild compromised systems from scratch, ensuring a clean state with no hidden malware or backdoors.

- **Security monitoring enhancements:** Enhancing security monitoring to detect if the attacker tries to return or if residual threats are still present.

The following table depicts the significant differences between short-term and long-term containment:

Aspect	Short-term containment	Long-term containment
Objective	Limit immediate damage and halt the spread of the attack	Ensure permanent control and prevention of future incidents
Timeframe	Immediate to hours or days	Days to weeks or months
Methods	Network segmentation, system quarantine, blocking IPs	Patching vulnerabilities, rebuilding systems, and firewall updates
Outcome	Temporary isolation of threat	Mitigating the risk of reoccurrence

Table 7.2: Key differences between short-term and long-term containment

Eradication

Eradication removes malicious code, malware, or other threats from an organization's environment. This phase focuses on cleaning the affected systems and addressing the root cause of the incident, preventing the attacker from regaining access in the future. The three significant steps of eradication are explained here:

- **Removing malicious code:** The first step in eradication is eliminating the malicious code or payload that caused the incident. This may involve a variety of methods, including:

  o **Antivirus/malware removal tools:** Using specialized software to scan and remove malware from infected systems. These tools can automatically detect and remove known threats.

  o **Manual cleanup:** For sophisticated attacks that involve custom malware or advanced persistence mechanisms, manual investigation and removal by CyberSecurity experts may be required. This can include searching for unauthorized files, backdoors, and modified system settings.

  o **Reimage systems:** In some cases, it may be faster and more effective to completely wipe and reimage the compromised system, restoring it to a known good state from backups.

- **System restoration:** After removing the malicious code, the next step is restoring the affected systems to full operational status. This includes:

  o **Restoring from backups:** If available, organizations can restore clean backups of the compromised systems. However, ensuring that the backup itself was not compromised during the attack is essential.

  o **Reconfiguring Systems:** Reconfigure security settings to ensure that any weaknesses that were exploited are appropriately addressed.

  o **Reinstalling Software:** If the software was corrupted during the incident, reinstalling critical applications and updating them with the latest patches may be necessary.

- **Post-eradication validation:** Before declaring the eradication process complete, security teams must verify that the systems are immaculate and secure. Key steps include:

  o **Vulnerability scans:** Conducting a complete system vulnerability scan to ensure that no additional exploits remain.

  o **Penetration testing:** Running penetration tests to confirm that all attack vectors have been closed.

  o **System logs review:** Reviewing logs for any signs of remaining malicious activity.

This table provides details regarding various eradication techniques:

Technique	Description
Antivirus/malware removal	Automated tools that detect and remove known threats.
Manual investigation	Expert analysis to identify and remove sophisticated or unknown threats.
Reimaging systems	Wiping the system entirely and restoring from a clean backup.
Vulnerability scanning	Automated scans to identify any remaining weaknesses or vulnerabilities.
Penetration testing	Simulated attacks to ensure that all attack vectors have been closed.

Table 7.3: Various eradication techniques

Forensic analysis

Forensic analysis is a crucial component of containment and eradication, as it helps organizations understand the full scope of the incident. By investigating the root cause, security teams can identify exploited vulnerabilities, determine how far the attack has spread, and gather evidence for possible legal action.

NIST SP 800-86 outlines a comprehensive forensic process for investigating computer security incidents. It involves the following key steps:

1. **Preparation:**

    a. **Establish policies and procedures:** Develop clear policies and procedures for handling digital evidence, including chain of custody, documentation, and analysis techniques.

    b. **Acquire tools and resources:** Invest in appropriate forensic tools, hardware, and software to collect, preserve, and analyze digital evidence.

    c. **Train personnel:** Train personnel in forensic techniques, legal and ethical considerations, and incident response procedures.

2. **Incident identification and response:**

    a. **Identify the incident:** Detect and recognize the occurrence of a security incident.

    b. **Initiate response:** Activate the IRP and notify relevant stakeholders.

    c. **Contain the incident:** Isolate affected systems to prevent further damage and data compromise.

3. **Collection:**

   a. **Identify data sources:** Determine relevant data sources, such as hard drives, network devices, and log files.

   b. **Collect data:** Use appropriate forensic techniques to collect data without altering the original evidence.

   c. **Document the collection process:** Maintain detailed documentation of the collection process, including dates, times, and actions taken.

4. **Examination:**

   a. **Analyze the data:** Use forensic tools to examine the collected data for evidence of malicious activity.

   b. **Identify artifacts:** Look for IOCs, such as malicious files, network traffic, or system modifications.

   c. **Correlate evidence:** Connect the dots between different pieces of evidence to build a comprehensive understanding of the incident.

5. **Analysis:**

   a. **Interpret the evidence:** Analyze the collected data to determine the incident's root cause and the damage's extent.

   b. **Identify vulnerabilities:** Identify any vulnerabilities or weaknesses that may have contributed to the incident.

   c. **Develop a timeline:** Create a timeline of the incident to understand the sequence of events.

6. **Reporting:**

   a. **Document findings:** Prepare a detailed report summarizing the investigation findings.

   b. **Share information:** Share the report with relevant stakeholders, such as management, legal counsel, and law enforcement.

   c. **Provide recommendations:** Offer recommendations for improving security practices and preventing future incidents.

Figure 7.3 represents the generic forensic process for any incident:

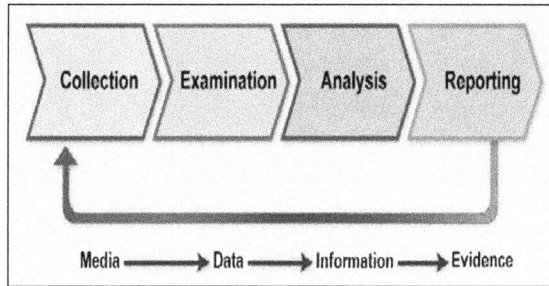

¹Figure 7.3 Forensic process

Incident spread analysis

Forensic analysis also involves understanding how the incident spread within the organization. The key activities include:

- **Lateral movement tracking:** Identifying how the attacker moved between systems, if applicable.

- **Data exfiltration analysis:** Determining whether any sensitive data was exfiltrated and, if so, how much and what type.

- **Persistence mechanisms:** Investigating whether the attacker installed backdoors or other mechanisms to maintain access over time.

Forensic analysis provides valuable insights that can be used to strengthen future defenses. Key outcomes include:

- **Vulnerability patching:** Identifying and patching vulnerabilities exploited during the attack.

- **Improved monitoring:** Enhancing monitoring and detection capabilities based on the attacker's techniques.

- **Incident response plan updates:** Updating the IRP to incorporate lessons learned from the incident.

Communication during containment

Effective communication during the containment and eradication phases is essential to ensure that all stakeholders are informed and the response process runs smoothly. Organizations' handling of communication can significantly impact the incident's outcome, both in terms of technical resolution and reputational management.

---

1. https://nvlpubs.nist.gov/nistpubs/legacy/sp/nistspecialpublication800-86.pdf

Internal communication

Internally, clear communication among team members is crucial for a coordinated response. Key practices include:

- **Establishing a communication plan**: Creating a plan that outlines who will communicate what information, to whom, and when. This should be predetermined to avoid confusion during an incident.

- **Regular updates**: Regular updates to stakeholders, including IT management, the executive team, and other relevant departments. This keeps everyone informed and aligned.

- **Utilizing collaboration tools**: Leveraging secure communication channels (such as encrypted messaging apps or dedicated incident response platforms) to share real-time information and coordinate actions.

External communication

External communication can be compassionate, involving how the organization presents itself to customers, partners, and the public. Important considerations include:

- **Transparency**: While providing accurate information is essential, organizations should avoid overwhelming stakeholders with technical details that may cause panic.

- **Timing**: It is critical to determine when to communicate with external stakeholders. It is crucial to balance transparency and avoid premature disclosure of details that could hinder the investigation.

- **Designating a spokesperson**: A designated spokesperson (often from the public relations or legal department) ensures consistent messaging and reduces the risk of mixed messages.

Table 7.4 reveals the details of key communication strategies:

Communication type	Description
Internal updates	Regular updates to the internal team on the status of the incident and response efforts.
Communication plan	A predefined plan outlining roles and responsibilities for communication during an incident.
External messaging	Clear messaging to customers and stakeholders, avoiding technical jargon, and focusing on reassurance.
Designated spokesperson	A single point of contact for all external communications to ensure consistency and clarity.

Table 7.4: Key communication techniques

Recovery and lessons learned

Recovery is not the end; it is the start of preventing the next incident.

The final phases of any effective incident response strategy are recovery and lessons learned. Recovery's primary objective is to bring the affected systems back online, restore business operations to normalcy, and validate the environment's security. However, recovery is not merely about restoring systems; it involves a broader and more critical process of reflection and improvement.

Once recovery is complete, conducting a **post-incident analysis** is imperative to understand the weaknesses that allowed the breach and improve the organization's overall security posture. This subchapter explores how organizations can ensure they recover effectively and how to document and apply lessons learned from the incident to prevent future occurrences.

System recovery

System recovery after a CyberSecurity incident involves more than just getting the systems back online; it encompasses re-establishing trust in the integrity of the infrastructure and ensuring that the vulnerabilities that led to the breach are addressed. Recovery can be seen as a multi-step process that begins as soon as containment measures are complete.

The key steps in system recovery are as follows:

1. **Restoring systems and services**: This step involves restoring affected systems, data, and applications to their pre-incident state. This could be achieved through backup restoration, reconfiguration, or a complete system rebuild. In critical infrastructure or highly regulated environments, a well-defined recovery protocol ensures minimal disruption to business operations.

2. **Infrastructure validation**: Once systems are restored, it is essential to validate that they function properly. Validating the recovery ensures that no residual malicious code remains and that all business-critical systems have been converted to their total operational capacity. This may involve redeploying system images from backups, rechecking firewall settings, and ensuring configurations meet security standards.

    The following table summarizes the critical system recovery actions.

Action	Description
Restoring systems	Restore affected systems and applications from backups or system images.
Data recovery	Recover data from backups or alternative storage if necessary.
Network and access controls	Re-check firewall, IDS/IPS, and access control settings to ensure correct configurations.
Operational validation	Test systems for functionality and ensure business processes can resume usually.

Table 7.5: System recovery actions

Validating the recovery

Restoration is one thing, but verification is the primary need. It is essential to ensure that every restored system or application functions without residual malware or vulnerabilities. Part of this process is known as post-recovery validation, and it ensures that the restored environment is secure and fully operational.

The steps in validation are as follows:

1. **Penetration testing:** After recovery, a series of penetration tests or vulnerability assessments should be conducted to ensure the security posture of the restored environment.

2. **Log monitoring:** Continuous monitoring of logs post-recovery helps identify any anomalies or hidden malware that may have evaded detection during the incident response phase.

3. **Functional testing:** Ensure that the restored systems work and fulfill the business requirements they did before the incident.

The key validation metrics are as follows:

- **Uptime metrics**: Measure system availability post-recovery.

- **Incident recurrence**: Track if the same or related incidents reoccur within a certain period.

- **System performance**: Ensure that the performance of restored systems matches pre-incident levels.

Post-incident analysis

PIA is a critical step in the CyberSecurity incident response process. It involves thoroughly examining the incident to understand its root causes, impact, and the effectiveness of the response. By analyzing the incident timeline, identifying vulnerabilities, and reviewing security controls, organizations can learn from the experience and implement necessary improvements to prevent future attacks. This analysis helps strengthen security posture, improve incident response capabilities, and minimize the potential damage from future cyber incidents.

Once normalcy is restored, organizations must undertake a PIA to uncover exploited vulnerabilities and missteps in the response process. This analysis should include a detailed examination of all events leading to and during the incident, identifying areas of strength and improvement in the IRP.

The components of PIA are as follows:

- **Incident timeline construction**: Create a detailed timeline of the incident, identifying the initial compromise, escalation points, and containment actions.

- **Root cause analysis (RCA):** This process involves determining the root cause of an incident, focusing on vulnerabilities, system weaknesses, or misconfigurations.

- **Response gaps**: Identify where response protocols were lacking or delays occurred and how to address these in the future.

A sample of PIA questions is tabulated as follows:

Question	Description
How did the breach occur?	Understanding the initial entry point of the attack and the vulnerabilities exploited.
How effective was the response?	Analyzing whether containment, eradication, and recovery procedures were timely and efficient.
What went wrong?	Identifying gaps in communication, delays in detection, or inefficiencies in the response process.
What can be improved?	Suggestions for procedural improvements, technical adjustments, or team training.

Table 7.6: Sample PIA questions

Updating security policies

PIA should not be limited to a theoretical exercise. It must inform practical changes in an organization's security policies and incident response procedures. Every incident should be a learning experience, providing opportunities to update and strengthen the organization's defenses.

Some critical updates to consider are as follows:

- **Access controls**: Were compromised credentials a major attack vector? If so, it may be time to implement more stringent access control measures, such as multi-factor authentication or least privilege principles.

- **Patch management**: Did an unpatched vulnerability cause the breach? Updating patch management policies and ensuring systems are patched on time can help prevent future breaches.

- **Training and awareness**: Did employees inadvertently cause the incident by falling for phishing attacks or clicking on malicious links? Implementing ongoing security training programs is essential to raise awareness and reduce human error.

Documentation

One of the most critical yet often overlooked elements of the recovery and lessons learned phase is documentation. Proper documentation is a reference for future incidents, legal inquiries, audits, and training. Thorough records can also aid in regulatory compliance and reduce liability.

The key documentation elements are as follows:

- **Incident report**: A detailed report documenting the incident, response, and recovery efforts, including timeframes, actions taken, and outcomes.

- **Lessons learned document**: A summary of key takeaways from the incident, highlighting improvements to be made in the future.

- **Compliance and legal considerations**: Depending on the industry, detailed documentation may be required to comply with regulatory requirements, such as GDPR or PCI-DSS.

Testing and training for effective incident response

Preparedness is the only antidote to surprise.

In the fast-paced world of CyberSecurity, where attackers continually develop new strategies and exploits, having an IRP is just the beginning. The real test of an organization's preparedness lies in how well its response plans are tested and how effectively its teams are trained. This subchapter emphasizes the importance of continuous, rigorous testing and training to ensure that when an incident does occur, the response is swift, effective, and well-coordinated.

Without regular testing, an IRP can become outdated or irrelevant. As threats evolve and change, so must the processes and strategies for responding to them. Testing helps identify weaknesses within the plan and ensures that the response team is well-versed and confident in handling incidents. Testing and training aim to minimize damage, shorten the response time, and restore normal operations as quickly as possible. Furthermore, continuous improvements must be implemented based on the outcomes of these exercises to remain adaptable to new threat vectors.

Case study, Capital One data breach: In 2019, Capital One faced a massive data breach that exposed the personal data of over 100 million customers. The breach was later traced back to a misconfigured firewall that allowed a former AWS employee to gain unauthorized access to customer data. While Capital One had an IRP, the incident revealed several gaps in its detection and response capabilities, particularly in its communication and escalation procedures. Testing its response plan more rigorously may have uncovered these issues earlier, allowing for faster containment and mitigation.

Types of testing

Incident response testing is not a one-size-fits-all approach. Different types of testing provide various benefits, from theoretical walkthroughs to real-time, full-scale simulations. Here, we break down the primary types of incident response testing and their advantages and disadvantages:

- **Walkthroughs:** Walkthroughs involve reviewing the IRP step by step with key team members. The goal is to ensure that everyone understands their roles and responsibilities, identify potential oversights, and verify that all necessary resources are available.

    o **Pros:** Walkthroughs are low-cost, easy to organize, and can be done frequently without requiring extensive resources. They are particularly helpful in reinforcing team members' understanding of their roles and familiarizing them with the incident response process.

    o **Cons**: Walkthroughs lack the realism of other testing methods. They do not test the team's ability to act under pressure, and technical skills are not tested. For this reason, walkthroughs should not be the only form of testing.

- **Tabletop exercises:** Tabletop exercises are a step up from walkthroughs and are particularly useful for testing how well team members communicate and coordinate their efforts. These exercises simulate hypothetical scenarios, and participants discuss their responses as if they were facing a real incident.

    The goal is to test the IRP in theory and identify potential procedural weaknesses, communication breakdowns, or areas where resources may be lacking. Tabletop exercises are also useful for testing scenarios where multiple departments, such as legal, PR, and HR, need to be involved.

    o **Pros:** Tabletop exercises are highly practical for testing coordination and communication between departments. They allow for detailed discussion and analysis of each team's responsibilities, ensuring everyone is on the same page. They are also a cost-effective way to test scenarios that are difficult to simulate in real-time, such as long-term investigations or legal ramifications.

- ○ **Cons**: Like walkthroughs, tabletop exercises lack the intensity and realism of live scenarios. They do not test technical readiness or the team's ability to respond quickly to evolving threats. Tabletop exercises are valuable for strategy discussions but should be supplemented with more dynamic tests.

- **Simulations:** Simulations involve mimicking real-world conditions in a controlled environment, allowing teams to test their response to cyberattacks in real-time. These exercises are much more technical and hands-on than walkthroughs or tabletop exercises, requiring the team to defend against simulated attacks actively, contain threats, and recover affected systems.

  Although simulations are typically more involved and require dedicated resources, they offer the most accurate representation of how the team will perform during an actual incident. They test both the technical and procedural aspects of incident response, offering invaluable insights into the team's readiness and ability to act under pressure.

  - ○ **Pros**: Simulations provide a realistic, immersive experience that tests technical and procedural skills. They help teams practice their ability to respond quickly to evolving threats and allow them to refine their strategies in real-time. Simulations also provide critical insights into whether tools, systems, and technologies function as expected during an incident.

  - ○ **Cons**: Simulations require significant time, resources, and planning. They may also disrupt regular business operations if mishandled, mainly if live network environments are used. Additionally, simulations are resource-intensive and can be challenging to organize frequently.

- **Live drills:** Live drills are the most comprehensive form of incident response testing, simulating a full-scale cyberattack in real-time. These exercises involve launching attacks on live systems to test the response team's ability to contain the threat, recover systems, and communicate with stakeholders. Live drills push the team to react as they would during an actual attack and are particularly valuable for assessing the effectiveness of the IRP under actual conditions.

  - ○ **Pros:** Live drills offer the most accurate measure of the team's readiness and provide the highest level of realism. They reveal the strengths and weaknesses of the IRP and the team's response capabilities. By testing live systems, live drills also uncover potential technical issues that may not be apparent in other forms of testing.

  - ○ **Cons**: The primary downside of live drills is the potential for business disruption. Testing live systems comes with inherent risks, such as unintentional downtime or data loss, if the drill is not carefully planned. Live drills are also time-consuming and resource-intensive, requiring coordination across multiple departments.

The following table provides details on the comparison of Incident response testing methods:

Method	Pros	Cons
Walkthroughs	Low-cost, easy-to-schedule	Lacks real-time pressure; does not test technical skills
Tabletop exercises	Suitable for team coordination and communication	Limited in testing technical response and speed
Simulations	Realistic, tests technical and procedural readiness	More expensive, time-consuming
Live drills	Closest to real-world conditions	The risk of system disruption requires significant resources

Table 7.7: Comparison of incident response testing methods

Role-playing scenarios

One of the most effective ways to prepare an IRT for real-world incidents is through role-playing scenarios. These scenarios place team members in hypothetical situations where they must respond to security incidents as if they were occurring in real-time. Role-playing scenarios can be as simple as responding to a phishing attack or as complex as handling a multi-stage, coordinated cyberattack. The goal is to simulate the chaos and uncertainty of an actual incident, allowing teams to practice their response in a controlled environment.

Role-playing scenarios are invaluable for training teams to handle common threats like phishing, ransomware, or DDoS attacks. However, they also allow for exploring more sophisticated attack vectors, such as insider threats, supply chain attacks, or APTs. By incorporating a range of scenarios, organizations can prepare their teams for the full spectrum of cyber threats they may encounter.

Some of the common role-playing scenarios are as follows:

- **Phishing attacks**: Phishing remains one of the most common methods cybercriminals use to access sensitive data. In this scenario, team members are asked to respond to a simulated phishing email that contains a malicious link or attachment. The goal is to assess how well the team can identify and respond to phishing threats, including whether they can prevent the attack from spreading and mitigate any potential damage.

- **Ransomware outbreak**: Ransomware attacks have become increasingly common and can have devastating consequences for organizations that are not prepared. In this scenario, the response team must handle a simulated ransomware outbreak where multiple systems have been encrypted, and the attackers are demanding a ransom. The team is tested on its ability to isolate the affected systems, communicate with stakeholders, and restore operations using backups.

- **Distributed Denial of Service (DDoS)**: DDoS attacks are designed to overwhelm a network or service with an excessive amount of traffic, rendering it unavailable to legitimate users. In this scenario, the team must handle a simulated DDoS attack, working to mitigate the impact on service availability while identifying and neutralizing the source of the attack.

- **Insider threat**: Insider threats are particularly challenging because they involve individuals with legitimate access to the organization's systems. In this scenario, the team must respond to a trusted employee leaking sensitive information or sabotaging internal systems. The response team must navigate the complexities of identifying the insider, collecting evidence, and mitigating the threat without causing undue disruption.

- **Advanced persistent threat**: APTs are prolonged and sophisticated cyberattacks where attackers maintain a foothold within an organization's network over an extended period. In this scenario, the team must respond to an APT, working to identify the scope of the attack, remove the threat, and secure the network from further exploitation.

The benefits of role-playing scenarios are as follows:

- **Hands-on training**: Role-playing scenarios offer hands-on training that allows team members to apply their skills in real-time. This is particularly valuable for developing the technical and procedural expertise to respond effectively to incidents.

- **Skill enhancement**: Role-playing scenarios help to enhance the skills of the IRT by exposing them to various attack vectors and challenges. This ensures that team members are prepared for various incidents and can adapt to evolving threats.

- **Real-world relevance**: Role-playing scenarios are based on real-world threats, allowing teams to practice responding to the types of incidents they are most likely to encounter. This makes the training highly relevant and practical.

Example of phishing simulation scenario

In a phishing simulation, the IRT is presented with a series of simulated phishing emails designed to mimic real-world attacks. The emails may contain links to fake login pages, attachments with malicious payloads, or requests for sensitive information. The team must identify the phishing emails, report them to the appropriate channels, and ensure that no sensitive information is compromised.

As the scenario unfolds, the team may discover that one or more employees have fallen victim to the phishing attack, providing the attackers with access to the organization's network. The IRT must work to isolate the compromised accounts, remove any malware or backdoors, and restore normal operations.

Continuous improvement

Incident response is not a one-and-done process. Instead, it is an ongoing cycle of improvement, where each test or real-world incident provides valuable feedback that can be used to strengthen the organization's response capabilities. Continuous improvement is critical to staying ahead of evolving threats and ensuring that the IRP remains adequate.

Debriefing sessions

It is important to hold a debriefing session with all relevant stakeholders after every incident response test or live incident. The goal of the debriefing session is to review the actions taken during the incident, identify what worked well, and highlight areas where improvements are needed. This feedback loop ensures that lessons learned are captured and incorporated into future iterations of the IRP.

Key questions to ask during a debriefing session include:

- Were the appropriate team members involved in the response?
- Was the incident detected quickly enough?
- Were communication protocols followed, and were they effective?
- Did the team have access to the necessary resources and tools?
- What challenges did the team face during the response, and how can they be addressed in the future?

Post-mortem reports

In addition to debriefing sessions, post-mortem reports that document the details of each incident or test are essential. These reports should provide a comprehensive overview of the incident, including how it was detected and handled and the outcome of the response. The report should also include any lessons learned, recommendations for improvement, and a timeline of events.

Post-mortem reports serve as valuable references for future incidents and can help ensure that the same mistakes are not repeated. They also provide a historical record of incidents that can be used to track trends and identify recurring issues.

Updating the IRP

Based on the feedback gathered from debriefing sessions and post-mortem reports, the IRP should be updated to address any identified gaps or weaknesses. This may involve revising procedures, updating communication protocols, or adding new tools and resources to the incident response toolkit.

It is important to review and update the IRP regularly, even if no major incidents have occurred. As new threats emerge and the organization's infrastructure changes, the plan must evolve to remain effective.

Need for regular testing

CyberSecurity threats are becoming increasingly complex, and sophisticated attackers continuously develop new ways to infiltrate organizations. Regularly testing an IRP is the only way to ensure that the team and the technology are ready to face modern threats.

Organizations often fall into the trap of creating an IRP that looks impressive on paper but fails to deliver when faced with real-world incidents. This discrepancy often stems from a lack of regular and comprehensive testing. Without continuous testing, an organization might be unable to identify gaps in its processes, unprepared staff, or deficiencies in its technical capabilities.

IRPs are designed to provide clear and systematic steps during a security event. However, as cyber threats evolve and change, plans that are not regularly tested may become outdated or inadequate. Regular testing helps to:

- **Identify gaps and weaknesses:** Testing ensures that any shortcomings in the IRP are identified and corrected before an actual incident occurs. It helps organizations uncover procedural gaps, communication bottlenecks, or technical inadequacies that may have been overlooked.

- **Adapt to new threats:** The cyber threat landscape is dynamic, and testing allows organizations to adapt their IRP to emerging threats, new technologies, and evolving business requirements.

- **Ensure team readiness:** The readiness of the IRT is a direct outcome of how frequently they participate in drills and simulations. Testing boosts confidence and ensures that the team can respond effectively under pressure.

  Enhance communication: Testing allows teams to refine internal and external communication protocols during incidents, ensuring the right people are informed at the right time.

Adjusting training programs

Continuous improvement also extends to training programs. If weaknesses are identified during testing or in real-world incidents, the training program should be adjusted to address those areas. For example, if the team struggles to respond to a phishing attack, additional training on phishing detection and response may be necessary.

Training programs should be dynamic and adaptable, evolving alongside the threat landscape and the organization's needs. Regularly updating training materials and incorporating lessons learned from past incidents ensures that the IRT remains well-prepared.

Training the entire organization

Incident response is not the sole responsibility of the IRT. In today's interconnected digital environment, every employee plays a role in maintaining the organization's security. Whether it is identifying phishing attempts, reporting suspicious activity, or adhering to security best practices, the actions of non-technical staff can significantly impact the effectiveness of the incident response.

Security awareness training for non-technical staff

Security awareness training is essential for ensuring that all employees understand their role in protecting the organization from cyber threats. This training should cover a wide range of topics, including:

- **Phishing and social engineering**: Employees should be trained to recognize phishing emails, social engineering tactics, and other attempts to manipulate them into revealing sensitive information.

- **Incident reporting**: Employees need to know how and when to report suspicious activity. This could be anything from an unusual email to a system malfunction that may indicate a security breach.

- **Data protection**: Employees should be educated on how to handle sensitive data, including encryption practices, password management, and data storage protocols.

By educating non-technical staff on these topics, organizations can reduce the likelihood of human error leading to a security breach. In many cases, employees are the first line of defense against cyber threats, making their awareness and vigilance critical to incident response.

Training for executives and leadership

Incident response is not just a technical issue; it is also a business issue. When a security incident occurs, executives and leadership teams play a key role in managing the fallout, communicating with stakeholders, and making critical decisions about how to respond. For this reason, it is important to provide specialized training for executives that focuses on the business impact of CyberSecurity incidents and the decision-making process during a crisis.

Key areas of training for executives and leadership include:

- **Crisis management**: Executives need to be trained on how to manage a crisis, including how to communicate with external stakeholders (customers, partners, regulators) and how to allocate resources to support the incident response effort.

- **Legal and regulatory requirements**: Many security incidents, such as data breaches, come with legal and regulatory implications. Executives should be aware of the organization's obligations under data protection laws (e.g., GDPR, CCPA) and know how to work with legal teams to ensure compliance.

- **Business continuity and recovery**: Executives need to understand how to prioritize business continuity and recovery efforts during an incident. This includes making decisions about when to shut down systems, how to minimize operational disruption, and how to restore normal operations as quickly as possible.

By involving executives in the incident response process and providing them with the necessary training, organizations can ensure that leadership is prepared to act swiftly and decisively during a CyberSecurity incident.

Training for legal and public relations teams

In addition to technical and leadership training, it is important to provide training for legal and public relations teams. These teams play a crucial role in managing a CyberSecurity incident's legal, regulatory, and reputational impact.

Legal teams should be trained on handling the legal implications of a security incident, including how to notify regulatory bodies, protect the organization from liability, and respond to legal inquiries. Public relations teams should be trained on how to manage communication with the media, customers, and other stakeholders during an incident.

Example of Equifax data breach

The Equifax data breach of 2017, which exposed the personal information of 147 million people, is a prime example of the importance of legal and public relations training. Equifax's response to the breach was widely criticized for its lack of transparency and poor communication with affected individuals. The company's failure to provide timely and accurate information about the breach further damaged its reputation and led to legal action from regulators and consumers. Proper training for legal and PR teams could have mitigated some of the damage caused by the breach.

Conclusion

Chapter 7, Incident Response, emphasizes the importance of proactive preparation, intelligence gathering, and organized response to manage CyberSecurity incidents effectively. It begins with threat hunting and intelligence, which enables organizations to detect and respond to threats before they materialize. Establishing a skilled IRT with clear roles and communication protocols is crucial for rapid response. Incident detection, classification, containment, and eradication are essential in controlling threats and eliminating malicious actors. Recovery focuses on restoring normal operations and learning from incidents through PIA, strengthening defenses for the future. Testing and training are vital for ensuring effective response plans and that all team members, including non-technical staff, are prepared. The chapter underscores that incident response is a continuous process of adaptation and improvement, combining human expertise and technology to safeguard against evolving cyber threats.

Points to remember

- **Proactive threat hunting and intelligence:** Constantly searching for signs of compromise, paired with actionable intelligence, helps organizations detect and prevent threats before they escalate, forming a proactive defense strategy.

- **Establishing a strong incident response team:** A well-defined IRT with cross-functional expertise and clear communication protocols is crucial for coordinated, effective responses to incidents. Roles should be specific, and the team must be trained for decisive action.

- **Incident detection and classification:** Quick identification of incidents using tools like SIEM, IDS, and IPS ensures faster containment. Classification based on severity and risk helps prioritize incidents for immediate action.

- **Containment and eradication:** Containment focuses on isolating the threat to prevent further damage, while eradication eliminates it completely. Short-term and long-term strategies are essential to fully neutralize incidents without disrupting business operations.

- **Recovery and learning:** After containment, systems must be restored with integrity. The PIA identifies gaps, updates security policies, and ensures continuous improvement to bolster defenses.

- **Testing and training for preparedness:** Regular testing, including simulations and drills, ensures the response plan is effective. Extending training beyond the core response team to include the entire organization ensures that everyone is prepared for incidents.

Join our book's Discord space

Join the book's Discord Workspace for Latest updates, Offers, Tech happenings around the world, New Release and Sessions with the Authors:

https://discord.bpbonline.com

CHAPTER 8

Legal and Ethical Considerations

Introduction

In CyberSecurity, the true test of leadership lies not just in defending against threats but in navigating the intricate web of laws and ethics that define our digital world. Compliance and integrity are not mere obligations but the pillars of trust and resilience.

In an increasingly interconnected digital world, understanding the legal and ethical frameworks that govern CyberSecurity is vital. Laws shape how organizations protect data, while ethics guide professionals in responsible conduct. This chapter explores the intersection of law, policy, and morality, providing insights into compliance, ethical hacking, and **intellectual property** (**IP**) management. CyberSecurity leaders can navigate complex legal landscapes by mastering these aspects while upholding integrity and trust.

Structure

The chapter covers the following topics:

- CyberSecurity laws and regulations
- Ethical hacking and responsible disclosures
- Intellectual property and digital rights

Objectives

Chapter 8, Legal and Ethical Considerations, aims to equip CyberSecurity professionals with a comprehensive understanding of the legal and ethical dimensions that underpin modern security practices. A solid grasp of CyberSecurity laws and regulations is essential in an era where digital infrastructure is integral to economic stability and societal function. This knowledge allows organizations to ensure compliance, mitigate risks, and avoid legal repercussions from data breaches or mishandling sensitive information. By exploring critical global and industry-specific regulations, readers will gain insights into the evolving legal landscape and its implications for CyberSecurity strategies across different sectors.

Beyond legal frameworks, the chapter emphasizes the importance of **ethical conduct** in CyberSecurity operations. It explores the principles and practices of ethical hacking, highlighting the significance of responsible disclosure in identifying and addressing vulnerabilities before malicious actors can exploit them. Understanding these ethical considerations is crucial for security professionals to navigate the fine line between safeguarding digital assets and respecting legal boundaries. This section also delves into ethical hackers' challenges and responsibilities, including potential legal risks and the importance of adhering to established protocols.

This chapter seeks to foster a holistic understanding of how legal and ethical considerations intersect with CyberSecurity practices. It prepares readers to navigate the complexities of compliance, make ethically sound decisions, and uphold the principles of integrity and responsibility in their professional roles.

CyberSecurity laws and regulations

*Compliance is not just a requirement — it is a **cornerstone of trust**. Understanding the law means knowing where security ends and liability begins.*

In an era dominated by data-driven decisions and interconnected networks, CyberSecurity is not just a technical necessity but a legal imperative. Modern businesses rely heavily on technology to store, manage, and process sensitive data, from customer information to proprietary corporate data. This reliance brings significant risks, including data breaches, cyber espionage, and regulatory penalties. Consequently, governments and regulatory bodies worldwide have established robust CyberSecurity laws to protect individuals' privacy, ensure data integrity, and maintain national security.

Historically, CyberSecurity laws evolved in response to specific threats or high-profile incidents. For instance, the **Health Insurance Portability and Accountability Act (HIPAA)** in the United States emerged in the late 1990s to address the growing digitization of healthcare records. Similarly, the European Union's **General Data Protection Regulation (GDPR)** was introduced to harmonize European data privacy laws and provide citizens greater control over their personal information. These laws set strict standards for data handling, imposing severe penalties for non-compliance.

However, compliance is not merely about avoiding fines. It is about fostering trust. Consumers and business partners expect organizations to protect their data and uphold their privacy rights. Compliance demonstrates a commitment to ethical data management, which can enhance an organization's reputation and competitiveness. Understanding these laws is crucial for CyberSecurity professionals to meet legal obligations and design security frameworks that align with regulatory requirements and industry best practices.

This subchapter explores key global CyberSecurity regulations, their impact on various industries, and the challenges businesses face in achieving compliance. We will delve into significant regulations such as GDPR, CCPA/CPRA, HIPAA, and India's DPDP Act, highlighting their core principles, enforcement mechanisms, and real-world implications. We will also examine industry-specific frameworks like PCI DSS for financial services and NIST guidelines for government entities, offering insights into how organizations can navigate the complex regulatory landscape effectively.

General Data Protection Regulation

The GDPR, enacted in May 2018, is one of the most comprehensive data protection laws globally. It applies to organizations operating within the **European Union (EU)** and those outside the EU that process the personal data of EU residents. GDPR's primary objective is to enhance individuals' privacy rights and harmonize data protection laws across EU member states.

The key provisions are as follows:

- **Lawfulness, fairness, and transparency**: Organizations must process personal data lawfully and transparently. Data subjects must be informed about how their data is collected, used, and stored.

- **Purpose limitation**: Personal data should only be collected for specific, legitimate purposes and not further processed in a manner incompatible with those purposes.

- **Data minimization**: Only data necessary for the intended purpose should be collected.

- **Accountability and governance**: Organizations must demonstrate compliance through documentation, the appointment of **Data Protection Officers (DPOs)**, and impact assessments.

Enforcement and penalties

GDPR violations can result in fines of up to €20 million or 4% of an organization's global annual revenue, whichever is higher. High-profile cases, such as the €746 million fine imposed on Amazon, underscore the regulation's stringent enforcement.

Case study British Airways breach

In 2018, British Airways suffered a data breach affecting 500,000 customers. The UK's **Information Commissioner's Office (ICO)** fined the airline £20 million for failing to implement adequate security measures, highlighting the importance of GDPR compliance.

The impact on businesses:

- **Cross-border operations:** Companies must ensure data transfers outside the EU comply with GDPR standards, using mechanisms like **Standard Contractual Clauses (SCCs)** and **Binding Corporate Rules (BCRs)**.

- **Consumer trust:** GDPR compliance enhances customer trust by demonstrating a commitment to privacy.

California Consumer Privacy Act

The **California Consumer Privacy Act (CCPA/CPRA)**, enacted in January 2020, is the first comprehensive consumer privacy law in the United States. It gives California residents control over their personal information and imposes obligations on businesses that collect or sell this data. In 2023, the **California Privacy Rights Act (CPRA)** expanded the CCPA's scope and introduced additional rights and enforcement mechanisms.

The key provisions are as follows:

- **Right to know**: Consumers can request information about the data a business collects and how it is used.

- **Right to delete**: Consumers can ask businesses to delete their personal data.

- **Right to opt-out**: Consumers can prevent businesses from selling their personal data.

- **Data portability**: Consumers can receive their data in a portable format.

Differences from GDPR

While both laws aim to protect personal data, GDPR focuses on broader principles, whereas CCPA emphasizes consumer rights and business obligations. CCPA also has a narrower geographic scope, applying only to California residents.

The impact on businesses:

- **Compliance challenges:** U.S. nationwide companies must adapt their data practices to meet CCPA requirements.

- **Legal risks:** Non-compliance can lead to fines and lawsuits, especially after data breaches.

Health Insurance Portability and Accountability Act

HIPAA, enacted in 1996, sets standards for protecting sensitive health information in the United States. It applies to healthcare providers, insurers, and their business associates.

The key rules are as follows:

- **Privacy rule**: Governs the use and disclosure of **Protected Health Information (PHI)**.

- **Security rule**: Sets standards for protecting electronic PHI.

- **Breach notification rule**: Requires covered entities to notify affected individuals and regulators of data breaches.

Real-world implications

Healthcare data breaches can have severe consequences. In 2015, *Anthem Inc.* suffered a breach affecting 78.8 million individuals, leading to a $16 million settlement with the U.S. Department of **Health and Human Services (HHS)**.

India's Digital Personal Data Protection Act

India's **Digital Personal Data Protection Act (DPDP)**, enacted in 2023, is a comprehensive legal framework designed to protect individuals' digital privacy. It aligns closely with global data protection laws like the GDPR but reflects India's unique socioeconomic and digital landscape. DPDP applies to personal data collected, processed, and stored digitally within Indian territory, including data processed outside India for business purposes.

The key provisions are as follows:

- **Data principal rights**: The DPDP Act empowers individuals (Data Principals) with rights, including access to their data, correction, and erasure. They also have the right to know how their data is being processed and can seek remedies in case of violations.

- **Data fiduciary obligations:** Organizations, termed *data fiduciaries*, must ensure transparency, fairness, and accountability in data processing. They must implement adequate security measures and obtain explicit consent from individuals before processing their data.

- **Consent management**: Consent must be explicit, specific, and informed. Data Fiduciaries are responsible for demonstrating that consent was obtained and can be withdrawn at any time.

- **Cross-border data transfers**: Like GDPR, DPDP regulates cross-border data flows, requiring organizations to ensure adequate safeguards when transferring personal data outside India. Approved jurisdictions and binding contracts may be necessary for such transfers.

- **Penalties and enforcement:** Violations of the DPDP Act can result in hefty penalties, up to ₹250 crore (~ USD 30 million) for severe breaches. The Data Protection Board of India oversees enforcement and compliance.

Impact on businesses

Organizations operating in India or processing Indian citizens' data must overhaul their data management practices to comply with the DPDP Act. Compliance involves significant investments in technology, staff training, and legal consultations.

Case study, of Indian startups and compliance challenges

Many Indian startups, particularly in the fintech and e-commerce sectors, have faced challenges adapting to the stringent requirements of the DPDP Act. Ensuring compliance while maintaining business agility has been a balancing act.

Key points to keep in mind are as follows:

- **Impact on international business:** International businesses operate in an environment characterized by a patchwork of CyberSecurity laws. Each jurisdiction has unique requirements, from GDPR in the EU to CCPA in California and the DPDP Act in India. This creates complexity, as organizations must tailor their CyberSecurity policies to comply with multiple legal frameworks.

- **Challenges in cross-border data transfers:** Data localization laws, such as those in Russia and China, require that data about citizens be stored within national borders. For multinational corporations, this means establishing localized data centers and ensuring compliance with divergent laws. Mechanisms like **Standard Contractual Clauses (SCCs** and **Data Protection Agreements (DPAs)** are commonly used to manage cross-border transfers.

- **Legal conflicts and harmonization efforts:** One of the significant challenges international businesses face is the potential for legal conflicts. For example, compliance with U.S. government data requests might breach GDPR requirements if the data concerns EU residents. Harmonization efforts like the EU-U.S. Data Privacy Framework aim to resolve conflicts and provide more precise guidelines.

- **Strategic approaches for businesses:** To navigate these complexities, organizations adopt a proactive compliance strategy. This involves regular audits, appointing global Data Protection Officers (DPOs, and leveraging compliance management software. Businesses prioritizing compliance mitigate legal risks and enhance their reputation and customer trust globally.

Industry-specific compliance frameworks

Industry-specific compliance frameworks are essential for safeguarding sensitive data, ensuring privacy, and maintaining regulatory standards across various sectors. These frameworks provide structured guidelines to mitigate risks, enforce security controls, and achieve regulatory compliance. Below is an overview of some widely adopted frameworks:

Financial sector, PCI DSS

The **Payment Card Industry Data Security Standard (PCI DSS)** is a set of security standards designed to protect cardholder data. It applies to all entities involved in payment processing, including merchants, banks, and service providers. Compliance is mandatory for any organization handling credit card transactions.

The key requirements are as follows:

- **Secure network architecture**: Maintain firewalls and avoid using default security settings.

- **Data protection:** Encrypt cardholder data during transmission and storage.

- **Access control**: Implement strict access controls, ensuring only authorized personnel can access sensitive data.

- **Monitoring and testing**: Regularly test security systems and processes, including vulnerability assessments and penetration testing.

Case study of target data breach (2013):

The target data breach, affecting over 40 million credit card numbers, highlighted the importance of PCI DSS compliance. The breach occurred due to inadequate third-party vendor management, emphasizing the need for comprehensive security measures across the supply chain.

Government sector, FISMA and NIST frameworks

Governments worldwide are prime targets for cyberattacks due to the sensitive nature of the data they handle, ranging from national security intelligence to personal information about citizens. As cyber threats grow in sophistication and frequency, robust CyberSecurity frameworks are crucial for protecting public infrastructure and maintaining citizen trust. In the United States, the **Federal Information Security Management Act (FISMA)** and the guidelines established by the **National Institute of Standards and Technology (NIST)** form the backbone of federal CyberSecurity efforts. Together, they provide a structured approach to securing federal information systems, setting standards for risk management, and ensuring accountability across government agencies.

Federal Information Security Management Act

Enacted in 2002 as part of the **E-Government Act**, the FISMA was designed to bolster information security within the U.S. federal government and its contractors. Recognizing the growing dependency on digital infrastructure, FISMA aimed to establish a comprehensive framework for safeguarding federal information systems against unauthorized access, use, disclosure, disruption, modification, or destruction.

In 2014, FISMA was amended through the **Federal Information Security Modernization Act**, updating the original legislation to address emerging CyberSecurity challenges and enhance the **Department of Homeland Security's** (**DHS**) role in overseeing federal CyberSecurity.

The key objectives of FISMA are as follows:

- **Risk-based approach:** Agencies must adopt a risk-based approach to information security, prioritizing resources based on the potential impact of a security breach.

- **Continuous monitoring** Implementing continuous monitoring programs to promptly detect and respond to security incidents.

- **Accountability and oversight:** Federal agencies must maintain comprehensive security policies, conduct regular audits, and report their compliance status to Congress annually.

- **Security controls and assessments:** FISMA mandates the use of security controls based on NIST standards and requires agencies to assess their effectiveness regularly.

National Institute of Standards and Technology Frameworks

NIST plays a pivotal role in FISMA compliance by developing the guidelines and standards that federal agencies must follow. NIST's publications provide detailed instructions on implementing robust security controls and managing risks effectively.

The key NIST publications are as follows:

- **NIST Special Publication (SP) 800-53:** This publication, "Security and Privacy Controls for Federal Information Systems and Organizations," is the cornerstone of FISMA compliance. It provides a catalog of security controls federal agencies must implement to protect their information systems.

- Categories of controls:

  - **Access control (AC):** Ensures that only authorized individuals can access sensitive data and systems. This includes policies on multi-factor authentication, least privilege, and session management.

  - **Incident Response (IR):** Establishes procedures for detecting, responding to, and recovering from security incidents. Agencies must have IR teams and conduct regular drills.

  - **Risk Assessment (RA):** Requires agencies to conduct periodic RAs to identify vulnerabilities and assess the potential impact of threats.

  - **System and Communications Protection (SC):** Focuses on securing communications and information systems through encryption, secure protocols, and network segmentation.

  - **Continuous monitoring (CM):** Mandates ongoing monitoring of information systems to detect and mitigate risks in real-time.

- **NIST CyberSecurity Framework (CSF):** Introduced in 2014 and revised in 2018, the NIST CSF provides a voluntary framework for organizations, including private sector entities, to manage CyberSecurity risks. Although not mandatory under FISMA, many federal agencies adopt the CSF as a best practice.

  - Core components of NIST CSF:

    - **Identify:** Understand the organization's assets, systems, and data, and identify potential risks.

    - **Protect:** Implement safeguards to ensure the delivery of critical services.

    - **Detect:** Develop capabilities to identify CyberSecurity events.

    - **Respond:** Establish procedures to respond to detected incidents effectively.

    - **Recover:** Implement plans to restore capabilities and services after a CyberSecurity incident.

- **NIST SP 800-37:** This publication, titled *Risk Management Framework (RMF) for Information Systems and Organizations*, provides guidelines for integrating security and risk management activities into the system development lifecycle. The RMF process includes six steps:

  1. **Categorize:** Define the information system and categorize its data based on sensitivity.

  2. **Select:** Choose appropriate security controls from NIST SP 800-53.

  3. **Implement:** Apply the selected controls within the system.

4. **Assess:** Evaluate the effectiveness of the implemented controls.

5. **Authorize:** Obtain official authorization to operate the system.

6. **Monitor:** Continuously monitor the system for compliance and vulnerabilities.

Implementing FISMA and NIST guidelines

Federal agencies must follow a rigorous process to implement FISMA and NIST guidelines. This involves conducting comprehensive RAs, selecting and deploying appropriate security controls, and regularly testing the system's resilience. Agencies must also develop policies and procedures to address various aspects of CyberSecurity, from data encryption to IR.

Role of continuous monitoring

CM is a critical aspect of FISMA compliance. Agencies must establish processes for real-time detection and response to security incidents, ensuring that vulnerabilities are addressed promptly. Automated tools like **Security Information and Event Management (SIEM)** systems facilitate CM.

Common challenges are as follows:

- **Resource constraints:** Implementing FISMA and NIST standards requires significant resources, including skilled personnel and advanced technologies. Smaller agencies often struggle to allocate sufficient budgets for CyberSecurity initiatives.

- **Complexity of compliance:** The sheer volume of security controls and guidelines can be overwhelming. Ensuring compliance across large, complex systems requires meticulous planning and execution.

- **Evolving threat landscape:** Cyber threats constantly evolve, making it challenging for agencies to keep their security measures current. Continuous training and threat intelligence are essential to address this challenge.

- **Third-party risk management:** Federal agencies rely on third-party contractors and service providers. Ensuring that these third parties comply with FISMA and NIST standards is critical but challenging.

Case studies of FISMA in action

The following section discusses some case studies.

Department of Veterans Affairs (VA)

The VA handles vast amounts of sensitive health information for veterans. In 2019, the VA implemented NIST SP 800-53 controls to enhance its CyberSecurity posture, focusing on access control, data encryption, and CM. Regular audits have shown significant improvements in the VA's ability to detect and respond to threats.

NASA's compliance journey

NASA faced challenges in implementing FISMA due to the complexity of its systems and the need for real-time data sharing. By adopting the NIST RMF, NASA improved its risk management processes and enhanced collaboration between IT and security teams.

FISMA and NIST frameworks form the foundation of CyberSecurity in the U.S. federal government, establishing rigorous standards for protecting sensitive information. While compliance can be complex and resource-intensive, it is essential for safeguarding national security and maintaining public trust. By adopting a risk-based approach and leveraging CM, federal agencies can mitigate cyber threats effectively. As cyber challenges evolve, FISMA and NIST will continue to play a crucial role in shaping the future of government CyberSecurity.

Legal challenges and future trends in CyberSecurity

The rapid evolution of technology continually reshapes the CyberSecurity landscape, creating opportunities and challenges for legal frameworks worldwide. As emerging technologies like **artificial intelligence** (**AI**) and the **Internet of Things** (**IoT**) become integral to modern infrastructure, they introduce complex regulatory considerations. Additionally, global data flows raise questions about jurisdiction, compliance, and conflict resolution, particularly as countries implement diverse and sometimes conflicting laws. Understanding these dynamics is crucial for organizations aiming to stay compliant and resilient in an increasingly interconnected world.

Emerging laws for AI and IoT

AI technologies, from machine learning algorithms to autonomous systems, are transforming industries and raising ethical and legal concerns. Governments are beginning to address these challenges through new legislation and guidelines.

Key regulatory considerations for AI:

- **Transparency and explainability:** Regulators emphasize the need for AI systems to be transparent and explainable. This ensures accountability, particularly in sectors like healthcare and finance, where AI decisions can have profound impacts.

- **Bias and fairness:** AI systems can perpetuate or amplify biases present in training data. Emerging regulations require organizations to demonstrate fairness and mitigate discriminatory outcomes.

- **Data privacy:** AI relies heavily on data, raising privacy concerns. Regulations like the GDPR mandate strict data handling protocols, including rights to access, rectify, and erase personal data.

Example legislation:

- **EU AI Act:** Proposed by the European Commission, this framework categorizes AI applications by risk level (minimal, limited, high, and unacceptable). High-risk AI systems face stringent transparency, accuracy, and human oversight requirements.

- **US Algorithmic Accountability Act:** This proposed legislation addresses biases in automated systems by requiring impact assessments for AI tools used in critical decision-making processes.

Challenges and opportunities:

- **Global Standards vs. fragmented regulations:** Different jurisdictions independently develop AI laws, creating compliance challenges for multinational organizations. A unified global standard could streamline compliance but remains a distant goal.

- **Ethical dilemmas:** Balancing innovation with ethical considerations requires continuous dialogue between policymakers, technologists, and ethicists.

Regulatory complexity and security imperatives in IoT

IoT devices, from smart home appliances to industrial sensors, are increasing rapidly. However, their interconnected nature introduces significant security vulnerabilities, making regulation essential.

Key regulatory considerations for IoT:

- **Device security:** Ensuring IoT devices are secure by design is a priority. Regulations increasingly mandate built-in security features, such as strong default passwords and regular software updates.

- **Data privacy:** IoT devices collect vast amounts of personal data, often without users' explicit consent. Regulations require transparency in data collection and storage practices.

- **Interoperability standards:** As IoT ecosystems expand, ensuring interoperability between devices from different manufacturers is crucial. Regulatory bodies are promoting open standards to facilitate this.

Example legislation:

- **California IoT Security Law:** Effective since 2020, this law requires manufacturers of connected devices to implement reasonable security features to protect against unauthorized access.

- **EU CyberSecurity Act:** This legislation establishes a certification framework for IoT devices, ensuring they meet defined security standards before reaching consumers.

Challenges and opportunities:

- **Legacy devices:** Many older IoT devices lack the security features now required by regulations, posing ongoing risks.

- **Global interconnectivity:** Cross-border regulatory inconsistencies can complicate IoT deployments for multinational companies. Establishing global norms is a priority but remains challenging.

Cross-border data transfers and legal conflicts

In an interconnected digital economy, data frequently moves across borders. However, this raises legal and regulatory challenges, mainly when data protection standards vary significantly between countries.

The key regulatory frameworks impacting cross-border transfers are as follows:

- **GDPR (EU):** The GDPR imposes strict conditions on transferring personal data outside the EU. Transfers are only permitted to countries with adequate data protection laws or through mechanisms like SCCs and BCRs.

- **US CLOUD Act:** This legislation allows US law enforcement agencies to access data stored by US-based companies, even if the data is stored overseas. This can conflict with local privacy laws in other countries.

- **China's CyberSecurity Law:** China imposes stringent requirements on transferring data outside its borders, particularly for critical information infrastructure operators.

Legal conflicts and challenges:

- **Jurisdictional conflicts:** When data privacy laws in different countries conflict, organizations face the challenge of navigating these legal tensions. For example, complying with US data access requests may violate EU data protection laws.

- **Schrems II decision:** This landmark ruling by the European Court of Justice invalidated the EU-US Privacy Shield framework, highlighting concerns about US government surveillance and emphasizing the need for robust protections when transferring data to non-EU countries.

Case study of Schrems II and its aftermath

Following the Schrems II decision, companies must conduct detailed assessments of their data transfer arrangements, ensuring they offer equivalent protections to the GDPR. This has led to increased reliance on SCCs, which also face scrutiny.

Potential solutions are as follows:

- **Data localization:** Some countries mandate that data be stored locally, reducing cross-border transfer issues but potentially raising costs and creating data silos.

- **International agreements:** Efforts like the proposed **EU-US Data Privacy Framework** aim to establish consistent standards for data transfers, but achieving global consensus remains challenging.

Anticipating regulatory evolution

Several factors will shape the future of CyberSecurity regulations:

- **Technological advancements:** Emerging technologies like quantum computing and blockchain will introduce new security and regulatory considerations.

- **Evolving threat landscape:** As cyber threats become more sophisticated, regulations must adapt. This includes addressing threats from state-sponsored actors and emerging attack vectors like AI-driven attacks.

- **Public and political pressure:** High-profile data breaches and privacy scandals have increased public awareness and demand for stronger regulations. Governments are responding with more stringent laws and enforcement actions.

The key trends to watch are as follows:

- **Unified global standards:** There is a growing push for global CyberSecurity standards to simplify compliance and enhance cooperation. Organizations like the **International Telecommunication Union (ITU)** and **ISO** play critical roles in this effort.

- **Focus on supply chain security:** Regulations increasingly address supply chain vulnerabilities, requiring organizations to assess and secure their third-party vendors.

- **Integration of AI and ethics:** Future regulations will likely include ethical considerations for AI, particularly around transparency, accountability, and fairness.

Regulatory sandbox models

Some jurisdictions are adopting **regulatory sandbox** models to encourage innovation while ensuring compliance. These models allow companies to test new technologies in a controlled environment with regulatory oversight.

The future of CyberSecurity regulation is marked by complexity and constant evolution. As emerging technologies like AI and IoT introduce new risks, regulatory frameworks must adapt to address these challenges. Cross-border data transfers remain contentious, highlighting the need for international cooperation and consistent standards. By anticipating regulatory trends and preparing for future changes, organizations can navigate this dynamic landscape effectively, ensuring compliance while fostering innovation.

Ethical hacking and responsible disclosure

Ethical hacking bridges the gap between security and vulnerability. Transparency in disclosure transforms risk into resilience.

Ethical hacking has emerged as a critical component of CyberSecurity, aiming to identify vulnerabilities before malicious hackers can exploit them proactively. Unlike criminal hackers, ethical hackers operate within legal boundaries and ethical frameworks to strengthen an organization's security posture. This section studies the principles guiding ethical hacking, protocols for responsible disclosure, and the legal landscape that governs these practices.

Figure 8.1: *Symbolic representation of an ethical hacker*

Principles of ethical hacking

Ethical Hacking involves simulating cyber-attacks to assess an organization's security. Ethical hackers, often called **white-hat hackers**, use the same tools and techniques as malicious hackers but with the authorization to identify and remediate vulnerabilities. Here are some of the key types of ethical hacking:

- **Network penetration testing:** Network penetration testing involves simulating attacks on an organization's network infrastructure to identify vulnerabilities and weaknesses. This can include:

  - **External network scanning:** Scanning the organization's external network for open ports, services, and vulnerabilities.

  - **Internal network scanning:** Assessing the security of internal networks, including servers, workstations, and network devices.

  - **Vulnerability scanning:** Identifying and prioritizing vulnerabilities in network devices and systems.

  - **Exploit testing:** Attempting to exploit vulnerabilities to gain unauthorized access.

  - **Post-exploitation assessment:** Simulating the actions of a malicious attacker after gaining access to the network.

- **Web application testing:** Web application testing focuses on identifying vulnerabilities in web applications, such as:

  - **SQL injection:** Exploiting vulnerabilities in web applications to manipulate databases.

  - **Cross-Site Scripting (XSS):** Injecting malicious scripts into web pages to steal user data or hijack sessions.

  - **Cross-Site Request Forgery (CSRF):** Tricking users into performing unauthorized actions on web applications.

  - **Insecure direct object references:** Accessing sensitive data by manipulating URLs or parameters.

- **Social engineering assessments:** Social engineering assessments test the human element of security by simulating attacks that exploit human psychology. These attacks can include:

  - **Phishing:** Sending deceptive emails to trick users into revealing sensitive information.

  - **Vishing:** Using voice calls to deceive users into providing personal information.

  - **Smishing:** Using SMS messages to trick users into clicking malicious links or revealing sensitive information.

  - **Tailgating:** Following authorized individuals into restricted areas.

- **Wireless network assessments:** Wireless network assessments focus on the security of Wi-Fi networks, including:

- o **Wardriving:** Identifying and analyzing Wi-Fi networks in a specific area.

- o **Wi-Fi hacking:** Cracking Wi-Fi passwords and gaining unauthorized access to networks.

- o **Man-in-the-Middle attacks:** Intercepting and manipulating communication between devices on a Wi-Fi network.

Organizations can proactively identify and address security vulnerabilities by conducting these ethical hacking assessments, reducing the risk of successful cyberattacks. The following table summarizes the key differences between ethical and unethical hacking:

Criteria	Ethical hacking	Unethical hacking
Purpose	Improve security	Exploit for personal/financial gain
Authorization	Legal, with permission	Unauthorized access
Intent	Protect assets and data	Damage, theft, or disruption
Accountability	Reports findings to the organization	Operates anonymously

Table 8.1: Ethical vs. unethical hacking

Ethical considerations and boundaries

Ethical hacking is a powerful tool for improving security, but it must always be conducted with the utmost integrity and respect for legal and moral boundaries. Ethical hackers can contribute to a safer and more secure digital landscape by adhering to the ethical considerations and boundaries mentioned as follows:

- **Consent and authorization:** Ethical hacking must always be conducted with explicit permission. Unauthorized penetration testing, even with good intent, is illegal and can lead to severe consequences. Obtaining written consent from the organization or individual owning the system is crucial. This consent should clearly outline the scope of the testing, the expected outcomes, and any limitations.

  - o **Scope and limitations:** Defining the scope of the ethical hacking engagement is essential to prevent unintentional disruptions and maintain focus. Clear guidelines should ensure that testers concentrate on authorized areas only. This includes:

    - ▪ **Target systems:** Clearly define the specific systems or networks that will be tested.

    - ▪ **Testing methods:** Specifying the techniques and tools that can be used.

    - ▪ **Timeframes:** Setting a timeline for the testing to minimize disruption.

    - ▪ **Acceptable risks:** Identifying the acceptable level of risk that can be tolerated during the testing.

- o **Transparency and reporting:** Ethical hackers must document all findings accurately and transparently. This ensures that vulnerabilities are reported responsibly and can be addressed effectively. A detailed report should include:

  - **Vulnerability identification:** A clear description of each vulnerability found.

  - **Impact assessment:** An evaluation of the potential impact of each vulnerability.

  - **Exploitability:** An assessment of how easily a vulnerability can be exploited.

  - **Recommendations:** Specific recommendations for mitigating or eliminating the vulnerabilities.

- o **Skills and certifications:** Ethical hacking requires technical skills, moral integrity, and continuous learning. Key areas include networking, programming, cryptography, and system administration.

- o **Notable certifications:** To validate their skills and knowledge, ethical hackers often pursue industry-recognized certifications. Here are some of the most prominent certifications in the field:

  - **Certified Ethical Hacker (CEH):** The CEH certification covers a broad range of fundamental ethical hacking techniques. It equips individuals with the knowledge and skills to identify, assess, and exploit vulnerabilities in systems and networks. By earning this certification, professionals demonstrate their understanding of various hacking tools, techniques, and methodologies.

  - **Offensive Security Certified Professional (OSCP):** The OSCP is a highly respected certification focusing on hands-on penetration testing. It requires candidates to complete a rigorous practical exam exploiting real-world vulnerabilities. By passing this challenging certification, individuals prove their ability to think like an attacker and identify critical security weaknesses.

  - **GIAC Penetration Tester (GPEN):** The certification of GPEN emphasizes advanced penetration testing methodologies. It covers web application security, wireless network security, and network infrastructure security. By earning this certification, professionals demonstrate their expertise in conducting in-depth penetration tests and developing effective mitigation strategies.

The following table provides a broader comparison summary of notable certifications:

Certification	Focus area	Difficulty level	Ideal candidate
CEH	Broad ethical hacking knowledge	Intermediate	IT Security Professionals
OSCP	Practical penetration testing	Advanced	Experienced security practitioners
GPEN	Detailed penetration methodologies	Advanced	Technical analysts, consultants

Table 8.2: Comparison between notable certifications

- **Responsible disclosure protocols:** Responsible disclosure ensures that vulnerabilities are reported to organizations in a structured and ethical manner, allowing them to address issues before public exposure.

  - **Discovery and documentation:** Ethical hackers must first **identify and document vulnerabilities comprehensively**. This involves meticulous research, testing, and evidence gathering. Clear documentation is essential for effective communication with the affected organization.

  - **Initial contact:** The ethical hacker should report a vulnerability to the organization's security team through designated channels once a vulnerability is confirmed. This typically involves sending a detailed report outlining the vulnerability, its potential impact, and recommended remediation steps.

  - **Verification and remediation:** The ethical hacker should **work with the organization to verify the vulnerability and assist with necessary remediation**. This collaboration can involve providing technical advice, sharing exploit code (in a controlled manner), or offering guidance on patching and security updates.

  - **Public disclosure:** After the organization has had a reasonable amount of time to address the vulnerability, the ethical hacker can consider **public disclosure with the organization's consent**. This transparency builds trust within the security community and educates the broader public about potential threats. However, public disclosure should be a last resort, used only when necessary to motivate organizations to act.

  - **Challenges and ethical dilemmas:** Ethical hackers often face challenges and dilemmas in their work. Some of the common challenges include:

    - **Delayed responses:** Organizations may delay or ignore reports, leaving vulnerabilities unpatched.

    - **Fear of legal repercussions:** Ethical hackers may face legal threats, even when acting in good faith, significantly if they exceed the scope of their authorization or cause unintended damage.

- **Zero-day vulnerabilities:** The ethical dilemma of disclosing or selling zero-day vulnerabilities raises complex questions about responsibility, public safety, and financial gain.

  o **Case studies:** Successful and controversial disclosures:

    - **Successful disclosure: Google Project Zero:** Known for its rigorous disclosure process, Project Zero has uncovered critical vulnerabilities in significant software, driving industry-wide improvements.

    - **Controversial case: The Heartbleed Bug:** Public awareness led to rapid global remediation efforts despite initial disclosure delays.

- **Legal implications for ethical hackers:** Understanding the legal framework is crucial for ethical hackers to avoid unintended consequences. Here's a look at some key laws and considerations:

  o **Computer Fraud and Abuse Act (CFAA) - US:** Enacted in **1986**, the CFAA criminalizes unauthorized access to computer systems. To avoid legal issues, ethical hackers must obtain explicit authorization from the system owner, which means obtaining written permission that clearly outlines the scope of their activities. Violations of the CFAA can result in severe penalties, including fines and imprisonment.

  o **UK Computer Misuse Act:** Like CFAA, this law, passed in **1990**, penalizes unauthorized access to computer systems. However, it offers defenses for individuals with lawful authority to access the system. This includes security professionals conducting authorized penetration testing. The UK Computer Misuse Act has been amended several times to address evolving cyber threats and technologies.

  o **Rights and responsibilities of ethical hackers:** Ethical hackers occupy a unique space in the CyberSecurity landscape. They are entrusted with sensitive information and powerful tools and must navigate a complex legal and moral landscape. Understanding below rights and responsibilities is crucial for maintaining trust and operating within the bounds of the law:

    - **Legal protections:** While laws like the CFAA and the UK Computer Misuse Act focus on unauthorized access, some countries offer limited legal protections for ethical hackers who follow responsible disclosure guidelines. For example, the **Digital Millennium Copyright Act (DMCA)** has exemptions for "good faith" security research in the US. However, these protections are not absolute and can vary significantly by jurisdiction. Ethical hackers should always consult legal counsel if they have questions about their legal standing.

- **Documentation:** Meticulous documentation of all actions and findings is essential. This is legal evidence in disputes and demonstrates a commitment to transparency and accountability. Documentation should include:

- **Scope of authorization:** Documented permission from the system owner, including specific systems and testing methods allowed.

- **Timeline of activities:** Detailed records of all actions taken, including dates, times, and targets.

- **Vulnerability findings:** Comprehensive reports on all discovered vulnerabilities, including their potential impact and recommended remediation steps.

- **Communication records:** Records of all communications with the organization, including emails, phone calls, and meeting notes.

o **Navigating legal protections and potential risks:** While ethical hacking is a valuable practice, it comes with inherent risks. To mitigate these risks and operate within legal boundaries, ethical hackers must take the proactive steps mentioned here to protect themselves:

1. **Engagement contracts:** Before undertaking any ethical hacking engagement, it's crucial to have a clear and comprehensive contract in place. This contract should outline the scope of the engagement, including the specific systems and networks that can be tested. It should also define the ethical hacker's responsibilities, the organization's obligations, and the legal protections afforded to both parties. A well-drafted contract can help mitigate legal risks and provide a clear framework for the engagement.

2. **Bug bounty programs:** Many organizations have established bug bounty programs, which provide a legal and financial framework for responsible disclosure. These programs offer a safe and incentivized way for ethical hackers to report vulnerabilities. By participating in bug bounty programs, ethical hackers can receive rewards for their findings while adhering to the program's terms and conditions. However, it's essential to carefully review the terms of service of each program to ensure compliance and avoid unintended consequences.

Ethical hacking is essential for identifying and mitigating CyberSecurity risks, but it must be conducted within strict legal and moral boundaries. Responsible disclosure protocols ensure that vulnerabilities are addressed collaboratively, benefiting organizations and the wider community. Ethical hackers play a crucial role in enhancing global CyberSecurity resilience by understanding legal implications and adhering to established frameworks.

Intellectual property and digital rights

*Intellectual property is the backbone of innovation in the digital age, while **digital rights** are the keys to fair access. CyberSecurity protects these pillars of progress from erosion.*

Intellectual property (IP and digital rights have become invaluable in today's knowledge-driven economy. From technological innovations to creative works, IP fuels industries and underpins competitive advantages. However, as the world embraces digital transformation, the complexities surrounding IP protection and digital rights enforcement are magnified. Cyber threats like espionage, piracy, and unauthorized reproduction challenge creators, businesses, and policymakers globally. This subchapter explores the intricate dynamics of IP in cyberspace, strategies for safeguarding it, and emerging challenges in the ever-evolving digital landscape.

Understanding intellectual property in cyberspace

IP represents the creations of the mind, such as inventions, literary and artistic works, designs, symbols, signs, images, and names used in commerce. These creations are legally protected to ensure exclusivity and incentivize innovation. There are three primary types of IP:

- **Copyrights:** Copyrights protect artistic and literary works such as software, music, films, books, and articles. This protection grants the creator the exclusive right to reproduce, distribute, perform, display, and adapt their work. In cyberspace, this includes:

  o **Software**: Source codes, executable programs, and software architectures.

  o **Media**: Digital art, videos, and e-books.

  o **Databases**: Structured data collections.

  o **Duration**: In many jurisdictions, copyright protection lasts the creator's lifetime plus 70 years.

  o **Example**: Unauthorized downloading of copyrighted movies or using copyrighted code without permission.

- **Trademarks:** Trademarks secure distinctive signs, logos, or slogans associated with brands. They help consumers identify the source of goods and services and prevent confusion in the marketplace.

  o **Renewable indefinitely**: Trademark protection can be renewed indefinitely if the trademark is actively used in commerce.

  o **Example**: The Nike swoosh or the golden arches of McDonald's.

- **Patents:** Patents grant exclusive rights to inventions, ensuring innovators can profit from their ideas. This protection encourages innovation by providing a legal framework for inventors to commercialize their creations.

    o **Duration**: Patents typically last for 20 years from the filing date.

    o **Example**: Patented drug formulas or new software algorithms.

By understanding these different types of IP, individuals and organizations can protect their IP rights and avoid legal disputes.

The following table summarizes the key differences of different Intellectual properties:

Feature	Copyright	Trademark	Patent
Purpose	Protects original creative works (literary, artistic, musical, and software).	Protects brand identity (logos, slogans, business names, and distinctive symbols).	Protects inventions, processes, or designs that are novel and useful.
Duration	Life of the author + 50 to 70 years (varies by country).	It is indefinite but requires renewal (typically every 10 years).	Generally, 20 years from the filing date (for utility patents).
Scope	Prevents unauthorized reproduction, distribution, or adaptation of works.	Prevents unauthorized use of a brand identifier in commerce.	Grants exclusive rights to make, use, sell, or distribute the invention.
Examples	Books, movies, songs, paintings, software code.	Logos (Nike Swoosh), brand names (Coca-Cola), slogans ("Just Do It").	Pharmaceuticals, mechanical devices, software algorithms, industrial designs.

Table 8.3: Comparison of IP types

Digital Rights Management systems

Digital Rights Management (**DRM**) systems are tools that control how digital content is accessed and used. They are integral in preventing unauthorized duplication and ensuring fair compensation for creators.

The functions of DRM:

- Restricts unauthorized copying.

- Manages licensing agreements.

- Enforces geographical or time-based access limitations.

The challenges in DRM:

- Ethical concerns over consumer rights, like fair use.

- Technical bypass methods, such as DRM removal tools.

The case studies of IP theft and cyber espionage are mentioned as follows:

- **Stuxnet and industrial espionage:** Stuxnet, a cyber weapon targeting Iranian nuclear centrifuges, illustrated the intersection of IP theft and state-sponsored cyber espionage.

- **TikTok algorithm theft allegation:** ByteDance faced accusations of replicating patented recommendation algorithms from Western firms, highlighting IP risks in cross-border tech competition.

Figure 8.2 *Symbolic figure of IP theft*

Protecting intellectual property in the digital age

In today's hyper-connected world, IP has become the lifeblood of innovation-driven businesses. From proprietary algorithms and source code to confidential designs and trade secrets, digital assets represent a significant portion of an organization's value. However, this increasing reliance on digital IP exposes it to many cyber threats. Protecting IP through CyberSecurity is no longer a secondary concern; it's a fundamental business imperative.

Evolving landscape of IP theft

Before the digital age, IP theft often involved someone physically taking or copying sensitive paperwork. While those threats still exist, the digital age has ushered in a new era of cyber espionage and IP theft. Attackers, ranging from lone hackers to state-sponsored actors, are increasingly targeting digital assets due to their high value and the relative ease with which they can be exfiltrated and monetized. It is important to note that Protecting IP through CyberSecurity can help mitigate some of these risks.

Motivations behind IP theft:

- **Financial gain**: Stolen IP can be sold on the black market, used to create counterfeit products, or leveraged for competitive advantage.

- **Competitive espionage**: Companies may use cyber espionage to gain an edge over their rivals by stealing trade secrets, product designs, or market research.

- **State-sponsored espionage**: Governments may target IP to advance their national interests, bolster their domestic industries, or gain a military advantage.

- **Ideological or political motivations**: Hacktivists may target IP to expose perceived wrongdoing or advance a political agenda.

Methods of IP theft:

- **Phishing and social engineering**: Tricking employees into revealing credentials or downloading malware.

- **Malware attacks**: Using viruses, Trojans, or ransomware to gain unauthorized access to systems and data.

- **Exploiting vulnerabilities**: Taking advantage of unpatched software or weak security configurations.

- **Insider threats**: Malicious or negligent employees who intentionally or inadvertently leak sensitive data.

- **Supply chain attacks**: Targeting third-party vendors or partners with weaker security to gain access to the primary target's network.

- **Cloud-based attacks**: Targeting cloud storage services or applications to access sensitive data.

Strategies for safeguarding digital assets

Protecting IP through CyberSecurity requires a multi-layered approach encompassing people, processes, and technology.

Foundational CyberSecurity practices are as follows:

- **Strong access controls:**
  - **Principle of Least Privilege (PoLP):** Grant users only the necessary access to perform their jobs.
  - **Multi-factor authentication (MFA):** Require multiple forms of authentication (e.g., password, OTP, biometrics) for all users, especially for sensitive systems.

- o **Regular access reviews**: Periodically review user access rights and revoke unnecessary permissions.

- **Robust network security:**

  - o **Firewalls**: Implement firewalls to control network traffic and block unauthorized access.

  - o **Intrusion Detection and Prevention Systems (IDS/IPS):** Monitor network traffic for malicious activity and block suspicious connections.

  - o **Virtual Private Networks (VPNs):** Encrypt network traffic, especially for remote access.

- **Endpoint protection:**

  - o **Antivirus/Anti-malware**: Deploy and regularly update endpoint security software on all devices.

  - o **Endpoint Detection and Response (EDR):** Provide advanced threat detection and response capabilities.

  - o **Data Loss Prevention (DLP):** Monitor and prevent sensitive data from leaving the organization's control.

- **Data encryption:**

  - o **Encryption at rest:** Encrypt sensitive data stored on servers, laptops, and other devices.

  - o **Encryption in transit:** Use protocols like TLS/SSL to encrypt data transmitted over networks.

- **Regular security assessments:**

  - o **Vulnerability scanning:** Regularly scan systems and applications for known vulnerabilities.

  - o **Penetration testing:** Simulate real-world attacks to identify security weaknesses.

- **Patch management:** Implement a robust patch management process to address known vulnerabilities in operating systems and applications promptly.

- **Secure Software Development Lifecycle (SDLC):** Integrate security considerations into every stage of the software development process. This includes using secure coding practices and performing code reviews to identify security flaws.

IP-specific security measures are as follows:

- **Data classification and labelling:** Categorize data based on its sensitivity and apply appropriate security controls. Labeling helps employees understand the sensitivity of the information they handle. Protecting IP through CyberSecurity includes classifying your most sensitive data.

- **Digital Rights Management:** Use DRM technologies to control access to and usage of sensitive digital assets, such as documents, designs, and code.

- **Watermarking:** Embed digital watermarks in sensitive documents and images to deter unauthorized sharing and identify the source of leaks.

- **Secure collaboration platforms:** Use secure platforms for sharing and collaborating on sensitive IP, with features like access controls, audit trails, and encryption.

- **Monitoring and auditing:**

  o Implement systems to monitor user activity, data access, and network traffic for suspicious behavior that could indicate IP theft.

  o Regularly audit security logs and access records to detect and investigate potential security incidents.

Role of CyberSecurity in IP compliance

Protecting IP through CyberSecurity is not just a best practice; it's increasingly becoming a legal and regulatory requirement. Several industry standards and regulations mandate specific CyberSecurity measures to protect sensitive data, including IP:

- **General Data Protection Regulation:** While primarily focused on personal data, GDPR also has implications for IP protection, mainly when IP includes personal data. Organizations must implement appropriate technical and organizational measures to protect all data, including IP.

- **NIST CyberSecurity Framework**: This framework provides comprehensive guidelines for managing CyberSecurity risk, including protecting sensitive information like IP.

- **ISO 27001:** An international standard for **information security management systems (ISMS)**, ISO 27001 provides a framework for establishing, implementing, maintaining, and continually improving an organization's information security posture, which includes IP protection.

- **Trade Secrets Laws**: Many countries have laws protecting trade secrets, and these laws often require organizations to take reasonable steps to maintain the secrecy of their information. Protecting IP through CyberSecurity measures is essential for demonstrating compliance with these laws.

- **Industry-Specific Regulations**: Certain industries, such as healthcare (HIPAA) and finance (PCI DSS), have specific regulations that mandate CyberSecurity controls to protect sensitive data, including IP.

Compliance with these standards and regulations helps protect IP, demonstrate due diligence, reduce legal liability, and enhance an organization's reputation.

Insider risks and external breaches

Threats to IP: Insider risks and external breaches represent two sides of the same coin. Organizations must address both to protect their valuable digital assets effectively.

Insider **threats** Insider threats are often considered the most challenging to detect and mitigate because they involve individuals who have legitimate access to sensitive information. Protecting IP through CyberSecurity is an essential part of mitigating these risks.

Types of insider threats:

- **Malicious insiders:** Employees or contractors who intentionally steal or leak IP for personal gain, revenge, or other motives.

- **Negligent insiders:** Employees or contractors who unintentionally expose IP due to carelessness, lack of awareness, or poor security practices.

- **Compromised insiders:** Individuals whose credentials or devices have been compromised by external actors.

Mitigating insider threats:

- **Background checks:** Conduct thorough background checks on employees and contractors who will have access to sensitive IP.

- **Security awareness training**: Educate employees about the importance of IP protection and the risks of insider threats.

- **User activity monitoring:** Implement systems to monitor user activity for suspicious behavior, such as unusual data access patterns or attempts to exfiltrate data.

- **Data Loss Prevention:** DLP solutions detect and prevent unauthorized data transfers.

- **Principle of Least Privilege:** Limit access to sensitive IP to only those who need it

- **Separation of duties:** Divide critical tasks among multiple individuals to prevent anyone from having too much control over sensitive IP.

External breaches: External breaches are typically carried out by hackers, cybercriminals, or state-sponsored actors targeting organizations outside their networks:

- **Common attack vectors:**

    o **Phishing:** Tricking employees into revealing credentials or downloading malware.

o **Malware:** Using viruses, Trojans, or ransomware to gain unauthorized access to systems and data.

o **Vulnerability exploits:** Taking advantage of unpatched software or weak security configurations.

o **Denial-of-Service (DoS) attacks:** Disrupting access to systems or services, often as a distraction for other malicious activities.

o **Supply chain attacks:** Targeting third-party vendors or partners to gain access to the primary target's network.

- **Mitigating external breaches:**

  o **Strong perimeter security:** Implement firewalls, IDS/IPS, and other network security controls.

  o **Regular security assessments:** Conduct vulnerability scans and penetration tests to identify and address security weaknesses.

  o **Patch management:** Promptly apply security patches to operating systems and applications.

  o **Endpoint protection:** Deploy and maintain up-to-date antivirus, anti-malware, and EDR solutions.

  o **Threat intelligence:** Leverage threat intelligence feeds to stay informed about the latest threats and vulnerabilities.

  o **Incident response plan:** Develop and regularly test an IR plan to ensure a coordinated and effective response to security breaches. Protecting IP through CyberSecurity is a key consideration when building such a plan.

The following table shows a comparative summary of security controls:

Feature	Description	Benefits for IP Protection
Access control	Restricts access to systems and data based on user roles and permissions.	Prevents unauthorized access to sensitive IP. Enforces PoLP.
Encryption	Protects data at rest and in transit by converting it into an unreadable format.	Safeguards IP from theft or unauthorized disclosure even if a breach occurs.
DLP	Monitors and prevents sensitive data from leaving the organization's control.	Detects and blocks attempts to exfiltrate IP, whether intentional or accidental.

Feature	Description	Benefits for IP Protection
DRM	Controls access to and use of digital assets like documents, designs, and code.	Limits the ability to copy, share, or modify IP without authorization.
Watermarking	Embeds digital fingerprints in documents and images.	Deters unauthorized sharing and helps trace leaks back to the source.
SIEM	Aggregates and analyses security logs from various sources to detect and respond to threats in real-time.	Provides visibility into potential IP theft attempts and enables rapid response.
UEBA	**User and Entity Behavior Analytics (UEBA)** uses machine learning to detect anomalous user behavior.	Identifies insider threats by detecting deviations from standard user activity patterns that could indicate IP theft.
Training	Educates employees about CyberSecurity threats and best practices.	Reduces the risk of human error leading to IP theft. Improves awareness of social engineering and phishing attacks.
Auditing	Educates employees about CyberSecurity threats and best practices.	It helps identify security breaches and policy violations that could compromise IP.

Table 8.4: Comparative summary of security controls

Global challenges and future directions

The digital revolution has fundamentally reshaped the landscape of IP. While offering unprecedented opportunities for innovation and creativity, it has also created a complex web of challenges, particularly concerning enforcement, emerging technologies, and the delicate balance between fostering innovation and ensuring adequate protection. This exploration delves into the global challenges and future directions of IP, examining the difficulties of cross-border enforcement, the implications of digital rights trends like AI-generated content and NFTs, and the critical need to balance innovation with protection.

Cross-border IP enforcement challenges

The internet's borderless nature poses significant challenges to IP enforcement. While IP rights are typically territorial, online infringement often transcends national boundaries, making it difficult to identify perpetrators, gather evidence, and enforce judgments. Global challenges and future directions in IP are directly tied to how we address these issues:

- **Jurisdictional complexities:**
  - **Determining applicable law**: When infringement occurs online, it's often unclear which country's laws apply. The infringer's location, the server

hosting the infringing content, and the target audience can all be in different jurisdictions.

- o **Enforcing judgments abroad**: Even if a court issues a judgment against an infringer, enforcing that judgment in a foreign country can be a lengthy and expensive, requiring navigating different legal systems and procedures.

- o **Varying legal standards**: IP laws and enforcement mechanisms differ significantly across countries. What constitutes infringement in one jurisdiction may not in another, creating uncertainty and potential conflicts.

- **Challenges in the digital environment:**

  - o **Anonymity and pseudonymity**: The internet allows infringers to operate anonymously or under pseudonyms, making identifying and locating them difficult.

  - o **Rapid dissemination of infringing content**: Digital content can be copied and distributed globally within seconds, making it challenging to contain infringement once it occurs.

  - o **Domain name disputes**: The proliferation of domain names and the ease with which they can be registered has increased cybersquatting and other domain name disputes.

  - o **Challenges with intermediaries**: Determining the liability of online intermediaries, such as search engines, social media platforms, and e-commerce marketplaces, for hosting or facilitating access to infringing content is a complex and evolving area of law.

- **International cooperation and harmonization:**

  - o **Treaties and agreements:** International treaties like the Berne Convention, the Paris Convention, and the TRIPS Agreement provide a framework for international IP protection, but their enforcement mechanisms are often weak.

  - o **Bilateral and multilateral cooperation:** Effective cross-border enforcement requires cooperation between countries in information sharing, evidence gathering, and mutual legal assistance.

  - o **Harmonization of laws:** While complete harmonization of IP laws is unlikely, efforts to promote greater consistency and predictability in IP laws across jurisdictions can facilitate enforcement.

  - o **Capacity building:** Providing technical assistance and training to developing countries can help them strengthen their IP enforcement capabilities.

Emerging trends in digital rights

The digital landscape constantly evolves, and new technologies create opportunities and challenges for IP owners. How we manage these emerging trends will define global challenges and future directions. Some points to be kept in mind are as follows:

- **AI-generated content:** The rise of AI has blurred the lines of authorship and creation. AI systems can now generate text, images, music, and even code that are often indistinguishable from human-created works. This raises fundamental questions about:

  - **Copyright ownership:** Can AI be considered an author for copyright purposes? Most jurisdictions currently require human authorship for copyright protection.

  - **Infringement:** If an AI generates a work substantially like an existing copyrighted work, who is liable for infringement—the AI developer, the user, or no one?

  - **Training data:** AI systems are trained on vast amounts of data, which may include copyrighted works. Does using copyrighted works to train AI constitute infringement?

- **Non-Fungible Tokens (NFTs):** NFTs are unique digital assets verified and recorded on a blockchain. They have gained popularity as a way to represent ownership of digital art, collectibles, and other unique items.

  - **Copyright vs. ownership:** Owning an NFT does not necessarily mean owning the copyright to the underlying work. The copyright may remain with the original creator.

  - **Authenticity and provenance:** NFTs can help verify the authenticity and provenance of digital assets, but they do not prevent unauthorized copying or distribution of the underlying work.

  - **Smart contracts:** NFTs can be programmed with smart contracts that automatically execute specific actions, such as paying royalties to the original creator upon resale.

- **The metaverse and virtual worlds:** As virtual worlds and the metaverse become more immersive and interactive, new questions arise regarding IP protection in these digital realms:

  - **Virtual goods and avatars:** Can IP law protect virtual goods, avatars, and other digital creations?

  - **Infringement in virtual environments**: How can IP rights be enforced in virtual worlds where users can easily copy and modify digital objects?

    o   **Jurisdiction and enforcement:** Which country's laws apply to infringements in the metaverse?

Balancing innovation and protection

One of the most critical global challenges and future directions in the IP sphere involves striking the right balance between incentivizing innovation and ensuring adequate protection for creators.

The role of IP in innovation:

- **Incentives for creation:** IP rights, particularly patents and copyrights, provide creators exclusive rights to their works, incentivizing them to invest time and resources in developing new ideas and creations.

- **Promoting competition:** IP can foster competition by allowing businesses to differentiate their products and services based on unique features and designs.

- **Attracting investment:** A strong IP system can attract investment in research and development by providing a degree of certainty that investors can recoup their investments.

The risks of overprotection are:

- **Stifling creativity:** Overly broad or strong IP protection can stifle creativity and innovation by making it difficult for others to build upon existing works.

- **Limiting access to knowledge:** Restrictive IP laws can limit access to knowledge and information, particularly in developing countries.

- **Creating monopolies:** In some cases, strong IP protection can lead to monopolies, harming consumers by reducing choice and increasing prices.

Finding the right balance:

- **Tailoring IP protection:** IP laws should be tailored to the specific characteristics of different industries and technologies.

- **Promoting open innovation:** Open innovation models, such as open-source software and Creative Commons licenses, can encourage collaboration and knowledge sharing while protecting creators to some degree.

- **Exceptions and limitations:** IP laws should include exceptions and limitations, such as fair use or fair dealing, to allow for specific uses of copyrighted works without permission, such as for research, education, or criticism.

- **Public domain:** Ensuring that works eventually enter the public domain, where anyone can freely use them, is essential for fostering creativity and innovation.

Table 8.5 reflects the feature differences in IP enforcement mechanisms:

Feature	Civil litigation	Criminal prosecution	Administrative remedies	Border measures
Nature of action	Private lawsuit between IP owner and infringer.	Government-led prosecution of IP crimes.	Actions taken by government agencies (e.g., customs).	Measures to prevent the import/export of infringing goods.
Remedies	Injunctions, damages, account of profits.	Fines, imprisonment.	Seizure of goods, warnings, fines.	Seizure and destruction of infringing goods.
Burden of proof	Balance of probabilities (generally).	Beyond a reasonable doubt.	Varies by jurisdiction and agency.	Varies by jurisdiction and agency.
Cost	High	It can be high but often borne by the state.	Generally lower than litigation.	Relatively low.
Speed	It can be slow.	It can be slow.	It can be faster than litigation.	It can be fast.
Effectiveness	Depends on factors like the infringer's assets and jurisdiction.	The deterrent effect but may not provide compensation.	It can be effective for specific types of infringement.	Effective for preventing physical goods from crossing borders.
Nature of action	Private lawsuit between IP owner and infringer.	Government-led prosecution of IP crimes.	Actions taken by government agencies (e.g., customs).	Measures to prevent the import/export of infringing goods.

Table 8.5: *Comparative summary of IP enforcement mechanism*

Future directions and recommendations

Addressing the global challenges and future directions of IP in the digital age requires a multi-faceted approach involving:

- **Strengthening international cooperation:**
  - **Enhanced information sharing**: Establish mechanisms for more effective information sharing about IP infringers and enforcement actions between countries.
  - **Joint investigations:** Conducting joint investigations and enforcement actions against cross-border infringers.
  - **Capacity building:** Providing technical assistance and training to developing countries to help them strengthen their IP enforcement capabilities.

- o **Harmonization of standards:** Promoting greater consistency in IP laws and enforcement procedures across jurisdictions.

- **Adapting IP laws to new technologies:**

  - o **Clarifying copyright in AI-generated works:** Developing clear legal frameworks for determining authorship and ownership of works created by AI.

  - o **Addressing the challenges of NFTs:** Providing greater clarity on the relationship between NFT ownership and copyright and exploring the potential of smart contracts for managing digital rights.

  - o **Developing IP frameworks for the metaverse:** Establishing clear rules for IP protection in virtual worlds, including protecting virtual goods and enforcing rights in virtual environments.

- **Promoting a balanced approach to IP protection:**

  - o **Tailoring IP laws to specific industries:** Different industries have different needs, and a one-size-fits-all approach to IP protection may not be appropriate.

  - o **Strengthening exceptions and limitations:** Ensuring IP laws include robust exceptions and limitations for fair use, research, education, and other socially beneficial uses of protected works.

  - o **Supporting open innovation models:** Encouraging the adoption of open innovation models that promote collaboration and knowledge sharing while providing adequate protection for creators.

  - o **Educating the public:** Raising public awareness about the importance of IP and the need to respect creators' rights.

Conclusion

This chapter highlights the critical role of legal and ethical frameworks in ensuring CyberSecurity practices align with societal, organizational, and individual expectations. The chapter underscores that CyberSecurity is not just a technical domain but a deeply legal and ethical responsibility. From understanding global CyberSecurity laws to navigating the moral boundaries of hacking, this chapter explores how organizations can foster compliance, maintain trust, and avoid liabilities. IP and digital rights, which form the backbone of innovation and creativity, also feature prominently, showcasing how robust CyberSecurity measures can safeguard these critical assets.

As cyber threats grow increasingly sophisticated, the need for clear laws, responsible disclosures, and practical compliance frameworks becomes paramount. Emerging challenges, such as AI, IoT regulations, and cross-border data transfers, demand proactive strategies to navigate the legal landscape. Ultimately, CyberSecurity leaders must blend technical expertise with a deep understanding of legal and ethical considerations to protect assets and uphold trust in the digital age.

Points to remember

- **CyberSecurity laws:** Global regulations like GDPR and CCPA set data protection and privacy compliance standards.

- **Ethical hacking:** Following responsible disclosure protocols builds trust while adhering to ethical boundaries.

- **IP protection:** Safeguarding IP requires robust CyberSecurity and strategic planning.

- **Emerging trends:** AI, IoT laws, and cross-border data transfers represent evolving legal challenges.

- **Balance of compliance and ethics:** Striking a balance between legal requirements and ethical conduct ensures long-term trust and innovation.

Join our book's Discord space

Join the book's Discord Workspace for Latest updates, Offers, Tech happenings around the world, New Release and Sessions with the Authors:

https://discord.bpbonline.com

CHAPTER 9

Emerging Trends in CyberSecurity

Introduction

As technology advances, the cyber landscape evolves. To stay ahead, mastering emerging trends is not just strategic—it is essential for resilience and foresight.

The only constant in CyberSecurity is change. Yesterday's cutting-edge defenses are today's vulnerabilities. The rapid evolution of technology presents unprecedented opportunities and significant challenges in CyberSecurity. Emerging trends like **artificial intelligence (AI)**, the **Internet of Things (IoT)**, **Quantum computing**, and **blockchain** reshape how security is approached and delivered. This chapter explores these innovations and prepares CyberSecurity professionals to anticipate and mitigate future threats. It emphasizes the need for proactive threat intelligence, blockchain's transformative potential, and quantum computing's disruptive power.

Structure

The chapter covers the following topics:

- Threat intelligence and information sharing
- Blockchain and distributed ledger technology
- Internet of Things

- Artificial intelligence and machine learning
- Quantum computing

Objectives

The CyberSecurity landscape is not static; it is a dynamic, ever-evolving battlefield where the only constant is change. Throughout the preceding chapters of this book, we've delved into the foundational principles, best practices, and essential tools that form the bedrock of effective CyberSecurity. We've explored network security, cryptography, risk management, and incident response, among other critical areas. However, just as technology continues its relentless march forward, so too do the tactics and techniques of cyber adversaries. This final chapter, *Emerging Trends in CyberSecurity*, is dedicated to peering into the future. We will examine five pivotal areas rapidly reshaping CyberSecurity: threat intelligence, blockchain, the IoT, AI, and quantum computing. These are not merely theoretical concepts; they are the realities shaping the future of cyber warfare, demanding our attention and understanding. Each of these technologies presents unprecedented opportunities and formidable challenges for CyberSecurity professionals. *Figure 9.1* is a symbolic image representing the future and emerging trends in the CyberSecurity domain:

Figure 9.1 *Emerging trends in CyberSecurity*

Threat intelligence and information sharing

In an interconnected world, sharing intelligence isn't a choice—it's a defense strategy.

In the digital age, where data is the new oil and technology drives critical infrastructure, the security of information assets is paramount. Cyber threats evolve daily, challenging traditional defense mechanisms and pushing organizations toward innovative solutions. Threat intelligence and information sharing are essential pillars of modern CyberSecurity strategies.

About threat intelligence

Threat intelligence is actionable information about existing or emerging cyber threats that organizations use to prevent, detect, or mitigate attacks. Unlike raw data, it involves contextualized insights—understanding the **who, what, when, why**, and **how** of potential threats. It transforms CyberSecurity from a reactive function into a proactive, intelligence-driven endeavor.

Defining threat intelligence and its various forms

Threat intelligence can be broadly categorized into four main types, each serving a different purpose and catering to different audiences within an organization:

- **Strategic threat intelligence:** This high-level intelligence provides a broad overview of the threat landscape, focusing on trends, emerging threats, and threat actors' motivations. It's typically consumed by executives and decision-makers to inform long-term security strategy and resource allocation. Strategic intelligence helps answer questions like: *What are the biggest cyber threats facing our industry?* or *How are geopolitical events impacting the cyber threat landscape?*

- **Tactical threat intelligence:** This type of intelligence focuses on the specific TTPs adversaries use. It provides detailed information about the tools, techniques, and procedures employed in attacks, allowing security teams to understand how attacks are carried out and develop specific countermeasures. Tactical intelligence helps answer questions like: *What malware variants are being used in current campaigns targeting our sector?* or *What vulnerabilities are being exploited by a specific threat actor?*

- **Operational threat intelligence:** This intelligence provides context around specific cyber events or incidents. It helps security analysts understand an attack's who, what, when, where, and why, enabling them to respond more effectively and efficiently. Operational intelligence helps answer questions like: *What is the likely motive behind this specific attack?* or *What other organizations have been targeted by this same threat actor?*

- **Technical threat intelligence:** This type of intelligence consists of technical **indicators of compromise (IOCs)**, such as IP addresses, domain names, file hashes, and malware signatures. Security tools and automated systems typically use it to detect and block malicious activity. Technical intelligence helps answer questions like: *Is this IP address associated with known malicious activity?* or *Does this file match the signature of a known malware variant?*

The following table outlines various types of threat intelligence, detailing their purpose, target audience, and illustrative questions they can help answer. Understanding these distinctions is crucial for developing a comprehensive and effective CyberSecurity strategy.

Type of threat intelligence	Description	Audience	Example questions answered
Strategic	High-level overview of the threat landscape, trends, and motivations of threat actors.	Executives, Board Members, CISOs	1. What are the most significant cyber threats facing our industry? 2. How are geopolitical events impacting the cyber threat landscape? 3. What are our long-term security risks?
Tactical	Specific TTPs used by adversaries, including tools, techniques, and procedures.	Security Teams, SOC Analysts, IR Teams	1. What malware variants are being used in current campaigns? 2. What vulnerabilities are being exploited by a specific threat actor? 3. How can we detect this attack?
Operational	Context around specific cyber events or incidents, including an attack's who, what, when, where, and why.	Security Analysts, Incident Responders	1. What is the likely motive behind this specific attack? 2. What other organizations have been targeted by this same threat actor? 3. What is the impact of this attack?
Technical	Technical IOCs include IP addresses, domain names, file hashes, and malware signatures.	Security Tools, Automated Systems, SOC Analysts	1. Is this IP address associated with known malicious activity? 2. Does this file match the signature of a known malware variant?

Table 9.1: Types of threat intelligence

Threat intelligence lifecycle

The threat intelligence lifecycle is a continuous process that involves several distinct phases:

- **Planning and direction:** This initial phase involves defining the goals and objectives of the threat intelligence program. Based on the organization's risk profile, assets, and business objectives, identifying its specific intelligence requirements is crucial. This phase sets the foundation for all subsequent activities. Example questions answered in this phase: What are our critical assets? What threats are most likely to target us? What information do we need to collect?

- **Collection:** This phase involves gathering raw data from various sources, both internal and external. The collected data can be structured or unstructured, including technical indicators, threat reports, news articles, social media posts, and dark web forums. The collection strategy should align with the intelligence requirements defined in the planning phase. Key considerations in this phase: What sources are most relevant to our needs? How will we access and collect the data? How will we ensure the reliability of the collected data?

- **Processing:** Once data is collected, it needs to be processed and normalized into a consistent format. This may involve data cleaning, deduplication, translation, and enrichment. The goal is to transform raw data into a format that can be easily analyzed and used to generate intelligence. Key considerations: How will we standardize the format of the collected data? How will we enrich the data with additional context?

- **Analysis:** This is the core of the threat intelligence process. Analysts examine the processed data to identify patterns, trends, and connections. They use various analytical techniques to assess the credibility of the information, identify threat actors, understand their motivations and TTPs, and generate actionable intelligence. The analysis phase answers key questions like: What are the implications of this data? What is the likelihood and impact of a potential attack?

- **Dissemination:** The insights generated during the analysis phase need to be communicated to the relevant stakeholders promptly and effectively. This may involve creating reports, dashboards, alerts, or briefings tailored to the specific needs of different audiences (e.g., executives, security analysts, incident responders). Key considerations: Who needs this information? What format is most appropriate for each audience? How will we ensure the timely delivery of the intelligence?

- **Feedback:** This crucial phase involves gathering feedback from intelligence consumers to assess its effectiveness and identify areas for improvement. Feedback helps refine the intelligence requirements, collection strategies, and analytical processes, ensuring the threat intelligence program remains relevant and effective. Key questions for gathering feedback: Was the intelligence actionable? Did it help improve our security posture? How can we improve the intelligence process?

Key sources of threat intelligence

Threat intelligence can be gathered from various sources, each providing a unique perspective on the threat landscape. The effectiveness of threat intelligence hinges on the quality and diversity of its sources. The table explores key sources of threat intelligence, briefly describing their respective advantages and disadvantages:

Source	Description	Pros	Cons
Open-Source Intelligence (OSINT)	Publicly available information from news, blogs, social media, forums, government reports, etc.	Free, readily accessible, provides broad coverage	It can be overwhelming, may contain inaccurate or outdated information, and requires careful vetting
Commercial Threat Intelligence Feeds	Subscription-based services provide curated and analyzed threat data.	High-quality data, often includes technical indicators, threat reports, and vulnerability information, can save time and resources	It can be expensive, may not be tailored to specific organizational needs
Government Agencies	Information shared by government agencies like CISA (US) or similar organizations worldwide.	It often provides insights into nation-state activities and can be highly reliable.	It may be limited in scope, may not be shared promptly, and may require security clearances.
Internal Telemetry and Logs	Data is collected from internal systems, such as network traffic, endpoint, and security event logs.	Provides insights into your environment, tailored to your specific infrastructure and threats	Requires robust logging and monitoring capabilities, can generate large volumes of data, analysis can be time-consuming
Honeypots	Decoy systems are designed to attract and trap attackers.	Provides insights into attacker TTPs, can generate high-fidelity alerts	Requires careful setup and management, may not attract all types of attacks
ISACs/ISAOs	Industry-specific or geographically focused communities where members share threat information and best practices and collaborate on incident response.	Sector-specific threat intelligence, peer-to-peer collaboration, access to a trusted network	Requires active participation, may be limited to specific industries or regions, information sharing may be subject to legal and regulatory constraints

Table 9.2: Sources of threat intelligence

Threat Intelligence Platforms

Threat Intelligence Platforms (TIPs) are specialized software solutions that streamline and automate the threat intelligence lifecycle. They act as central repositories for threat data, providing tools for aggregation, correlation, analysis, and visualization. TIPs have become essential tools for organizations of all sizes, enabling them to manage the ever-increasing volume and complexity of threat data.

Exploring the functionalities of TIPs

TIPs offer a wide range of functionalities that support various stages of the threat intelligence lifecycle:

- **Data aggregation and normalization:** TIPs can ingest data from a multitude of sources, including commercial feeds, open-source intelligence, internal logs, and security tools. They normalize this data into a standardized format, making it easier to analyze and correlate.

- **Data enrichment:** TIPs can automatically enrich threat data with additional context from various sources. For example, they can add information about the reputation of an IP address, the geolocation of a domain, or the known vulnerabilities associated with a particular software version.

- **Correlation and analysis:** TIPs provide powerful analytical capabilities to identify relationships between different pieces of threat data. They can correlate IOCs with specific threat actors, campaigns, or malware families.

- **Visualization:** TIPs often include dashboards and visualization tools that help analysts understand complex threat data more easily. They can display threat data in various formats, such as graphs, charts, and maps, making it easier to identify patterns and trends.

- **Alerting and reporting:** TIPs can generate alerts based on predefined rules or thresholds. For example, they can alert security teams when detecting a new IOC associated with a high-priority threat actor. They can also generate reports that summarize threat intelligence findings for different audiences.

- **Integration with security tools:** TIPs can integrate with other security tools, such as **Security Information and Event Management (SIEMs)**, **Security Orchestration, Automation, and Response (SOAR)**, and **firewalls**. This integration allows for automated actions based on threat intelligence, such as blocking malicious IP addresses or isolating infected endpoints.

Benefits of using TIPs

Implementing a TIP offers several significant benefits for organizations:

- **Improved threat detection:** TIPs help organizations detect threats faster and more accurately by providing a centralized view of threat data and automating the analysis process.

- **Faster incident response:** TIPs enable security teams to respond to incidents more quickly and effectively by providing contextualized threat intelligence. They can quickly identify the scope of an attack, understand the attacker's TTPs, and prioritize remediation efforts.

- **Better resource allocation:** TIPs help organizations prioritize their security resources by focusing on the most critical threats. They can identify the vulnerabilities that are most likely to be exploited and prioritize patching efforts accordingly.

- **Proactive threat hunting:** TIPs provide the tools and data needed to hunt for threats within an organization's network proactively. Analysts can use the platform to search for IOC, identify suspicious activity, and investigate potential threats before they cause damage.

- **Enhanced situational awareness:** TIPs provide a comprehensive view of the threat landscape, allowing organizations to understand their threats and make informed decisions about their security posture.

Selecting the right TIP for your organization's needs

Choosing the right TIP is crucial for maximizing its effectiveness. Organizations should consider the following factors when evaluating TIP solutions:

- **Scalability:** The TIP should be able to handle the volume of threat data your organization generates and ingests.

- **Integration capabilities:** The TIP should integrate seamlessly with your existing security tools and infrastructure.

- **Ease of use:** The TIP should have an intuitive interface that is easy for analysts to use and understand.

- **Data sources:** The TIP should support various data sources, including commercial feeds, open-source intelligence, and internal logs.

- **Analytical capabilities:** The TIP should provide robust analytical capabilities, including correlation, visualization, and reporting.

- **Cost:** The TIP should be cost-effective and provide a good return on investment.

- **Vendor support:** The vendor should provide reliable technical support and training.

ISACs and ISAOs

Information Sharing and Analysis Centers (ISACs) and **Information Sharing and Analysis Organizations (ISAOs)** play a crucial role in fostering collaboration and information sharing among organizations within specific sectors or across broader communities. They are trusted hubs for collecting, analyzing, and disseminating threat intelligence, best practices, and incident response strategies.

Understanding the role of ISACs and ISAOs

ISACs: ISACs are typically sector-specific organizations facilitating information sharing among members within a particular industry, such as financial services, healthcare, or energy. Industry associations or government agencies often establish them to address the unique CyberSecurity challenges faced by that sector.

ISAOs: ISAOs are like ISACs but are not limited to specific sectors. Organizations can form them from different industries, geographic regions, or even a single supply chain. President Obama created ISAOs as part of a 2015 executive order to encourage greater information sharing among private sector organizations.

ISACs and ISAOs share the common goal of improving the CyberSecurity posture of their members through collaboration and information sharing. They provide a forum for organizations to:

- **Share threat information:** Members can share information about cyber threats, vulnerabilities, and incidents they have experienced. This information is often anonymized to protect the confidentiality of the reporting organization.

- **Collaborate on incident response:** ISACs and ISAOs can facilitate coordinated incident response efforts among members, helping to contain and mitigate the impact of cyberattacks.

- **Share best practices:** Members can share best practices for CyberSecurity, including policies, procedures, and technical controls.

- **Receive early warnings:** ISACs and ISAOs often have access to early warning information about emerging threats and vulnerabilities, which they can disseminate to their members.

- **Conduct joint exercises:** Members can participate in joint CyberSecurity exercises to test their incident response capabilities and improve coordination.

Benefits of participating in ISACs/ISAOs

Participating in an ISAC or ISAO offers several significant benefits for organizations:

- **Access to sector-specific threat data:** ISACs, in particular, provide access to threat intelligence tailored to the specific challenges a particular industry faces. This information can be more relevant and actionable than generic threat intelligence feeds.

- **Peer-to-peer collaboration:** ISACs and ISAOs provide a forum for security professionals to connect with their peers, share experiences, and learn from each other. This peer-to-peer collaboration can be invaluable for developing effective CyberSecurity strategies.

- **Best practice sharing:** Members can learn from the experiences of other organizations and adopt effective best practices.

- **Improved situational awareness:** By participating in an ISAC or ISAO, organizations can better understand the overall threat landscape and the specific threats facing their sector or community.

- **Enhanced incident response capabilities:** ISACs and ISAOs can facilitate coordinated incident response efforts, helping to contain and mitigate the impact of cyberattacks.

- **Increased trust and collaboration:** ISACs and ISAOs foster a culture of trust and collaboration among members, leading to more effective information sharing and a more vigorous collective defense.

Building a threat intelligence program

Building an effective threat intelligence program requires careful planning, execution, and ongoing refinement. It's not just about purchasing tools; it is about developing a comprehensive strategy that aligns with your organization's risk profile and business objectives.

Developing a strategy for threat intelligence collection and analysis:

- **Define your intelligence requirements:** Identify the key questions your threat intelligence program needs to answer. What are your most critical assets? What threats are most likely to target your organization? What information do you need to make informed security decisions? These questions will shape your entire intelligence program.

- **Identify your assets and attack surface:** Understand what you're protecting. Catalog your critical assets (data, systems, applications) and map your attack surface. This includes understanding your network perimeter, cloud environments, third-party vendors, and any other potential entry points for attackers.

- **Prioritize threats:** Not all threats are created equal. Use a risk-based approach to prioritize the threats that pose the most significant risk to your organization based on their likelihood and potential impact.

- **Select appropriate sources:** Choose a mix of internal and external sources that align with your intelligence requirements. Consider open-source intelligence, commercial feeds, government sources, and information-sharing communities like ISACs or ISAOs.

- **Develop collection methods:** Establish processes and procedures for collecting data from your chosen sources. This may involve manual collection, automated tools, or a combination of both.

- **Establish analysis procedures:** Define how to analyze the collected data to extract meaningful insights. This includes identifying patterns, correlating data points, and generating actionable intelligence.

Integrating threat intelligence into existing security operations

Threat intelligence's actual value is realized when integrated into your existing security operations, enabling proactive threat detection, automated response, and informed decision-making.

- **SIEM:** Integrate your TIP with your SIEM to enrich security events with contextual threat intelligence. This allows your SIEM to:

    o **Improve alert triage:** Correlate security alerts with known threat actors, campaigns, or vulnerabilities, helping analysts prioritize the most critical alerts.

    o **Reduce false positives:** Use threat intelligence to filter out false positives, allowing analysts to focus on real threats.

    o **Enhance threat detection:** Create new detection rules based on threat intelligence, such as identifying communication with known malicious IP addresses or domains.

- **SOAR:** Integrate threat intelligence into your SOAR platform to automate incident response workflows. This enables your SOAR platform to:

    o **Automate threat containment:** Automatically block malicious IP addresses, isolate infected endpoints, or suspend compromised user accounts based on threat intelligence feeds.

    o **Enrich investigations:** Automatically gather additional context about an incident from threat intelligence sources, providing analysts with a more complete picture of the attack.

    o **Orchestrate response actions:** Trigger automated response actions across multiple security tools based on threat intelligence, such as updating firewall rules, initiating vulnerability scans, or notifying relevant stakeholders.

- **Firewalls and Intrusion Prevention Systems (IPS):** Feed threat intelligence, such as malicious IP addresses and domain names, into your firewalls and IPS to block known malicious traffic at the network perimeter.

- **Endpoint Detection and Response (EDR):** Integrate threat intelligence with your EDR solution to enhance endpoint protection. This allows your EDR to:

- o   **Detect malicious files:** Identify and block files with known malicious hashes.

- o   **Monitor for suspicious processes:** Detect processes communicating with known command-and-control servers.

- o   **Investigate endpoint activity:** Correlate endpoint activity with threat intelligence to identify potential compromises.

- **Vulnerability management:** Use threat intelligence to prioritize vulnerability patching efforts. Focus on patching vulnerabilities actively exploited by threat actors, as identified by your threat intelligence feeds.

Measuring the effectiveness of your threat intelligence program

It is crucial to measure the effectiveness of your threat intelligence program to demonstrate its value and identify areas for improvement. Key metrics to track include:

- **Mean Time to Detect (MTTD):** How long does it take to detect a security incident? A successful threat intelligence program should help reduce MTTD.

- **Mean Time to Respond (MTTR):** How long does responding to and remediate a security incident take? Threat intelligence should contribute to a faster MTTR.

- **Number of incidents prevented:** Track the incidents that were prevented due to proactive measures taken based on threat intelligence.

- **Reduction in false positives:** A good threat intelligence program should help reduce the number of false positives generated by security tools, freeing up analyst time.

- **Cost savings:** Estimate the cost savings realized by preventing security breaches or reducing the impact of incidents.

- **Number of IOCs shared with ISACs/ISAOs:** Track how much your organization contributes to the broader security community.

- **Number of actionable reports produced:** How many internal reports, based on collected intelligence, resulted in a security action or informed a strategic decision?

Challenges and best practices in threat intelligence

While threat intelligence offers significant benefits, organizations often face challenges in implementing and maintaining an effective program. Understanding these challenges and adopting best practices can help maximize the value of threat intelligence.

Addressing challenges such as data overload, false positives, and attribution difficulties:

- **Data overload:** The sheer volume of threat data available can be overwhelming.

  o **Best practice:** Collect and analyze data relevant to your organization's threat profile and intelligence requirements. Utilize a TIP to automate data aggregation, normalization, and prioritization.

- **False positives:** Threat intelligence feeds can sometimes generate false positives, wasting time and effort.

  o **Best practice:** Establish a process for validating threat intelligence before acting. Use multiple sources to corroborate information and tune your security tools to minimize false positives. Regularly review and update your whitelists and blacklists.

- **Attribution difficulties:** Attributing cyberattacks to specific threat actors can be challenging.

  o **Best practice:** Focus on understanding the TTPs used in attacks rather than solely focusing on attribution. While attribution can be valuable, it's often more important to understand how attacks are carried out so you can defend against them. When attempting attribution, be cautious and rely on substantial evidence. Recognize that attribution is often uncertain and may be subject to change as new information emerges.

- **Data quality and reliability:** The accuracy and reliability of threat intelligence data can vary depending on the source.

  o **Best practice:** Evaluate the credibility of your sources and establish processes for verifying the information you receive. Prioritize reputable commercial feeds and well-vetted open-source resources.

- **Skill gap:** Building and maintaining a threat intelligence program requires skilled analysts who can effectively collect, process, analyze, and disseminate threat intelligence.

  o **Best practice:** Invest in training for your security team and consider hiring experienced threat intelligence analysts. Partner with external providers for specialized expertise if needed.

- **Maintaining context:** Threat intelligence can quickly become outdated or lose its relevance if not correctly maintained and updated.

  o **Best practice:** Establish a process for regularly reviewing and updating your threat intelligence data. Continuously monitor the threat landscape and adapt your intelligence program accordingly.

- **Use standardized formats:** When sharing threat intelligence externally, use standardized formats like STIX and TAXII to ensure interoperability and facilitate automated processing.

Blockchain and distributed ledger technology

Blockchain is more than a financial tool—it's a paradigm shift in trust and security.

Blockchain technology has sparked considerable interest across various industries, and CyberSecurity is no exception. While initially known as the underlying technology for cryptocurrencies like Bitcoin, Blockchain's core principles of decentralization, immutability, and transparency offer a powerful new paradigm for enhancing security in the digital age. This subchapter will delve into the fundamentals of blockchain and its close relative, **distributed ledger technology** (**DLT**), exploring its potential to revolutionize various aspects of CyberSecurity.

Fundamentals of blockchain

Before we explore blockchain's CyberSecurity applications, it is essential to understand the fundamental concepts and principles that underpin this technology.

Defining blockchain and its key characteristics

A blockchain is a distributed, immutable ledger that records and verifies transactions securely and transparently. It's a growing list of records, called blocks, that are linked together using cryptography. Each block contains a cryptographic hash of the previous block, a timestamp, and transaction data.

Key characteristics of blockchain:

- **Decentralization:** Unlike traditional databases controlled by a central authority, a blockchain is distributed across a network of computers (nodes). No single entity controls the blockchain, making it resistant to censorship and single points of failure.

- **Immutability:** Once a block is added to the blockchain, it cannot be altered or deleted. This immutability is ensured through cryptographic hashing and the consensus mechanism. Any attempt to tamper with a block would require changing all subsequent blocks, which is computationally infeasible.

- **Transparency:** All transactions on a public blockchain are visible to anyone on the network. While the participants' identities may be pseudonymous, the transaction details are publicly accessible, promoting transparency and accountability. (Note: Private and permissioned blockchains offer varying degrees of transparency.)

- **Consensus mechanisms:** These algorithms ensure agreement among the nodes on the network about the validity of transactions and the order of blocks. They are crucial for maintaining the integrity and security of the blockchain. Common consensus mechanisms include **Proof-of-Work (PoW)**, **Proof-of-Stake (PoS)**, and **Delegated Proof-of-Stake (DPoS)**.

- **Cryptography:** Blockchain heavily relies on cryptography to secure transactions and maintain data integrity. Cryptographic hashes link blocks together, and digital signatures verify transaction authenticity.

Understanding different types of blockchains

Blockchains can be broadly classified into three main types:

- **Public blockchains:** These are permissionless blockchains, meaning anyone can join the network, participate in the consensus process, and view the transaction history. Examples include Bitcoin and Ethereum. Public blockchains are highly transparent but can face scalability challenges due to their open nature.

- **Private blockchains:** These are permissioned blockchains where access and participation are restricted to authorized entities. Private blockchains are typically used within organizations or consortia to improve efficiency and security in internal processes. They offer greater control and scalability than public blockchains but sacrifice some degree of decentralization.

- **Consortium (or federated) blockchains:** These are partially decentralized blockchains governed by a group of organizations rather than a single entity. They balance public blockchains' openness and private blockchains' control. Consortium blockchains are often used in industries where multiple organizations need to collaborate and share data securely, such as supply chain management or financial services.

Blockchain technology offers varying levels of access and control depending on the type implemented. The following table compares the features of public, private, and consortium blockchains, highlighting their key differences:

Feature	Public blockchain	Private blockchain	Consortium blockchain
Access	Permissionless	Permissioned	Permissioned
Participation	Open to anyone	Restricted to members	Restricted to members
Control	Decentralized	Centralized (single org)	Partially decentralized
Transparency	Fully transparent	Can be controlled	Can be controlled
Scalability	Can be challenging	More scalable	More scalable
Use Cases	Cryptocurrencies, Public Records	Internal processes, Data Management	Inter-organizational collaboration, Supply Chain
Examples	Bitcoin, Ethereum	Hyperledger Fabric, R3 Corda	Ripple, R3 Corda

Table 9.3: Comparison of blockchain types

Exploring the components of a blockchain

Let us break down the key components that make up a blockchain:

- **Blocks:** These are the fundamental building blocks of a blockchain. Each block contains a set of transactions, a timestamp, and a previous block's cryptographic hash, creating a blockchain.

- **Chain:** The sequence of blocks linked together through cryptographic hashes forms the blockchain. This chain creates an immutable record of all transactions.

- **Nodes:** These are the computers or servers participating in the blockchain network. Nodes maintain a copy of the blockchain, validate transactions, and participate in the consensus process.

- **Cryptographic hashes:** These are unique, fixed-size strings of characters generated from data using a hashing algorithm (e.g., SHA-256). Hashes are used to link blocks together and ensure data integrity. Any change to the data in a block will result in a different hash, making tampering easily detectable.

- **Digital signatures:** These are used to verify the authenticity and integrity of transactions. They ensure that only the owner of a private key can authorize a transaction and that the transaction data has not been tampered with during transit.

The following figure illustrates various components of blockchain:

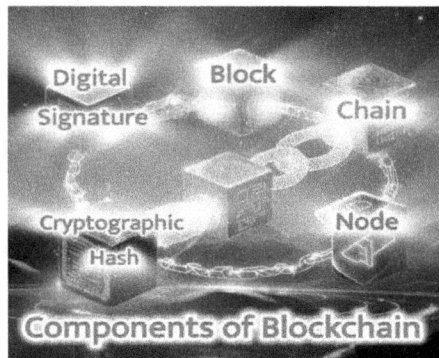

Figure 9.2 Components of blockchain

Blockchain for data integrity and security

One of the most promising applications of blockchain in CyberSecurity is enhancing data integrity and security. Blockchain's immutable nature makes it an ideal solution for protecting sensitive data from tampering and unauthorized modification.

Enhancing data integrity through immutable records and tamper-proof audit trails:

- **Immutable records:** Data cannot be altered or deleted once recorded on a blockchain. This immutability ensures that the data remains accurate and trustworthy over time. Any attempt to modify the data would be immediately detectable, as it would change the block's cryptographic hash and invalidate the entire chain.

- **Tamper-proof audit trails:** Blockchain provides a transparent and auditable trail of all transactions. Every change to the data is recorded on the blockchain, creating a permanent and verifiable record of who did what and when. This audit trail can be used to track data lineage, verify data authenticity, and investigate security incidents.

Securing digital identities and access management using blockchain-based solutions:

- **Decentralized Identifiers (DIDs):** Blockchain can be used to create decentralized digital identities that are not controlled by any single entity. DIDs are globally unique identifiers anchored to a blockchain, allowing individuals and organizations to maintain their digital identities and share verifiable credentials.

- **Self-Sovereign Identity (SSI):** SSI is a concept where individuals have complete control over their digital identities and can choose what information to share and with whom. Blockchain can enable SSI by providing a secure and tamper-proof platform for managing and sharing identity attributes.

- **Verifiable credentials:** These digital credentials can be cryptographically verified using a blockchain. They can represent various types of information, such as academic degrees, professional licenses, and employment history.

- **Improved access control:** Blockchain can enhance access control by providing a secure and transparent way to manage permissions and track access to sensitive resources. Smart contracts can be used to automate access control policies, ensuring that only authorized individuals can access specific data or systems.

Improving supply chain security and provenance tracking:

- **Transparency and traceability:** Blockchain can create a transparent and traceable record of every step in a supply chain, from the origin of raw materials to the delivery of the final product. This allows stakeholders to track the movement of goods, verify their authenticity, and identify potential issues or bottlenecks.

- **Counterfeit prevention:** Blockchain can help prevent counterfeiting by recording product information and tracking its movement on an immutable ledger. Consumers can verify a product's authenticity by scanning a QR code or other identifier linked to the blockchain record.

- **Enhanced security:** Blockchain can improve the security of supply chains by reducing the risk of data tampering and fraud. Its decentralized and immutable nature makes it difficult for malicious actors to manipulate supply chain data or introduce counterfeit products.

Blockchain in CyberSecurity applications

Beyond data integrity and supply chain security, blockchain is finding applications in various other areas of CyberSecurity:

- **Decentralized key management and encryption:**

  o **Secure key storage:** Blockchain can store cryptographic keys decentralized and securely, eliminating the risk of a single point of failure associated with traditional key management systems.

  o **Key recovery:** Blockchain-based key management systems can be designed to allow for secure key recovery in case of loss or compromise. This can be achieved through techniques like multi-signature schemes or sharding.

  o **Enhanced encryption:** Blockchain can facilitate the use of more robust encryption algorithms and protocols by providing a secure and transparent platform for key exchange and management.

- **Blockchain-based intrusion detection and prevention systems:**

  o **Immutable audit logs:** Blockchain can create immutable audit logs of network activity, making it difficult for attackers to cover their tracks. Intrusion detection systems can use these logs to identify suspicious patterns and anomalies.

  o **Decentralized threat intelligence sharing:** As discussed at the begining of the chapter, blockchain can facilitate secure and efficient information sharing among organizations, improving their collective ability to detect and respond to cyber threats.

  o **Reputation systems:** Blockchain-based reputation systems can track the behavior of network participants and identify malicious actors. This can help prevent attacks from known bad actors.

- **Securing DNS and mitigating DDoS attacks:**

  o **Decentralized DNS:** Blockchain can create a decentralized **Domain Name System (DNS)** that is more resistant to censorship and single points of failure. This can help to prevent DNS hijacking and other DNS-related attacks.

  o **DDoS mitigation:** Blockchain-based solutions can help mitigate **Distributed Denial of Service (DDoS)** attacks by providing a more resilient and distributed infrastructure. For example, blockchain can create decentralized **content delivery networks (CDNs)** less susceptible to DDoS attacks.

- **Enhancing the security of IoT devices and networks:**

  o **Device identity and authentication:** Blockchain can provide secure and verifiable identities for IoT devices. This can help prevent unauthorized access and ensure that only legitimate devices can connect to the network.

  o **Secure firmware updates:** Blockchain can be used to distribute and verify the integrity of firmware updates for IoT devices. This can help to prevent the installation of malicious or compromised firmware.

  o **Data integrity:** As discussed before, blockchain can ensure that data generated by IoT devices is tamper-proof and trustworthy.

  o **Micro-transactions and access control:** Blockchain can enable secure and efficient micro-transactions between IoT devices, allowing for automated access control and payment for services.

Smart contracts and security automation

Smart contracts are self-executing contracts in which the terms of the agreement between buyer and seller are directly written into lines of code. Some of the security challenges in smart contracts are mentioned as follows:

- **Code vulnerabilities:** If a smart contract's code contains vulnerabilities, attackers can exploit them, leading to financial losses or other security breaches. The DAO hack in 2016 is a prime example of a smart contract vulnerability that resulted in a significant loss of funds.

- **Immutability issues:** Its code cannot be changed once a smart contract is deployed. This can be a problem if a vulnerability is discovered after deployment.

- **Lack of standardization:** The lack of standardization in innovative contract development can make ensuring security and interoperability difficult.

- **Oracle problem:** Smart contracts often rely on external data feeds (oracles) to trigger their execution. The smart contract may execute incorrectly if the oracle is compromised or provides incorrect data.

Challenges and limitations of blockchain in CyberSecurity

While blockchain offers significant potential for enhancing CyberSecurity, it is not a silver bullet. Several challenges and limitations need to be considered:

- **Scalability issues:**

  o **Transaction throughput:** Public blockchains like Bitcoin and Ethereum have limited transaction throughput, meaning they can only process a certain number of transactions per second. This can be a bottleneck for applications that require high transaction volumes.

- **Latency:** The time it takes to confirm a transaction on a blockchain can vary depending on the network congestion and the consensus mechanism used. This latency can be an issue for applications that require real-time or near-real-time transaction processing.

- **Storage requirements:** As the blockchain grows, the storage required to store the entire transaction history increases. This can be a challenge for nodes with limited storage capacity.

- **Regulatory uncertainties:**

  - **Lack of clear regulations:** The regulatory landscape for blockchain technology is still evolving and varies significantly across different jurisdictions. This lack of clarity can create uncertainty for businesses and hinder the adoption of blockchain solutions.

  - **Compliance challenges:** It can be challenging for organizations to ensure their blockchain solutions comply with all applicable regulations, particularly in data privacy and **anti-money laundering (AML)**.

  - **Cross-border transactions:** The decentralized nature of blockchain can make it challenging to determine which jurisdiction's laws apply to a particular transaction, creating legal complexities for cross-border transactions.

- **Energy consumption:**

  - **Proof-of-Work (PoW) blockchains:** Blockchains that use the PoW consensus mechanism, like Bitcoin, require significant amounts of energy for mining. This has raised concerns about the environmental impact of these blockchains.

  - **Alternatives to PoW:** Other consensus mechanisms, like Proof-of-Stake (PoS, are being developed to address the energy consumption issue. However, these mechanisms also have their trade-offs in terms of security and decentralization.

- **51% attacks:**

  - **Concept:** A 51% attack occurs when a single entity or group controls more than 50% of the network's mining hash rate (in PoW systems) or stake (in PoS systems). This allows them to potentially manipulate the blockchain, for example, by double-spending coins or censoring transactions.

  - **Vulnerability:** While challenging to execute on large, established blockchains like Bitcoin, smaller or less secure blockchains are more vulnerable to this type of attack.

- **Private key management:**

  o **Security risks:** The security of blockchain assets and identities ultimately relies on the security of private keys. The corresponding assets can be irretrievably lost or compromised if a private key is lost or stolen.

  o **User responsibility:** Unlike traditional systems where a central authority can reset passwords or recover accounts, users are typically responsible for managing their own private keys in a blockchain environment.

  o **Custodial solutions:** While custodial services exist to manage private keys on behalf of users, they introduce a centralized point of trust and potential vulnerability.

Future trends in blockchain and CyberSecurity

The intersection of blockchain and CyberSecurity is a rapidly evolving field. Here are some key trends that are likely to shape the future:

- **Integration with other technologies (AI, IoT, Cloud):**

  o **AI and blockchain:** As discussed previously, AI can enhance blockchain security by detecting anomalies, automating incident response, and improving threat intelligence. Blockchain, in turn, can provide a secure and transparent platform for training and deploying AI models.

  o **IoT and blockchain:** Blockchain can enhance the security of IoT devices and networks by providing secure device identities, enabling secure communication, and ensuring data integrity.

  o **Cloud and blockchain:** Cloud providers increasingly offer **blockchain-as-a-service (BaaS)** platforms, making it easier for organizations to deploy and manage blockchain applications. Blockchain can also enhance cloud security by providing tamper-proof audit trails and secure data storage.

- **Advancements in scalability and performance:**

  o **Layer-2 solutions:** These solutions, such as state channels and sidechains, are being developed to improve the scalability of public blockchains by processing transactions off-chain and only periodically settling them on the main chain.

  o **Sharding:** This technique involves dividing the blockchain network into smaller, more manageable pieces called shards, allowing for parallel processing of transactions.

  o **New consensus mechanisms:** Research is ongoing to develop more efficient and scalable consensus mechanisms to improve transaction throughput and reduce latency.

- **Increased adoption in specific industries:**
  - **Supply chain management:** Blockchain is expected to see increased adoption in supply chain management, where it can be used to track goods, verify authenticity, and improve transparency.
  - **Healthcare:** Blockchain can be used to securely store and share patient medical records, manage access to sensitive data, and improve the efficiency of clinical trials.
  - **Financial services:** Blockchain has the potential to streamline cross-border payments, reduce fraud, and improve the efficiency of financial markets.
  - **Government:** Governments are exploring using blockchain for various applications, including voting, identity management, and land registry.

Internet of Things

IoT: Where connectivity meets vulnerability.

The IoT is no longer a futuristic concept; it's a rapidly expanding universe of interconnected devices transforming our lives, from smart homes to industrial automation. But with each new connection comes a new vulnerability. This subchapter will equip you to navigate the complex security landscape of the IoT, turning a potential security nightmare into a managed risk and unlocking the transformative power of connected devices while safeguarding against inherent risks.

Understanding the IoT landscape

To effectively address the IoT's security challenges, it's crucial first to understand the diverse landscape of connected devices, their applications, and the underlying architecture of IoT systems.

Defining the IoT and its various applications

The IoT encompasses various devices, applications, and industries. Here are some key examples:

- **Consumer IoT:** This category includes devices used in homes and personal settings, such as:
  - **Smart home devices:** Smart thermostats, lighting systems, security cameras, door locks, and voice assistants.
  - **Wearables:** Smartwatches, fitness trackers, and health monitoring devices.
  - **Smart appliances:** Refrigerators, ovens, washing machines, and other appliances that can be controlled and monitored remotely.

- **Industrial IoT (IIoT):** This refers to the use of IoT in industrial settings, such as:

  o **Manufacturing:** Predictive machinery maintenance, process automation, and supply chain optimization.

  o **Energy:** Smart grids, remote monitoring of pipelines, and optimization of energy consumption.

  o **Agriculture:** Precision farming, livestock monitoring, and automated irrigation systems.

- **Healthcare IoT:** This includes devices and systems used in healthcare settings, such as:

  o **Remote patient monitoring:** Devices that track vital signs and other health data remotely.

  o **Wearable medical devices:** Insulin pumps, pacemakers, and other implantable devices.

  o **Hospital asset tracking:** Tracking the location and status of medical equipment.

- **Smart cities:** This involves the use of IoT to improve urban infrastructure and services, such as:

  o **Traffic management:** Smart traffic lights and sensors to optimize traffic flow.

  o **Waste management:** Sensors in trash bins to optimize collection routes.

  o **Environmental monitoring:** Air quality sensors and noise pollution monitoring.

- **Transportation:** Integrating IoT technologies into vehicles for communication and data exchange.

  o **Fleet management:** GPS tracking, fuel efficiency monitoring, preventative maintenance.

  o **Autonomous vehicles:** Self-driving cars rely on a vast network of sensors and data analysis.

  o **Traffic optimization:** Real-time traffic data analysis for improved traffic light control and congestion management.

Exploring the architecture of IoT systems

While specific implementations vary, most IoT systems share a typical architectural pattern, typically consisting of four main components:

- **Devices (things):** These physical objects are embedded with sensors, actuators, and communication capabilities. They collect data from the environment and may also perform actions based on that data or commands from other system parts.

- **Sensors**: Devices that measure physical properties (temperature, pressure, motion, etc.) and convert them into electrical signals.

- **Actuators**: Devices that receive signals and cause a physical action (e.g., turning on a motor, opening a valve).

- **Gateways:** These act as intermediaries between devices and the cloud. They often perform protocol translation, data filtering, and local processing before forwarding data to the cloud. They may also provide security features like firewalls and intrusion detection systems.

- **Network:** This communication infrastructure connects devices, gateways, and the cloud. Various communication protocols are used in IoT, including Wi-Fi, Bluetooth, Zigbee, Z-Wave, cellular (4G/5G), and **Low-Power Wide-Area Network** (**LPWAN**) technologies like Lora WAN and Sigfox.

- **Cloud platform:** This is where device data is stored, processed, and analyzed. Cloud platforms provide data management, device management, application development, and analytics services. They often offer dashboards and APIs for interacting with the IoT system.

Analyzing key characteristics of IoT devices impacting security

Several characteristics of IoT devices contribute to their unique security challenges:

- **Resource constraints:** IoT devices have limited processing power, memory, and storage capacity. Implementing robust security measures, such as strong encryption and complex authentication mechanisms, isn't easy.

- **Heterogeneity:** The IoT ecosystem is incredibly diverse, with devices from numerous manufacturers using various operating systems, communication protocols, and hardware platforms. This heterogeneity makes it challenging to develop standardized security solutions.

- **Long lifecycles:** Some IoT devices, particularly in industrial settings, are designed to operate for many years or even decades. This can lead to security vulnerabilities becoming outdated and unpatched over time.

- **Physical accessibility:** Many IoT devices are deployed in publicly accessible locations, making them vulnerable to physical tampering or theft.

- **Lack of updates and patching:** Many IoT devices lack mechanisms for automatic updates or are not regularly patched by their owners, leaving them vulnerable to known exploits.

- **Default or weak credentials:** Many IoT devices come with default usernames and passwords that are easily guessable or publicly known. Users often fail to change these credentials, making the devices easy targets for attackers.

The proliferation of IoT devices presents unique security challenges. This table outlines the key characteristics of these devices and their corresponding security implications:

Characteristic	Security implication
Resource constraints	Difficult to implement strong security measures like encryption and complex authentication.
Heterogeneity	Challenging to develop standardized security solutions; interoperability issues.
Long lifecycles	Vulnerabilities may become outdated and unpatched over time.
Physical accessibility	Devices are vulnerable to physical tampering or theft.
lack of updates	Devices may remain vulnerable to known exploits if not regularly patched.
Default credentials	Many devices have default or weak credentials that can be easily guessed or publicly known, making them easy targets for attackers.
Scale and volume	The sheer number of deployed devices creates a massive attack surface and makes monitoring and managing security for each device challenging.
Interconnectivity	A compromise of one device can provide access to an entire network, including other connected devices and sensitive data.

Table 9.4: Security challenges of IoT devices

Security challenges in the IoT

The unique characteristics of the IoT ecosystem create a wide range of security challenges across the device, network, and data layers.

Device vulnerabilities are as follows:

- **Weak authentication:** As mentioned earlier, many IoT devices use default or easily guessable passwords. This makes them vulnerable to brute-force attacks and unauthorized access.

- **Insecure firmware:** The firmware running on IoT devices may contain vulnerabilities that attackers can exploit. These vulnerabilities can arise from coding errors, outdated libraries, or a lack of secure development practices.

- **Lack of patching mechanisms:** Many IoT devices lack mechanisms for automatic updates or are not regularly patched by their owners. This leaves them vulnerable to known exploits that could be quickly addressed with a software update.

- **Physical tampering:** Physically accessible devices can be tampered with or stolen. Attackers may try to extract sensitive information from the device's memory, modify its firmware, or use it to launch attacks on other parts of the network.

- **Side-channel attacks:** These attacks exploit information leaked through a device's physical implementation, such as power consumption or electromagnetic emissions, to extract cryptographic keys or other sensitive data.

- **Lack of secure boot:** Secure boot is a process that ensures that only authorized code is executed during the device's startup. Many IoT devices lack secure boot capabilities, making them vulnerable to malicious code injection.

- **Use of outdated or insecure components**: Some devices use outdated hardware or software components with known vulnerabilities.

Network vulnerabilities are as follows:

- **Insecure communication protocols:** Many IoT devices use insecure communication protocols that do not encrypt data in transit. This makes it possible for attackers to eavesdrop on communications and intercept sensitive information.

- **Lack of network segmentation:** In many IoT deployments, all devices are connected to the same network. An attacker can access all other network devices if one device is compromised.

- **Man-in-the-Middle (MitM) attacks:** Attackers can intercept and modify communications between devices and the cloud or between devices. This can allow them to steal data, inject malicious code, or disrupt the operation of the IoT system.

- **Denial-of-Service (DoS) and Distributed Denial-of-Service (DDoS) attacks:** IoT devices, particularly those with weak security, can be hijacked and launched against other systems. The Mirai botnet is a prime example of this type of attack.

- **Lack of encryption**: Many IoT devices either do not use encryption or use weak encryption for communication, leaving data vulnerable to interception.

- **Inadequate access control**: Insufficient access control mechanisms on the network can allow attackers to move laterally between devices after an initial breach.

Data security and privacy concerns are as follows:

- **Unauthorized data collection:** IoT devices often collect large amounts of personal and sensitive data, such as location information, health data, and usage patterns. This data may be collected without the user's explicit consent or knowledge.

- **Data breaches:** If the data collected by IoT devices is not adequately secured, it can be vulnerable to data breaches. This can have serious consequences for individuals' privacy and security.

- **Data integrity:** If the data collected by IoT devices is tampered with or modified, it can lead to incorrect decisions or actions. For example, if the data from a medical device is altered, it could lead to a misdiagnosis or incorrect treatment.

- **Lack of transparency:** Users often lack visibility into what IoT devices are collecting data, how it is being used, and with whom it is being shared.

- **Data retention and disposal**: Unclear policies on how long data is retained and how it is disposed of can lead to privacy risks.

- **Cross-border data flows**: Data collected by IoT devices may be transferred across borders, raising concerns about compliance with different privacy regulations.

Lack of standardization and interoperability:

- **Fragmented ecosystem:** The IoT ecosystem is highly fragmented, with numerous vendors, platforms, and protocols. This lack of standardization makes it difficult to ensure interoperability and security across different devices and systems.

- **Security by obscurity:** Some vendors rely on proprietary protocols and security measures, making it difficult for independent security researchers to assess the security of their products.

- **Difficulty in implementing uniform security policies:** The lack of standardization makes it challenging to implement and enforce consistent security policies across all devices and systems in an IoT deployment.

Securing the IoT ecosystem

Addressing the security challenges of the IoT requires a multi-faceted approach that encompasses device hardening, network security, data protection, and ongoing monitoring and management.

Implementing device-level security:

- **Secure boot:** Implementing secure boot mechanisms ensures that only authorized firmware can be executed during startup. This helps prevent attackers from loading malicious code onto the device.

- **Firmware integrity verification:** Regularly check the integrity of the device's firmware to ensure it has not been tampered with. This can be done using cryptographic hashes and digital signatures.

- **Strong authentication:** Enforcing strong, unique passwords or other robust authentication methods, such as **multi-factor authentication** (**MFA**) or biometric authentication. Avoid default credentials.

- **Hardware Security Modules (HSMs):** These use dedicated hardware modules to store cryptographic keys and perform cryptographic operations. They provide a higher level of security than software-based solutions.

- **Tamper resistance and detection:** Implementing mechanisms to detect and respond to physical tampering with the device. This may include using tamper-evident seals, sensors that detect when the device's enclosure is opened, or mechanisms that erase sensitive data if tampering is detected.

- **The Principle of Least Privilege involves granting devices only the necessary permissions** for their function, limiting the potential damage from a compromised device.

- **Regular security audits**: Conduct periodic security audits of IoT devices to identify vulnerabilities and ensure adequate security controls.

Securing IoT networks:

- **Network segmentation:** Dividing the IoT network into smaller, isolated segments to limit the impact of a security breach. If one segment is compromised, the attacker's ability to move laterally to other network parts is restricted.

- **Firewalls and Intrusion Prevention Systems:** Deploying firewalls and IPS at the network perimeter and between network segments to block unauthorized access and detect malicious activity.

- **Secure communication protocols:** Using secure communication protocols, such as TLS/SSL, to encrypt data in transit and authenticate devices.

- **Virtual Private Networks (VPNs):** Implementing VPNs to create secure tunnels for communication between devices and the cloud or between different parts of the IoT network.

- **Access Control Lists (ACLs):** Defining and enforcing strict ACLs to control which devices can communicate with each other and external networks.

- **Network monitoring and anomaly detection:** Continuously monitoring network traffic for suspicious activity and using anomaly detection techniques to identify potential threats. This includes monitoring for unusual communication patterns, unexpected data transfers, or attempts to access unauthorized resources.

- **Regular security assessments**: Periodic vulnerability assessments and penetration testing of the IoT network are conducted to identify and address security weaknesses.

- **Intrusion Detection and Prevention Systems (IDPS)**: Deploying IDPS specifically designed for IoT protocols and traffic patterns to detect and block malicious activity.

Protecting data in transit and at rest:

- **Encryption:** Encrypting data in transit and at rest is crucial for protecting sensitive information.

  o **Data in transit:** Encrypt data as it travels between devices, gateways, and the cloud using secure communication protocols like TLS/SSL.

- o **Data at rest:** Encrypt data stored on devices, gateways, and cloud servers using strong encryption algorithms.

- **Data minimization:** Collect and store only the minimum amount of data necessary for the IoT system's intended purpose. This reduces the potential impact of a data breach.

- **Data masking and anonymization:** Techniques for protecting sensitive data by replacing it with pseudonyms or removing identifying information.

- **Secure key management:** Implementing robust key management practices to protect the cryptographic keys used for encryption and decryption.

- **Data Loss Prevention (DLP):** Implementing DLP solutions to monitor and prevent sensitive data from leaving the network without authorization.

- **Access control:** Implementing strict access control policies ensures that only authorized users and devices can access sensitive data.

- **Data retention and disposal policies**: Establishing clear guidelines for how long data should be retained and how it should be securely disposed of when no longer needed.

Utilizing IoT security gateways and platforms:

- **IoT security gateways:** These specialized gateways act as intermediaries between IoT devices and the network, providing a range of security functions, such as:

  - o **Protocol translation:** Translating between different IoT communication protocols to ensure interoperability.

  - o **Firewalling:** Blocking unauthorized access to devices and the network.

  - o **Intrusion detection and prevention:** Monitoring network traffic for malicious activity.

  - o **Data filtering and aggregation:** Reducing the data sent to the cloud and filtering out sensitive information.

  - o **Device authentication and authorization:** Verifying the devices' identity and controlling their network access.

- **IoT security platforms:** These cloud-based platforms provide a centralized management point for securing IoT deployments. They often include features such as:

  - o **Device management:** Onboarding, provisioning, and managing the lifecycle of IoT devices.

  - o **Security monitoring and analytics:** Collecting and analyzing security data from devices and the network.

○ **Threat intelligence integration:** Integrating with threat intelligence feeds to identify known threats.

○ **Automated response:** Automating security responses, such as isolating compromised devices or updating security policies.

○ **Vulnerability management:** Identifying and managing vulnerabilities in IoT devices and systems.

IoT security best practices and standards

To improve the overall security posture of the IoT ecosystem, it is essential to adopt best practices and adhere to relevant industry standards and frameworks:

- **Implementing security by design principles:**

  ○ **Threat modeling:** Threat modeling is conducted during the design phase of an IoT project to identify potential security risks and develop appropriate mitigation strategies. This involves analyzing the system's architecture, identifying potential attackers and their motivations, and assessing the likelihood and impact of various threats.

  ○ **Secure Development Lifecycle (SDL):** Integrating security into every stage of the software development lifecycle, from requirements gathering to deployment and maintenance. This includes conducting security code reviews, penetration testing, and vulnerability scanning.

  ○ **Minimizing attack surface:** Reducing the number of potential entry points for attackers by disabling unnecessary features, closing unused ports, and limiting the amount of data collected and stored.

  ○ **Principle of least privilege:** Granting devices and users only the minimum necessary permissions required to perform their intended functions.

  ○ **Secure by default:** Configuring devices and systems with the most secure settings by default, rather than relying on users to enable security features.

- **Adhering to industry standards and frameworks:** Several industry standards and frameworks provide guidance for securing IoT devices and systems:

  ○ **Open Web Application Security Project (OWASP) IoT top 10:** This list identifies the top 10 security risks for IoT applications and provides recommendations for mitigating them. (Website: **https://owasp.org/**)

  ○ **NIST CyberSecurity for IoT program:** The **National Institute of Standards and Technology** (**NIST**) has developed a framework for improving the CyberSecurity of IoT devices. This framework guides device security, data security, and privacy protection. (Website: **https://www.nist.gov/**)

- o **IoT Security Foundation (IoTSF):** This industry organization promotes best practices for IoT security and provides resources for developers and manufacturers. (Website: **https://www.iotsecurityfoundation.org/**)

- o **CTIA CyberSecurity Certification Program for IoT devices:** This program provides a framework for evaluating the security of IoT devices and certifying those that meet specific security standards. (Website: **https://www.ctia.org/**)

- o **ISO/IEC 27030:2021:** This international standard provides guidelines for security and privacy on the IoT.

- o **EN 303 645**: A European standard establishing a CyberSecurity baseline for consumer IoT products.

Addressing IoT security requires adherence to recognized standards and frameworks. This table compares prominent IoT security standards and frameworks, outlining their focus and key features:

Standard/ Framework	Focus	Key features
OWASP IoT top 10	Identifying and mitigating the top 10 security risks for IoT applications	Provides a prioritized list of vulnerabilities and recommendations for addressing them.
NIST CyberSecurity for IoT	Comprehensive guidance on device security, data security, and privacy	Outlines core CyberSecurity features for IoT devices, guides manufacturers and developers, and addresses considerations for federal agencies deploying IoT.
IoTSF	Promoting best practices and providing resources for IoT security	It offers a security assurance framework, a vulnerability disclosure program, and educational resources.
CTIA Certification	Evaluating and certifying the security of IoT devices	Provides a testing and certification program based on industry-developed security standards.
ISO/IEC 27030:2021	Guidelines for security and privacy on the IoT	Offers a comprehensive framework addressing various aspects of IoT security and privacy, including risk management, security controls, and data protection.
EN 303 645	CyberSecurity baseline for consumer IoT products	It defines specific security requirements for consumer IoT devices sold in Europe, including provisions for secure software updates, vulnerability management, and personal data protection.

Table 9.5: Comparison of IoT security standards and frameworks

- Conducting regular security assessments and penetration testing:

  - o **Vulnerability scanning:** Regularly scanning IoT devices and networks for known vulnerabilities using automated vulnerability scanning tools.

  - o **Penetration testing:** Simulating real-world attacks on IoT systems to identify security weaknesses and assess the effectiveness of security controls.

  - o **Security audits:** Conduct periodic security audits to evaluate the overall security posture of IoT deployments and ensure compliance with relevant standards and regulations.

  - o **Red teaming:** Employing a **red team** of ethical hackers to simulate attacks on the IoT environment and identify vulnerabilities that traditional security assessments might miss.

Future trends in IoT security

IoT security is constantly evolving as new technologies and threats emerge. Some key trends that are likely to shape the future of IoT security include:

- **Anomaly detection**: AI and ML algorithms can analyze large volumes of data from IoT devices and networks to detect unusual patterns or behaviors that may indicate a security threat.

- **Threat intelligence:** AI can automate the process of collecting, analyzing, and disseminating threat intelligence, providing more timely and accurate insights into emerging threats.

- **Automated response:** AI-powered security systems can automatically respond to security incidents, such as isolating compromised devices or blocking malicious traffic.

- **Predictive security**: Using AI and ML to anticipate and prevent attacks before they occur by identifying patterns and predicting likely attack vectors.

- **Adaptive security**: Developing security systems that can dynamically adapt to changing threat landscapes and evolving attack techniques.

Artificial intelligence and machine learning

AI defends—and threatens—the digital frontier.

In CyberSecurity, AI and ML offer a powerful arsenal of tools for automating tasks, analyzing vast datasets, detecting anomalies, and responding to threats in real-time. They can augment human capabilities, enabling security teams to be more efficient and effective in protecting against cyberattacks. For example, AI-powered systems can analyze network traffic to detect malicious activity that traditional signature-based detection methods might miss.

AI and ML in CyberSecurity defense

AI and ML are invaluable tools for enhancing CyberSecurity defenses across various domains. They enable organizations to automate threat detection, accelerate incident response, and improve their security posture.

Key point regarding anomaly detection are as follows:

- **Concept:** Anomaly detection involves identifying unusual patterns or behaviors that deviate from the established norm. In CyberSecurity, this can be used to detect malicious activity that might otherwise go unnoticed. For instance, a sudden spike in network traffic from a particular device or an unusual login attempt from an unfamiliar location could be flagged as an anomaly.

- **How AI/ML enhance it:** ML algorithms can be trained on large datasets of normal network traffic, user behavior, or system activity. Once trained, they can identify deviations from this baseline in real time, flagging potential threats. Think of an AI system that learns your network's typical communication patterns and then alerts you when it sees something unusual.

- **Benefits**:

  o **Detects unknown threats:** Unlike signature-based detection systems, anomaly detection can identify novel attacks that haven't been seen before. This is crucial in a constantly evolving threat landscape.

  o **Reduces false positives:** By focusing on deviations from normal behavior, anomaly detection can reduce the false positives generated by security systems.

  o **Provides Early Warning:** Anomaly detection can provide early warning of a potential attack, allowing security teams to respond before significant damage is done. **Early detection is often the key to minimizing the impact of a breach.**

- **Examples**:

  o **Network Intrusion Detection Systems (NIDS):** AI-powered NIDS can analyze network traffic in real time to identify anomalous patterns that may indicate an intrusion.

  o **User and Entity Behavior Analytics (UEBA):** UEBA systems use ML to create behavioral profiles of users and devices, and then flag any deviations from these profiles.

  o **Fraud detection:** Financial institutions use AI to detect fraudulent transactions by identifying unusual spending patterns.

Threat intelligence analysis

Threat intelligence involves gathering, processing, and analyzing information about potential and current cyber threats. This information can come from various sources, including open-source intelligence, commercial threat feeds, and internal security logs. The goal is to understand threat actors' **tactics, techniques, and procedures (TTPs)** to anticipate and defend against attacks.

- **How AI/ML enhance it:**
  - **Automated data processing:** AI can automate collecting and processing large volumes of threat data from multiple sources. **Natural Language Processing (NLP)** can extract relevant information from unstructured text, such as threat reports and security blogs.

  - **Correlation and analysis:** ML algorithms can identify patterns and correlations in threat data that human analysts might miss. For example, AI can link seemingly unrelated IOCs to identify a specific threat actor or campaign.

  - **Threat prioritization:** AI can help prioritize threats based on their severity, likelihood, and potential impact on the organization. This enables security teams to focus their efforts on the most critical threats.

- **Benefits:**
  - **Faster threat detection:** AI can analyze threat data much faster than humans, enabling organizations to detect threats more quickly.

  - **Improved accuracy:** AI can identify subtle patterns and correlations that might be missed by human analysts, improving the accuracy of threat intelligence.

  - **Enhanced situational awareness:** AI-powered TIPs can comprehensively view the threat landscape, helping organizations understand their threats.

Malware detection and classification

Malware detection involves identifying malicious software, such as viruses, worms, and Trojans. Malware classification involves categorizing malware into families based on their characteristics and behavior. Traditional methods rely on signatures, which are unique patterns that identify known malware.

- **How AI/ML enhance it:**
  - **Signature-less detection:** ML algorithms can be trained to identify malware based on its behavior rather than relying solely on signatures. This enables them to detect new and unknown malware variants, including zero-day exploits.

- o **Polymorphic and metamorphic malware detection:** AI can detect malware that changes its code to evade signature-based detection. This is achieved by analyzing the underlying behavior and functionality of the malware.

- o **Automated malware analysis:** AI can automate analyzing malware samples, extracting key features, and classifying them into different families.

- **Benefits:**

  - o **Detects unknown malware:** AI-powered malware detection systems can identify new and previously unseen malware variants.

  - o **Faster analysis:** AI can analyze malware samples much faster than humans, accelerating incident response.

  - o **Improved accuracy:** Reduces reliance on signatures that can be easily bypassed.

Vulnerability management

Vulnerability management involves identifying, assessing, prioritizing, and remediating vulnerabilities in software and systems. The goal is to reduce the attack surface and prevent attackers from exploiting known weaknesses.

- **How AI/ML enhance it:**

  - o **Vulnerability prioritization:** AI can help prioritize vulnerabilities based on their exploitability, the criticality of the affected asset, and the likelihood of exploitation. This goes beyond traditional severity scores by considering the real-world threat landscape.

  - o **Predictive vulnerability analysis:** ML algorithms can be trained on historical vulnerability data to predict which vulnerabilities will most likely be exploited. This allows organizations to patch vulnerabilities before they are actively targeted proactively.

  - o **Automated patch management:** AI can automate identifying and applying patches to vulnerable systems, reducing the time it takes to remediate vulnerabilities.

- **Benefits:**

  - o **Focus on critical vulnerabilities:** Helps security teams prioritize patching efforts.

  - o **Proactive remediation:** Enables organizations to address vulnerabilities before they are exploited.

  - o **Improved efficiency:** Automates many of the manual tasks involved in vulnerability management.

Automated incident response

Incident response involves the steps taken to identify, contain, eradicate, and recover from a security incident. Traditionally, this process has been largely manual, requiring significant human effort and expertise.

- **How AI/ML enhance it:**
  - **Automated threat detection and investigation:** AI can automatically detect and investigate security incidents, reducing the time it takes to identify and respond to threats.
  - **Automated containment and eradication:** AI-powered systems can automatically take actions to contain and eradicate threats, such as isolating infected systems, blocking malicious traffic, or disabling compromised accounts.
  - **Orchestration and automation:** AI can orchestrate and automate incident response workflows across multiple security tools, streamlining the response process and reducing manual effort. Think of a system that automatically isolates an infected endpoint, triggers a vulnerability scan, and generates a report for the security team.

- **Benefits:**
  - **Faster response times:** AI can respond to incidents much faster than humans, minimizing the impact of a breach.
  - **Reduced workload:** Automates many of the manual tasks involved in incident response.
  - **Improved consistency:** Ensures incident response procedures are followed consistently and accurately.

AI-powered attacks

While AI and ML offer significant benefits for CyberSecurity defense, they also present new challenges as adversaries adopt these technologies to enhance their attacks. It is important to remember that AI is a tool; like any tool, it can be used for good and bad.

Evasion techniques:

Attackers can use AI to develop malware that evades traditional security defenses, such as signature-based detection systems and antivirus software. The details are as follows:

- **How it is done:**
  - **Polymorphic and metamorphic malware:** AI can generate polymorphic and metamorphic malware that constantly changes its code to avoid detection

by signature-based systems. This is like a chameleon constantly changing its skin to blend in with its surroundings.

- o **Adversarial machine learning:** Attackers can use adversarial machine learning techniques to fool AI-powered security systems. This involves crafting malicious inputs designed to cause the AI system to misclassify them as benign. For example, an attacker might make subtle changes to a malware sample that cause an AI-based detection system to classify it as a legitimate file.

- **Examples:**
  - o **Deep locker:** A proof-of-concept malware that uses AI to conceal its malicious payload until it reaches a specific target.

Automated vulnerability discovery and exploitation

Attackers can use AI to automate finding and exploiting vulnerabilities in software and systems. This can significantly accelerate the attack process and make it more difficult for defenders to keep up. The details are as follows:

- **How it is done:**
  - o **Automated vulnerability scanning:** AI-powered tools can scan systems for known vulnerabilities much faster and more efficiently than traditional methods.

  - o **Exploit generation:** AI can automatically generate exploits for newly discovered vulnerabilities, reducing the time attackers take to weaponize them.

  - o **Fuzzing:** AI can enhance fuzzing techniques by feeding random data to a program to identify vulnerabilities. AI-powered fuzzers can learn from previous results to generate more effective inputs, increasing the likelihood of finding exploitable bugs.

AI-powered phishing and social engineering attacks

AI can create more convincing and targeted phishing emails and social engineering attacks. These attacks often trick users into revealing sensitive information or taking actions that compromise their security. The details are as follows:

- **How it is done:**
  - o **Natural Language Generation (NLG):** AI can generate highly realistic and personalized phishing emails that are difficult to distinguish from legitimate communications. Imagine an email that perfectly mimics the writing style of your CEO, asking you to transfer funds to a new account urgently.

- o **Deepfakes:** AI-generated synthetic media, such as audio and video, can impersonate trusted individuals, such as CEOs or colleagues, in social engineering attacks.

- o **Automated social engineering:** AI-powered chatbots can interact with victims in real time, gathering information and manipulating them into taking actions that compromise their security.

Adversarial machine learning

Adversarial machine learning is a specific type of attack that targets AI and ML models themselves. The goal is to manipulate the model's inputs or training data to cause it to make incorrect predictions or classifications. The details are as follows:

- **How it is done:**

  - o **Evasion attacks:** Attackers craft malicious inputs designed to be misclassified by the AI model. For example, adding small perturbations to an image that are imperceptible to humans but cause an image recognition system to misclassify the object.

  - o **Poisoning attacks:** Attackers inject malicious data into the training dataset used to train the AI model. This can cause the model to learn incorrect patterns and make inaccurate predictions.

  - o **Model stealing:** Attackers try to replicate the functionality of a target AI model by querying it with carefully crafted inputs and observing its outputs. This can allow them to create a copy of the model or gain insights into its inner workings.

Building AI-resilient security systems

As AI-powered attacks become more prevalent, it is crucial to develop resilient security systems for these threats. This requires a combination of techniques to protect AI models from manipulation and to detect and mitigate AI-powered attacks, as explained here:

- **Developing robust ML models:**

  - o **Adversarial training:** Training ML models on datasets that include adversarial examples makes them more robust to evasion attacks. This helps the model learn to identify and correctly classify inputs that have been intentionally manipulated. Think of it as exposing the model to various "trick" inputs during training so it's not fooled later.

  - o **Defensive distillation:** This technique involves training a second model to mimic the behavior of the first model but with a smoother decision surface. This makes it more difficult for attackers to find adversarial examples.

- **Input validation and sanitization:** Strict input validation and sanitization techniques are implemented to prevent malicious inputs from being processed by the AI model. This is like having a security guard check every piece of data that enters the system.

- **Feature squeezing:** Reducing the complexity of the input data by compressing or smoothing features, making it harder for attackers to craft adversarial examples.

- **Ensemble methods:** Using multiple ML models in combination to improve robustness. If an adversarial example fools one model, the others may still correctly classify it.

- **Detecting and mitigating AI-powered attacks:**

  - **Monitoring model behavior:** Continuously monitoring AI models for signs of adversarial manipulation, such as unexpected changes in prediction accuracy or unusual patterns in model outputs. This is like regularly checking the vital signs of your AI system.

  - **Adversarial example detection:** Developing techniques to detect adversarial examples before the AI model processes them. This may involve analyzing the input data for subtle perturbations or comparing the model's prediction with the predictions of other models.

  - **Input reconstruction:** Attempting to reconstruct the original input from a potentially adversarial example to identify malicious modifications.

  - **Network monitoring:** Monitoring network traffic for signs of AI-powered attacks, such as unusual communication patterns or attempts to access sensitive data.

  - **Human-in-the-loop systems:** Maintaining human oversight of AI-powered security systems to ensure they make accurate and reliable decisions. Humans can provide crucial judgment and context that AI systems may lack.

- **Ensuring the security and privacy of data used to train ML models:**

  - **Data sanitization and anonymization:** Removing sensitive information from training datasets to protect privacy and prevent data breaches.

  - **Differential privacy:** A technique that adds noise to the training data to protect the privacy of individual data points while still allowing the model to learn valuable patterns.

  - **Federated learning:** A technique allowing multiple parties to train an ML model collaboratively without sharing their raw data. This can be useful for training models on sensitive data that cannot be centralized due to privacy or security concerns. Think of it as training a model across multiple devices without the data ever leaving those devices.

- o **Secure data storage:** Implementing robust security measures to protect training data from unauthorized access and modification.

- o **Data provenance tracking:** Maintaining a record of the origin and history of training data to ensure its integrity and trustworthiness.

Employing Explainable AI

Explainable AI (XAI) aims to make AI decision-making more transparent and understandable to humans. This is crucial in CyberSecurity, where understanding why an AI system made a particular decision can be critical for building trust and ensuring accountability.

How it helps:

- **Debugging and improvement:** XAI can help developers understand why an AI model is making errors and identify areas for improvement.

- **Trust and transparency:** XAI can increase trust in AI-powered security systems by providing insights into the model's decision-making process.

- **Auditing and compliance:** XAI can help organizations demonstrate that their AI systems are making fair and unbiased decisions, which is essential for regulatory compliance.

The techniques are as follows:

- **Local Interpretable Model-agnostic Explanations (LIME):** Explains individual predictions of any ML model.

- **SHapley Additive exPlanations (SHAP):** Assigns an importance value to each feature for a particular prediction.

- **Decision trees:** Inherently interpretable models that can be used to explain the decision-making process.

Ethical considerations of AI in CyberSecurity

The use of AI in CyberSecurity raises several important ethical considerations that must be addressed to ensure that these technologies are deployed responsibly and ethically. The ethical considerations are as follows:

- **Addressing biases in AI algorithms:**

  - o **Problem:** AI algorithms are trained on data, and if that data reflects existing societal biases, the algorithms may perpetuate and even amplify those biases. For example, a facial recognition system trained on a dataset that underrepresents certain demographic groups may be less accurate for those groups. This can lead to discriminatory outcomes in security applications.

- o **Solutions:**

    - **Careful data selection and preprocessing:** Ensuring that training datasets are diverse, representative, and free of bias.

    - **Bias detection and mitigation techniques:** Using algorithms to detect and mitigate bias in AI models.

    - **Auditing AI systems:** Regularly auditing AI systems for bias and taking corrective action when necessary.

- **Ensuring transparency and accountability:**

    - o **Problem:** Some AI algorithms' "black box" nature can make it difficult to understand why they made a particular decision. This lack of transparency can erode trust and make it difficult to hold anyone accountable for errors or unintended consequences.

    - o **Solutions:**

        - **Explainable AI (XAI):** As discussed earlier, XAI techniques can help make AI decision-making more transparent and understandable.

        - **Documentation and auditing:** Maintain detailed documentation of AI system design, development, and deployment, and conduct regular audits to ensure they operate as intended.

        - **Clear lines of responsibility:** Establishing clear lines of responsibility for developing, deploying, and using AI systems.

- **Balancing the benefits of AI with potential risks to privacy and civil liberties:**

    - o **Problem:** AI-powered security systems can collect and analyze vast amounts of personal data, raising concerns about privacy and civil liberties. For example, the widespread use of facial recognition technology for surveillance could have a chilling effect on freedom of expression and assembly.

    - o **Solutions:**

        - **Privacy by design:** Integrating privacy considerations into the design and development of AI systems from the outset.

        - **Data minimization and anonymization:** Collecting and storing only the minimum amount necessary for the intended purpose and anonymizing data whenever possible.

- **Strict access controls:** Implementing strict access controls ensures that only authorized individuals can access sensitive data.

- **Transparency and user consent:** Being transparent with individuals about how their data is collected and used and obtaining informed consent whenever possible.

- **Independent oversight:** Establishing independent oversight mechanisms to ensure AI systems are used responsibly and ethically.

As AI becomes more prevalent, weighing its potential benefits against its inherent ethical risks is crucial. The following figure depicts this dilemma, contrasting AI's advancements in efficiency and security with challenges related to transparency and bias:

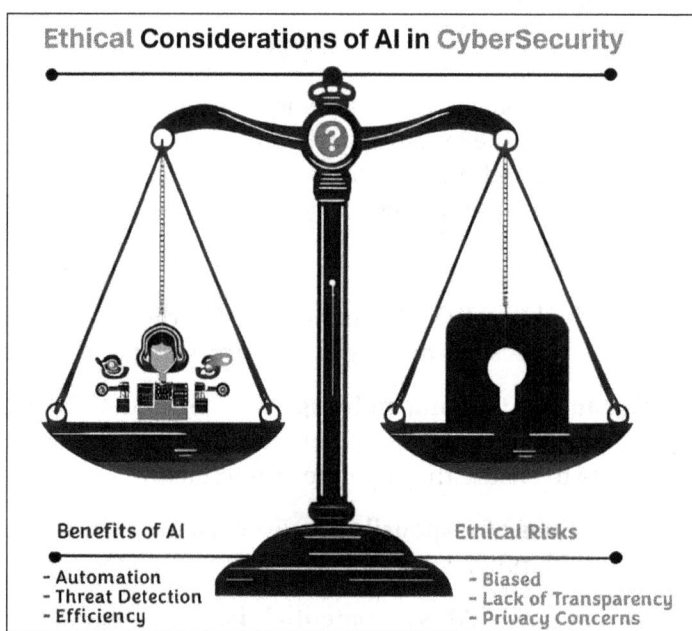

Figure 9.3 Ethical considerations of AI in CyberSecurity

Future of AI in CyberSecurity

The role of AI in CyberSecurity will only grow in the coming years. As AI technology matures and adversaries become more sophisticated, we expect to see even greater AI integration into defensive and offensive cyber operations. Some future trends are as follows:

- **Convergence of AI, automation, and orchestration:** The future of CyberSecurity will likely involve the convergence of AI, automation, and orchestration to create more intelligent and autonomous security systems. These systems can detect, respond to, and predict threats with minimal human intervention.

- Benefits:

    - **Faster and more efficient response:** Automated and orchestrated responses can dramatically reduce the time it takes to detect and respond to incidents.

    - **Reduced workload for security teams:** Automation can free up security teams to focus on more strategic tasks.

    - **Improved scalability:** AI-powered systems can scale more efficiently than traditional security solutions.

- **Development of AI-powered threat hunting and proactive defense:** AI will enable more proactive threat hunting, allowing organizations to identify and neutralize threats before they cause damage. This involves using AI to analyze vast datasets to identify patterns and IOC that traditional methods might miss.

    - Benefits:

        - **Early threat detection:** AI can help identify threats earlier in the attack lifecycle.

        - **Reduced dwell time:** By detecting threats earlier, organizations can reduce the time attackers can access their systems.

        - **Proactive threat mitigation:** AI can help organizations proactively address vulnerabilities and prevent attacks before they occur.

- **Potential for AI to revolutionize security training and awareness:** AI can create more engaging and effective security training programs tailored to individual users' needs and learning styles. Imagine an AI-powered training platform that can simulate realistic phishing attacks and provide personalized feedback to users.

    - Benefits:

        - **Improved user awareness:** AI-powered training can help users develop better security habits and become more resilient to social engineering attacks.

        - **Personalized learning:** AI can tailor training content to individual users' needs and learning styles.

        - **Gamification:** AI can create gamified training experiences that are more engaging and effective than traditional methods.

        - **Continuous learning:** AI-powered platforms can provide ongoing training and reinforcement to update users on the latest threats.

- **Quantum-safe/resistant algorithm implementation:** Quantum computing has the potential to break many encryption algorithms. In anticipation, researchers and security professionals are developing quantum-resistant algorithms designed to withstand attacks from quantum computers.

○ **Benefits**:

- ▪ **Future-proofing security:** Implementing quantum-resistant algorithms helps prepare for a future where quantum computers could compromise existing cryptographic systems.

- ▪ **Long-term data protection:** Ensuring that data encrypted today remains secure even when quantum computers become more prevalent.

AI is increasingly being leveraged to enhance CyberSecurity defenses. The following table explores the impact of AI across different CyberSecurity use cases, including their benefits and associated challenges:

Use case	Description	Benefits	Challenges
Anomaly detection	Identifying unusual patterns that may indicate malicious activity.	Detects unknown threats, reduces false positives, and provides early warning.	It requires large datasets for training and can be challenging to tune.
Threat intelligence	Automating the collection, processing, and analysis of threat data.	Faster threat detection, improved accuracy, enhanced situational awareness.	Data quality issues and difficulty integrating with existing systems.
Malware detection	Identifying malware based on its behavior rather than relying solely on signatures.	Detects unknown malware, faster analysis, improved accuracy.	It can be computationally expensive, and susceptible to evasion techniques.
Vulnerability management	Prioritizing vulnerabilities based on their exploitability and potential impact.	Focus on critical vulnerabilities, proactive remediation, and improved efficiency.	Requires accurate and up-to-date vulnerability data.
Incident response	Automating the detection, investigation, containment, and eradication of security incidents.	Faster response times, reduced workload, improved consistency.	It requires careful planning and configuration, and unintended consequences are potentially possible.
Adversarial attacks	Using AI to create more sophisticated and evasive attacks.	Increased attack success rate bypasses traditional defenses.	Requires significant expertise and may be detectable by AI-powered defenses.
Building AI resilience	Developing security systems that are robust to AI-powered attacks.	Protects against adversarial machine learning and ensures the reliability of AI-powered security systems.	Requires ongoing research and development.

Table 9.6: Comparison of AI use cases in CyberSecurity

Quantum computing

Quantum computing: CyberSecurity's next frontier—or its greatest threat?

Quantum computing is on the horizon, and its implications for CyberSecurity are profound. This is not just an incremental change; it is a paradigm shift that will shatter the foundations of modern cryptography, rendering many of our current encryption standards obsolete. This subchapter will prepare you for the quantum revolution, ensuring you can navigate a world where today's encryption standards are rendered outdated and equipping you with the knowledge to transition to a quantum-resistant future. The quantum age is not a matter of *if*, but *when*, and its impact on CyberSecurity will be monumental.

Fundamentals of quantum computing

To understand quantum computing's implications for CyberSecurity, it is essential to grasp the basic principles of quantum mechanics that underpin this technology.

Introduction to quantum mechanics principles

Quantum mechanics is a branch of physics that describes the behavior of matter and energy at the atomic and subatomic levels. It is a complex and often counterintuitive field, but a few key principles are essential for understanding quantum computing:

- **Superposition:** One of the most fundamental principles of quantum mechanics. Unlike classical bits that can be either 0 or 1, a qubit can exist in a superposition, representing a combination of both 0 and 1 simultaneously. Imagine a coin spinning in the air; it is neither heads nor tails until it lands. Similarly, a qubit is in a probabilistic state until it is measured. This allows quantum computers to explore multiple possibilities simultaneously.

- **Entanglement:** A phenomenon where two or more qubits become linked together to share the same fate, even if they are physically separated. If you measure the state of one entangled qubit, you instantly know the state of the other, regardless of the distance between them. This interconnectedness allows for powerful parallel computations.

- **Quantum measurement:** Measuring a qubit's state causes it to collapse from a superposition into a definite state of either 0 or 1. This is like the spinning coin finally landing on either heads or tails. The measurement outcome is probabilistic, based on the qubit's superposition state.

- **Quantum gates:** Like logic gates in classical computing, quantum gates are operations that manipulate the state of qubits. These gates can be combined to create complex quantum circuits that perform computations.

Overview of different quantum computing architectures

Several different approaches are being pursued to build quantum computers, each with its advantages and challenges:

- **Superconducting qubits:** These are based on superconducting circuits that operate at extremely low temperatures. They are one of the most advanced technologies currently being used to build quantum computers, and companies like Google and IBM are heavily invested in this approach.

- **Trapped ions:** These qubits are based on individual ions trapped and manipulated using electromagnetic fields. They offer long coherence times (when a qubit can maintain its quantum state) but can be challenging to scale up.

- **Photonic qubits:** These use photons (light particles) as qubits. They can operate at room temperature and are less noise-resistant than other qubits, but manipulating them can be challenging.

- **Topological qubits:** These are based on exotic quasiparticles called **Anyons**. They are theoretically more resistant to errors than other qubits but are still in the early stages of development.

- **Silicon spin qubits:** These use the spin of electrons in silicon as qubits. They leverage existing semiconductor manufacturing technology, offering a potential path to scalability.

- **Neutral atoms:** These use individual atoms trapped in optical lattices (created by lasers) as qubits. They offer reasonable control and scalability potential.

Several architectures are being pursued in the development of quantum computers. The following table provides a comparative overview of these architectures, including their qubit implementation, benefits, and limitations:

Architecture	Qubit representation	Advantages	Challenges
Superconducting qubits	Current loops in superconducting circuits	Fast gate operations, sound control, relatively scalable	Requires extremely low temperatures, susceptible to noise and decoherence
Trapped ions	Energy levels of trapped ions	Long coherence times, high gate fidelity	It isn't easy to scale up to large numbers of qubits
Photonic qubits	Polarization or path of photons	Can operate at room temperature, less susceptible to noise	Difficult to create strong interactions between photons
Topological qubits	Anyons (quasiparticles)	Theoretically more robust to errors	Still in the early stages of development, experimentally challenging

Architecture	Qubit representation	Advantages	Challenges
Silicon spin qubits	Electron spins in silicon	Leverages existing semiconductor technology, potentially scalable	Requires precise control of individual electron spins
Neutral atoms	Internal states of neutral atoms	Reasonable control, scalability potential	Requires complex laser systems for trapping and manipulation

Table 9.7: Comparison of quantum computing architectures

Understanding the potential of quantum algorithms

Specific quantum algorithms have the potential to break widely used cryptographic systems:

- **Shor's algorithm:** This algorithm can factor large numbers exponentially faster than the best-known classical algorithms. This directly threatens RSA and ECC, which rely on the difficulty of factoring large numbers for their security.

- **Grover's algorithm:** This algorithm can search an unsorted database quadratically faster than the best-known classical algorithms. While not as dramatic as Shor's algorithm, it could weaken the security of symmetric key ciphers like AES by effectively reducing the key length.

Quantum computing's impact on cryptography

The most significant CyberSecurity threat this emerging technology poses is the potential for quantum computers to break widely used cryptographic algorithms.

The threat to RSA and ECC encryption from Shor's algorithm:

- **RSA:** The RSA cryptosystem relies on the difficulty of factoring large numbers into their prime factors. Shor's algorithm can perform this factorization exponentially faster than classical algorithms, breaking RSA encryption. This would compromise the security of digital signatures, key exchange, and data encryption that relies on RSA.

- **Elliptic Curve Cryptography (ECC):** ECC is a type of public-key cryptography based on the algebraic structure of elliptic curves over finite fields. It offers similar security to RSA but with significantly shorter key lengths, resulting in faster processing and lower bandwidth usage.

The impact on symmetric key cryptography from Grover's algorithm:

- **Advanced Encryption Standard (AES):** AES is a widely used symmetric-key algorithm. Grover's algorithm can speed up the search for the correct key, effectively reducing the security offered by AES. For example, AES-256, which has a 256-bit key, would be reduced to a security level roughly equivalent to a 128-bit key against a quantum attack.

- **Implications:** While not wholly breaking AES, Grover's algorithm necessitates using longer key lengths to maintain the same level of security in a post-quantum world. This means that organizations will need to transition to AES with longer keys (e.g., AES-256) sooner rather than later.

Potential for Quantum Key Distribution

Quantum Key Distribution (QKD) is a method for securely exchanging cryptographic keys between two parties using the principles of quantum mechanics. Unlike traditional key exchange methods that rely on mathematical problems, QKD's security is based on the laws of physics. The details are as follows:

- **How it works:** QKD leverages the properties of quantum mechanics, such as the no-cloning theorem (which states that it's impossible to create an identical copy of an unknown quantum state) and the fact that measurement disturbs a quantum state, to detect any eavesdropping attempt. If an eavesdropper tries to intercept the key, their actions will inevitably alter the quantum state, alerting the legitimate parties to the attempted intrusion.

- **Benefits:**

  - **Information-theoretically secure:** QKD offers security that is not based on computational assumptions but on the fundamental laws of physics.

  - **Eavesdropping detection:** Any attempt to intercept the key is detectable.

- **Limitations**:

  - **Distance limitations:** QKD is currently limited by the distance over which quantum signals can be transmitted reliably.

  - **Specialized hardware:** QKD requires specialized hardware, which can be expensive and complex to deploy.

  - **Authentication:** While QKD provides secure key exchange, it doesn't address the issue of authenticating the communicating parties. You still need a secure way to verify who you are exchanging keys with.

- **Scalability**: Implementing and maintaining QKD infrastructure on a large scale is challenging and costly.

Post-quantum cryptography

In response to the quantum threat, researchers are actively developing cryptographic algorithms that are believed to resist attacks from classical and quantum computers. This field is known as **post-quantum cryptography (PQC)** or quantum-resistant cryptography.

Exploring potential replacements for current standards

Several families of cryptographic algorithms are considered potential replacements for RSA and ECC in a post-quantum world. With the advent of quantum computing, new cryptographic families are being developed to ensure future security. This table compares different PQC families, outlining their security basis, advantages, and disadvantages:

Family	Security based on	Advantages	Disadvantages
Lattice-based	Difficulty of solving lattice problems	Relatively efficient, versatile, strong security arguments	Some schemes have large public keys
Hash-based	Security of hash functions	Robust security, well-understood	This can result in large signatures
Code-based	Difficulty in decoding error-correcting codes	The long history of study, good security	Large key sizes
Multivariate	Difficulty of solving multivariate equations	Small key sizes, fast operations	Some schemes have faced security challenges, and ongoing research is needed
Supersingular Isogeny-based	Difficulty in finding isogenies between curves	Very small key sizes	Relatively new, computationally intensive, ongoing security analysis required

Table 9.8: Comparison of post quantum cryptography family

NIST post-quantum cryptography standardization process

The **National Institute of Standards and Technology (NIST)** runs a multi-year process to select and standardize one or more quantum-resistant public-key cryptographic algorithms. This is crucial to preparing for the transition to a post-quantum world. The goal is to have new standards that can replace RSA, ECC, and other algorithms vulnerable to quantum attacks.

- **Process:** NIST initiated the process in 2016, soliciting proposals for quantum-resistant algorithms. The submissions have gone through multiple rounds of evaluation, analysis, and public review. NIST has selected a few finalists and is expected to finalize the standards shortly.

- **Evaluation Criteria:** NIST is evaluating the candidate algorithms based on:

  o **Security:** The primary consideration is the algorithm's ability to resist attacks from classical and quantum computers.

  o **Performance:** Efficiency in computational speed, key, and signature sizes is essential for practical use.

  o **Other Properties:** Flexibility, simplicity, and ease of implementation are also considered.

Challenges and considerations in migrating to post-quantum cryptographic algorithms:

- **Performance overhead:** Some PQC algorithms can be computationally more expensive than current algorithms, potentially impacting performance, especially on resource-constrained devices.

- **Key and signature sizes:** Some PQC algorithms have more significant key or signature sizes than current algorithms, impacting storage and bandwidth requirements.

- **Implementation complexity:** Implementing new cryptographic algorithms can be complex and requires careful consideration of security and performance trade-offs.

- **Interoperability:** Ensuring interoperability between systems using different PQC algorithms will be challenging during the transition period.

- **Software and hardware updates:** Migrating to PQC will require updates to software, hardware, and cryptographic libraries across a vast range of systems and devices.

- **Cryptographic agility:** The ability to switch to new cryptographic algorithms relatively easily and quickly. This will be essential for adapting to future advances in cryptanalysis and the potential discovery of new vulnerabilities.

- **Lack of real-world testing**: Many PQC algorithms are relatively new and haven't been subjected to the same level of real-world testing and scrutiny as RSA or ECC.

- **"Drop-in" replacement is not always possible**: PQC algorithms may require different implementation approaches and may not be directly compatible with existing protocols and systems.

- **Side-channel attacks**: Vulnerabilities in implementing an algorithm rather than the algorithm itself. Variations in power consumption or timing during execution can leak information. PQC algorithms, like any other, are susceptible to these attacks if not implemented carefully.

Quantum-resistant security strategies

Preparing for the post-quantum era requires a proactive and multi-faceted approach. Organizations must start planning to ensure a smooth transition to quantum-resistant security measures.

Developing a quantum risk assessment:

- **Identify critical assets:** Determine which data, systems, and processes are most vulnerable to quantum attacks and would have the most significant impact if compromised. Focus on assets that rely on public-key cryptography for confidentiality, integrity, or authentication.

- **Assess cryptographic dependencies:** Identify all instances where vulnerable algorithms like RSA and ECC are used within your organization and by your third-party vendors. This includes applications, protocols, hardware, and cryptographic libraries.

- **Evaluate the lifetime of data:** Consider how long your data needs to remain confidential. Data that needs to be protected for many years is at higher risk from quantum attacks.

- **Estimate a timeline for quantum threat:** While the exact timeline for developing a large-scale quantum computer is uncertain, making an informed estimate based on current research and expert opinions is essential. This will help you prioritize your migration efforts.

- **"Harvest now, decrypt later" attacks**: Consider the possibility of attackers collecting encrypted data today, even if they can't, hoping to decrypt it later when quantum computers become available.

Implementing cryptographic agility

Design systems and applications that can easily switch to new cryptographic algorithms without requiring major overhauls. This involves modular design, standardized interfaces, and crypto libraries that support multiple algorithms:

- **Benefits**:
    - **Flexibility:** Allows organizations to adapt to new cryptographic standards and address emerging threats more quickly.
    - **Reduced migration costs:** Minimizes the cost and effort required to transition to new algorithms.
    - **Futureproofing:** Prepares systems for future changes in the cryptographic landscape.

- **Implementation strategies:**

  o Using modular design principles in software development.

  o Employing cryptographic libraries that support multiple algorithms and are regularly updated.

  o Designing systems with well-defined interfaces for cryptographic operations.

Using hybrid approaches

Concept: During the transition period, it may be prudent to use hybrid approaches that combine classical and quantum-resistant algorithms. This provides a layered defense, ensuring security even if one of the algorithms is broken. Details are as follows:

- **Example:** Using both RSA and a lattice-based algorithm for key exchange.

- **Benefits:**

  o **Defense in depth:** Provides multiple layers of security.

  o **Mitigates transition risks:** Allows for a gradual transition to PQC while maintaining security during the interim period.

- **Considerations:**

  o **Performance impact:** Using multiple algorithms can increase computational overhead.

  o **Complexity:** Managing hybrid systems can be more complex than using a single algorithm.

Participating in the development and standardization of PQC:

- **Engage with the research community:** Stay informed about the latest research on PQC and contribute to developing new algorithms and techniques.

- **Provide feedback to NIST:** Participate in the NIST PQC standardization process by providing feedback on candidate algorithms and draft standards.

- **Support open standards:** Advocate for developing and adopting open, interoperable PQC standards.

- **Collaborate with industry peers:** Share information and best practices with other organizations to prepare for the post-quantum era.

Planning for long-term data protection:

- **Identify data with long-term confidentiality needs:** Determine which data needs to remain confidential for an extended period (e.g., decades). This might include sensitive personal data, intellectual property, or government secrets.

- **Prioritize the protection of this data:** This data is most at risk from the "harvest now, decrypt later" threat.

- **Consider using symmetric-key cryptography with longer key lengths:** For data that only needs confidentiality and not authentication or non-repudiation, symmetric key cryptography with sufficiently long keys (e.g. AES-256) might be a good choice for now.

- **Evaluate and test PQC algorithms**: As PQC algorithms mature and are standardized, they are tested and implemented for long-term data protection.

Future of quantum computing and CyberSecurity

The interplay between quantum computing and CyberSecurity will evolve rapidly in the coming years:

- **Quantum-safe security considerations for emerging technologies (IoT, Cloud, etc.):** As technologies like IoT and cloud computing become increasingly prevalent, it is vital to consider their security in a post-quantum world.

  - **IoT:** Many IoT devices have long lifecycles and limited resources, making them particularly challenging to secure against quantum threats. Solutions might involve:

    - Using lightweight PQC algorithms.

    - Implementing secure firmware update mechanisms.

    - Leveraging edge computing to perform computationally intensive cryptographic operations.

  - **Cloud:** Cloud providers must adopt PQC algorithms to protect data stored and processed in the cloud. This includes:

    - Offering quantum-resistant encryption services.

    - Implementing QKD for secure communication between data centers.

    - Supporting hybrid approaches during the transition period.

  - **Blockchain**: While some blockchains rely on ECC and are vulnerable, others are exploring post-quantum alternatives.

    - Researching and implementing quantum-resistant consensus mechanisms.

    - Hash-based cryptography is generally considered quantum-resistant.

  - **AI/ML**: Protecting AI/ML models from potential quantum attacks will also be essential.

- Researching quantum-resistant machine learning algorithms.

- Applying PQC to secure training data and model parameters.

- **Ongoing evolution of quantum algorithms and cryptanalysis:**

  o The field of quantum computing is still in its early stages, and new quantum algorithms and cryptanalytic techniques are constantly being developed.

  o It is essential to stay informed about the latest research and to continuously evaluate the security of cryptographic systems.

  o **Continuous monitoring:** Regularly reassess the security of your cryptographic systems, considering new developments in quantum computing.

  o **Collaboration and information sharing:** Share information and best practices with other organizations and participate in research initiatives.

- **Role of governments and regulatory bodies:**

  o Governments and regulatory bodies will be crucial in setting standards, promoting research, and guiding the transition to a post-quantum world.

  o This includes:

    - Funding research on PQC and quantum computing.

    - Developing and enforcing security standards for PQC algorithms.

    - Guiding organizations on how to prepare for the quantum threat.

    - Promoting international cooperation on quantum security.

Conclusion

The chapter underscores the dynamic and evolving nature of the field. We've explored how threat intelligence, blockchain, IoT, AI, and quantum computing reshape the landscape. These technologies offer powerful tools for defenders but also introduce new challenges and attack vectors. Proactive threat intelligence and information sharing are crucial for staying ahead of threats. Blockchain promises enhanced data integrity and security, while the expanding IoT ecosystem demands robust security measures. AI and ML are revolutionizing both defense and offense, demanding AI-resilient systems. Finally, the looming quantum computing era necessitates a shift toward PQC. Successfully navigating this future requires continuous learning, adaptation, and collaboration to build a more secure digital world.

Points to remember

- **Threat intelligence is key:** Proactive threat intelligence and information sharing are essential for anticipating and mitigating emerging threats.

- **Blockchain's potential:** Blockchain offers significant potential for improving data integrity, identity management, and supply chain security.

- **IoT security is paramount:** The expanding IoT landscape presents unique security challenges that require a multi-faceted approach.

- **AI is a double-edged sword:** AI and ML transform CyberSecurity, empowering defenders and enhancing attacker capabilities.

- **Adversarial ML is a real threat:** Be aware of and prepare for attacks designed to manipulate or evade AI-based security systems.

- **Quantum computing looms large:** The advent of quantum computing will necessitate a transition to PQC to protect sensitive data.

- **Cryptographic agility is crucial:** Organizations must design systems that can quickly adapt to new cryptographic standards.

- **Collaboration is essential:** Sharing threat intelligence and best practices within the CyberSecurity community is vital.

Join our book's Discord space

Join the book's Discord Workspace for Latest updates, Offers, Tech happenings around the world, New Release and Sessions with the Authors:

https://discord.bpbonline.com

Index

www.ingramcontent.com/pod-product-compliance
Lightning Source LLC
Chambersburg PA
CBHW061744210326
41599CB00034B/6789